KU-495-774

Acknowledgements

We gratefully acknowledge permission to reprint the articles published in this volume from the following sources:

Reading 1   *Southern Economic Journal* and F. Machlup

Reading 2   *Social Research*

Reading 3   *Royal Economic Society* and Yew-Kwang Ng

Reading 4   *Economic Inquiry*

Reading 5   *Canadian Journal of Economics*

Reading 6   *Australian Economic Papers*

Reading 7   *Journal of Economic Literature* and L.A. Boland

Reading 8   *Journal of Economic Issues*

Reading 9   *Southern Economic Journal* and F. Machlup

Reading 10   *British Journal for the Philosophy of Science*

Reading 11   *Journal of Agricultural Economics* and
               L.D. McClements

Reading 12   *National Westminster Bank Quarterly Review*

Reading 13   *Journal of Economic Issues*

Reading 14   *Kyklos*

Reading 15   *Nobel Foundation* and H.A. Simon

Reading 16   *American Economic Review* and W. Leontief

Reading 17   *American Asssociation for the Advancement of
               Science* and W. Leontief

Reading 18   *American Economic Review* and W.W. Heller

Contents

iv

HOW
ECONOMISTS
EXPLAIN

A Reader in Methodology

Edited by

William L. Marr
Baldev Raj

Wilfrid Laurier University
School of Business and Economics
Waterloo, Ontario, Canada

UNIVERSITY
PRESS OF
AMERICA

LANHAM • NEW YORK • LONDON

All University Press of America books are produced on acid-free
paper which exceeds the minimum standards set by the National
Historical Publications and Records Commission.

Preface

Several years ago, the Economics Faculty at Wilfrid Laurier University introduced an undergraduate course on Economic Methodology. It was believed that the students of economics should study various methodological positions to increase their awareness about competing economic paradigms. We have both taught this course at one time or another and believe there is a need for a reader in this course. The volume is divided into nine parts and readers are introduced to selected readings in each part with a brief introduction and suggestions for further study.

It took us several years to collect enough courage and motivation actually to work on such a reader. The current reader is a by-product of that courage and perseverance. We are thankful to many of our colleagues, particularly John A. Weir and John R. Finlay, for their encouragement.

Some of our colleagues have given us the benefit of their wisdom either formally or informally and have prevented us from making errors of misinterpretation of the literature and its significance. In particular, Peter Sinclair has read the introductions to various parts and has given us written comments. Professors Åki Blomqvist, Ronald G. Bodkin, David Laidler and John Whalley have also commented on the introductions and the selection of readings. Professor Lawrence A. Boland brought to our attention several of his writings and his recent book referenced in the Introduction.

We would like to thank the Editor of the University Press of America for his assistance at various stages of the completion of this manuscript. We also would like to acknowledge various publishers of journals and the authors of the articles for giving us their kind permission to use their work.

We have attempted to gather together several important articles of relatively recent origin which could stand as a complete unit and complement the books that have recently appeared on methodology (listed in the references following the Introduction to this reader). The selection of these articles reflects our judgment on various topics. Undoubtedly, there are many other excellent articles which could have been included in the reader but haven't found their place in it. Their exclusion in no way reflects their contribution to the literature but merely indicates the space limitation that has prevented their inclusion.

We gratefully acknowledge the financial assistance from

Andrew Berczi, Director of Graduate Studies, and the Short-Term Research Grants Committee of Wilfrid Laurier University in the form of an initiatory research grant and a book publication grant.

The typing of the manuscript was done at Wilfrid Laurier University and we would like to thank Elsie Grogan for her exceptional care in putting the manuscript in camera-ready form. Margaret Dilworth and Karen Free proof-read and Dave Kroeker of DK Graphix copy-edited the manuscript; we would like to thank them for their diligence. A number of our students worked on the bibliography. We would like to thank in particular, Alan Marshall and Mee Leong Teoh. James Moore constructed the glossary of words. In no way are these individuals responsible for any errors that may remain.

Finally, we wish sincerely to thank Marion Marr, Jennifer Marr, Peter Marr, Balbeer Raj and Rahul Raj for their affection and moral support which helped immensely in the completion of this reader.

William L. Marr

Baldev Raj

Introduction

The public esteem of economics as a science, as well as the profes-sional euphoria of economists, were at an all time high during the 1960s. Governments in particular looked to economics as a means of achieving simultaneously the many economic goals of full em-ployment, relatively low inflation, economic growth, stable ex-change rates and a balance in the country's international pay-ments in a more or less automatic and routine manner. Economics appeared to wed the necessary ingredients of a deductive theory and empirical, statistical and econometric research methods into a coherent discipline which could solve any economic problem. Economists generally accepted this view of their activities and questioned very little the underlying basis of their discipline; their attitude seemed to be: let's get on with the work of curing the world's ills and enhancing the welfare of all. Then, the talk of crisis, revolution, and counter-revolution began to be heard during the 1970s and self-criticism on the part of some economists replaced the earlier attitude of self-assured singlemindedness. There are signs that the 1980s will be a decade devoted to debate on what is wrong versus what is right about economics, and that this debate will include a thorough study of the methodology of economics or how economists explain.

Methodology is sometimes used as a synonym for "methods" which include an examination of data collection, sampling, survey methods, and how to use hypotheses in empirical research. This use of the word is inappropriate to this book, however. Following the usage of Mark Blaug, economic methodology investigates the concepts, theories, and basic principles of reasoning which are part and parcel of the discipline of economics, or the philosophy of science as applied to economics. To give the reader a single example which clarifies this distinction, this book does not deal with how someone might verify or falsify a particular hypothesis (such as if price increases, the quantity demanded falls, all else the same): instead, this book deals with whether the terms "verification" and "falsification" have any place in economics at all.

As evidence of a reawakening of interest in their methodology among economists, the past few years saw the appearance of a number of textbooks which could be used in one-term undergrad-uate courses in economic methodology: Mark Blaug, *The Method-ology of Economics* (1980), Ian Stewart, *Reasoning and Method in Economics* (1979), Homa Katouzian, *Ideology and Method in Economics* (1980), Lawrence A. Boland, *The Foundations of Economic Method* (1982) and Bruce Caldwell, *Beyond Posi-*

tivism - Economic Methodology in the Twentieth Century (1982). These books are addressed mainly to students of economics who, having studied economics, find it is difficult to choose among competing theories and principles. While these books serve to fill a void in the training of modern economists, there is a need for a book of readings on methodology, so as to help students obtain a thorough grounding in the alternative methodological foundations of economics. This collection is meant to supplement the textbooks which are noted above, where often only a synthesis of the views of the leading exponents of alternative positions is presented. It is important that students form independent opinons on various positions through reading original sources. This collection of papers selects some of the best examples of writings on economic methodology and makes them available to the undergraduate student. The issues which are covered are wide ranging; the journals from which the works are taken are also numerous which makes the collection in one place of several notable pieces all the more useful.

Although this reader is primarily designed to fulfill the need of training students in economics, we have not overlooked the needs of general readership interested in the question of how economists explain. Moreover, the reader would serve equally well for students in business, geography, history, political science, psychology, social work, sociology, and other disciplines of social sciences. The selection of titles and subtitles in this reader are chosen to make these readings attractive to the general readership in an international market. Each section is introduced with a brief introduction on how the selection or selections fit into the overall methodological issues at hand. The introductions help to place the pieces in a wider framework and to suggest how they relate to each other. Each section also contains suggestions for further reading which the interested reader may follow up if more detail and further elaboration would be useful. A glossary of the main philosophical and methodological terms which the reader will come across in these articles is included at the end of the readings.

References

M. Blaug. *The Methodology of Economics* (London: Cambridge University Press, 1980).

L.A. Boland, *The Foundations of Economic Method* (London: George Allen and Unwin, 1982).

B. Caldwell. *Beyond Positivism - Economic Methodology in the Twentieth Century* (London: George Allen and Unwin, 1982).

H. Katouzian. *Ideology and Method in Economics* (New York: New York University Press, 1980).
I.M.T. Stewart. *Reasoning and Method in Economics* (Toronto: McGraw-Hill, 1979).

Other Readings

M. Hollis and E. Nell. *Rational Economic Man* (Cambridge: Cambridge University Press, 1975).
I. Krimerman. *The Nature and Scope of Social Science. A Critical Anthology* (New York: Meredith, 1969).
J.J. Latsis (editor). *Methods and Appraisal in Economics* (Cambridge: Cambridge University Press, 1976).
F. Machlup. *Methodology of Economics and Other Social Sciences* (New York: Academic Press, 1978).

Part One   **The Nature of Economics**

Especially since the 1930s when Lionel Robbins published *An Essay on the Nature and Significance of Economic Science*, economists have been concerned with the dual issues of what is economics and how does it compare to the natural or physical sciences. The readings in this section address the latter question.

Fritz Machlup examines the position that the social sciences, including economics, are inferior to the natural sciences. He reacts to the feeling among some social scientists that their disciplines are unable to reach the heights of the "better" natural sciences and so have developed an inferiority complex. He also implicitly attacks the view of other investigators who argue that the social sciences are equal in all respects to the natural sciences and therefore can and should adopt the theoretical and empirical methodology and methods of the latter. Machlup looks at nine bases of comparison between the two sciences and finds that the social sciences are "inferior" in some respects. He then asks if this is important. He seems to conclude that it is not; the greater complexities and difficulties in the social sciences present a greater challenge but must not act as a deterrent to research and analysis.

A different view is held by Mark Blaug. He writes that:

> to hold that the social sciences should employ a methodology distinct from the natural sciences is to advocate the startling view that theories or hypotheses about social questions should be validated in ways that are radically different from those used to validate theories or hypotheses about natural phenomena.

Karl Popper presents the view called methodological monism which asserts that both the physical and social sciences use the same methods. Both services set up deductive causal explanations and test them using the hypothetical-deductive method. Furthermore, Popper goes on to argue that a study of society should be done in terms of the attitudes, expectations, and relations of individuals. This view is known as methodological individualism.

1

1 Are The Social Sciences Really Inferior?

Fritz Machlup*

If we ask whether the "social sciences" are "really inferior," let us first make sure that we understand each part of the question.

"Inferior" to what? Of course to the natural sciences. "Inferior" in what respect? It will be our main task to examine all the "respects," all the scores on which such inferiority has been alleged. I shall enumerate them presently.

The adverb *"really"* which qualifies the adjective "inferior" refers to allegations made by some scientists, scholars, and laymen. But it refers also to the "inferiority complex" which I have noted among many social scientists. A few years ago I wrote an essay entitled "The Inferiority Complex of the Social Sciences."[1] In that essay I said that "an inferiority complex may or may not be justified by some 'objective' standards," and I went on to discuss the consequences which "the *feeling* of inferiority"--conscious or subconscious--has for the behavior of the social scientists who are suffering from it. I did not then discuss whether the complex has an objective basis, that is, whether the social sciences are "really" inferior. This is our question today.

The subject noun would call for a long disquisition. What is meant by *"social sciences,"* what is included, what is not included? Are they the same as what others have referred to as the "moral sciences," the "Geisteswissenschaften," the "cultural sciences," the "behavioral sciences"? Is Geography, or the part of it that is called "Human Geography," a social science? Is History a social science--or perhaps even *the* social science *par excellence*, as some philosophers have contended? We shall not spend time on this business of defining and classifying. A few remarks may later be necessary in connection with some points of methodology, but by and large we shall not bother here with a definition of "social sciences" and with drawing boundary lines around them.

The Grounds of Comparison

The social sciences and the natural sciences are compared and con-

Reprinted by permission from the *Southern Economic Journal*, 27 (1961), 173-84.

trasted on many scores, and the discussions are often quite un-systematic. If we try to review them systematically, we shall encounter a good deal of overlap and unavoidable duplication. None the less, it will help if we enumerate in advance some of the grounds of comparison most often mentioned, grounds on which the social sciences are judged to come out "second best":

1. Invariability of observations
2. Objectivity of observations and explanations
3. Verifiability of hypotheses
4. Exactness of findings
5. Measurability of phenomena
6. Constancy of numerical relationships
7. Predictability of future events
8. Distance from every-day experience
9. Standards of admission and requirements

We shall examine all these comparisons.

Invariability of Observations

The idea is that you cannot have much of a science unless things recur, unless phenomena repeat themselves. In nature we find many factors and conditions "invariant". Do we in society? Are not conditions in society changing all the time, and so fast that most events are unique, each quite different from anything that has happened before? Or can one rely on the saying that "history repeats itself" with sufficient invariance to permit general-izations about social events?

There is a great deal of truth, and important truth, in this comparison. Some philosophers were so impressed with the in-variance of nature and the variability of social phenomena that they used this difference as the criterion in the definitions of natural and cultural sciences. Following Windelband's distinction between generalizing ("nomothetic") and individualizing ("ideo-graphic") propositions, the German philosopher Heinrich Rickert distinguished between the generalizing sciences of nature and the individualizing sciences of cultural phenomena; and by individ-ualizing sciences he meant historical sciences.[2] In order to be right, he redefined both "nature" and "history" by stating that reality is "nature" if we deal with it in terms of the *general* but becomes "history" if we deal with it in terms of the *unique*. To him, geology was largely history, and economics, most similar to physics, was a natural science. This implies a rejection of the contention that all fields which are normally called social sciences suffer from a lack of invariance; indeed, economics is here con-sidered so much a matter of immutable laws of nature that it is handed over to the natural sciences.

4

This is not satisfactory, nor does it dispose of the main issue that natural phenomena provide *more* invariance than social phenomena. The main difference lies probably in the number of factors that must be taken into account in explanations and predictions of natural and social events. Only a small number of reproducible facts will normally be involved in a physical explanation or prediction. A much larger number of facts, some of them probably unique historical events, will be found relevant in an explanation or prediction of economic or other social events. This is true, and methodological devices will not do away with the difference. But it is, of course, only a difference in degree.

The physicist Robert Oppenheimer once raised the question whether, if the universe is a *unique* phenomenon, we may assume that *universal* or *general* propositions can be formulated about it. Economists of the Historical School insisted on treating each "stage" or phase of economic society as a completely unique one, not permitting the formulation of universal propositions. Yet, in the physical world, phenomena are not quite so homogeneous as many have liked to think; and in the social world, phenomena are not quite so heterogeneous as many have been afraid they are. (If they were, we could not even have generalized concepts of social events and words naming them.) In any case, where reality seems to show a bewildering number of variations, we construct an ideal world of abstract models in which we create enough homogeneity to permit us to apply reason and deduce the implied consequences of assumed constellations. This artificial homogenization of types of phenomena is carried out in natural and social sciences alike.

There is thus no difference in invariance in the sequences of events in nature and in society as long as we theorize about them --because in the abstract models homogeneity is assumed. There is only a difference of degree in the variability of phenomena of nature and society if we talk about the real world-- as long as heterogeneity is not reduced by means of deliberate "controls." There is a third world, between the abstract world of theory and the real unmanipulated world, namely, the artificial world of the experimental laboratory. In this world there is less variability than in the real world and more than in the model world. But this third world does not exist in most of the social sciences (nor in all natural sciences). We shall see later that the mistake is often made of comparing the artificial laboratory world of manipulated nature with the real world of unmanipulated society.

We conclude on this point of comparative invariance, that there is indeed a difference between natural and social sciences, and that the difference--apart from the possibility of laboratory experiments--lies chiefly in the number of relevant factors, and hence of possible combinations, to be taken into account for explaining or predicting events occurring in the real world.

Objectivity of Observations and Explanations

The idea behind a comparison between the "objectivity" of observations and explorations in the natural and social sciences may be conveyed by an imaginary quotation: "Science must be objective and not affected by value judgments; but the social sciences are inherently concerned with values and, hence, they lack the disinterested objectivity of science." True? Frightfully muddled. The trouble is that the problem is "subjective value," which is at the very root of the social sciences, is quite delicate and has in fact confused many, including some fine scholars.

To remove confusion one must separate the different meanings of "value" and the different ways in which they relate to the social sciences, particularly economics. I have distinguished eleven different kinds of value-reference in economics, but have enough sense to spare you this exhibition of my pedagogic dissecting zeal. But we cannot dispense entirely with the problem and overlook the danger of confusion. Thus, I offer you a bargain and shall reduce my distinctions from eleven to four. I am asking you to keep apart the following four meanings in which value judgment may come into our present discussion: (a) The analyst's judgment may be biased for one reason or another, perhaps because his views of the social "Good" or his personal pecuniary interests in the practical use of his findings interfere with the proper scientific detachment. (b) Some normative issues may be connected with the problem under investigation, perhaps ethical judgments which may color some of the investigator's incidental pronouncements--obiter dicta--without however causing a bias in his reported findings of his research. (c) The interest in solving the problems under investigation is surely affected by values since, after all, the investigator selects his problems because he believes that their solution would be of value. (d) The investigator in the social sciences has to explain his observations as results of human actions which can be interpreted only with reference to motives and purposes of the actors, that is, to values entertained by them.

With regard to the first of these possibilities, some authorities have held that the social sciences may more easily succumb to temptation and may show obvious biases. The philosopher Morris Cohen, for example, spoke of "the subjective difficulty of maintaining scientific detachment in the study of human affairs. Few human beings can calmly and with equal fairness consider both sides of a question such as socialism, free love, or birth-control."[3] This is quite true, but one should not forget similar difficulties in the natural sciences. Remember the difficulties which, in deference to religious values, biologists had in discussions of evolution and, going further back, the troubles of astronomers in discussions of the heliocentric theory and of geologists in discussions of the age of the earth. Let us also recall that only 25 years ago, German mathematicians and physicists rejected "Jewish" theorems and theories, including physical relativity, under the pressure of nationalistic values, and only ten years ago Russian biologists stuck to a mutation theory which was evidently affected by political values. I do not know whether one cannot detect in our own period here in the United States an association between political views and scientific answers to the question of the genetic dangers from fall-out and from other nuclear testing.

Apart from political bias, there have been cases of real cheating in science. Think of physical anthropology and its faked Piltdown Man. That the possibility of deception is not entirely beyond the pale of experimental scientists can be gathered from a splendid piece of fiction, a recent novel, *The Affair*, by C.P. Snow, the well-known Cambridge don.

Having said all this about the possibility of bias existing in the presentation of evidence and findings in the natural sciences, we should hasten to admit that not a few economists, especially when concerned with current problems and the interpretation of recent history, are given to "lying with statistics." It is hardly a coincidence if labor economists choose one base year and business economists choose another base year when they compare wage increases and price increases; or if for their computations of growth rates expert witnesses for different political parties choose different statistical series and different base years. This does not indicate that the social sciences are in this respect "superior" or "inferior" to the natural sciences. Think of physicists, chemists, medical scientists, psychiatrists, etc., appearing as expert witnesses in court litigation to testify in support of their clients' cases. In these instances the scientists are in the role of analyzing concrete individual events, of interpreting recent history. If there is a difference at all between the natural and social sciences in this respect, it may be that economists these days have more opportunities to present biased findings than their colleagues in the physical sciences. But even this may not be so. I may underestimate the opportunities of scientists and engineers to submit expert testimonies with paid-for bias.

The second way in which value judgments may affect the investigator does not involve any bias in his findings or his reports on his findings. But ethical judgments may be so closely connected with his problems that he may feel impelled to make evaluative pronouncements on the normative issues in question. For example, scientists may have strong views about vivisection, sterilization, abortion, hydrogen bombs, biological warfare, etc., and may express these views in connection with their scientific work.

7

Likewise, social scientists may have strong views about the right to privacy, free enterprise, free markets, equality of income, old-age pensions, socialized medicine, segregation, education, etc., and they may express these views in connection with the results of their research. Let us repeat that this need not imply that their findings are biased. There is no difference on this score between the natural and the social sciences. The research and its results may be closely connected with values of all sorts, and value judgments may be expressed, and yet the objectivity of the research and of the reports on the findings need not be impaired.

The third way value judgments affect research is in the selection of the project, in the choice of the subject for investigation. This is unavoidable and the only question is what kinds of value and whose values are paramount. If research is financed by foundations or by the government, the values may be those which the chief investigator believes are held by the agencies or committees that pass on the allocation of funds. If the research is not aided by outside funds, the project may be chosen on the basis of what the investigator believes to be "social values," that is, he chooses a project that may yield solutions to problems supposed to be important for society. Society wants to know how to cure cancer, how to prevent hay fever, how to eliminate mosquitoes, how to get rid of crab grass and weeds, how to restrain juvenile delinquency, how to reduce illegitimacy and other accidents, how to increase employment, to raise real wages, to aid farmers, to avoid price inflation, and so on, and so forth. These examples suggest that the value component in the project selection is the same in the natural and in the social sciences. There are instances, thank God, in which the investigator selects his project out of sheer intellectual curiosity and does not give "two hoots" about the social importance of his findings. Still, to satisfy curiosity is a value too, and indeed a very potent one. We must not fail to mention the case of the graduate student who lacks imagination as well as intellectual curiosity and undertakes a project just because it is the only one he can think of, though neither he nor anybody else finds it interesting, let alone important. We may accept this case as the exception to the rule. Such exceptions probably are equally rare in the natural and the social sciences.

Now we come to the one real difference, the fourth of our value-references. Social phenomena are defined as results of human action, and all human action is defined as motivated action. Hence, social phenomena are explained only if they are attributed to definite types of action which are "understood" in terms of the values motivating those who decide and act. This concern with values--not values which the investigator entertains but values he understands to be effective in guiding the actions which bring about the events he studies-- is the crucial difference between the social sciences and the natural sciences. To explain the motion of molecules, the fusion or fission of atoms, the paths of celestial bodies, the growth or mutation of organic matter, etc., the scientist will not ask why the molecules want to move about, why atoms decide to merge or to split, why Venus has chosen her particular orbit, why certain cells are anxious to divide. The social scientist, however, is not doing his job unless he explains changes in the circulation of money by going back to the decisions of the spenders and hoarders, explains company mergers by the goals that may have persuaded managements and boards of corporate bodies to take such actions, explains the location of industries by calculations of such things as transportation costs and wage differentials, and economic growth by propensities to save, to invest, to innovate, to procreate or prevent procreation, and so on. My social-science examples were all from economics, but I might just as well have taken examples from sociology, cultural anthropology, political science, etc., to show that explanation in the social sciences regularly requires the interpretation of phenomena in terms of idealized motivations of the idealized persons whose idealized actions bring forth the phenomena under investigation.

An example may further elucidate the difference between the explanatory principles in non-human nature and human society. A rock does not say to us: "I am a beast,"[4] nor does it say: "I came here because I did not like it up there near the glaciers, where I used to live; here I like it fine, especially this nice view of the valley." We do not inquire into value judgments of rocks. But we must not fail to take account of valuations of humans; social phenomena must be explained as the results of motivated human actions.

The greatest authorities on the methodology of the social sciences have referred to this fundamental postulate as the requirement of "subjective interpretation," and all such interpretation of "subjective meanings" implies references to values motivating actions. This has of course nothing to do with value judgments impairing the "scientific objectivity" of the investigators or affecting them in any way that would make their findings suspect. Whether the postulate of subjective interpretation which *differentiates* the social sciences from the natural sciences should be held to make them either "inferior" or "superior" is a matter of taste.

9

Verifiabiltiy of Hypotheses

It is said that verification is not easy to come by in the social sciences, while it is the chief business of the investigator in the natural sciences. This is true, though many do not fully understand what is involved and, consequently, are apt to exaggerate the difference.

One should distinguish between what a British philosopher has recently called "high-level hypotheses" and "low-level generalizations."[5] The former are postulated and can never be *directly* verified; a single high-level hypothesis cannot even be *indirectly* verified, because from one hypothesis standing alone nothing follows. Only a *whole system* of hypotheses can be tested by deducing from some set of general postulates and some set of specific assumptions the logical consequences, and comparing these with records of observations regarded as the approximate empirical counterparts of the specific assumptions and specific consequences.[6] This holds for both the natural and the social sciences. (There is no need for *direct* tests of the fundamental postulates in physics--such as the laws of conservation of energy, of angular momentum, of motion--or of the fundamental postulates in economics--such as the laws of maximizing utility and profits.)

While entire theoretical systems and the low-level generalizations derived from them are tested in the natural sciences, there exist at any one time many unverified hypotheses. This holds especially with regard to theories of creation and evolution in such fields as biology, geology, and cosmogony; for example (if my reading is correct), of the theory of the expanding universe, the dust-cloud hypothesis of the formation of stars and planets, of the low-temperature or high-temperature theories of the formation of the earth, of the various (conflicting) theories of granitization, etc. In other words, where the natural sciences deal with non-reproducible occurrences and with sequences for which controlled experiments cannot be devised, they have to work with hypotheses which remain untested for a long time, perhaps forever.

In the social sciences, low-level generalizations about recurring events are being tested all the time. Unfortunately, often several conflicting hypotheses are consistent with the observed facts and there are no crucial experiments to eliminate some of the hypotheses. But everyone of us could name dozens of propositions that have been disconfirmed, and this means that the verification process has done what it is supposed to do. The impossibility of controlled experiments and the relatively large number of relevant variables are the chief obstacles to more efficient verification in the social sciences. This is not an inefficiency on the part of our investigators, but it lies in the nature of things.

Exactness of Findings

Those who claim that the social sciences are "less exact" than the natural sciences often have a very incomplete knowledge of either of them, and a rather hazy idea of the meaning of "exactness." Some mean by exactness measurability. This we shall discuss under a separate heading. Others mean accuracy and success in predicting future events, which is something different. Others mean reducibility to mathematical language. The meaning of exactness best founded in intellectual history is the possibility of constructing a theoretical system of idealized models containing abstract constructs of variables and of relations between variables, from which most or all propositions concerning particular connections can be deduced. Such systems do not exist in several of the natural sciences--for example, in several areas of biology--while they do exist in at least one of the social sciences: economics.

We cannot foretell the development of any discipline. We cannot say now whether there will soon or ever be a "unified theory" of political science, or whether the piecemeal generalizations which sociology has yielded thus far can be integrated into one comprehensive theoretical system. In any case, the quality of "exactness," if this is what is meant by it, cannot be attributed to all the natural sciences nor denied to all the social sciences.

Measurability of Phenomena

If the availability of numerical data were in and of itself an advantage in scientific investigation, economics would be on the top of all sciences. Economics is the only field in which the raw data of experience are already in numerical form. In other fields the analyst must first quantify and measure before he can obtain data in numerical form. The physicist must weigh and count and must invent and build instruments from which numbers can be read, numbers standing for certain relations pertaining to essentially non-numerical observations. Information which first appears only in some such form as "relatively" large, heavy, hot, fast, is later transformed into numerical data by means of measuring devices such as rods, scales, thermometers, speedometers. The economist can begin with numbers. What he observes are prices and sums of moneys. He can start out with numerical data given to him without the use of measuring devices.

The compilation of masses of data calls for resources which only large organizations, frequently only the government, can muster. This, in my opinion, is unfortunate because it implies

11

that the availability of numerical data is associated with the extent of government intervention in economic affairs, and there is therefore an inverse relation between economic information and individual freedom.

Numbers, moreover, are not all that is needed. To be useful, the numbers must fit the concepts used in theoretical propositions or in comprehensive theoretical systems. This is rarely the case with regard to the raw data of economics, and thus the economic analyst still has the problem of obtaining comparable figures by transforming his raw data into adjusted and corrected ones, acceptable as the operational counterparts of the abstract constructs in his theoretical models. His success in this respect has been commendable, but very far short of what is needed; it cannot compare with the success of the physicist in developing measurement techniques yielding numerical data that can serve as operational counterparts of constructs in the models of theoretical physics.

Physics, however, does not stand for all natural sciences, nor economics for all social sciences. There are several fields, in both natural and social sciences, where quantification of relevant factors has not been achieved and may never be achieved. If Lord Kelvin's phrase, "Science is Measurement," were taken seriously, science might miss some of the most important problems. There is no way of judging whether non-quantifiable factors are more prevalent in nature or in society. The common reference to the "hard" facts of nature and the "soft" facts with which the student of society has to deal seems to imply a judgment about measurability. "Hard" things can be firmly gripped and measured, "soft" things cannot. There may be something to this. The facts of nature are perceived with our "senses," the facts of society are interpreted in terms of the "sense" they make in a motivational analysis. However, this contrast is not quite to the point, because the "sensory" experience of the natural scientist refers to the *data*, while the "sense" interpretation by the social scientist of the ideal-typical inner experience of the members of society refers to basic *postulates* and intervening variables.

The conclusion, that we cannot be sure about the prevalence of non-quantifiable factors in natural and social sciences, still holds.

Constancy of Numerical Relationships

On this score there can be no doubt that some of the natural sciences have got something which none of the social sciences has got: "constants," unchanging numbers expressing unchanging relationships between measurable quantities.

The discipline with the largest number of constants is, of course, physics. Examples are the velocity of light (c = 2.99776 x 10^{10} cm/sec), Planck's constant for the smallest increment of spin or angular momentum (h = 6.624 x 10^{-27} erg. sec), the gravitation constant (G = 6.6 x 10^{-8} dyne cm^2 $gram^{-2}$), the Coulomb constant (e = 4.8025 x 10^{-10} units), proton mass (M = 1.672 x 10^{-24} gram), the ratio of proton mass to electron mass (M/m = 1836.13), the fine-structure constant (α^{-1} = 137.0371). Some of these constants are postulated (conventional), others (the last two) are empirical, but this makes no difference for our purposes. Max Planck contended, the postulated "universal constants" were not just "invented for reasons of practical convenience, but have forced themselves upon us irresistibly because of the agreement between the results of all relevant measurements."[7]

I know of no numerical constant in any of the social sciences. In economics we have been computing certain ratios which, however, are found to vary relatively widely with time and place. The annual income-velocity of circulation of money, the marginal propensities to consume, to save, to import, the elasticities of demand for various goods, the savings ratios, capital-output ratios, growth rates--none of these has remained constant over time or is the same for different countries. They all have varied, some by several hundred per cent of the lowest value. Of course, one has found "limits" of these variations, but what does this mean in comparison with the virtually immutable physical constants? When it was noticed that the ratio between labor income and national income in some countries has varied by "only" ten per cent over some twenty years, some economists were so perplexed that they spoke of the "constancy" of the relative shares. (They hardly realized that the 10 per cent variation in that ratio was the same as about a 25 per cent variation in the ratio between labor income and non-labor income.) That the income velocity of circulation of money has rarely risen above 3 or fallen below 1 is surely interesting, but this is anything but a "constant." That the marginal propensity to consume cannot in the long run be above 1 is rather obvious, but in the short run it may vary between .7 and 1.2 or even more. That saving ratios (to national income) have never been above 15 per cent in any country regardless of the economic system (communistic or capitalistic, regulated or essentially free) is a very important fact; but saving ratios have been known to be next to zero, or even negative, and the variations from time to time and country to country are very large indeed.

Sociologists and actuaries have reported some "relatively stable" ratios--accident rates, birth rates, crime rates, etc.-- but the "stability" is only relative to the extreme variability of other numerical ratios. Indeed, most of these ratios are subject to "human engineering," to governmental policies designed to change them, and hence they are not even thought of as constants.

The verdict is confirmed: while there are important numerical constants in the natural sciences, there are none in the social sciences.

Predictability of Future Events

Before we try to compare the success which natural and social sciences have had in correctly predicting future events, a few important distinctions should be made. We must distinguish hypothetical or conditional predictions from unconditional predictions or forecasts. And among the former we must distinguish those where all the stated conditions can be controlled, those where all the stated conditions can be either controlled or unambiguously ascertained before the event, and finally those where some of the stated conditions can neither be controlled nor ascertained early enough (if at all). A conditional prediction of the third kind is such an "iffy" statement that it may be of no use unless one can know with confidence that it would be highly improbable for these problematic conditions (uncontrollable and not ascertainable before the event) to interfere with the prediction. A different kind of distinction concerns the numerical definiteness of the prediction: one may predict that a certain magnitude (a) will change, (b) will increase, (c) will increase by at least so-and-so much, (d) will increase within definite limits, or (e) will increase by a definite amount. Similarly, the prediction may be more or less definite with respect to the time within which it is supposed to come true. A prediction without any time specification is worthless.

Some people are inclined to believe that the natural sciences can beat the social sciences on any count, in unconditional predictions as well as in conditional predictions fully specified as to definite conditions, exact degree and time of fulfilment. But what they have in mind are the laboratory experiments of the natural sciences, in which predictions have proved so eminently successful; and then they look at the poor record social scientists have had in predicting future events in the social world which they observe but cannot control. This comparison is unfair and unreasonable. The artificial laboratory world in which the experimenter tries to control all conditions as best as he can is different from the real world of nature. If a comparison is made, it must be between predictions of events in the real natural world and in the real social world.

14

Even for the real world, we should distinguish between predictions of events which we try to bring about by design and predictions of events in which we have no part at all. The teams of physicists and engineers who have been designing and developing machines and apparatuses are not very successful in predicting their performance when the design is still new. The record of predictions of the paths of moon shots and space missiles has been rather spotty. The so-called "bugs" that have to be worked out in any new contraption are nothing but predictions gone wrong. After a while predictions become more reliable. The same is true, however, with predictions concerning the performance of organized social institutions. For example, if I take an envelop, put a certain address on it and a certain postage stamp, and deposit it in a certain box on the street, I can predict that after three or four days it will be delivered at a certain house thousands of miles away. This prediction and any number of similar predictions will prove correct with a remarkably high frequency. And you don't have to be a social scientist to make such successful predictions about an organized social machinery, just as you don't have to be a natural scientist to predict the result of your pushing the electric-light switch or of similar manipulations of a well-trained mechanical or electrical apparatus.

There are more misses and fewer hits with regard to predictions of completely unmanipulated and unorganized reality. Meteorologists have a hard time forecasting the weather for the next 24 hours or two or three days. There are too many variables involved and it is too difficult to obtain complete information about some of them. Economists are only slightly better in forecasting employment and income, exports and tax revenues for the next six months or for a year or two. Economists, moreover, have better excuses for their failures because of unpredictable "interferences" by governmental agencies or power groups which may even be influenced by the forecasts of the economists and may operate to defeat their predictions. On the other hand, some of the predictions may be self-fulfilling in that people, learning of the predictions, act in ways which bring about the predicted events. One might say that economists ought to be able to include the "psychological" effects of their communications among the variables of their models and take full account of these influences. There are, however, too many variables, personal and political, involved to make it possible to allow for all effects which anticipations, and anticipations of anticipations, may have upon the end results. To give an example of a simple self-defeating prediction from another social science: traffic experts regularly forecast the number of automobile accidents and fatalities that are going to occur over holiday weekends, and at the same time they hope that their forecasts will influence drivers to be more careful and thus to turn the forecasts into exaggerated fears.

15

We must not be too sanguine about the success of social scientists in making either unconditional forecasts or conditional predictions. Let us admit that we are not good in the business of prophecy and let us be modest in our claims about our ability to predict. After all, it is not our stupidity which hampers us, but chiefly our lack of information, and when one has to make do with bad guesses in lieu of information the success cannot be great. But there is a significant difference between the natural sciences and the social sciences in this respect: Experts in the natural sciences usually do not try to do what they know they cannot do; and nobody expects them to do it. They would never undertake to predict the number of fatalities in a train wreck that might happen under certain conditions during the next year. They do not even predict next year's explosions and epidemics, floods and mountain slides, earthquakes and water pollution. Social scientists, for some strange reason, are expected to foretell the future and they feel badly if they fail.

Distance from Every-Day Experience

Science is, almost by definition, what the layman cannot understand. Science is knowledge accessible only to superior minds with great effort. What everybody can know cannot be science.

A layman could not undertake to read and grasp a professional article in physics or chemistry or biophysics. He would hardly be able to pronounce many of the words and he might not have the faintest idea of what the article was all about. Needless to say, it would be out of the question for a layman to pose as an expert in a natural science. On the other hand, a layman might read articles in descriptive economics, sociology, anthropology, social psychology. Although in all these fields technical jargon is used which he could not really understand, he might think that he knows the sense of the words and grasps the meanings of the sentences; he might even be inclined to poke fun at some of the stuff. He believes he is— from his own experience and from his reading of newspapers and popular magazines-- familiar with the subject matter of the social sciences. In consequence, he has little respect for the analyses which the social scientists present.

The fact that social scientists use less Latin and Greek words and less mathematics than their colleagues in the natural science departments and, instead, use everyday words in special, and often quite technical, meanings may have something to do with the attitude of the layman. The sentences of the sociologist, for example, make little sense if the borrowed words are understood in their non-technical, every-day meaning. But if the layman is told of the special meanings that have been bestowed upon his words, he gets angry or condescendingly amused.

16

But we must not exaggerate this business of language and professional jargon because the problem really lies deeper. The natural sciences talk about nuclei, isotopes, gallaxies, benzoids, drosophilas, chromosomes, dodecahedrons, Pleistocene fossils, and the layman marvels that anyone really cares. The social sciences, however,--and the layman usually finds this out--talk about--him. While he never identifies himself with a positron, a pneumococcus, a coenzyme, or a digital computer; he does identify himself with many of the ideal types presented by the social scientists, and he finds that the likeness is poor and the analysis "consequently" wrong.

The fact that the social sciences deal with man in his relations with fellow man brings them so close to man's own everyday experience that he cannot see the analysis of this experience as something above and beyond him. Hence he is suspicious of the analysts and disappointed in what he supposes to be a portrait of him.

Standards of Admission and Requirements

High school physics is taken chiefly by the students with the highest I.Q.'s. At college the students majoring in physics, and again at graduate school the students of physics, are reported to have on the average higher I.Q.'s than those in other fields. This gives physics and physicists a special presitge in schools and universities, and this prestige carries over to all natural sciences and puts them somehow above the social sciences. This is rather odd, since the average quality of students in different departments depends chiefly on departmental policies, which may vary from institution to institution. The pre-eminence of physics is rather general because of the requirement of calculus. In those universities in which the economics department requires calculus, the students of economics rank as high as the students of physics in intelligence, achievement and prestige.

The lumping of all natural sciences for comparisons of student quality and admission standards is particularly unreasonable in view of the fact that at many colleges some of the natural science departments, such as biology and geology, attract a rather poor average quality of students. (This is not so in biology at universities with many applicants for a pre-medical curriculum.) The lumping of all social sciences in this respect is equally wrong, since the differences in admission standards and graduation requirements among departments, say between economics, history, and sociology, may be very great. Many sociology departments have been notorious for their role as refuge for mentally under-privileged undergraduates. Given the propensity to over-

17

generalize, it is no wonder then that the social sciences are being regarded as the poor relations of the natural sciences and as disciplines for which students who cannot qualify for the sciences are still good enough.

Since I am addressing economists, and since economics departments, at least at some of the better colleges and universities, are maintaining standards as high as physics and mathematics departments, it would be unfair to level exhortations at my present audience. But perhaps we should try to convince our colleagues in all social science departments of the disservice they are doing to their fields and to the social sciences at large by admitting and keeping inferior students as majors. Even if some of us think that one can study social sciences without knowing higher mathematics, we should insist on making calculus and mathematical statistics absolute requirements—as a device for keeping away the the weakest students.

Despite my protest against improper generalizations, I must admit that averages may be indicative of something or other, and that the average I.Q. of the students in the natural science departments is higher than that of the students in the social science department.[8] No field can be better than the men who work in it. On this score, therefore, the natural sciences would be superior to the social sciences.

The Score Card

We may now summarize the tallies on the nine scores.

1. With respect to the invariability or recurrence of observations, we found that the greater number of variables—— of relevant factors—— in the social sciences makes for more variation, for less recurrence of exactly the same sequences of events.

2. With respect to the objectivity of observations and explanations, we distinguished several ways in which references to values and value judgments enter scientific activity. Whereas the social sciences have a requirement of "subjective interpretation of value-motivated actions" which does not exist in the natural sciences, this does not affect the proper "scientific objectivity" of the social scientist.

3. With respect to the verifiability of hypotheses, we found that the impossibility of controlled experiments combined with the larger number of relevant variables does make verification in the social sciences more difficult than in most of the natural sciences.

4. With respect to the exactness of the findings, we decided to mean by it the existence of a theoretical system from which most propositions concerning particular connections can be deduced. Exactness in this sense exists in physics and in economics, but much less so in other natural and other social sciences.

5. With respect to the measurability of phenomena, we saw an important difference between the availability of an ample supply of numerical data and the availability of such numerical data as can be used as good counterparts of the constructs in theoretical models. On this score, physics is clearly ahead of all other disciplines. It is doubtful that this can be said about the natural sciences in general relative to the social sciences in general.

6. With respect to the constancy of numerical relationships, we entertained no doubt concerning the existence of constants, postulated or empirical, in physics and in other natural sciences, whereas no numerical constants can be found in the study of society.

7. With respect to the predictability of future events, we ruled out comparisons between the laboratory world of some of the natural sciences and the unmanipulated real world studied by the social sciences. Comparing only the comparable, the real worlds—and expecting the special case of astronomy—we found no essential differences in the predictability of natural and social phenomena.

8. With respect to the distance of scientific from every-day experience, we saw that in linguistic expression as well as in their main concerns the social sciences are so much closer to prescientific language and thought that they do not command the respect that is accorded to the natural sciences.

9. With respect to the standards of admission and requirements, we found that they are on the average lower in the social than in the natural sciences.

The last of these scores relates to the current practice of colleges and universities, not to the character of the disciplines. The point before the last, though connected with the character of the social sciences, relates only to the popular appreciation of these disciplines; it does not aid in answering the question whether the social sciences are "really" inferior. Thus the last two scores will not be considered relevant to our question. This leaves seven scores to consider. On four of the six no real differences could be established. But on the other three scores, on "Invariance," "Verifiability," and "Numerical Constants," we found the social sciences to be inferior to the natural sciences.

The Implications of Inferiority

What does it mean if one thing is called "inferior" to another with regard to a particular "quality"? If this "quality" is something that is highly valued in any object, and if the absence of this "quality" is seriously missed regardless of other qualities present, then, but only then, does the noted "inferiority" have any evaluative implications. In order to show that "inferiority" sometimes means very little, I shall present here several statements about differences in particular qualities.

"Champagne is inferior to rubbing alcohol in alcoholic content."

"Beef steak is inferior to strawberry jello in sweetness."

"A violin is inferior to a violoncello in physical weight."

"Chamber music is inferior to band music in loudness."

"Hamlet is inferior to Joe Palooka in appeal to children."

"Sandpaper is inferior to velvet in smoothness."

"Psychiatry is inferior to surgery in ability to effect quick cures."

"Biology is inferior to physics in internal consistency."

It all depends on what you want. Each member in a pair of things is inferior to the other in some respect. In some instances it may be precisely this inferiority that makes the thing desirable. (Sandpaper is wanted *because* of its inferior smoothness.) In other instances the inferiority in a particular respect may be a matter of indifference. (The violin's inferiority in physical weight neither adds to nor detracts from its relative value.) Again in other instances the particular inferiority may be regrettable, but nothing can be done about it and the thing in question may be wanted none the less. (We need psychiatry, however much we regret that in general it cannot effect quick cures; and we need biology, no matter how little internal consistency has been attained in its theoretical systems.)

We have stated that the social sciences are inferior to the natural sciences in respects, for example, in verifiability. This is regrettable. If propositions cannot be readily tested, this calls for more judgment, more patience, more ingenuity. But does it mean much else?

20

The Crucial Question: "So What?"

What is the pragmatic meaning of the statement in question? If I learn, for example, that drug E is inferior to drug P as a cure for hay fever, this means that, if I want such a cure, I shall not buy drug E. If I am told Mr. A. is less inferior to Mr. B. as an automobile mechanic, I shall avoid using Mr. A when my car needs repair. If I find textbook K inferior to textbook S in accuracy, organization, as well as exposition, I shall not adopt textbook K. In every one of these examples, the statement that one thing is inferior to another makes pragmatic sense. The point is that all these pairs are *alternatives* between which a choice is to be made.

Are the natural sciences and the social sciences alternatives between which we have to choose? If they were, a claim that the social sciences are "inferior" could have the following meanings:

1. We should not study the social sciences.

2. We should not spend money on teaching and research in the social sciences.

3. We should not permit gifted persons to study social sciences and should steer them toward superior pursuits.

4. We should not respect scholars who so imprudently chose to be social scientists.

If one realizes that none of these things could possibly be meant, that every one of these meanings would be preposterous, and that the social sciences and the natural sciences can by no means be regarded as alternatives but, instead, that both are needed and neither can be dispensed with, he can give the inferiority statement perhaps one other meaning:

5. We should do something to improve the social sciences and remedy their defects.

This last interpretation would make sense if the differences which are presented as grounds for the supposed inferiority were "defects" that can be remedied. But they are not. That there are more variety and change in social phenomena; that, because of the large number of relevant variables and the impossibility of controlled experiments, hypotheses in the social sciences cannot be easily verified; and that no numerical constants can be detected in the social world-- these are not defects to be remedied but fundamental properties to be grasped, accepted, and taken into account. Because of these properties research and analysis

21

in the social sciences hold greater complexities and difficulties. If you wish, you may take this to be a greater challenge, rather than a deterrent. To be sure, difficulty and complexity alone are not sufficient reasons for studying certain problems. But the problems presented by the social world are certainly not unimportant. If they are also difficult to tackle, they ought to attract ample resources and the best minds. Today they are getting neither. The social sciences are "really inferior" regarding the place they are accorded by society and the priorities with which financial and human resources are allocated. This inferiority is curable.

Footnotes

* This was the Presidential Address delivered at the thirtieth annual conference of the Southern Economic Association, Atlanta, Georgia, on November 18, 1960.

1. Published in *On Freedom and Free Enterprise: Essays in Honour of Ludwig von Mises,* Mary Sennholz, ed. (Princeton: Van Nostrand, 1956), pp. 161-172.

2. Heinrich Rickert. *Die Grenzen der naturwissenschaftlichen Begriffsbildung* (Tübingen: Mohr-Siebeck, 1902).

3. Morris Cohen, *Reason and Nature: An Essay on the Meaning of Scientific Method* (New York: Harcourt, Brace, 1931), p. 348.

4. Hans Kelsen, *Allgamiene Staatslehre* (Berlin: Springer, 1925), p. 129. Quoted with illuminating comments in Alfred Schütz, *Der sinnhafte Aufbau der sozialen Welt* (Wien: Springer, 1932).

5. Richard B. Braithwaite, *Scientific Explanation: A Study of the Function of Theory, Probability and Law in Science* (Cambridge, Mass.: Harvard University Press 1953).

6. Fritz Machlup, "The Problem of Verification in Economics," *Southern Economic Journal,* July 1955.

7. Max Planck, *Scientific Autobiography and Other Papers* (New York: Philosophical Library, 1949), p. 173.

8. The average I.Q. of students receiving bachelor's degrees was, according to a 1954 study, 121 in the biological sciences, and 122 in economics, 127 in the physical sciences, and 119 in business. See Dael Wolfe, *America's Resources of Specialized Talent: The Report of the Commisson on Human Resources and Advanced Training* (New York: Harpers, 1954), pp. 319-322.

Part Two   Economics and Value Judgment

One of the methodological issues which has divided economists for decades is whether economics ever can be or even should be value free. The two readings in this section give the reader two views on a value-free economics and, by design, should cause some controversy. Robert Heilbroner argues that economics is value-laden because the objects of study all possess an attitude of consciousness. For him, economists should duplicate the methods but not the models of the natural sciences. These issues are related to the important issue of whether science should only study what is (called positive economics in that discipline) or can as well enter the domain of what ought to be (or normative economics). To Heilbroner, economic analysis can never be separated from considerations of a judgmental or normative kind because economists deal with a different subject matter than natural scientists.

Although Heilbroner is somewhat vague in the distinction between value judgments and positive or value-free statements, Yew-Kwang Ng attempts carefully to draw a distinction among what he refers to as factual judgments, value judgments proper, and subjective judgments of fact because he believes that value judgments have been confused with untestable factual judgments. A factual statement or judgment describes a fact as it is, and, therefore, must be either true or false; economists can certainly deal with such judgments. Subjective judgments of fact are "value judgments" based on scientific analysis and subjective opinion which can be true or false; Ng argues that economists should deal with such statements because they are better able than laymen to cover all the issues.

Turning to other writings on this topic, at the one extreme, Ronald Meek notes that:

> ... by the second half of the eighteenth century the so-called 'rule of law' in the economic sphere was becoming very much more apparent... The main job of economists ... has indeed been to take the economic machine to pieces to see how it works.... The motives of this study ... may well involve

value-judgments, but the study in itself does not necessarily do so. The core of traditional economic analysis ... consists of the simple law governing the inter-relations of supply, demand and price....

While Meek does not necessarily hold the viewpoint espoused in this quotation, Gunnar Myrdal does espouse the opposite position:

... every study of a social problem ... is and must be determined by valuations. A 'disinterested' social science has never existed and ... can never exist....

... valuations express our ideas of how it ought to be, or ought to have been.

For those who want to sample the view of economics as a value-free exercise, at least to some extent, the writings of Max Weber, an exponent of this view, should be consulted. His ideas are set out and analyzed by W.G. Runciman, and W.J. Cahnman discusses the Weberian methodology in the context of the other viewpoints that prevailed before and during the time period when Weber wrote.

Much of the writing about the use and abuse of value judgments in economics had revolved around the distinction between positive and normative economics. While different authors have put forward various definitions, usually a positive statement has been defined as dealing with facts while a normative statement concerns feelings and tastes. Normative economics spreads over into the domain of value-judgments and thus relates to the idea that economists should recognize at which points value-judgments enter their argument and analysis. T.W. Hutchison introduces and discusses the different types, sources, and entry-points of value-judgments and bias in economics; he distinguishes value judgments which are logically inevitable in any science from value-judgments which are not inevitable. As this suggests, much of this literature deals with types of statements which economists may or may not want to deal with.

Kurt Klappholz presents and then criticizes five arguments in support of the idea that value impregnation affects economics. The role of values in economics is shown by Fritz Machlup to resemble closely the physical sciences; thus he questions the inferiority complex of economists. Finally, Scott Gordon argues for objectivity as a criterion of performance in economics.

2 Economics as a "Value-free" Science

Robert L. Heilbroner*

Is economics a science? Partly that depends on how we choose to define the word. Does science mean a search for "repeatable patterns of dependence" among variables, the definition suggested by Ernest Nagel?[1] This nicely fits the current fashion for functional models in economics, but omits large areas of economic scrutiny, including economic history or economic taxonomy (comparative economic systems). Do we mean by science a reliance on the experimental method?[2] This throws into limbo certain central ideas of economics, such as value or utility, for which no experiments seem to be possible. Do we mean only the acceptance of a common paradigm, as suggested by Kuhn?[3] This then presents us with the problem of which economic paradigm to choose among a number of competing claimants: neoclassicism, institutionalism, Marxism.

I do not propose to explore here the question of which definition of science best applies to economics. Rather, my concern will be the relevance for economics of an idea that runs through all ideas of science - the conviction that science must be "value-free." By this I means that all scientists agree that their work should be carried on in a manner quite independent of the biases and hopes, not to mention the willful interference, of the scientist. In a word, science exists to explain or clarify things that exist independently of the values of the observer. It is the study of what "is," not of what "ought to be."

We shall have occasion later to glance at the purity with which science keeps its vows. But I think it fair to state that the vow itself constitutes an ideal to which almost all economists gladly and wholeheartedly subscribe. However they may define their task, nearly all would include "value-neutrality" as a necessary condition for the performed of those tasks in a "scientific" manner.

It is this central contention that I wish to challenge here. I will deny that the vital element of economic analysis (and I will define in a moment what I mean by this "vital element") can ever be wholly devoid of considerations of a normative of judgmental kind. To put it more strongly, I will try to show that the economic investigator is in a fundamentally different relationship *vis-a-vis* his subject from that of the natural scientist, so that advocacy or

Reprinted by permission from the *Social Research*, 40 (1973), 129-43.

value-laden interpretation becomes an inescapable part of social inquiry-- indeed, a desirable part.

That, however, is not all I wish to argue. For having sought to demonstrate that economics is not and should not be value-free, I will then turn around and insist that it should nonetheless retain as an objective the methods of science. The resolution of this seeming conflict will constitute the second objective of my paper.

Let me begin with the simpler part of my task, which is to argue that the work of the economist is laden with value judgments. Perhaps the best way to do so is to observe an economist at work. Let us say that he is collecting certain data--say the size distribution of corporations or the movement of prices. This is assuredly a procedure as objective and value-free as that of the natural scientist collecting data on the sizes of natural objects or the movements of the planets. (There are, to be sure, value considerations hidden in his *choice* of research object, but we will let that problem rest for the moment.) Our economist may then relate his first set of data to a second set--say the profit rates of corporations ranked by size, or the quantities of goods exchanged at various prices. Here, too, he breaches no rules of value-neutrality, assuming of course that he does not winnow his facts or doctor his observations, and that he avoids falsely imputing causal relationships to his resulting correlations.

Is not such work quite as value-free as that of the natural scientist who performs similar observations or correlations on the objects of the physical universe? Indeed it is. Furthermore, these findings of the economist may be of the utmost importance. But what he has performed up to this point is not yet economic analysis, or at least not that "vital element" of analysis to which I earlier called attention. Thus far he has only performed the task of an economic statistician. If economic analysis stopped at this point, the basic contention of my paper would be false.

But an *economist*--not an economic statistician--does not stop here. Indeed, his task now begins--the task of ascribing meaning to the data and the relationships that he has so painstakingly acquired. This meaning takes the form of efforts to "explain," postdictively or predictively, how and why the social organism displays the objective characteristics he has unearthed. And here is where value judgments inevitably insinuate themselves into his work.

Consider a very simple case. In every elementary textbook on economics (including my own), we find a standard example of economic analysis in the discussion of the social result of imposing a price ceiling below the "equilibrium" price for commodity, say, a rent ceiling on apartments. At the below-equilibrium price, we are told, there will be more would-be buyers (renters) "in the market" than before the ceiling was imposed. The result is the classic instance of a "shortage"--that is, a situation in which the quantity of a commodity demanded at a given price exceeds that which is offered at that price.

Now, is this not also a "value-free" finding, as removed from the wishes or biases of the economist as the finding of a natural scientist that a compass needle swings when a magnet is placed near it? Has not the unduly depressed price of the commodity "attracted" buyers in the first case, in the same way that the force field of the magnet has "attracted" the needle in the second? The question brings us to the critical parting of the ways between value-free natural science and value-laden social science. But the answer is not as simple as it might first appear, so I shall take some pains to spell it out carefully.

As perhaps you have anticipated, there is one very easy mode of demonstrating the value-laden content of economic analysis as contrasted with that of the natural scientist. It is that economists do not remain content with a simple observation (presumably derived by empirical techniques) that there co-exist a rent ceiling and a large number of disgruntled apartment-seekers. Invariably they go on to *prescribe* social remedies for this situation, usually remedies that fall back on the workings of the market system. "Thus," writes Paul Samuelson, "France had practically no residential construction from 1914 to 1948 because of rent controls. If new construction had been subject to such controls after World War II, the vigorous boom in French residential building since 1950 would never have taken place..." He concludes: "To protect the poor from being gouged by landlords, maximal rentals are often fixed by law. These fiats may do short-run good, but they also do long-run harm."[4]

It is not difficult to spot the value judgments latent in this example of economic analysis. There is a silent acquiscence in the propriety of the market as the mechanism for allocating apartments to would-be renters, rather than government allocations, or other means. There is also the assumption that the "long-run harm" cannot be overcome by non-market means, e.g., the provision of additional dwelling space by state construction. Now, Samuelson may have sound philosophical grounds for preferring the market means of allocation to non-market means, and he may be correct in his contention that the market will ultimately provide more housing than will a program of government construction. But it is quite clear that neither his preference nor his policy judgment follow as "value-free" conclusions from the raw data of ceiling prices and disgruntled apartment-seekers.

29

Since I have already declared that I do not believe that economists should aim at value-free analysis, it is not my intent to chastise Samuelson for introducing what are clearly value-laden statements into his text. (I *am* concerned about his failure to alert his readers to his value assumptions, but that is another matter, to which I will return later.) Therefore I will not further pursue the easy course of calling to attention other such institutional biases that affect the manner in which economists consciously or unconsciously move from initially neutral facts to ultimately loaded conclusions. Instead I shall set forth a more intricate and abstract, but I think more fundamental, argument. This is the argument that the inherent and inescapable value-content of economic analysis lies in the fact that the "behavior" of objects of social analysis is *not* like the behavior of the needle of the compass. In the difference between the two meanings of the word "behavior" lie the roots of the value problem for social science.

Of course we all know that human beings do not behave like so many iron filings or compass needles. Yet, when we inquire into the reasons for, or the nature of, the difference, the answer is not immediately apparent. Take the scientist who has observed the effect of a magnet on a compass a hundred times, and the economist who has observed the effects of lower prices on expenditures a hundred times. Assume that all the treacherous problems of extraneous influences are eliminated--that *ceteris paribus* truly prevails. In what way is the economist prevented from describing the behavior of his social universe by "laws" that are just as objective as those of the natural scientist?

The answer is obvious, but its implications may not be. The difference is that the objects observed by the social scientist all possess an attribute that is lacking in the objects of the natural universe. This is the attribute of consciousness--of cognition, of "calculation," of volition. Individuals and social organizations *do* often behave in ways that are as regular as those of the objects of physics and chemistry--if they did not, society would have long ago disintegrated. Yet, even in the most routine human actions there resides an element of latent willfulness that is lacking from even the most spectacular processes of nature. Indeed, one of the decisive attributes that distinguishes the social world from the physical is that social events are not merely interactions of forces, but contests of wills.

Thus behavior has both a purposiveness and a capriciousness that makes predictions infinitely more difficult than for the natural scientist. It is for these reasons that our efforts to predict economic behavior--however accurate in the "normal" case--suddenly become inaccurate when behavior changes its purpose or displays its caprices. The record of prediction with regard to stock market fluctuations, foreign exchange rates, price levels, or even the growth rate of vast aggregates like GNP, is all evidence of this "distressing" unreliability of behavioral regularity.

But what is the relevance of this unreliability to the problem of the value judgments concealed in economic analysis? The relevance lies in the central role played by behavior (and by the prediction of behavior) in the progress from value-free facts to value-laden conclusions. *Without assumptions about behavior, no conclusions whatsoever can be drawn from any set of social facts.* The problem, then, becomes one of discovering the value-component which is intrinsically part of our behavioral assumptions.

But why "intrinsically?" The answer is a curious one. If the economist hews to a strictly empirical description of behavior, given its latent unpredictability, he retains his value-neutrality, *but at the cost of any usable theory.* To put it differently, if the economist wishes to move from economic statistics to economic analysis, he must go beyond "observations" into "assumptions" with regard to behavior, and it is at this juncture that value judgments enters the picture. For when we examine the analytical work of economists, we do not find that their behavioral propositions are carefully framed to reflect the fundamental uncertainty that beclouds all behavioral "laws". Instead, we discover that economic behavior is almost universally described in precisely the "magnetic" fashion of the needle and the compass. The ruling "law" of behavior which is assumed to apply to consumers, workers, and businessmen alike is that they seek to "maximize"--consumers maximize their "utilities," workers their incomes, businessmen their profits.

Do they? The question is embarrassing on at least two counts. The first is that we have a great deal of difficulty in specifying exactly what kind of behavior we mean by "maximizing." For example, how shall we specify the behavior of a corporation which seeks to "maximize" its profits, presumably for a very long period of time, with respect to its price policies, its labor policies, its governmental relations, etc.?[5]

Second, there is the awkward probability that whatever behavior presumably "maximizes" utility or profits in one period is not likely to be that which maximizes in another. Lowered rents will not attract renters, as a magnet attracts a needle, if the renters expect the rent ceilings to be still *lower* in the future. So, too, we must taken into account changes in the state of mind of the economic actors over history. However consumers may have behaved in the days of the Industrial Revolution when they sought to maximize their utilities, it is surely not the way they behave in the days of the Advertising Age; nor do the entre-

31

preneurs of the New Industrial State, wrestling with the difficulties of maximization of which I just spoke, resemble the entrepreneurs of Dickensian England, couting up each day's receipts.

Thus the claim to knowledge of economic "laws" requires a
degree of "insight" wholly different from that required to enun-
ciate natural laws. The natural scientist does not care about how
his needle feels about magnetism, but the social scientist *has
to know* how his buyers and sellers feel about the "attraction"
of prices if his analysis is to be grounded on anything other than
guesswork or blind faith.

This crucial aspect in the meaning of social behavior infuses
economic analysis with values in two ways. The first has to do
with the fact that economists arbitrarily apply to economic reasoning "laws" that they know to be at best partial descriptions of
reality and at worst outright mis-descriptions of it. This is
surely an attitude at variance with the willingness of the scientist
to abandon a hypothesis when it no longer conforms with observations.

Why do economists persist in their *mumpsimus*--a term
Joan Robinson has unearthed (no doubt from English crossword
puzzles) that means "persistence in a belief one knows to be mistaken?" The answer is, I believe, embarrassingly simple. It is
that economists must have *some* kind of behavioral assumptions to make their theories "work." Lacking any better generalization, economists have retained the convenient assumption of
maximization because it serves this purpose--even if the resulting
theory often works very badly as a predictive instrument.

A second reason for the retention of the assumption of maximization introduces the problem of value-judgment from a different perspective. It is that maximization, for all its vagueness and
error, generally accords with the prevailing orientation of most
economists that "more is better." The idea of maximization
thereby gives a certain "scientific" authority to textbook statements that the consumer who climbs to the peak of his indifference map is more "satisfied" than one who camps out, like a
vagabond, on some lower contour, or that an economy with a high
growth rate if "better off" than one with a lower rate. In a
word, maximization becomes a prescription for conduct. Since we
are all now acutely aware that more is not necessarily better, I
will not belabor the value implications of this belief, other than to
equate it with a latter-day version of Benthamism, in which
pushpin, poetry, and pollution are all the same, so long as they
get counted in the Gross National Product.

The charge that economics is deeply immersed in value orien-
tations is not a new one, and I shall not spend more time in

seeking to prove the point. Indeed, many readers may have wondered why I did not make a much more immediate attack. This is to point out that the value-judgments of economics can be discerned at a simpler level than the one to which I have paid attention--to wit, the ideological biases exemplified in my dis cussion of rent ceilings. There is an obvious political bias observable in the choice of research tasks arrogated to itself by the profession--the doubter may wish to compare the contents of *The American Economic Review* with that of the *Review of Radical Political Economics*. There is the general failure on the part of economists to recognize that the essential terms of their vocabulary--labor, capital, interest, even wealth--are all historical concepts fraught with socio-political implications.

If I have not chosen this road, it is not because it is not relevant to the topic (indeed, I will return to it later), but because it has been well covered by others.[6] My purpose, therefore, was to call attention to a less well-explored aspect of the problem lodged in the interstices of economic analysis itself, rather than in the underlying premises of economic thought.

But all this is, in a sense, preamble to the more difficult task that I set myself at the outset. This is to question the legitimacy of the idea of "value neutrality" as an ideal for economics, and at the same time to defend the idea of "science" as an appropriate ideal for economics. The task sounds like a contradiction in terms, so I shall proceed with care, trying to specify with precision what I believe are the elements at stake.

The first problem with "value freedom" concerns the psychological or sociological relationship between the observer and the thing observed. Presumably the scientist approaches his research object in a frame of mind that is without conscious prejudice-- fearlessly open to an acceptance of results, however unexpected or unwelcome these may be.

This attribute of scientific inquiry has come under sharp attack in the natural sciences. The work of both Polanyi and Kuhn has made it abundantly clear that scientists do not in fact behave with indifference to their observed results, but struggle desperately to fit "anomalies" into preconceived patterns or paradigms, explaining away or simply ignoring results that fly in the face of prevailing expectations.[7] If this is the case with the natural sciences, it is far more so with the social sciences. Within the field of economics many instances can be cited to demonstrate the absence of that scientific detachment that supposedly characterizes the scientist at work. Let me only mention in passing the long intellectual struggle against Keynesianism and in more recent days the equal unwillingness to abandon the Keynesian notion that inflation was incompatible with substantial unemployment. Or

I might call attention to the unwillingness of economists to admit the phenomenon of imperialism as a proper subject for economic investigation, or their dogged adherence to a benign theory of international trade in the face of disquieting evidence that trade has failed to benefit the poorer lands.

As in my previous discussion involving Paul Samuelson's unwitting use of value criteria, my purpose is not to scold economists for their lack of objectivity. It is rather to point to the cause for this universally observed state of affairs. This cause lies in the fact that the process of social investigation inescapably embroils the investigator in his subject in a way that is different from that of the natural scientist. For the latter, the discovery of an anomaly may constitute a blow to his intellectual "security," perhaps even to his phychological "integrity." *But it does not threaten his moral position as a member of a social order.*

On the contrary, the discovery of unexpected results in the social universe almost invariably threatens or confirms the legitimacy of the social system of which the social investigator is unavoidably a part. Indeed, at the risk of making an assertion that verges on a confession, I would venture the statement that every social scientist approaches his task with a wish, conscious or unconscious, to demonstrate the workability or unworkability of the social order he is investigating. It is not a matter of indifference to the neoclassicist or to the Marxist whether his data fit the hypothesis he is testing, and each struggles mightily to explain away, to minimize, or to reject results that go counter to his initial beliefs.

Moreover, this extreme vulnerability to value judgments is not a sign of deficiency in the social investigator. On the contrary, he belongs to a certain order, has a place in it, benefits or loses from it, and sees his future bound up with its success or failure. In the face of this inescapable existential fact, an attitude of total "impartiality" to the universe of social events is psychologically unnatural, and more likely than not leads to a position of moral hypocrisy. It is not one of their flaws, but one of their claims to greatness as economists that Smith, Ricardo, Mill, Marx, Marshall and Keynes were explicit in their use of facts and theories as instruments of advocacy. Smith's great model of the economic system was written not merely to "analyze" late eighteenth-century England, but to plead for a policy of "perfect liberty" and to assail the policies of mercantilism. Ricardo used his theory as the underpinnings of his attack against the Corn Laws. Mill's *Principles* advocated a stationary state and income redistribution. Marx espoused social revolution, based on his economic model of the "immanent" tendencies of capitalism. Marshall was a partisan of cautious and careful social change, the rationale for which was spelled out in his *Principles.*

Keynes sought the social control over investment, for reasons that the *General Theory* made clear.

These "policy" prescriptions were not afterthoughts. On the contrary, they were an inextricable part of the great contributions of these economists to social understanding. Yet in every case, they rested on value-laden assumptions. The most obvious of these, to which I have referred in passing but have purposely not discussed in this paper, lay in their beliefs in the propriety or impropriety of the *class relations* of the societies they analyzed. Take away the sociological or institutional parameters from the thought of the classical economists (or from Marshall and Keynes) and there is nothing in their systems that could not have led them to conclusions similar to those of Marx. But--and this is the element I have chosen to highlight--there is also in every instance the assumption that maximization is the behavioral force that makes the social universe move. Take away maximization, and the conclusions of Marx can be rather easily made to conform with the mild policy prescriptions for the stationary state proposed by John Stuart Mill.[8]

Thus value judgments, partly of a sociological kind, partly with respect to behavior, have infused economics from its earliest statements to its latest and most sophisticated representations. And indeed, insofar as economic analysis is concerned with social change, in which the fortunes of men (including the analyst) must be affected, how could it be otherwise?

But this leads me to my final contention--that despite its immersion in values, norms and advocacy, economics should nonetheless attempt to embrace "scientific" canons of procedure. How is it possible to reconcile such seemingly contradictory positions?

The reconciliation involves as its first step a return to our earlier dichotomy between economic statistics and economic analysis. So far as the former is concerned, there is little to trouble us. Precisely the same standards and precisely the same pitfalls confront the economic statistician as the biologist or the physicist. Both must struggle against the inhibitions imposed by the reigning paradigm, first in their choice of research objects, and second in their treatment of research results. Both confront, albeit in somewhat different ways, the problem of the interaction of the observer with the things he observes. It is not here that the problem lies.

The question is, rather, how the economic analyst, whose analysis *must* include normative elements, can aspire to the position of the scientist. Here, at this critical last juncture, I must first state with all the force at my command that I do not believe that the economist has the right, in the name of value-

35

advocacy, to tamper with data, to promote or promulgate policy recommendations without supporting evidence, or to pass off his value-laden conclusions as possessing "scientific" validity. Indeed, one of my objections to much of the contemporary economics is that it lends a gloss of such "objective" validity to conclusions that in fact only follow from arbitrary and value-laden assumptions--I refer, for example, to the use of neoclassical economics to "disprove" the usefulness of minimum wage laws, etc. Of course minimum wage laws *may* bring consequences other than those desired by their sponsors. But I hope that my labors in analyzing the dubious nature of the usual assumptions about economic behavior now make it possible for me to state that no economic predictions or prescriptions that rest on these assumptions can lay claim to any "scientific" validity.

How then can the economist possibly aspire to the standards of a social *scientist?* The answer does not lie in efforts to produce behavioral "laws" that will be the counterpart of the laws of nature--that is a chimerical task.[9] The answer lies rather in his efforts to duplicate the methods, not the models, of the natural sciences.

What are these methods? They are to be found, above all, in the openness of the procedures by which science goes about its task, exposing itself to informed criticism at every stage of its inquiry, engaging in painful self-scrutiny with regard to its premises, experiments, reasoning, conclusions. Revelation, "truths beyond question," unstated premises, missing links in the chain of deduction may all be found in "scientific" analysis, but they are by common consent its weakness to which criticism is rightly directed.

This element of science can be transposed in its entirety to economic analysis. Like the natural scientist, the economist (or for that matter, any social scientist) is expected to keep his journal, recording as best he can his starting points, his successive steps, his final conclusions. He records, with all the honesty and fidelity of which he is capable, not only his data and his processes of reasoning, but his initial commitments, hopes, and disappointments. Since economists perform few experiments that can be rerun in a laboratory, his results cannot be so easily falsified as those of the natural scientist, but they can be equally subject to scrutiny and criticism in the forum of expert opinion.

Thus when I urge the abandonment of the idea of a "value free" economics, I do not thereby seek to abandon the idea of an economics committed to scientific standards. Rather, I want economics to make a virtue of necessity, exposing for all the world to see the indispensable and fructifying value-grounds from which it begins its inquiries so that these inquiries may be fully exposed to--and not falsely shielded from--the public examination that is the true strength of science.

Footnotes

* This was a paper prepared for delivery at the 1972 annual meeting of the American Political Science Association, Washington, D.C., September, 5-9.

1. Ernest Nagel, *The Structure of Science* (1961), p. 4.

2. P.W. Bridgman, *The Way Things Are* (1959), p. 130.

3. Thomas S. Kuhn, *The Structure of Scientific Revolutions* (1962, 1970).

4. Paul A. Samuelson, *Economics*, 8th edn., p. 372.

5. A problem into which we cannot enter here, but which warrants passing mention, is the similarly empty content of "maximization" with regard to consumers. Of all the terms of economics, none is so cavalierly dealt with as "utility", which is presumably the *summum bonum* of individual economic behavior. Samuelson disposes of it in one sentence: "As a consumer you will buy a good because you feel it will give you satisfaction or utility" (op. cit., p. 410). Yet, in a famous earlier work, *The Foundations of Economic Analysis* (1965, pp. 90-91), Samuelson warned against definitions of utility that are "consistent with all conceivable behavior, while refutable by none!" For a discussion of the difficulties of giving operational content to the "maximizing" behavior of corporations, see Marris and Wood, *The Corporate Economy* (1971), pp. xviii-xx, and A. Lowe, *On Economic Knowledge* (1965), pp. 34-35, 47-48.

6. The literature of "ideological" criticism is substantial. Let me cite here only a few examples. The founding father is no doubt Marx, especially the three volumes of wbTheories of Surplus Value. There is the well-known critique by Myrdal, The Political Element in the Development of Economic Thought (first published in 1928). For more recent statements see W. Leontief, *The American Economic Review*, March 1961; Benjamin Ward, *What's Wrong with Economics?* (1972); Assar Lindbeck, *The Political Economy of the New Left* (1971), and my review of it in *Political Science*

Review, September, 1972; and numerous essays in the *Review of Radical Political Economics*, especially Vol. 3, No. 2 (July, 1971), entitled "Special Issue on Radical Paradigms in Economics."

7. Michael Polanyi, *Personal Knowledge* (1958); Kuhn, op. cit.

8. Lowe (op. cit.) maintains that short-run maximizing behavior--i.e., behavior that seeks to maximize receipts and minimize expenditures within very short time horizons--may well have been a reasonably accurate generalization with respect to behavior in the early days of industrial capitalism, but that the rise of consumer affluence and corporate oligopoly have progressively enlarged the area of "discretionary" activity, and thus also enlarged the degree of unpredictability that afflicts statements about behavior. This introduces an historical element into the problem, whose implications I shall not pursue further in this paper. Lowe maintains that economic theory (including its inescapable behavioral suppositions) was empirically defensible in the early to mid-nineteenth century, but has become progressively less so in the early to mid-twentieth century. His treatise *On Economic Knowledge* is essentially an effort to circumvent this problem by urging that moden economic theory cease its efforts to create "predictive" theory (which depends on reliable behavioral laws), turning instead toward an "instrumental" approach which seeks to specify a range of behavioral responses and patterns that are compatible with the attainment of a postulated "goal." I return briefly to this redefinition of the task of economics in footnote 9.

9. As Lowe has argued (op. cit.), it well may be that the problem for economic analysis lies in specifying the behavior that is required to attain certain postulated goals or targets. His suggestion thus changes the paradigm of economics from that of a "positive" science, predicting future states on the basis of "laws" of behavior, to that of a means-ends science, investigating the various behavioral paths by which a society may attain a goal. This does not, of course, make economics "value-free," since the selection of alternative routes will inevitably reflect the preconceptions of the investigator. It does, however, free economics from the particular value-orientations implicit in the laws of behavior which it now takes as "constants" of the social universe.

3 Value Judgments and Economists' Role in Policy Recommendation[1]

Yew-Kwang Ng

It is generally held that economists, *per se*, should refrain from making "value judgments." Economists' (and other social scientists') role in policy recommendations is therefore seriously limited. In many cases, economists do make these judgments out of necessity, but usually with an uneasy conscience. This paper argues that many so-called "value judgments" are not value judgments at all, but subjective judgments of fact. Since economists are more qualified than many others for making subjective judgments of fact closely related to their fields of study, they can have a quieter conscience in making them. If this argument is accepted, economists' role in making policy recommendations can be considerably enhanced.

I

While this is not the place to go into the controversy of the philosophical problems of meta-normative theory, a definition of value judgment, the usage of which is so confused and confusing, is not out of place.

Value judgments, as the term implies, are meant to be contrasted with factual judgments. Factual statements are descriptive, value judgments are evaluative and/or prescriptive. A factual statement describes a fact as it is, and hence must be either true or false. In principle, it can be verified or falsified under ideal conditions. On the other hand, value judgments assert the moral worthiness of certain things, *e.g.*, whether an object is good, a behavior is right or something ought to be done. They cannot, by their very nature, be true or false, in the same sense as a factual statement. Thus, we cannot prove or disprove a value judgment as we verify a factual statement. However, a value judgment can be persuasive, *i.e.*, it may appeal to us because it agrees with our ethical codes. The statement that "you ought to help the poor" is a value judgment. The statement that "the depth of this well is over ten feet" is a factual statement.[2]

Reprinted by permission from the *Economic Journal*, 82 (1972), pp. 1014-18.

Value judgments have been widely confused with untestable factual judgments.

It should be obvious that, while value judgments are untestable, not all untestable judgments are value judgments. Thus the factual statement that "there is a winged pig (somethere in the universe)" is untestable. However, it is untestable only because it is physically impossible to search every corner in the universe and not because the statement cannot be true or false.

Some factual judgments are regarded as value judgments because they either cannot be proved or are difficult to prove in practice, and hence they usually reflect personal values. The difficulty of proving may be due to practical difficulty of measurement (as may be the case in certain interpersonal comparisons), the complexity of inter-relationships (including ends-means relationship) typical of social phenomena, or some other factors. These difficulties render universal agreement impossible and hence factual judgments in these areas usually reflect personal values and personal or sectional interests as well. For example, it is pointed out (Klappholz, 1964, p. 103) that, gazing at the same statistics, left-wing economists tend to "infer" from them that progressive taxation does not have a disincentive effect, while right-wing economists tend to "infer" that it does.

It seems, therefore, that if "value judgment" is defined widely to include every judgment which reflects the values of the person making it, many judgments of fact which are difficult to prove *could* be value judgments. This may be a matter of definition. But to be useful, a definition must reflect the main characteristics of the set it defines. Value judgments proper and judgments of fact which reflect personal values are logically distinct; the one cannot, the other can be true or false; hence, even if we insist on the wide definition, we must sub-define them into value judgments proper and secondary value judgments. I propose to call the latter "subjective judgments of fact" and reserve the word "value" to those judgments which in themselves are statements of values.

Now there is some agreement among economists (and other scientists) that, as economists, they are not entitled to make any value judgment, and as citizens, they are no more qualified than any other citizen in making value judgments. I have no quarrel with this standpoint if "value judgments" refer to value judgments proper. However, most economists tend to subsume under "value judgments" what I call "subjective judgments of fact." It is my contention that economists are often more qualified than non-economists in making subjective judgments of fact closely related to their fields of study. This should be acceptable to anyone who has any faith in the supposed usefulness of learning economics. I limit myself here to those subjective judgments of fact that are closely related to economics; economists need not be better qualified in making other subjective judgments. But many subjective judgments of fact are subjective only because the relationships or inter-relationships are too complicated to be determined precisely. For example, an economist may be hard put to it to judge the effects on economic growth of two alternative balance-of-payments policies. But a layman is likely to know nothing about the effects at all. For another example, given a set of statistics, economists are more qualified to infer whether progressive taxation has a disincentive effect. Though their personal ideology or interest may influence their inference, they are still better qualified than non-economists, *ceteris paribus*. That is to say, left-wing economists are better qualified than left-wing non-economists, neutral economists are better qualified than neutral non-economists and so on.

Economists are commonly asked by government agencies to make subjective judgments of fact. They usually do out of necessity make them, but only with an uneasy conscience that they are making "value judgments" which they are not supposed to make. If my argument above is accepted, economists can have quieter consciences in doing so.

It is quite true that economists and sociologists must as scientists be as objective as possible in making subjective judgments of fact. Both left and right wings must struggle to free themselves from ideological biases. They are, however, free as citizens to advocate their particular brand of ideology.

It is also quite true that subjective judgments of fact my not be correct and hence must be taken with a grain of salt. Economists will help to clarify this by stating explicitly in their recommendations or reports which parts are scientifically established facts, which are judgments of fact partly based on scientific analysis and partly on subjective opinion, and which are pure value judgments. While subjective judgments of fact do not have the same status as well-established scientific propostions, they are needed in aking many important policy decisions. Thus, unless these decisions are to be left unmade, or to be made on even more arbitrary judgments, economists and other scientists must stand up and make them.

II

Recognising the distinction between subjective judgments of fact and value judgments proper not only enhances economists' (and other scientists') role in policy recommendation, it also calls for a revaluation of the logical status of such disciplines as welfare economics.

It is widely held that welfare economics is necessarily normative. For example, Nath (1969, chs. I, VI, X) argues that welfare economics is necessarily based on value judgments. It seems to me that some of the main propositions of welfare economics can be quite free of value judgments.[3] Apart from the purely technological propostions on which Nath places exception, such a proposition as "under classical environments, a perfectly competitive equilibrium is also a Paretian optimum" is purely positive; it is not based on the Paretian value judgments. Only where it is reformulated for example into "a perfectly competitive equilibrium is optimal," is it based on the Paretian value judgment. As a matter of fact, the proposition in its first formulation has been proved by mathematical economists (Arrow, 1951).

To descend to a more practical plane, such a statement as "this particular policy will result in a Pareto improvement" is also not based on any value judgment, but rather on positive economic analysis and perhaps on some subjective judgments of fact. On the other hand, the statement that "this policy should be adopted as it will result in a Pareto improvement" is certainly based on some Pareto value judgment. In general, it may be said that any policy recommendation must be based on some value judgment but economic analysis itself need not be value-loaded; and economic analysis (including welfare economics) and economic policy are two different things. It is by confusing these two logically distinct concepts that Nath (1969, p. 131) is led to deny the existence of theoretical welfare economics.

A similar approach to that of Nath is also adopted by Machlup (1969) when he asserts that welfare economics is necessarily normative. "Where the objectives are fully and unambiguously specified, the analysis of the best ways to attain the objectives is instrumental, not normative. But where there is any deficiency or ambiguity in the specification, the analyst cannot provide the answer without (consciously or unconsciously) filling the gaps *ad hoc* according to value judgments he himself entertains at the moment... this kind of economic analysis--welfare economics--is normative" (Machlup, 1969, p. 119, p. 116).

The deficiency in the specification of objectives means that no definite conclusion can be drawn without additional value judgments. Where a conclusion (e.g., a policy of policy suggestion) must be drawn, it is true that value judgment is involved. This is usually true for economists as advisers, though many of the "value" judgments are actually subjective factual judgments. But for theoretical welfare economics, the analysis can go short of making personal value judgments. It is true that for the analysis

42

to go a step further, value judgments are involved, but these judgments may be put in conditional clauses so that the analysis itself is value-free.

Take the example of external effects. The general proposition that, where externality exists, the utility maximizing behaviors of atomistic actors will result in a non-Paretian situation, is entirely value-free. However, to derive policy conclusions, a certain value judgment is needed which may be put in a conditional clause: "If the sole objective is the achievement of a Paretian optimum, then a tax should be imposed on X." On the other hand, in deciding whether to impose a tax on a particular firm A, without definite specification of objectives from outside, the decision is necessarily normative.

From the above discussion, it may be concluded that positive welfare economics exists, but in applying welfare economics to make definite recommendation or policy decisions, value judgments must be involved (either given from outside or being made by the applied economist). However, if the argument of Section I is valid, economists need not be inhibited from or have an uneasy conscience in making those "value judgments" which are actually subjective judgments of fact.

Footnotes

1. This paper is a revised version of a paper presented to the Second Conference of Australian Economists, Sydney, August 1971. I have benefited from the conference discussion, especially the comments by Dr. K.D. Rivett and Mr. M. Weisser.

2. Some statements seem to fall on the borderline. For example, there is some controversy whether the following statement is a value judgment: "This painting is beautiful." However, as far as the recommendatory role of economists is concerned, such difficulty is usually irrelevant.

3. Cf. Archibald (1959, p. 325).

References

C.G. Archibald, "Welfare Economics, Ethics, and Essentialism," *Economica*, November 1959.

K.J. Arrow, "An Extension of the Basic Theorems of Classical Welfare Economics," in J. Neyman (ed.), *Proceedings of the Second Berkeley Symposium on Mathematical Statistics and Probability*, (Berkeley, University of California Press, 1951).

K. Klappholz, "Value Judgments and Economics," *British Journal of Philosophy of Science*, August 1964.

F. Machlup, "Positive and Normative Economics," in R.L. Heilbroner (ed.), *Economic Means and Social Ends*, (Englewood Cliffs: Prentice-Hall, 1969).

S.K. Nath, *A Reappraisal of Welfare Economics*, (London: Routledge and Kegan Paul, 1969).

L. Robbins, *An Essay on the Nature and Significance of Economic Science*, (London: Macmillan, 1932, 1935).

L. Robbins, "Interpersonal Comparisons of Utility," *Economic Journal*, December 1938.

P.J.D. Wiles, *The Political Economy of Communism*, Harvard University Press, 1964).

Part Three   **The Goal of Economics as a Hard Science**

In Part One the question of whether social sciences like economics are in some sense inferior to the hard sciences such as physics and chemistry was formally examined. In this part the reader looks at another aspect of that same question from a pragmatic point of view. Since World War II two developments have greatly aided the work of many applied economists. These developments were the invention and expansion of the computer and computing facilities, and the growth of what has become known as econometrics. The former development will not be explained further here since the reading in this part by Thomas Mayer does not deal with it explicitly, but it is worth noting that the empirical aspects of econometrics (as opposed to the theoretical aspects) would be much less developed without the use of computers; computers permit organization and manipulation of masses of data in a speedy and efficient manner (see Mayes, 1981, Chapter 10).

The term econometrics may be new to some readers so it should be defined in an elementary way. If we take the broadest view of this branch of economics, it may be defined as methods of study which develop and apply statistical techniques to economic models. For a more formal definition see G. Tintner (1953) or the main and supplementary texts on econometrics.

There are normally two parts to an econometric model. The first part is comprised of an equation and more generally a system of equations connecting observable economic variables and unobservable random disturbances (representing the influence of social, political and other events not directly accounted for in the equations and the error of measurements in the observation of the economic variable). The second part is comprised of a set of assumptions about the properties of the random disturbances (including the assumptions about their probability distributions, if needed). Sometimes it is convenient to speak of econometrics in terms of its functions. These include: (i) the specification of causal econometric models based on economic theory, (ii) the estimation and statistical testing (using conventional predictive and non-predictive statistical tests) of the econometric models against observed data, (iii) the use of these models for policy and prediction purposes and finally, (iv) the respecification and replication of the model, if necessary (see Bergstrom 1967).

It should be pointed out that the econometric models are often a simplified representation of complex real-world phenomena. Accordingly, they are open to the "usual" criticisms of oversimplification and unrealistic assumptions. The use of simpler models has been defended by Koopmans (1957). He states that: "The study of simple models is protected from the reproach of unreality by the consideration that these models may be prototypes of a more complicated subsequent model" (pp. 142-143). Nevertheless, the adequacy of econometric models does depend critically on the assumptions regarding the disturbances of the model. For example, the usual statistical tests for the econometric models are valid only when the disturbances of the model are serially independent. Thus proper econometric model building requires that these assumptions are carefully formulated and adequate tests are performed to verify them. The challenging role of an econometrician is nicely summed up by Malinvaud (1970). He writes that: "The art of the econometrician consists as much in defining a good model as in finding an efficient statistical procedure. Indeed, this is why he cannot be purely a statistician, but must have a solid grounding in economics" (p. 723).

It may have seemed to many, and may still appear to a few, that econometrics with its model-building and testing methods provided economists with a first-rate means of establishing causal relationships and predicting the course of economies. But, following up on the work of G. Tintner and O. Morgenstern, Mayer introduces a sobering note to these optimistic expectations. He argues that empirical econometric work faces many problems in its causal and predictive roles, and that these difficulties have often been ignored or dealt with only superficially by economists who have perhaps not been trained to deal with them as have people in the physical or natural sciences. Mayer concludes his article, however, on an optimistic note by suggesting eight means by which econometrics can better serve or be better used by economists. Because of the widespread use of econometrics, students of economics should be aware of the problems which Mayer raises. The readers should also be made aware of another probable problem (which is not covered by Mayer's paper) associated with econometrics of macroeconomic models. It has come to light in the past few years that a priori restrictions used to identify these macroeconometric models are unlikely to be implied by acceptable dynamic economic theories; for example, see Sims (1980). Some economists have gone as far as suggesting that the conventional approach to econometric modelling be abandoned in favor of a rational expectation approach. For it is argued that expectations rationally formed by economic agents are essentially the same as the predictions of the relevant economic theory. The reader

46

should consult Lucas (1972) and Sargent and Wallace (1975) and references therein for an introduction to this approach of econometric modelling. The reader may also consult the Swamy, Barth and Tinsley (1982) paper for a critical analysis of the rational expectation approach. They have argued that "conventional formulation of rational expectations in these models violate the axiomatic basis of modern statistical theory by confounding 'objective' and 'subjective' notions of probability" (p. 125). Most of these readings, however, are rather involved and are recommended to readers with a solid background in econometrics. The basic ideas of rational expectations may be obtained by reading Maddock and Carter (1982). Kantor (1979) discusses the position of rational expectations in the history of economic thought and method.

Some other economists prefer the strengthening of traditional macroeconometric methodology by integrating it with the time series methodology. They favor more open specification searches for the model, and an open data analysis to uncover the mysteries of lags and the links to causality than carried out in the traditional macroeconometric approach. The proponents of this integrative methodology favor: a careful specification of disturbance terms in the model, a thorough testing of constraints imposed by the econometric theory, and a testing of exogeneity assumptions in the model. The interested reader may consult Leamer (1978) and Zellner (1979), and references therein for details. A comprehensive discussion on the methodology of time-series analysis can be found in Granger and Watson (1982).

A dynamic econometric model may be represented as a multivariate *autoregressive - moving average* (ARMA) process whose parameters are restricted on *a priori* basis of economic theory. Thus there is a natural link between time series models and conventional econometric models. An excellent survey of dynamic specification in econometrics is provided by Hendry *et al.*, (1982).

4 Economics as a Hard Science: Realistic Goal or Wishful Thinking?

Thomas Mayer*

Many economists believe that we should strive to turn economics into a hard science. Indeed, if this goal is feasible it is hard to see how anyone could possibly object to it. But, I will argue that it is overly ambitious, premature, and more likely to do harm than good. I do not deny that economics may perhaps ultimately become a hard science. To be sure, at present it is hard to see how we can ever achieve such a high degree of certainty, given the limited potential for meaningful controlled experiments, and also the fact that our conclusions affect the data (human behavior) they apply to. But the fact that one cannot see at present how something could be invented in the future is hardly evidence that it will never be invented (Cf. Popper, 1961). My argument that economics is currently very different from a hard science, therefore, does not rest on any fundamental dichotomy between the natural and the social sciences, but is based on much more mundane considerations.

I

Those who claim that economics is becoming a hard science point to the greatly increased use of mathematics in economics. And, indeed, economists no longer are differentiated from the hard scientists by their ignorance of advanced mathematics. If knowledge of mathematics is all that would be required to make a hard science, then many, though certainly not all economists could indeed claim to be hard scientists. But mathematics itself is not an empirical science. To make economics into a rigorous *empirical* science requires that we have reliable methods of testing hypotheses.[1] With all due respect to the great contribution that mathematical economics has made, it is the ability to test hypotheses rather than the use of advanced mathematics to formulate hypotheses that is the distinguishing mark of a hard empirical science.[2] Hence, to see whether economics is within hailing distance of being a hard empirical science, we have to see how reliable our techniques for testing hypotheses are.

Reprinted by permission from *Economic Inquiry*, 18 (1980), 165-78.

49

II

The answer, unfortunately, is that they are not at all good. This judgment is based, not on any sophisticated and subtle criticism of *theoretical* econometrics, but on the actual procedures followed by the workaday econometrician in turning out the "applied econometrics" papers that appear so frequently in our journals.[3] Techniques that are not subject to many of the following criticisms may exist, but they are not the ones being used in most of the applied work.

Suppose a new question arises and econometric studies are undertaken to answer it. Will we be much closer to an answer after these studies are completed than before? This is surely the acid test of whether economics is a hard science. And the answer is disheartening. After the first study is completed one can easily feel optimistic; arguments based on arm-waving can now be replaced with precise coefficients calculated to several decimal places, t-statistics, Durbin-Watson statistics, etc. So far so good. But sooner or later some of the other studies that have been undertaken will also be completed. Then optimism is likely to vanish. It is highly probable that some of these studies will reach conflicting conclusions. And what is just as bad, we do not really have an effective way of deciding which ones are correct. Hence, everyone can continue to adhere to the position he or she held prior to the appearance of the empirical tests, and justify this position by citing the supportive econometric results.[4] All that has happended is that arm-waving has been replaced by t coefficient waving. Perhaps this is a bit of an overstatement-- a few false hypotheses are rejected, but many hypotheses-- however contradictory-- cannot be rejected and hence coexist.

And what is just as bad, even if all or most of the econometric evidence points in the same direction, those who hold the contrary view need not be intimidated by this since there is now some empirical evidence that many econometric results are not reliable. The prime piece of evidence is a study by Michael Lovell (1975) in which he used a Monte-Carlo technique to test a standard applied econometrics procedure. His first step was to take consumption functions and use them to generate consumption data. He then added random error terms of reasonable size, so that he got a set of consumption data such as those that would be generated by stochastic consumption functions. His next step was to act as though these were data generated by the real world, and to try to see, by the usual econometric procedure, which of several possible consumption functions generated each of them. And what happened? It turned out that someone who did not know ahead of time which independent variables generated the data would usually not have been able to discover this by looking at the diagnostic statistics of the various consumption functions. This is not necessarily the fault of the theoretical econometrics; it simply means that, given the limited powers of these tests, the available data are insufficient to distinguish sharply between valid and invalid hypotheses. The theoretically correct thing is, therefore, not to try to do so, and instead to devote more effort to data collection. But our journals are full of papers that use the techniques which Lovell's paper shows to be unreliable.

A similar conclusion is indicated by Robert Ferber's (1953 and 1956) comparisons of consumption functions. He showed that the consumption function that predicts best during the sample period frequently does not do so during the post-sample period. Similarly, Martin Schupak (1962) in looking at the demand for various types of food products, beverages, tobacco and fuels found that there was only a weak relation between the fit over a ten-year sample period, and predictive accuracy. Comparing five different regressions, it turned out that in less than a quarter of the cases did the regression that gave the best sample period fit also predict best. When I extended this approach by looking at the use of regression equations for a wide variety of problems, investment functions, money supply and demand functions, econometric models, etc. it again turned out that goodness of fit during the sample period is an unreliable guide to performance in the post-sample period (Mayer, 1975). Even if one compares only three hypotheses, the probability turns out to be less than two thirds that the one that performed best in the sample period also performed best in the postsample period. And if one compares four hypotheses, the probability drops to about one third. While this is better than one would expect on a completely random basis, it is a far distance from our claim to verify hypotheses at the 5 percent level.[5]

To be sure, one might well argue that the results of just a few studies like this are not sufficient to invalidate our standard testing procedures. But where is the opposing empirical evidence that these techniques actually work in the sense of furnishing reliable guides to policy?

It would, therefore, be interesting to see the results of some further tests of the validity of applied econometrics. One possible test is to rerun a sample of regressions several times, each time omitting a year, to see if this changes the results substantially. It shouldn't, but the only time I did rerun someone's regression, leaving out a single year in which circumstances were unusual, it changed the results entirely (Mayer, 1978). Similarly, when Howrey and Hymans (1978, p. 666) dropped a single year from a consumption function that had been used to estimate the effect of interest rates of saving, the t-value of the coefficient of the yield on savings fell from -3.24 to -1.62.[6] Another test is to take a series of empirical studies that rely heavily on the National

51

Income Accounts data and rerun them, substituting the recently revised data for the ones used in the original study. In principle, the use of more accurate data should lead to a better fit, but if the fit was raised artificially by data mining, then it is likely to deteriorate when revised data are substituted for the data originally used. A third test is to take a sample of empirical studies and rerun them to see what proportion of them contain careless errors large enough to change the conclusions significantly. Until we have the results of these or other studies, and can say that they support our standard econometric results, we should conclude, on the admittedly limited empirical evidence that is currently available, that our procedures are just not adequate.

III

Lovell's results suggest that the procedures actually followed in much applied econometrics work do not enable us to distinguish between true and false hypotheses, presumably because of high multicollinearity and the paucity of data points. This is an inherent problem faced by economics, as is the familiar and more general problem that behavior parameters are not as stable as those in the natural sciences. But to these unavoidable problems we have added avoidable ones, and it is these that I mainly want to discuss. In doing so I do not want to sound like a hellfire preacher. Not only do we find examples of "unscientific" behavior also in the hard sciences,[7] but the fact that despite the high pay-off that publication has, there is a limit to the gilding of weeds that economists do, suggests that the moral standards of our profession are fairly high.

But even so, econometric work includes far too many examples of game playing, or what Frisch (1970) in his criticism of certain types of mathematical economics has called "playometrics." Admittedly, game playing has an obvious role in science since it provides a stimulus to work, and economics is not the only field in which game playing occurs in its undesirable as well as its desirable aspects (see Mahoney 1976). But I suspect that it is a particularly serious problem in economics because of the very fact that so few studies of the validity of econometric methods of testing hypotheses have been undertaken. In a field in which there is, on the one hand, so much methodological contention, and on the other hand, so much emphasis on testing, one would surely expect our standard testing techniques to be themselves subject to many more tests than have actually been undertaken. In this connection, the experience I had upon completing the previously discussed comparison of the forecasting performance of hypotheses within and beyond their sample periods was rather strange. The response of econometricians was usually: yes, you are right, but there is nothing new here, we have known this all along. But then how can one explain the continuation of these regression studies, unless it is a matter of "playing the game"?

Moreover, the rewards for publishing a paper are usually high, while both the chance - and the cost - of being caught in game playing, as long as it is not too egregious, are both low.

One aspect of game playing is that certain mundane aspects of research that are critical in obtaining correct conclusions are deemphasized relative to another aspect, the use of the latest complex techniques. These techniques are used not so much because they are likely to lead to the right answer, but probably as much, or more, because their very complexity creates a fascinating challenge, and also generates the applause of one's peers.[8] The deemphasis of that most mundane and unglamorous of tasks, getting the arithmetic right, also suggests that econometrics is in large part, "game playing." While obviously no data on this are available, it is likely that most econometricians do not bother to check their arithmetic, that is the copying of the data from the source onto the sheets from which cards are punched, and then the copying from computer print-out to the tables. The fact that few textbooks warn students about the need to check data suggests that they are infrequently checked. Yet, as anyone who does check his or her data has probably observed, data errors are quite common. This raises a rather nasty question. Suppose there are two conflicting econometric studies, one using sophisticated state of the art techniques but unchecked data, and the other using much less sophisticated techniques but (you happen to know) checked data. Which one should you believe? The most advanced methods do little good, if in transcribing the results a decimal point is allowed to slip one digit.[9]

A related point is the apparently frequent nonreplicability of results, i.e., the inability to determine what data were used in a published paper, and to use these same data to reproduce the results. Yet it is one of the most basic rules of scientific practice that one's methods must be reproducible, so that one's results can be checked.[10] A study of the criteria used by scientists in evaluating scientific publications found that 62 percent of natural scientists considered "replicability of research techniques" to be "essential", 18 percent considered it to be "very important but not essential", 12 percent to be "somewhat important", and only 7 percent "not very, or not at all important". Neither originality, logical rigor, or any other criterion was ranked as "essential" by so many natural scientists as was replicability.[11] In this respect, economists differ very sharply from natural scientists. Again, there are no data on what proportion of the published econometric literature can be replicated, but word of mouth folklore at least is that much of it cannot be. Many economists who have tried to reproduce results of others have probably experienced an author being unable to provide either his data or sources. In general, we do not teach our students, and to not practice ourselves, one of the standard techniques of the sciences, that is, to keep adequate lab books. Yet I suspect that the maintenance of adequate research records is at least as much a basic requirement for real scientific status of a subject as is the use of advanced mathematics.[12]

Another example of the game elements in applied econometrics (though certainly not in theoretical econometrics) is the automatic pardon for the crime of using upside-down significance tests. Although undergraduates are warned about this in statistics courses, one can find many examples in professional journals where authors grossly missuse significance tests. They treat the fact that a certain coefficient has a t value that is not significant at the 5 percent level as *evidence* that variable A has no effect on variable B. Even though it may be significant at, say the 20 percent level, the authors then conclude that they have shown that A has *no* effect on B. In this way, by using a small enough sample, it would be easy to prove that price has no effect on the quantity bought, income has no effect on consumption, and so on. Now these authors know better. But the rules of the game permit them to make this elementary mistake, while they prohibit the sin of using a simple technique, when there exists a more complex and reliable technique.

Another peculiarity with respect to significance tests in applied econometrics is the blanket exemption from having to use them that is extended to maximum likelihood methods. An economist may draw important conclusions from the fact that the regression selected as best by the computer has, say a positive gamma coefficient, without bothering to test whether the difference in the goodness of fit between this regression and one with a negative gamma is actually significant at any meaningful level. It is not clear why the "rules of the game" permit this.

Moreover, as William White (1967) has pointed out, econometricians often seem satisfied with having demonstrated that a certain variable is significant. But the policy-maker must usually be concerned, not just with the question of whether variable A has an effect on variable B, but he needs to know also how large this effect is. A 50 percent error in the point estimate can make a big difference to the success of a policy! But given a normal distribution, a variable that is just significant at the 5 percent level on a two-tailed test will, 16 percent of the time, have a point estimate that is at least 50 percent too low. And if one makes allowance for the usual data mining, this 16 percent figure should be raised substantially (White, 1967, pp. 28-34).

A further example of our doing something which all of us know to be wrong is the common tendency to interpret an insignificant regression coefficient or low correlation as evidence that a certain independent variable has no effect on the dependent variable. But surely all it means is that there is no *stable* relationship between the two variables. The independent variable could still have a high, though variable, effect on the dependent variable.

Another game aspect of economics is the way in which we ignore the quality of the data. As Wassily Leontief (1971, p. 3) has complained: "in all too many instances sophisticated statistical analysis is performed on a set of data whose exact meaning and validity are unknown to the author or rather so well known to him that at the very end he warns the reader not to take the material conclusions of the entire 'exercise' seriously." Moreover, it is probably quite common for economists to go to the library (or send their research assistants) to copy some data with which they are unfamiliar without reading the description of the data given in the source. This could lead to some peculiar results.[13]

To cite a specific instance of how questions about the quality of the data are ignored, Paul Taubman (1968) pointed out that the data used in time series studies of postwar saving are just one of three different sets of saving estimates that can be derived from government data, all of which purport to measure the same thing. He then used all three sets of data to see if they yield similar results when plugged into regressions. It turned out that, "judging both by the significance and size of the coefficients, the character of the saving function depends crucially on the choice of the savings series" (Taubman 1968, p. 128). And what is just as bad, there is no way of determining which one of the series is the best. This is a result that should surely have shaken up everyone working on savings functions and consumption functions. Yet this paper has had only little impact.

Moreover, the computer revolution, by allowing us to work with masses of data has an unfortunate by-product. We tend to dump the data into a computer without ever looking at them. Yet if the data are subject to large errors, (e.g., household budget data) a sample of, say, 300 observations for which the researcher has actually read each questionnaire with some care may be more reliable than a sample of 3000 observations that were dumped into the computer with very little editing for inappropriate responses.

It would be interesting to discover what would happen if econometricians were offered the following gamble: "You will get $1000 if you are right, but have to pay me $3000 if you are wrong." How many (even among those with little risk aversion) would take this gamble, and what does this tell us about our claim to have established something at the 5 percent significance level?[14]

IV

Given all of these problems, what can be done? One possible answer is that we should abandon applied econometrics altogether. But this is an unappetizing alternative because it would usually leave us with no way of selecting, from among a plethora or possible explanations, the one that actually *does* explain events. For example, there used to be a large number of business cycle theories. Each author pointed to some factor that, in principle, could generate cycles, without offering any evidence that it was *this factor*, and not some other, that actually did cause the observed cycle (see Mitchell, 1927, Chapter 4). Perhaps the particular factor singled out by his theory, while capable of generating a cycle, is much too small to account for the observed fluctuations. But without econometrics we will never know. Hence, my own attitude towards econometrics is like that of the person who upon being told that the craps game he was about to participate in is crooked, replied, "Sure, I know that, but it is the only game in town." Admittedly, this is a bit of an overstatement since at least some hypotheses could be tested by economic history, or by a simple cross-country comparison without the use of econometrics. But not many could be tested in these ways.

Hence, instead of abandoning applied econometrics altogether, we should do two things. One is to be more skeptical of our results. Instead of treating an econometric result as evidence from a "crucial experiment," we should think of it more as circumstantial evidence.[15] Only if a whole number of separate studies using different data, e.g., cross section data as well as time series data, and perhaps data for various countries, tell us the same thing, should we take it seriously. Such evidence from repetitive "experiments" is much more convincing than is the fact that the critical coefficient in a single study is highly significant (see Tukey, 1969, pp. 84-85). Until we have such massive evidence, we should not pretend, particularly to policy-makers, that we have the answer merely because we have some significant regression coefficients. If we are thus to rely on the weight of many pieces of evidence rather than on a single crucial experiment, then it would be most useful to have, from time to time, surveys that pull the evidence together, in the sense, not just of describing what various studies show, but by resolving any contradictions between them.[16] At present on too many questions we are buried in an inchoate mass of seemingly contradictory evidence.

Second, it would surely help if we can raise the standards of what is acceptable work by evaluating research more on the basis of the likely validity of its results, and less on the technical sophistication of its techniques. For example, it is likely that despite their well-known problems survey methods would be used more in economics if it were not for the fact that since they seem so simple, there is little kudos to be gained by using them.[17] Third, much more emphasis should be placed on collecting relevant data (Leontief, 1971).

Fourth, we should guard against data mining. Admittedly, not all data mining is necessarily bad, and it is often the fault of the theory for not specifying such critical "details" as the appropriate lags. As Griliches (1967) has pointed out, one should not expect the data both to specify the lag and to test the hypothesis embodying it. Moreover, Leamer (1978) has recently set out rules and safeguards for valid data mining. But he agrees that "without judgment and purpose [i.e., the way data mining is usually done] a specification search is merely a fishing expedition and the product of the search will have a value that is difficult or impossible to assess" (p.2). It is particularly important to guard against mere fishing expeditions at present when there is such a strong tendency in economics to carry the rationality assumption to extremes. It is usual to justify reliance on an implausible rationality assumption by saying that this assumption is validated by the fact that the hypothesis based on it is consistent with the data. But there is then strong temptation to run regressions until one of them finally "confirms" the hypothesis. Hence, there is a case for requiring researchers to list all the regressions they ran, and not just to present the particular regression, perhaps the only one of a large number, that happens to support their hypothesis.[18]

But this may not be sufficiently stringent. Suppose a researcher who planned to run, if necessary, say fifty regressions is lucky, and the very first regression happens to support the hypothesis. This regression may have been chosen quite arbitrarily, and data mining that just happens to hit a vein of gold on the first strike of the pick-axe is still, in a way, data mining (Bronfenbrenner, 1972), p. 57). Hence, before taking the results seriously, it would be reasonable to require that authors run their regressions in all or many of the numerous and varied forms that are consistent with their hypotheses, and are both plausible and econometrically valid. One should then accept only those results that are robust with respect to a wide variety of reasonable techniques. They could be robust in the sense that all the variants that are run generate similar results, or in the sense that the one variant that does support the maintained hypothesis gives a substantially better prediction. If they are not robust in either of these ways, then any support they provide to the maintained hypothesis should be considered as highly tentative.[19]

Requiring such tests of robustness would substantially

toughen the standards of acceptability, and should also work towards reducing the frequency of contradictory results in the literature. Authors would, so to speak, be their own critics by mining the data *against* themselves, and bring out objections that are now frequently raised by others in comments. This raising of standards is justified because those who present new results should have the burden of the proof thrust upon them, and the burden of the proof amounts to more than just showing that there happens to be one particular form of the basic regression equation that yields the desired result.[20] As both Keynes (1973, pp. 287 and 294) and Friedman (1951, p. 108) for once in agreement, have pointed out, one can get a good statistical fit merely by repeated testing, but such a fit proves very little.[21]

Fifth, it is important that authors not use up all their data in *fitting* their regressions, but leave some as a hold-out sample against which to *test* the regressions. This would not really waste data points because, once the hypothesis has been successfully tested, the regression can be rerun using all the data points to refine the coefficient estimates.

Sixth, the journals should publish papers that find statistically insignificant results. This would not only remove the great pressure to stomp on the data until they give in and yield a t value of 2 or more (as a saying has it: "if you just torture the data long enough, they will confess"), but it would also prevent others from wasting time replicating an unsuccessful project (see Feige, 1975). Journals should also encourage economists to replicate previously published results.[22] In other sciences replication is done continually. Presumably this is because replication is a good way of training students in laboratory techniques. But in economics we do this much less frequently probably, in part, because, in the absence of lab experiments that produce new data, all the "replication" we can do is rerunning the old regressions. Hence, erroneous results are allowed to remain in the literature. This lack of replications is particularly serious because, as just discussed, economists pay insufficient attention to avoiding calculating errors. Some foundation should finance a program wherein graduate students would rerun each year, say 10 percent of the empirical work published the previous year in the journals. This would not only catch many mistakes, but the potential embarrassment of being caught in a calculating error should make researchers more careful.

Seventh, authors using unpublished data should be required to make them available so that their work can be verified by others.[23] Some may object to this since they want to enjoy a monopoly while they exploit their data source for additional papers. This is something that occurs in the hard sciences too (Barnes and Dolby, 1970, p. 15). And indeed, like patent protection, such a temporary monopoly may provide a desirable incentive to look for new data. Hence, there is a case for allowing authors perhaps a one or two year leeway on such a rule. One or two years, combined with the usual publication lag for the initial paper should give them sufficient time to exploit their data mine ahead of others. Another requirement that journals should impose is that the author state whether, and to what extent, the reported computations were checked for transcription errors, etc.[24]

Finally, given all the weaknesses of econometric techniques, we should be open-minded enough to accept that truth does not always wear the garb of equations, and is not always born inside a computer. Other ways of testing, such as appeals to qualitative economic history, should not be treated as archaic.

V

To return to the earlier theme, I have so far given reasons why economics appears to be still far from a hard science. But is anything lost by taking this as a goal? I believe the answer is yes, because we then tend to act as though we are already close to that goal, which causes us to oversell the validity of our results both to policy-makers and the general public. Moreover, it induces us to reject the plausible in favor of the seemingly "proven". This can easily result in the choice of the wrong hypothesis, since we may then reject an hypothesis that accords with common sense in favor of one that appears to fit the data much better only because of one of the weaknesses of our methods just discussed. It also distracts us from looking for merely plausible evidence because we believe a paper based on plausible evidence rather than on seeming "scientific" evidence will not be published, or if published, will receive little recognition. As a result, we lose not only some interesting evidence, but in addition, some important problems get much too little discussion. Furthermore, the gathering of much-needed data is underemphasized. In addition, the stress on using advanced mathematical tools allows us to have a good conscience while ignoring some very elementary rules of good research procedure. Much of the published research consists of taking a new technique out for a walk rather than of really trying to solve a problem. And also, economics has become much too isolated from other social sciences, since being hard scientists we do not want to use either the results or tools of those who cannot claim our exalted status (Cf. Leontief, 1971).

59

Footnotes

* University of California, Davis. Presidential address delivered at the 54th Annual Conference of the Western Economic
Association, Las Vegas, 1979. I am indebted for helpful comments to Cliff Attfield, George Benston, Martin Bronfenbrenner, Robert Ferber, Jay Helms, David Laidler, Alan
Clemstead, Boris Pesek, Robert Renshaw, Steven Sheffrin,
Paul Strassmann, and R.M. Sundrum, who are not responsible
for any remaining errors.

1. Another possibility is, of course, to turn economics into a
deductive science; i.e., praxeology as advocated by the
Austrian school. But most economists, rightly I believe,
reject this course.

2. Norman Storer (1967) has argued that the hard sciences are
distinguished from the soft sciences by their greater use of
mathematics. The hard sciences are those in which "error,
irrelevance or sloppy thinking" can be detected relatively
easily, and mathematics facilitates such detection. However,
Storer includes statistical testing in his concept of mathematics, and as I will try to show below, in economics such
testing has not eliminated sloppy thinking. Moreover, it
would be hard to argue that mathematics has helped to purge
economics of irrelevance.

3. For criticisms of theoretical econometrics, see Brunner (1972)
as well as Streissler (1970) who also discusses some problems
in actually applying econometrics. In the subsequent discussion my focus will be primarily on the use of applied
econometrics in macroeconomics. In other fields of economics,
such as agricultural economics (see Leontief, 1971, p. 4) the
problem may be less severe. For a criticism of the literature
in finance along the lines of this paper see Friend (1973).

4. As Don Patinkin (1972, p. 142) has remarked, "I will begin to
believe in economics as a science when out of Yale there comes
an empirical Ph.D. thesis demonstrating the supremacy of
monetary policy in some historical episode and out of Chicago,
one demonstrating the supremacy of fiscal policy."

5. For an interesting discussion of how to evaluate the forecasting
accuracy of regressions, see Armstrong (1978a, Chapter 13).
He ranks goodness of fit in the sample period, which we use
so much in econometrics as the least reliable method. Since I
am dealing with hypothesis testing rather than with forecasting, it is not necessary to consider the questions whether
econometric models forecast better than naive models. For

evidence on this, see Armstrong (1978b) and Zarnowitz (1979). Any superiority of econometric models need not result from their being an accurate representation of the economy, but could result from their picking up various autoregressive features of the economy, as well as from the ad hoc adjustments that the managers of models usually make to the raw output of their models.

6. This problem could be ameliorated by the use of some techniques suggested by Belsley, Kuh and Welsch (forthcoming).

7. Thus the great physicist Max Planck lamented that "a new scientific truth does not triumph by convincing its opponents and making them see the light, but rather because its opponents eventually die, and a new generation grows up that is familiar with it. (Cited in Kuhn, 1962, p. 150).

8. The use of complex procedures is, of course, not the only possible type of game playing. For example, assume that mathematical sophistication would be held in low esteem by economists, but that wide-ranging scholarship would be highly regarded. In this case, articles would contain many totally irrelevant footnotes to esoteric sources. Whatever the standards that are used as proxies for the hard-to-discern true worth of research, there will be a tendency to meet these standards in ways that add little to the true worth of the project. I certainly do *not* mean to imply that econometricians are more "careerist" than are other economists: nor do I mean to imply that I am better than others in this respect. I certainly do not claim to have always met the standards recommended below.

9. Failure to check one's data is not the only example of carelessness in economic research. My colleague, Alan Olmstead, informs me that in refereeing articles in economic history (in which quotations play an important role) he has his research assistant check them against their source. He finds that most papers have mistakes in quotations, sometimes serious ones, such as omitting the word "not". While no data are available on the extent to which this occurs in other fields too, carelessness is probably more common in economics than in the majority of other fields. One reason is that scholarship is not held in high esteem in economics. The story is told about a Princeton historian who failed a graduate student's paper because in a footnote a page number was wrong. This is hardly likely to occur in economics! And while the natural sciences too do not place much weight on scholarship, their students are trained to be careful and painstaking in laboratory work.

10. The alternative criterion, "exportability" preferred by some scientists (see Agnew and Pyke, 1978, pp. 162-63) to take account of the fact that no laboratory experiment can be precisely reproduced, amounts to the same thing here.

11. (Chase, 1970). For social scientists, the ratios are 41.9 percent, 24.4 percent, 29.1 percent and 4.7 percent. However, in psychology, the reproducibility criterion seems to be largely ignored. (See Wolin, 1962 and Mahoney, 1976, pp. 53 and 97). Mahoney states (p.97) "the average physical scientist would probably shudder at the number of social science" facts "which rest on unreplicated research."

12. Moreover, adherence to rules of replicability should help to inhibit cases of outright fraud such as the recent Cyril Burts scandal in psychology.

13. Thus, many years ago, a then well-known economist used some Census Bureau data and complained that he could not carry his analysis up to date because, for some reason, the Census Bureau no longer published the data. But the description of the data said that they are untrustworthy and were published only because Congress insisted on it. And eventually Congress no longer insisted. Another potentially serious problem, that research assistants may have low morale and do slipshod work, is discussed by Roth (1966) who also suggests a way of amerliorating it.

14. Admittedly, this test may not be quite fair because it is said that "no one believes an hypothesis except its originator, but everyone believes an experiment except the experimenter," (Beveridge, 1957, p. 47).

15. For a general argument that economics should model itself on law rather than on the exact sciences, see Benjamin Ward (1972).

16. For an attempt to do this with respect to some of the consumption function literature, see Mayer (1972, Part 2).

17. Actually, survey techniques are not at all so simple to use. There exists an extensive literature in sociology on questionnaire construction. For a plea to use survey techniques more see Friend (1973).

18. There is, of course, no way this requirement could be enforced. But if authors would know that not reporting regression results that contradict their hypothesis is considered flagrant intellectual dishonesty, they would be reluctant to do this.

19. Unfortunately, there are many possible tests for robustness aside from the standard ones, such as using in alternative regression logs instead of natural members, yearly instead of quarterly data, and first differences instead of levels. For example, Evans (1967) showed that the Ball-Drake model, while confirmed by a time series regression in which the data are deflated by the GNP deflator, is rejected by the same data if they are deflated by the CPI instead. Obviously, it is not always feasible to run all reasonable variants of a regression, but enough should be run to give at least a presumption of robustness.

20. Would this requirement result in journals having to close down because they have an insufficient number of acceptable manuscripts? No it would not, because a paper that shows that a particular hypothesis cannot at present be tested because some forms of the underlying regression equation support it, while others reject it, is a contribution that warrants publication.

21. For a rigorous demonstration, see Bacon (1977).

22. Currently at least two journals, the *Journal of Political Economy* and *Journal of Consumer Research* have offered to publish replications.

23. The way to enforce this would be for journals to require that authors send, perhaps with the final revised draft of the paper, a copy of their data. The journal, and not the author, would then be responsible for making the data available.

24. There is, of course, no way this could be verified, but the mere fact of having to make a statement about it should induce economists to be more careful in their treatment of data.

References

Agnew, Neil and Sandra Pyke, *The Science Game* (1978) Englewood Cliffs, N.J.: Prentice-Hall.

Armstrong, J. Scott, (1978a) *Long Range Economic Forecasting,* New York: John Wiley & Sons.

_____, (1978b) "Forecasting with Econometric Methods: Folklore versus Fact," *Journal of Business*, 51 (October), pp. 549-64.

Bacon, Robert (1977), "Some Evidence on the Largest Squared Correlation Coefficient from Several Samples," *Econometrica*, 45 (November), pp. 1997-2001.

Barnes, S.B., and Dolby, R.G.A. (1970), "Scientific Ethos: A Deviant Viewpoint," *European Journal of Sociology*, No. 1, pp. 3-25.

Belsley, David, Kuh, Edwin, and Welsch, Roy (forthcoming), *Regression Diagnostics: Identifying Influential Data and Sources of Collinearity*, New York: John Wiley & Sons.

Beveridge, W.I.B. (1957), *The Art of Scientific Investigation*, New York: W.W. Norton.

Bronfenbrenner, Martin (1972), "Sensitivity Analysis for Econometricians," *Nebraska Journal of Economics*, II (Winter), pp. 57-66.

Brunner, Karl (ed.) (1972), *Problems and Issues in Current Econometric Practice*, Columbus: Ohio State University Press.

Chase, Janet (1970), "Normative Criteria for Scientific Publication," *American Sociologist*, 5 (August), pp. 262-64.

Evans, Michael (1967), "The Importance of Wealth in the Consumption Function," *Journal of Political Economy*, 75-Part I (August), pp. 333-351.

Feige, Edgar (1975), "The Consequences of Journal Editorial Policies and a Suggestion for Revision," *Journal of Political Economy*, 83 (December), pp. 1291-96.

Ferber, Robert (1953), *A Study of Aggregate Savings Functions*, NBER Technical Paper No. 8, New York: National Bureau of Economic Research.

_____(1956), "Are Correlations any Guide to Predictive Value," *Applied Statistics*, 5 (June), pp. 113-31.

Friedman, Milton (1951), "Comment," in Universities-National Bureau Committee for Economic Research, *Conference on Business Cycles*, New York, NBER.

Friend, Irwin (1973), "Mythodology in Finance," *Journal of Finance,* 28 (May), pp. 257-72.

Frisch, Ragnar (1970), "Econometrics in the World Today," in W.E. Eltis, M. Scott and J. Wolfe, *Induction, Trade and Growth,* Oxford: Oxford University Press.

Griliches, Zvi (1967), "Distributed Lags: A Survey," *Econometrica,* 35 (January), pp. 16-49.

Howrey, E. Phillip and Saul Hymans (1978), "The Measurement and Determination of Loanable Funds Savings," *Brookings Papers on Economic Activity,* 1978:3, pp. 655-85.

Keynes, J.M. (1973), *Collected Writings,* 14, London: Royal Economic Society, Vol. 14.

Kuhn, Thomas (1962), *The Structure of Scientific Revolutions,* Chicago: University of Chicago Press.

Leamer, Edward (1978), *Specification Searches,* New York: John Wiley & Sons.

Leontief, Wassily (1971), "Theoretical Assumptions and Nonobservable Facts," *American Economic Review,* 61 (March) pp. 1-7.

Lovell, Michael (1975), "Data Grubbing," unpublished manuscript.

Mahoney, Michael (1976), *Scientists as Subjects: The Psychological Imperative,* Cambridge, MA: Balinger Publishing Company.

Mayer, Thomas (1972), *Permanent Income, Wealth and Consumption,* Berkeley: University of California Press.

_____, (1975), "Selecting Economic Hypotheses by Goodness of Fit," *Economic Journal,* 85 (December), pp. 877-83.

_____, (1978), "Consumption in the Great Depression," *Journal of Political Economy,* 86 (February), pp. 139-45.

Mitchell, Wesley C. (1927), *Business Cycles, the Problem and its Setting,* New York: National Bureau of Economic Research.

Patinkin, Don (1972), "Keynesian Monetary Theory and the Cambridge School," Banca Nazionale del Lavoro, *Quarterly Review* (June), pp. 138-58.

Popper, Sir Karl (1961), *The Poverty of Historicism*, London: Routledge and Kegan Paul.

Roth, Julius (1966), "Hired Hands in Research," *American Sociologist*, I (August), pp. 190-96.

Schupak, Martin (1962), "The Predictive Accuracy of Empirical Demand Analyses," *Economic Journal*, 72 (September), pp. 550-75.

Storer, Norman (1967), "The Hard Sciences and the Soft: Some Sociological Observations," Bulletin of the Medical Library Association, 55 (January), pp. 75-84.

Streissler, Erich (1970), *Pitfalls in Econometric Forecasting*, London: Institute of Economic Affairs.

Taubman, Paul (1968), "Personal Saving: A Time Series Analysis of Three Measures of the Same Conceptual Series," *Review of Economics and Statistics*, 50 (February), pp. 125-29.

Tukey, John (1969), "Analyzing Data: Sanctification or Detective Work?" *American Psychologist*, 24 (February), pp. 83-91.

Ward, Benjamin (1972), *What's Wrong with Economics*, New York: Basic Books.

White, William H. (1967), "The Trustworthiness of 'Reliable' Econometric Evidence," *Zeitschrift fur Nationaloekonomie*, 27 (April), pp. 19-38.

Wolin, Leroy (1962), "Responsibility for Raw Data," *American Psychologist*, 17 (September), pp. 657-8.

Zarnowitz, Victor (1979), "An Analysis of Annual and Multiperiod Quarterly Forecasts of Aggregate Income, Output and the Price Level," *Journal of Business*, 52 (January), pp. 1-33.

Part Four   Should Prediction be the Goal of Economics?

Mainstream neoclassical economics seems to have followed two separate methodological approaches. These are: (i) the methodology of positive (or applied) economics, and (ii) the methodology of analytical (or theoretical) economics. The three readings in this section focus on the methodology of Positive Economics. An important requirement of this methodology is that not only must economic propositions (or theories) be empirically testable, but they must be supported (or tested) by available facts (or data).

A successful testing of economic propositions requires collection of enough hard facts, whose objective quality must be unquestionably guaranteed (see Leontief reading sixteen in Part Nine of this reader). Other critics argue that no quantity of available facts can ever prove the truth of an economic proposition, e.g. see Koopmans (1957), Samuelson (1963) among others. They are making an old point made by David Hume in the early part of the seventeenth century. Hume had observed the problem with inductive proofs in that a given general statement cannot be proved to be true with the help of any finite amount of singular statements. In other words, we cannot prove the general statement that the sun will rise every day by a singular statement that the sun rose on September 10, 1982 (see Boland (1982), Chapter 1).

Friedman (1953) in his article has attempted to overcome the problems with induction by side-stepping it. He favors the methodology of positive economics by saying that; "The ultimate goal of positive science is the development of a "theory" or hypothesis that yields valid and meaningful (i.e. not truistic) predictions about phenomena not yet observed."

The Boland article in this reader surveys the critique of Friedman's critics and provides a defense of Friedman's methodology, termed Institutionalism. Coddington's article discusses general issues involved in the methodology of positive economics. The purpose of a positivist's economic model with a policy orientation may be to generate good forecasts. Accordingly, he may not begin his analysis in search of true assumptions but rather the true (or successful) predictions. The Pope and Pope essay focuses on the debate concerning whether prediction should be the goal of economics.

The methodological approaches of the 'positive' economic and 'analytical' economics may be contrasted in the words of Boland (1982) from his recent book. He writes that:

> Unlike 'positive' analysis, which attempts to show that a particular theoretical proposition is logically supported by available data, the 'theory' article attempts to show that a articular theoretical proposition is logically supported by available mathematical theorems. Where 'positive' economics seeks objectivity in repeatable or observable data, 'theoretical' or, more properly, 'analytical' economics seeks objectivity in the autonomy of the discipline of mathematics.

The logical problem with the methodology of analytical economics is that the theory laden facts can become tautological. In order to avoid this problem, the proponents of analytical economics require that all economic models be logically supported by available data (i.e. testable) at the very least. For further details the reader may consult Koopmans (1979), Lucas (1980) and Boland (1982), chapters 1, 7 and 8.

5 Positive Economics

A. Coddington*

There is a tradition of thought which has been concerned to wed social theory and investigation to a positivist philosophy. This tradition goes back at least to Saint-Simon and Comte. The purpose of this essay is to enquire into the present state of this tradition as it manifests itself within the discipline of economics.

The term "positive economics" was introduced by J.N. Keynes as part of a three-fold distinction between economics as a source of uniformities, ideals and precepts.[1] Positive economics, then, is concerned with the discovery and expression of uniformities, in contrast to the value-laden activities involved in the formulation of ideals and the practicial considerations involved in the exposition of precepts.[2] More recently, Hutchison put forward a critique, on positivist lines, of the then-prevalent style of economic thought, which he took to be an "arm-chair theorizing" approach to the subject.[3] The term "positive economics" was adopted by Friedman in his manifesto of Chicago practice, "The Methodology of Positive Economics"[4] and, most recently, by Lipsey in his widely-used textbook, "An Introduction to Positive Economics."[5]

Attacks on positivist social science have been launched from a number of viewpoints. Such attacks may recognize the strong empiricist sentiments which motivate positivist thought, but nevertheless claim that the sentiments fail to be adequately embodied in positivist doctrine, e.g. that the positivist program is unworkable in practice, or rules out as illegitimate, concepts which are intellectually indispensable or processes which are either sanctioned by wide usage or which are obviously empirically respectable. The critical parts of the present essay fall within this category. What will be at issue, then, is not *whether* but *how* we are to be empiricists.

The first problem that we encounter is that the term "positive" has been used to mean many things: it has occurred as a synonym for non-evaluative, non-metaphysical, non-hypothetical, non-speculative, testable, observable, operational, and predictive.[6] In philosophy, logical positivism (sometimes called neo-positivism) is the (now discredited) view which took the verifiability criterion of meaning as its cornerstone.[7] What, then, are we to expect from "positive economics"? In examining the claims

Reprinted by permission from *The Canadian Journal of Economics*, 5 (1972), 1-15.

made on its behalf, it will become apparent that it is related to philosophical positivism only in the rough and ready sense of manifesting similar dispositions of thought--of being motivated by a strong urge for knowledge based on and closely related to "experience," "observation," "facts," "data" (or other empirical-sounding things) and a strong revulsion against speculation, metaphysics, covert moralizing and other nebulous processes. In short, those who adopt the term "positive" to qualify their practice wish to be thought scientific in much the same sense that they understand the physical sciences as being scientific. Indeed, it is such underlying sentiments, rather than what is explicitly claimed by those who adopt the term, which give coherence to a discussion of positive economics. It is not entirely clear, in any case, whether these claims are best labelled as positivist. In particular, Friedman's position is better described as an extreme form of pragmatism or instrumentalism, whereas Lipsey's position can be better described as a rather crude form of falsificationism. The philosophers having positions closest to those of Friedman and Lipsey are probably William James[8] and Karl Popper,[9] respectively. Neither of these are positivists. Indeed, James used his pragmatic conception of truth to give a justification of religious belief while Popper was highly critical of (as well as misunderstood by) the school of logical positivists known as the Vienna Circle.

If it is true that no very clear significance can be attached to the adoption of the term "positive," we must establish independently just what claims are made regarding the nature and pursuit of economic knowledge by those who adopt the term "positive economics." This task is not at all straightforward, since the accounts given by Friedman and Lipsey have both gaps in the argument and ambiguities in the exposition (as we shall see). I shall, however, attempt to present what is common to the pronouncements of those who adopt the term "positive economics" as four methodological propostions, which will form the basis for my discussion. My conclusion will be that these propositions together, if acted upon, would establish a style of empiricism which is unduly rigid and stultified. Whether the propositions are acted upon, even by their authors, or whether they *could* serve as a guide to practice, is a separate question that I will not discuss here.

(i) *The characteristic of a theory which alone is relevant in appraising it as a contribution to economic knowledge is its predictive performance.*

Thus: "The ultimate goal of positive science is the development of a 'theory' or 'hypothesis' that yields valid and meaningful (i.e. not truistic) predictions about phenomena not yet observed."[10] Also: "Viewed as a body of substantive hypotheses, theory is to

70

be judged by its predictive power for the class of phenomena which it is intended to 'explain'."[11] Furthermore: "...the only relevant test of the validity of a hypothesis is comparison of its predictions with experience."[12]

This first proposition follows from either of two possible arguments (or it may, of course, be taken as a primitive proposition, in no need of being derived from other principles). First, it can be argued that the task of economic theory is to *explain* economic phenomena, and that, furthermore, to explain something is to have been able to predict it. The thesis that explanation and prediction are identical in their logical structure then leads to the conclusion that predictive accuracy is entirely equivalent to explanatory power. It is interesting to note that Marshall subscribed to the view that explanation is the same as retrospective prediction.[13] He maintained that the difference between the two is merely that whereas prediction goes from cause to effect, explanation goes from effect to cause.[14]

The establishment of this link between explanation and prediction involves what has been termed the covering law or deductive model of explanation, i.e. that to explain an event is to subsume the event under a general law.[15] More accurately, it is to be able to deduce a statement describing the event from a law-like generalization together with certain initial conditions. But since prediction is also a deductive process of this same logical form (involving the deduction of a statement describing the predicted event from a general statement together with appropriate initial conditions), it follows that the two processes have the same logical structure.

The second way in which we can reach this conclusion is by denying that, in economics, we can ever explain anything in any deep or satisfying sense, and therefore concluding that we should set ourselves the more modest task of finding generalizations which "work" (in the sense of having a good predictive performance).[16] By any of these means we may arrive at the proposition which maintains that the predictive performance of a theory is the only aspect of it which is relevant in appraising it as a contribution to economic knowledge.

To dispute that the accuracy and scope of theory's predictive performance is, in itself, a guarantee of (or synonymous with) its explanatory power, calls for an examination of the thesis of the structural equivalence of explanation and prediction. Of course, one may always salvage the Friedman position by announcing that one is not concerned to explain economic phenomena at all, but only to be in a position to make predictions. This, at least, would reduce the discussion to a difference in those basic values about which, Friedman alleges, "men can ultimately only fight."[17]

The thesis of the structural equivalence of explanation and prediction has been subject to severe logical scrutiny and rejected by Sheffler.[18]   At a less formal level, I will argue that the structural equivalence of explanation and prediction can only be maintained by a rather drastic distortion of the customary concept of explanation.   It may be in half-conscious acknowledgement of this distortion that Friedman always puts the word "explain" in inverted commas.[19]   The point is that if the word "explain" is being used in its customary sense, why is it necessary to put it in inverted commas?   In asserting the equivalence of explanation and prediction, the words "explain" and "predict" have the same status, and yet the word "predict" escapes encapsulation.[20]   What this betokens is not so much the discovery of an equivalence, as the intention to shift the meaning of one term towards that of the other.   For could one really suppose that in the customary sense of "explanation" to explain why the sun rises, for example, is simply to say exactly when it will happen?

Let us consider this example further.   We may predict that the sun will rise tomorrow on the basis of the generalization that the sun rises every day.   But, to what explanation is such a prediction structurally equivalent?   We could say that the sun rose yesterday because it does so every day.   But it is doubtful if such a statement would be accepted, even by a small child, as an explanation in the sense of an answer to the question "Why did the sun rise yesterday?"

It seems evident that although there may be some relationship between predictive accuracy and explanatory power, it is not one of simple equivalence.   Friedman (and Blaug)[21] claim too much.   For if explanation and prediction were structually equivalent, predictive accuracy would be both a necessary and a sufficient condition for explanatory power.   But the existence of rules of thumb,   and *ad hoc* generalizations (such as so-called "naive" models) which yield relatively accurate predictions without providing any explanation of the phenomenon involved, shows that, although predictive accuracy may be a necessary condition, it is certainly not a sufficient condition for explanatory power. Whether or not it is true that explanation and prediction have the same structure (or logical form), what is more important is the interpretation we are able to give to the generalizations involved. It is here that the crucial difference between explanation and prediction resides.   As far as prediction is concerned, the generalization involved   may   be   seen   merely   as   a   *de facto* regularity, or it may be accompanied by a causal narrative concerning the process involved in, or underlying, the generalizations.   This difference has no effect on the predictive performance of the generalization.   But now consider whether an event could   be   explained   by   subsuming   it   under   a   *de facto* regularity.   Suppose the event is the occurrence of an A which is also

72

a B. Suppose, then, we purport to explain this by subsuming it under the generalization that all As are Bs. The alleged explanation is then of the form: "This happened this way because it always happens like that"; or, to put the same thing differently, it is purportedly to explain an event by pointing out that it is a member of a class of similar events (the class of events in which A is accompanied by B). This can hardly be regarded as *explaining* anything. As an answer to the question "Why?" it is not so much an evasion as an irrelevance. An answer to the question "Why?"--an explanation--would require some mention of the *process* (or we might want to say "underlying process"), which caused A to be accompanied by B. That is to say, an explanation requires some sort of causal narrative. Whereas a prediction states *that* something will be the case, an explanation concerns *how* it comes to be the case.

Of course, causal language involves us in going beyond what is revealed in experience or through observation. But this is just the point about an explanation--it is conceptually richer than the prediction to which it is structurally related; it involves the postulation of what are, by the standards of the generalization, theoretical entities out of which to construct a causal narrative.[22]

In speaking of "causal" narratives, the term "cause" is being used loosely and with full realization of the hazards involved. It may be that, at the deepest level of analysis, the distinction cannot be made between *de facto* regularities and causal processes: what we regard as causal processes may simply be *de facto* regularities of sufficient familiarity; and it would be a mistake to confuse the intelligible with the merely familiar. But at the level of analysis appropriate to the present discussion, the distinction seems sustainable, and, if any sense is to be made of the concept of explanation, indispensable. Not much harm would be done by thinking of causal narratives as accounts in which the various events would be linked together by familiar processes, these familiar processes including the way in which individuals make decisions in the light of certain reasons (which they could recount), and not being restricted to processes which are "causal" in any narrow, mechanical sense.

When we present a causal narrative to accompany some observed regularity and thereby convert a prediction-rule into an explanation, we make claims as to what is literally the case: how in fact the regularity comes to be. An explanation in this sense--which seems to accord well with the everyday sense of the word--therefore requires theoretical entities which are given a literal rather than an "as if" interpretation. Our theoretical explanations are to be taken at their face value--as asserting something to be the case--not merely instrumentally, as devices for organizing lower-level statements.

73

All this has implications for the conflict between operationalism and realism with regard to the status of theoretical entities. As far as prediction is concerned, one is free to take an operationalist position and make no claims to the literal truth of any of the theorizing that accompanies or surrounds the generalizations; one is free to use models which are given a purely "as if" interpretation, and are justifiable solely on the basis of the prediction-rules they generate. Uncompromising operationalism, however, would seem inconsistent with the concept of explaining an event. For if to explain an event involves making literal claims about underlying processes of forces--about causes, in a word--then we are not free to choose, at our convenience, stipulative definitions of the theoretical entities postulated. If theoretical entities are convenient fictions, they may be defined in any way we please; but if they are real, their correspondence with statements of observation or experience is not an arbitrary matter: it is itself an empirical matter. Put as briefly as possible, then, the issue as between operationalism and realism is whether the statements connecting theoretical terms to empirical ones are to be regarded as analytic or synthetic. The force of the present argument is that the ordinary sense of explanation appears to make demands which are inconsistent with the view--operationalism--which sees these connections as analytic.

All this may appear very abstract and general. Its relevance to the present discussion, however, will become clearer when we come to see that Friedman takes an "as if" interpretation of the theoretical assumptions of economics--a view which is compatible with operationalism and with the predictive but not the explanatory value of theories. It will be hardly surprising, then, when we note that he takes the predictive performance of a theory as the overriding criterion of its acceptability.

I turn now to a more detailed discussion of Friedman's position. In a nutshell, Friedmanesque methodology consists of the belief that the realism of the "assumptions" of a theory is of no importance in the decision to use the theory in a particular context; what is involved is its predictive performance in the context, i.e., the degree of correspondence of the predictions of the theory with the "facts," "evidence," "experience," or "observations" relevant to that context. Lipsey takes a similar line, although he does not stress the irrelevance of the realism of assumptions.

Friedman writes:[23] "Its [positive economics'] task is to provide a system of generalizations that can be used to make correct predictions about the consequences of any change in circumstances. Its performance is to be judged by the precision, scope and conformity with experience of the predictions it yields." And again:

Viewed as a body of substantive hypotheses, theory is to be judged by its predictive power for the class of phenomena which it is intended to "explain." Only factual evidence can show whether it is "right" or "wrong" or, better, tentatively "accepted" as valid or "rejected." As I shall argue at greater length below, the only relevant test of the *validity* of a hypothesis is comparison of its predictions with experience.[24]

In addition, Friedman introduces his "as if" principle: the hypothesis of, for example, maximizing behaviour is not to be interpreted as asserting that actors consciously maximize something, but rather that they behave as if they were maximizing something (such as expected returns or utility).[25] In adopting his "as if" principle, Friedman rejects the idea that the support or undermining of a microtheory of social behaviour can be influenced by whether the actor involved accepts the theory as a correct account of his behaviour. He writes:

> The billiard player, if asked how he decided where to hit the ball, may say that he 'just figures it out' but then also rubs a rabbit's foot just to make sure; and the businessman may well say that he prices at average cost, with of course some minor deviations when the market makes it necessary. The one statement is about as helpful as the other, and neither is a relevant test of the associated hypothesis.[26]

Further:

> A particularly clear example of criticizing a theory of the lack of realism of its assumptions is furnished by the recent criticisms of the maximization-of-returns hypothesis on the grounds that businessmen do not and indeed cannot behave as the theory "assumes" they do. The evidence cited to support this assertion is generally taken either from the answers given by businessmen to questions about the factors affecting their decisions--a procedure for testing economic theories that is about on a par with testing theories of longevity by asking octogenarians how they account for their long life--or from descriptive studies of the decision-making activities of individual firms. Little if any evidence is ever cited on the conformity of businessmen's actual market behaviour--what they do rather than what they say they do--with the implications' of the hypothesis being criticized, on the one hand, and of alternative hypotheses on the other.[27]

The argument appears to be that reasons for individual behaviour are largely subconscious, or that the behaviour is largely instinctive or habitual, or that proffered reasons may easily be rationalizations after the event. In other words, it is claimed that the individual is not in a position to give a proper account of the reasons for his own behaviour, nor even to judge the correctness of proferred accounts. In this way, the idea of microeconomic theory as the logic of choice becomes drastically attenuated. For, in Friedman's view, the "logic of choice" becomes merely a device for generating hypotheses: that is all. Strictly, the whole apparatus of microeconomic theory is no longer interpreted as a logic of choice but only as an apparent logic of choice-like acts.[28]

The over-all argument involves a metaphysical position which is extremely simple: that effects are intelligible, although causes are not. And such an over-all argument can readily be invoked as a licence for pragmatism with regard to truth.

(ii) *The primary yardstick for the acceptance or rejection of a theory is the compatibility of its predictions with something which is variously referred to as "facts," "evidence," "experience," or "observation."*

The force of the qualification "primary" is that other considerations such as simplicity, convenience, elegance may be involved in the acceptance or rejection of theories (or the choice between competing theories), but that these considerations must always be secondary; only when faced with a choice between theories which are equally consistent with the "facts," "evidence," "experience," or "observations" are these other considerations allowed to come into play.

The spirit of this proposition is entirely clear, but its expression leaves the exact import somewhat problematic.[29] Friedman talks about facts, evidence, experience, observation, observable phenomena, factual evidence, and empirical evidence. He mentions "reality" (his quotes) only in connection with assumptions, not predictions.[30] Lipsey talks about facts, observations, data, empirical observations, and evidence.[31] But terms like "facts," "evidence," "experience," and "observation" do not all refer to the same kind of things: a fact is a state of affairs which actually obtains, and of which some aspects may be described by statements; a piece of evidence is any object which may be interpreted as being relevant to a question at issue; "experience" is an account of events from a first-person viewpoint; and an "observation" is a deliberate, organized direction of attention towards some preselected aspect of things. One cannot have all these things being the primary yardstick for the appraisal of theories, for they may conflict with one another: "experience" may be conflict with what one has, until then, accepted as "facts"; "observation" may show that what was, until then, accepted as a piece of "evidence" has no bearing on the question at issue.

76

The issue is simply this: what class of things is to be regarded as the empirical base of economics? Friedman and Lipsey obviously regard this issue as quite unproblematic; they refer without qualification to facts, evidence, experience, observation, and phenomena as if these terms were perfectly interchangeable and as if it were obvious what is included. If we look at what Friedman and Lipsey treat as the empirical base in their own applied studies, it would appear that this consists largely of government statistics. It would be very hard to think of a convincing argument to present government statistics as the most fundamental ("raw") empirical materials of econmics, the ultimate yardstick against which all else must be judged. And such empirical materials as these (which are, of course, the ones typically used by economists) bear an extremely tenuous relation to experience, observation, and observable phenomena. They do constitute evidence of a kind and may be thought of (insofar as they are reliable and coherent) as descriptions of rather abstract and artificial facts.

It is worth pointing out that the recent controversies in monetary theory (monetarists versus neo-Keynesians) and in capital theory (neo-neo-classicists versus the Cambridge School) have not been brought any nearer to resolution by the introduction of evidence by either side, since part of the controversy in each case concerns the status and interpretation of such evidence; that is to say, what, if anything, it is to count as evidence *for*.

To sum up, then, the inadequacy of the methodology is precisely this: it is clear (and, indeed, dogmatic) on the quite indisputable point that evidence must count in deciding substantive questions; but it is silent on the crucial and controversial point of *what* is to count as evidence. Evidence provided by the senses? By history? By introspection? By the Central Statistical Office?[32]

The reason for our interest in the empirical base of economics is because of the part it plays in the testing of theories. Turning now to Lipsey's ideas on this issue, we find that he makes the following assertions: "The view that economics can be a science leads to the rejection of the critical nature of judgement in deciding when to test a theory and what facts to test it by."[33] "What the scientific method gives is an impersonal set of criteria for answering some questions: but what questions to ask and exactly how to obtain the evidence are difficult questions requiring great imagination."[34] "... as scientists we must always remember that, when theory and fact come into conflict, it is theory, not fact, that must give way."[35]

Although the quotations are taken out of context they are,

nevertheless, unequivocal. If the context is examined, we do find what might appear to be qualifications, but on close-examination these are seen to obscure rather than to modify the force of the doctrine. To be more specific: there are references to "evidence" and "the weight of evidence" rather than "facts," but there is no indication of the relation between these things, nor why the weighing of evidence should be an impersonal process; it is mentioned that, because of the fallibility of observation, testing can never lead to proof or refutation of a theory, but there is no attempt to reconcile this with the thesis that "theories" must always give way to "facts"; and the role of imagination and creativity in framing answerable questions, developing theories and searching for evidence is repeatedly stressed, but there is no indication of why these qualities are absent when evidence is interpreted or weighed.

It may be conceded that the development of economics is accomplished by some form of interplay between theoretical and empirical materials. But the view that this interplay, to qualify as a science, must consists of "tests" in which "theories" always give way to "facts" is a much stronger proposition which we are at liberty to reject. Of course, substantive questions can be settled only if there is an appear to evidence; so much is obvious. What is at issue here, however, is not whether there is any truth in the view but whether it constitutes an adequate methodology. It can be argued that Lipsey's over-mechanistic picture of the interplay of theory and evidence disqualifies it from serious consideration.[36] But that is not all. We may grant that the fruitful interplay of theory and evidence is a subtle, organic process; but still we may ask: in this process of interplay which items are to count as evidence?

An obvious issue which arises in this discussion is whether the dichotomy between theory and fact can be maintained. That anything we would want to call a "fact" can even be apprehended and interpreted independently of, or extricated from, theories and theoretical frameworks has been forcefully disputed.[37] If such a view is accepted, the positive doctrine may be dismissed not as incorrect but as failing even to make contact with the problem. Surprisingly, Friedman appears to subscribe to such a view when he writes "Known facts cannot be set on one side; a theory to apply 'closely to reality' on the other. A theory is the way to perceived 'facts,' and we cannot perceive 'facts' without a theory";[38] but he appears to be quite unaware that the implications of this view seriously undermine his general thesis. For if we perceive fact in different ways according to the theory we adopt, it would appear that the empirical base of the system dissolves into a hopeless relativism.

Essential to the positivist position is the idea that empirical testing is a *consequential* activity, i.e., an activity having definite and unambiguous implications for the theory in question. In contrast to this view, I intend to argue that a number of conditions must be satisfied before there is any possibility of a test being at all consequential; that these preconditions will never be satisfied in full; that in deciding whether the preconditions are *adequately* satisfied judgement must play a critical part; and that any criterion of adequacy will itself be a product of judgment.

The preconditions appear to me to be as follows: (i) the theory must be coherent and well-defined; (ii) the empirical materials must be reliable and must be satisfactory empirical counterparts of the concepts of the theory;[39] (iii) the assumptions made in designing the test must be of very low substantive content compared with the theory, or must be established independently of the test.

To elaborate these preconditions and discuss their implications for the theory of empirical testing would take us too far from the present argument, for the purposes of which it is sufficient to note that confronting a theory with some ostensibly relevant data may be a wholly inconsequential activity for a variety of reasons: the concepts of the theory may be vague; the data may be unreliable, or they may have a spurious precision unwarranted by the clarity of the underlying concepts; the system of conventions by means of which the theoretical concepts are delimited in practice may fail to yield a coherent and theoretically significant variable; or the variable so defined may fail to correspond to the original theoretical concept. The assumptions involved in the test may be very strong, or very dubious; the theory itself may be of such low substantive content that no data could discriminate, in practice, between its truth or falsity (or between its truth and that of an alternative theory of equally low substantive content).

It is apparent that only on very rare occasions will the conditions for consequential testing be fulfilled so manifestly that the issue is beyond dispute; in the usual run of things, one must appraise all the various aspects of the situation and try to arrive at an over-all decision as to whether the available data would unambiguously support or undermine the theory. More realistically, the question is a matter of degree in which a line must be drawn *somewhere* to delimit situations in which testing is to be regarded as sufficiently consequential to merit the effort involved.[40] One may engage in reflections along the following lines: the data appear to be reliable to two digits, but it is doubtful if the concepts can be defined so precisely without a great deal of arbitrariness. What do these data really mean? To what extent does their meaning overlap with the meaning of the theoretical concepts? Just how strong are the assumptions that have been made here? Are they strong enough to cast serious doubt on how the results would be interpreted? Does the theory have enough substantive content to make it sensibly testable? Or should it be classed as a near-tautology? All these are problems obviously requiring individual theoretical and practical judgement.

At the present stage of development of economics, there is an enormous potential for pseudo-testing, i.e., ostensible testing which is, in reality, wholly inconsequential. For example, it is pointless to attempt to test refined and well-articulated theories with inaccurate or even ambiguous data. But the situation is not easy to recognize, for the data which are commonly used by economists abound with instances of spurious precision--in statistics quoted to more digits than are warranted either by the precision of the corresponding concept, or by the processes by which the statistics are produced.[41] And this is not simply a problem of producing reliable statistics; it is a problem of the clarity of the underlying concepts; of what it is that we are saying in our theoretical discourse.

(iii) *There is no fundamental methodological difference between social and natural science.*

This thesis has been argued at length by Gibson[42] and has been disputed by a number of writers including Knight[43] and Winch.[44] This facet of positivist thought is clearly accepted by Friedman and Lipsey: Friedman states that "positive economics is, or can be, an "objective" science in precisely the same sense as any of the physical sciences,"[45] and goes on to conduct part of his argument in terms of the example of the law relating the distance travelled by a body falling under gravity to the time elapsed since it began its descent;[46] Lipsey quotes, at the beginning of his book, a passage from Lord Beveridge giving a (rather garbled) account of the allegedly pivotal role of facts in the history of physics, and attempting to extract a moral for the development of economics.[47]

It is evident that this proposition is closely related to the first one. Depending on what one means by "methodology," the claim of a common methodology for social and natural science could mean little more than that all theories must be appraised by their predictive performance.

The characteristic of social science which may involve it in radically different methodological problems from those of physical science is the circumstance that in social science there are two possible viewpoints: one may consider events and processes either from the viewpoint of the participant or from that of the observer. These viewpoints could be described as the first-person viewpoint and the third-person viewpoint, respectively. There is nothing quite comparable to this in the physical sciences. The social scientist is faced with a choice: he may attempt either to understand behavior in the actor's own terms, or to impose his own conceptual framework on it. (For example, "I was praying for forgiveness" could become "He was seeking emotional security by participating in organized ritual.") The physical scientist is without the former possibility--he cannot consider, as a basis for inquiry, the electron's own understanding of what it is doing.

The implications of this dualism of viewpoint are that there may be concepts which are intelligible to the actor/participant (and which may therefore appear in the reasons he gives for his actions) but which could not be translated without irremediable loss into the language of the observer. In other words, the third-person account of behaviour may leave no room for concepts which are essential to the actor's own understanding on his acts. If this is so, it could be argued that the third-person account is somehow necessarily impoverished and misleading. That this is to has been argued at length by Peter Winch.[48] The implication is that social science, in contrast to physical science, must derive from, or be based on, the actor's or participant's understanding of his situation. This would mean that it is quite improper and subversive of understanding for the social scientist to *impose* a conceptual framework on to the situations or events he wishes to understand. Rather, he must seek, as a foundation, at any rate, a grasp of the concepts which the participants themselves would understand and would use in describing and offering reasons for what they do: a first-person understanding of the situation.

Returning to Friedman's position we see the most uncompromising espousal of a third-person interpretation of microeconomics. Friedman's comments are, for once, perfectly unambiguous. He dismisses with some contempt the reasons which actors (businessmen and consumers) may give for their actions, or any account they may give of how they choose, as being entirely irrelevant to the acceptability of microeconomic theories of choice.-[49] His focusing on "predictions" to the complete exclusion of "assumptions," as the yardstick by which choice theories are to be judged is really the choice of a particular empirical base for his system: it is the choice of a third-person viewpoint for his theory and it therefore entails descriptions of "external" behaviour as the appropriate form of "empirical material."

The methodological unity of social and physical science is therefore achieved by restricting rather drastically the allowable empirical base of social science to exclude those empirical materials which would have no parallel in physical science. Provided the empirical materials of social science are restricted to records of "external" behaviour and exclude the accounts of "internal"

81

events--the intentions, expectation, reasons, goals, etc., of the actors, this unity can be maintained. And although such delimitation of the empirical base of the subject is consistent with the spirit of "positive economics," no arguments have been presented by its adherents in defence of such a restriction. It surely requires some good reasons for denying ourselves access to a class of empirical materials.

(iv) *Theory should be value-free.*

This is a facet of "positive economics" which involves the term "positive" in the sense of positive as opposed to normative. It could also be expressed as the proposition that economic theory should be ethically neutral. This aspect of positive doctrine is duly stressed by Friedman and Lipsey.[50] It is interesting to note that Friedman is also of the opinion that differences of opinion on economic policy derive primarily from differences over the positive rather than normative aspects of the policies. He writes:[51]

> I venture the judgement, however, that currently in the Western world, and especially in the United States, differences about economic policy among disinterested citizens derive predominantly from different predictions about the economic consequences of taking action--differences that in principle can be eliminated by the progress of positive economics--rather than from fundamental differences in basic values, differences about which men can ultimately only fight.

(It may be that this opinion is tautological, for Friedman is at liberty to disqualify, as failing to be "disinterested citizens" (a peculiar concept) those who claim that their basic values are fundamentally different from those of the consensus). Lipsey expresses a similar opinion when he writes "We may conclude that many hotly debated issues of public policy are positive and not normative ones, but that the scientific approach to such positive questions is very often ignored."[52] I do not propose to discuss this facet of positive economics, not because I regard it an unproblematic but because to do so would require a further article. I mention it here only for the sake of completeness.

My own view is that the chief defect of the approaches adopted by Friedman and Lipsey is the failure adequately to consider economic theory as a language. Friedman does briefly consider economic theory from this point of view when he writes:

> Viewed as a language, theory has no substantive content; it is a set of tautologies. Its function is to serve as a filing system for organizing empirical material and facilitating our understanding of it; and the criteria by which it is to be judged are those appropriate to a filing system. Are the

categories clearly and precisely defined? Are they exhaustive? Do we know where to file each individual item, or is there considerable ambiguity? Is the system of headings and sub-headings so designed that we can quickly find an item we want, or must we hunt from place to place? Are the items we shall want to consider jointly filed together? Does the filing system avoid elaborate cross-references.[53]

But the view of language as a filing system is surely grossly inadequate. Is Friedman unaware that language has syntactical as well as semantical properties, or does he simply choose to ignore the fact?

The language of economic theory, like any language, provides a framework for thought; but at the same time, it constrains thought to remain within that framework. It focuses our attention; determines the way we conceive of things; and even determines what *sort* of things can be said.[54] The commitment to use any language is also a commitment to conduct discourse in terms of assertions which are expressible in that language. A language, or conceptual framework is, therefore, at one and the same time both an opportunity and a threat. Its positive side is that (one hopes) it facilitates thought within the language or framework. But its negative side arises from the fact that the thought must be *within* the framework. In this sense, then, the framework of economic theory is (to introduce a rather hair-raising metaphor) both a springboard and a strait-jacket. Correspondingly, one aspect of the development of economic theory can be seen as an attempt to fight one's way out of the strait-jacket. It is this aspect which is neglected by positivistic thought. And a methodology which ignores the development of the conceptual framework itself suggests one of two things; that, conceptually, we have reached evolution's end--that the language of economic theory is at its highest stage of development; or that this language is, in any case, infinitely expressive and adaptable.

The unqualified emphasis on the testing of theories via their predictions suggests that the conceptual framework is regarded as a perfectly satisfactory language in which to make significant assertions about economic phenomena. There is no room left for the possibility that the conceptual framework itself is in need of enrichment - that it can be made more expressive by introducing distinctions, refining old concepts and inventing new ones. The apparent humility of the positivist programme (No armchair theorizing! Seek the relevant evidence!) is therefore seen to be rather superficial for the following reasons. The search for evidence, to be at all consequential, presupposes that what is to count as evidence is itself problematic. For with any interesting theory it is always possible to find some evidence which supports it and also sime which undermines it. In order to resolve the issue there must be some criterion of which kind of evidence has the greater claim to reflect reality. But, so far as the positive doctrine is concerned, the question of what constitutes reality for the purposes of economic analysis, of what things can be taken as "given" or "fundamental" for a satisfactory explanation of a phenomenon, and of what conceptual framework should be adopted for our theorizing, are allowed to be answered by the preconceptions with which we approach a problem. In other words, the unqualified emphasis of the positivist methodology on issues other than these suggests that our preconceptions are to be regarded as correct, and all the really *fundamental* issues in economics are to be regarded as solved. We see, therefore, that the demand for a justification of substantive assertions requires that the framework in which they are expressed and the criterion of justification are themselves accepted without justification.

Footnotes

*   I am grateful to G.L.S. Shackle and J.R. Ravetz for their help and encouragement with earlier drafts of this paper, and to Colette Bowe for patient criticism at all stages of its development.

1. J.N. Keynes, *The Scope and Method of Political Economy* (New York, 1965; first published, 1890; 4th ed., 1917).

2. Ibid., 31-6.

3. T.W. Hutchison, *The Significance and Basic Postulates of Economic Theory* (New York, 1965; first published, 1938).

4. M. Freidman, "The Methodology of Positive Economics," in *Essays in Positive Economics,* University of Chicago Press, 1953.

5. R.G. Lipsey, *An Introduction to Positive Economics* (1st ed., 1963; 2nd ed., 1966; 3rd ed., 1971). See also: "Can there be a valid theory of wages?" in B.J. McCormick and E. Owen Smith, eds., *The Labour Market* (London, 1968), 269-83.

6. See F. Machlup, "Positive and Normative Economics: An Analysis of the Ideas" in R.L. Heilbroner, ed., *Economic Means and Social Ends* (Englewood Cliffs, N.J., 1969).

7. Philosphers who wanted to establish the sort of claims which were previously derived from or associated with the verifiability criterion subsequently took to calling themselves logical empiricists.

8. W. James, *Pragmatism* (London, 1922).

9. K.R. Popper, *The Logic of Scientific Discovery* (London, 1968).

10. Friedman, *Essays, 7.*

11. Ibid., 8.

12. Ibid., 8-9.

13. A. Marshall, *Principles of Economics* (London, 1962), 638.

14. Ibid. In anticipation of later discussion, it should be mentioned that Friedman is not in a position to cite the authority of Marshall in support of his own position. For in Friedman's account not only is the notion of "cause" entirely absent but the account is in fact quite inconsistent with explanation or prediction involving "causes."

15. Also known as the deductive/nomological model. Such an account of explanation has been associated with Popper, Oppenheim, Hempel, Pap, and Nagel.

16. It might be some such view which makes Friedman use the word "explain" only in inverted commas. We shall return to this point leter.

17. See below, 14. I wonder if Friedman has empirical grounds for dismissing ethical and moral dialogue as entirely futile. Of course, the qualifications "basic" and "ultimately" may save the original statement from actually asserting anything.

18. I. Sheffler, *The Anatomy of Inquiry* (New York, 1963). See also D.V.T. Bear and D. Orr, "Logic and Expediency in Economic Theorising," *Journal of Political Economy,* 75 (April, 1967), 188-96.

19. Consider also this passage from Blaug: "Such methodologists as Senior, J.S. Mill, Cairnes, Sidgwick, Jevons, Marshall, John Neville Keynes, Bohm-Bawerk and Pareto frequently emphasised other matters and, of course, underemphasised the problem of devising appropriate emprical tests of theories, but nothing they wrote denied the idea that to "explain" is

simply to predict accurately." (M. Blaug, *Economic Theory in Retrospect,* 2nd ed. (London, 1968), 666).

20. The use of inverted commas by Blaug and Friedman is not (as in the above sentence) to distinguish between a word's being *mentioned* rather than *used*--as in "the meaning of 'meaning'" where the same word is first used and then mentioned.

21. See 19.

22. What we have to say here in no way prejudges the issue as to whether, in a different context, empirical counterparts could be discovered or inferred to correspond to those theoretical entities.

23. Friedman, *Essays,* 4.

24. Ibid., 8-9. Compare the spirit of these two quotations from Friedman with the following extracts from a chapter on pragmatism and religion in William James: "We cannot reject any hypothesis if consequences useful to life flow from it." "If the hypothesis of God works satisfactorily in the widest sense of the word, it is true." (*Pragmatisim,* 273, 299).

25. Friedman, *Essays,* 21-2.

26. Ibid., 22.

27. Ibid., 31.

28. I.M. Kirzner, writing within the tradition of subjective value theory which stresses the interpretation of microeconomics as the study of the logic of choice, distinguishes sharply between "positive" and "economic" concepts or categories. He regards the "positive" categories as related to technological rather than economic modes of thought. (I.M. Kirzner, *An Essay on Capital* (New York, 1966).)

29. Friedman and Lipsey are not alone. Bertrand Russell writes: "I found, when I began to think about theory of knowledge, that none of the philosophers who emphasise 'experience' tells us what they mean by the word." (B. Russell, *My Philosophical Development* (London, 1959), 131.)

30. Friedman, *Essays.*

31. Lipsey, *An Introduction.*

32. In a footnote (Lipsey, *An Introduction,* 7) there is a puzzling dismissal of introspection (along with appeals to authority and something that looks like essentialism) as a method of answering questions. The fruits of introspection are exemplified by any statement starting: "All reasonable men will surely agree..." But this example, looked upon simply as an unsupported (and vague) hypothesis about the (public) existence of a consensus is correctly seen as the product of thought, not of introspection. The example misses the point entirely: for the question of epistemological status of introspection concerns whether, in contrast to the behaviourist outlook, it can be a legitimate (private) source of knowledge about the reasons for one's actions.

33. Lipsey, *An Introduction,* 1st ed., 533.

34. Ibid., 6. Close variants of this statement appear in the second edition, p.8, and the third edition, p.7.

35. Ibid., 546; 2nd ed., 859; 3rd ed., 725.

36. Since one of the facets of positive economics is the view that social and physical science have fundamentally the same methodology, it is worth pointing out that the adequacy of the picture of testing as a consequential activity is subject to controversy in the context of physical science, too. T.S. Kuhn, for example, sees the overwhelming part of research activity not as a process of testing, but as a process of refining, extending and articulating a given framework of ideas. (T.S. Kuhn, *The Structure of Scientific Revolutions* (Chicago, 1962).)

37. See T.S. Kuhn, "The Function of Measurement in Modern Physical Science," in H. Woolf, ed., *Quantification: A History of the Meaning of Measurement in the Natural and Social Sciences* (New York, 1961), and *The Structure of Scientific Revolutions,* chap. X.

38. Friedman, *Essays,* p. 34.

39. For a discussion of the difficulties involved in meeting this requirement, see F. Machlup, "Operationalism and Pure Theory in Economics," in S.R. Krupp, ed., *The Structure of Economic Science* (Englewood Cliffs, N.J., 1966).

40. For a discussion, in a closely-related context, of the personal judgements which are essential to the activity of theorizing, see R.S. Rudner, "The Scientist *Qua* Scientist Makes Value Judgements," *Philosophy of Science,* 20 (Jan. 1953), 1-6.

41. If anything, the situation has worsened since O. Morgenstern made this clear (*On the Accuracy of Economic Observations* (Princeton, N.J., 1950)). The widespread availability of computing facilities has made it difficult to resist the temptation to engage in technically arcane but conceptually spurious statistical gymnastics.

42. Q. Gibson, *The Logic of Social Enquiry* (London, 1960).

43. F.H. Knight, *On the History and Method of Economics* (Chicago, 1963).

44. P. Winch, *The Idea of a Social Science* (London, 1958).

45. Friedman, *Essays*, 4.

46. Ibid., 16-9.

47. Lipsey, *An Introduction*, 1st ed., v-vi; 2nd ed., xi-xii; 3rd ed., xi-xii.

48. Winch, *The Idea of a Social Science*.

49. See above, 7.

50. Friedman, *Essays*, 3-5; Lipsey, *An Introduction*, 1st ed., 4-5; 2nd ed., 4-7; 3rd ed., 4-6.

51. Friedman, *Essays*, p. 5.

52. Lipsey, *An Introduction*, 1st ed., 7; 2nd ed., 9; 3rd ed., 8.

53. Friedman, *Essays*, p. 7.

54. D.W. Theobald, at some risk of overstatement, puts the point very neatly when he writes: "Reality is what you can say it is." (*Introduction to the Philosophy of Science* (London, 1968), 134).

6 In Defense of Predictionism

David and Robin Pope*

I

A central theme in Kenneth Rivett's original paper (repeated in his "Comment") is the need when confirming hypotheses to go beyond mathematical tests (specifically, significance tests). There is an emphasis on *further* evidence. But from the predictionist viewpoint, and from analysis of Rivett's elaboration of his overall test, what Rivett construes as further evidence is *already* incorporated in predictionist methods of confirmation – that is with the sole exception of a *logical fallacy*, the same fallacy which all assumptionists commit.

Rivett in his "Comment" now clarifies his "method for the confirmation of hypotheses" into a four-point schema. Let us examine it.

Point (i): whether "falsified by market transactions."[1] Here an implication (prediction) of the hypothesis is tested by observations (market transactions). If the observations disconfirm the prediction, this is diconfirming evidence for the hypothesis. We define this basic test a predictionist. Although assumptionists would not of course deny Point (i),[2] they are *characterised* by tacking on Point (ii).

Point (ii): whether "falsified by ... the aims, knowledge and rational capacity of the economic agents referred to." This part of the overall test does go beyond predictionist methods and is distinctly assumptionist, for aims, knowledge, rationality are the assumptions of theory.[3] However, to assert that falsification of the assumptions implies falsification of the hypothesis is invalid.[4] In classical Russell-Whitehead logic, the "consequent" of any proposition can be true though the "antecedent" is untrue. In this instance a hypothesis can be true though its assumptions are false. A simple example may help: My mother-in-law is expected today; I assume that she will come by air (she always has) and check schedules; and as the only plane arrives at 3:00 p.m., hypothesise that she will arrive at 3:00 p.m. She does indeed arrive at 3:00 p.m., but left her domicile a day earlier and came by bus; we cannot reject a hypothesis *merely* because the assumptions are false.[5] Assumptionists are forced to deny this

Reprinted by permission from the *Austrailian Economic Papers*, 11 (1972), 232-8.

implication of classical logic, i.e., assumptionism categorically embodies a *logical fallacy*. Rivett's Point (ii) completely embraces this fallacy and Rivett in his article (p. 137) and "Comment" (footnote 6) explicitly commits it: "The wish is expressed that he (Friedman) would go further and reject a hypothesis *merely because* its assumptions are false." (Our italics).

Rivett's Points (iii) and (iv) can be treated together since (iii), whether the hypothesis "has been suggested by a ... system which has suggested acceptable hypotheses in the past,"[6] is a subset of (iv), "to take account of ... the antecedent probability of the *hypothesis*." Thus (iv) is a plea, which we and all predictionists accept, namely that one should take account of prior probabilities of the hypothesis, and (iii) is an example of *one* factor which raises the antecedent or prior probability of a hypothesis. We say one, for predictionists also include, at least, consideration of how "old"[7] the hypothesis is, and whether the hypothesis under review derives "theoretical support"[8] from currently confirmed hypotheses.[9]

It is also important to emphasise that *a priori* evidence is not a *separate test* from Point (i). Rivett wrongly asserts that it is when he states, in his "Comment": "If the hypothesis survives (i) and (ii), then the outcome of (iii) and (iv) will determine whether it can be accepted." But test (i) cannot be properly conducted without reference to (iii) and (iv) and other relevant *a priori* information. For the *a priori* knowledge is used to determine whether the observations conform with the predictions of the hypothesis.

An example at this stage may help to make this clearer. Consider an economic historian interested in investigating the past effect of Australian unemployment rates and inter-country differences in real wages upon variation in annual migration to Australia. He might test the null hypothesis, H_0, that these factors had no influence against the alternative, H_1, that their influences were non-zero.[10] The prediction, more accurately retrodiction, which is the *test implication* of H_1 is that the partial regression coefficients[11] are non-zero. Now of course with limited data we can never know the true values of the regression coefficients; we can only estimate them with an expected margin of chance error. The question arises: How "large"[12] do our estimated regression coefficients (relative to their standard errors) have to be before we conclude that they are not non-zero merely by chance; in other words, what is the appropriate level of *statistical significance?*[13]

At this stage antecedent knowledge is crucial for the predictionists. In our example of historical migration, *a priori* considerations may run along the following lines: although economic betterment, as denoted by differences in real wages, may be a major motive to migrate to Australia, it is unlikely that expectations of differences in income will change greatly from one year to the next. Thus in a model explaining year-to-year changes in migration it may be expected, *a priori,* that changes in labour market conditions, which are on the whole short-term phenomena, are the more certain determinant. Such thoughts suggest then a low antecedent probability of the influence of the real wage differential and vice versa for unemployment rates.

How is such prior knowledge used in checking the predictions? The answer is that antecedent knowledge is one of the prime factors taken into account when deciding on the *level of significance*. In our example we set H_0, that variations in real wage rates between sender and recipient countries had no impact on migration, against H_1, that they did. Antecedent knowledge leads us to feel that the probability of such an effect operating is small; therefore we want the level of significance, the risk of wrongly rejecting H_0, to be very *low*. With Australian unemployment rates the opposite is the case. Prior information that unemployment is a very likely factor would prompt us to want the probability of rejecting H_0 (unemployment has zero effects), when indeed that is the case, to be very *high*. In other words we vary the *level of significance* directly in accord with the antecedent probability of the hypothesis.[14] And as the chosen *level of significance* affects which hypothesis (H_0 or H_1) is temporarily confirmed, it is abundantly clear that antecedent probability is a critical element in predictionist/postdictionist methodology.

The "central misunderstanding" to which Rivett refers now seems resolved. We are interested in methods of confirming empirical economic hypotheses. Rivett is too. But, as we hope we have demonstrated, the four-point schema in his "Comment" indicates that he *only* wants to use the predictionist test, Point (i) which utilises Points (iii) and (iv), *i.e.*, they are not further evidence beyond (i), plus a distinctly assumptionist test, Point (ii), which commits a *logical fallacy*.

II

The following are some related points, raised in Rivett's criticism of us, which have a general bearing on the central issue of "confirmation."

1. *"Entailment" and the Relevance of Assumptions*

Rivett's "entailment" is the *modus ponens* proof of traditional deductive logic[15] - if we know p (the assumptions) are *true,* and we know p logically implies q (the hypothesis), then q "must also be true."[16] This could be considered a test beyond the significance test. The problem is that it can never be applied. Rivett feels he is misquoted. We fail to see the importance of construing his claim as "it is never easy" to find an identity between the facts and the assumptions, rather than as "there seldom is" such an identity. Our argument is not that such an identity is "seldom" found to be true, but that it is *never* found to be true, *i.e.,* theory can never "help to entail ... a hypothesis" as Rivett again wrongly contended can be "the occasional case" in his "Comment". The reason is that in order to apply the test, the assumptions must be *known to be true.* But, as elaborated in our earlier paper, this is never the case, for assumptions are themselves hypotheses, and hence can only be tentatively confirmed or diconfirmed.[17] Rivett recognises this on one occasion,[18] but ignores it in his "Comment" when proposing "entailment" can be the "occasional case".

When the assumptions are not *known to be true,* but merely temporarily confirmed the entailment of the hypothesis is impossible. Evidence of the truth of the assumption is still relevant, however, since tentatively confirming evidence for a set of assumptions that imply the hypothesis p raises the prior probability of p. Thus tentative confirmation of the assumptions of p offers one more criterion for determining the antecedent probability of p.[19]

2.   *Stock Exchange Argument*

Rivett still want to reiterate the standard assumptionist critique of predictionims--predictionists do not reject hypotheses *simply* on the grounds that the assumption or assumptions are inaccurate. Ironically, in the preceding paragraph of his "Comment", Rivett wholeheartedly concurs that a hypothesis could be true when the assumptions are false, *i.e.,* in the previous paragraph he *accepts* the predictionist line: "In the example used in my paper, MR, AR, MC and AC ... could be equal--even though competition was far from perfect", *i.e.,* even though assumptions were false. Yet, despite this, when it comes to the stock exchange example, Rivett reverses and castigates the predictionists for not rejecting a hypothesis merely because its assumptions are false.[20]

3.   *The Level of Significance*

An implication of Rivett's comments, particularly his citation of Frisch,[21] is that the level of significance is a narrow mechanical concept, something which we need to go beyond. We disagree. Our answer, as demonstrated above, is that the level of significance becomes a *variable* with respect to antecedent probability.[22]

Rivett and ourselves have considered in our papers what evidence is needed for a hypothesis to be tentatively confirmed. Answers have been given in assumptionist and predictionist terms, with Rivett emphasising *a priori* knowledge. Frisch's point is a different one. His is the notion of widening the competing hypotheses: test hypothesis A against hypothesis B. But then how do we know we should not have tested A against C or D or N? Since Frisch wrote, there has been a great deal of development (within the framework of significance tests) for comparing diverse families of hypotheses,[23] *i.e.*, there are available statistical tests for choosing between widely divergent hypotheses, or in Frisch's words, for testing "the *applicability* of the model itself."

4. *Antecedent Probability*

Rivett in his "Comment" raises the interesting question: "Who will spell out the determinants of antecedent probability...?" We have cited formal criteria[24] for varying antecedent probability. A related question, implied by Rivett's, is: Who specifies the actual numerical value? Our answer is that if the individual researcher spells out his personal antecedent probability which greatly differs from that generally considered by his colleagues, then that researcher is unlikely to convince many of his colleagues that his test is at all powerful--a researcher is therefore likely to compromise and choose prior probabilities at least close to those held by the profession. Of course, this raises the further question--what if there is no agreement in the profession? Our answer is that this is a short-run problem. In the long run one can expect that differences in antecedent probability will disappear as observational evidence (from testing hypotheses) expands. For instance, successive observational evidence favourable to the hypothesis will push everyone's prior probability of the hypothesis for future tests towards unity; and successive observational evidence unfavourable to the hypothesis will induce everyone to revise his prior probability of that hypothesis downwards and towards zero. The procedure for revising the prior probabilities in the light of observational evidence could follow Bayes' procedure. In the meantime, in the short run, before there is general agreement, one solution is to select the prior probability by paying due weight to the various schools of thought.[25]

5. *Is Economics Inherently Different from the Physical Sciences?*

Our support for the straight application of predictionist methods in economics partly rests on the proposition that those methods have proved useful in the physical sciences. Rivett in his "Comment" contends, however, "that the concept of 'law' in the physicists' sense is not equally applicable in economics." Rivett asserts that the "basic concepts" of economics are observational terms, they "already carry meanings which no actual or possible advance in economic science will allow us to alter" in contrast to "the concepts used in 'theoretical' laws" in physics: in economics we deal with observable things such as the actions of consumers and producers, while in physics we deal with non-observable theoretic concepts such as atoms. There are two objections to Rivett's distinction:

(a) The logical positivists' dichotomy of observational and theoretical terms alluded to by Rivett has been shown to be invalid on any plausible definition--there are no *pure* observation terms.[26]

(b) Historically, terms used in a theory which start with a fixed meaning derived from the outside world (by "observation") have changed their meaning as the discipline develops --hence even though the meaning of "purpose" and "knowledge" are currently fixed in economics, this is no guarantee that they will retain these meanings, *i.e.*, their meanings may change because of the way they are used by economists.[27]

6.   *Opponents of Predictionism*

According to Rivett in his "Comment" opponents of predictionism constitute "perhaps most of the economics profession." We absolutely agree. However, assumptionism is indefensible for two reasons:

(a) Assumptionism categorically embodies a *logical fallacy* -- the "fallacy of denying the antecedent."

(b) Assumptionism has been responsible for none of the discoveries in the physical sciences since such a school of thought does not exist. Predictionism/postdictionism, on the other hand, has been the general method of verification which has proved useful. We think it regrettable that economists have so solidly aligned themselves with assumptionist methodology in testing their empirical hypotheses.

REJOINDER

KENNETH RIVETT

I am not guilty of the 'fallacy of denying the antecedent' and then purporting to deduce that the consequent is false, for the simple reason that, in my account of economic method, the hypothesis is not the consequent but the explanation of the consequent. The typical economic hypothesis is not the observation that prices rise, but the explanation that increased demand causes them to rise. In terms of the Popes' example, it is not the observation of a mother-in-law arriving at 3 p.m., but the explanation that she arrives at 3 p.m. because she comes by air.

The Popes write that

> even though the meaning of 'purpose,' knowledge' are currently fixed in economics, this is no guarantee that they will retain these meanings, *i.e.*, their meanings may change because of the way they are used by economists.

They may have in mind the changes that have occurred in the technical meanings of "value" and "utility." But nothing useful had to be surrendered when those words were allowed to acquire a different content. To use "purpose" and "knowledge" in senses distinctive to economics is to deny ourselves the huge explanatory power of each concept as currently understood. Unless the Popes envisage such a sacrifice, the meanings of the two terms cannot be changed--only ignored. This goes to the heart of the disagreement between us. Do the Popes reject the warning of the eminent chemist N.V. Sidgwick, quoted in a footnote on p. 141 of my article and including the words: "The chemist must not employ the language of physics unless he is willing to accept its laws"?

The fact that all empirical statements are tentative has no bearing on whether reality is sometimes identical with a situation described in the premises and conclusion of an analytical proposition.

Mention is made of Brunner's view that almost no propositions of economic theory have so far been formulated in a way which makes them analytical. If the others can be so formulated, the fact that they may not have been does not tell against my argument. If, on the other hand, they cannot be so formulated, the point is so important that, frankly, it should have been raised at an earlier stage in this controversy. It cannot be discussed now, and therefore briefly, without injustice to both standpoints.

The Popes' account of how antecedent probability affects the acceptable level of statistical significance is valuable. Their point against Frisch (footnote 23) seems well taken.

EPILOGUE

DAVID and ROBIN POPE

It does not matter how much explanation is embodied in a hypothesis. A hypothesis is simply a testable statement. Nor does it matter if the hypothesis, q, is absurdly simple (q = prices rise) or complex (q = if demand increases and if supply remains constant and if ... then prices rise). Whatever the hypothesis, the whole hypothesis, q, can be cast as the consequent of the assumptions (in Rivett's case, the rationality of men and other "alities"). Indeed Rivett formerly did exactly this--see "'Suggest' or 'Entail'" pp. 141-2. And when this is done, the logical fallacy embodied in Rivett's assumptionist position is revealed, *i.e.*, a hypothesis, q, is not falsified merely by falsifying its assumptions.

We have suggested that there is no fundamental methodological difference between the physical and social sciences with respect to hypothesis testing. Rivett rejects this proposition in asserting that physicists change the meanings of terms through time, but economists do not. But when Rivett notes that the meaning of "value" and "utility" have changed over time--in his own words, "'value' and 'utility' ... were allowed to acquire a different content"--he is explicitly admitting that the contents of terms are changed in economics as in physics, *i.e.*, he accepts our contention. As this was the *only* distinction made by Rivett between the methodology of the physical and social sciences, then that distinction no longer seems a point of debate. Rivett by his own argument is led to agree with us.

In his "Rejoinder," Rivett claims that this issue (whether economists can change the meanings of terms) "goes to the heart of the disagreement between us". Our interpretation of this debate has been that Rivett in his original article claimed to forward a schema for the confirmation of hypotheses that went beyond the simple mathematical significance tests of the predictionists. We have tried, via the role of antecedent probabilities and alpha errors in standard significance tests, to show that Rivett in no sense goes beyond classical predictionist methods. Rivett now agrees with us.

In reply to the third paragraph, the issue is not 'whether reality is ... identical with ... the premises'; the question is whether it can ever be *known to be* identical.

Footnotes

*   We are grateful for views and comments received from Professors Virgil Hinshaw, Peter Machamer and, particularly, Ronald Laymon (Department of Philosophy, Ohio State University); Professor Karl Brunner (Department of Economics, University of Konstanz Germany, and the University of Rochester); Professor P.A.V.B. Swamy (Department of Economics, Ohio State University); N.F. Roberts (New Zealand Wool Research Organization); and S. Payne (Department of Labour, New Zealand).

1. Rivett's language should still have been clearer. Whether the hypothesis is "falsified by market transactions" is such a general statement as to beg the whole controversy between assumptionists and predictionists. What market transactions falsify a hypothesis?--only those that tell against the predictions of a hypothesis; or *also* those that tell against the assumptions of a hypothesis?

2. How does one test assumptions? By predictions of assumptions. One set of predictions of the assumptions are the predictions of the hypothesis itself (via the transitivity of logical implication). Hence Rivett is mistaken in claiming our description of the assumptionist test - verifying the truth of the assumptions - does not include test (i). Why we regard the assumptionist position as untenable is not their stance on (i) but the logical fallacy embodied in Point (ii).

3. Ibid., p. 129.

4. This error is called the "fallacy of denying the antecedent," so named because it is *wrongly* deduced from denying the antecedent that the consequent is false. This erroneous form of deduction arises from its resemblance to the perfectly valid *modus tollens* form of argument. See for example, Wesley C. Salmon, *Logic,* Foundations of Philosophy Series (New Jersey: Prentice Hall, 1963), p. 27.

5. The prior probability of the hypothesis falls if I discover that she is not arriving by plane, but this is *not* a reason for rejecting the hypothesis before checking my wristwatch at 3:00 p.m. in the joint transport terminal (*i.e.,* the test).

6. The view that this raises the prior probability of a hypothesis first gained currency in the seventeenth century. For instance, the stages of this inductive argument are investigated by Descartes in his "Disclosure on Methods," Parts V and VI in *Optics, Geometry and Meteorology* (U.S.A.: Robbs Merrill, 1965). On the role of approximations in science in this context, see Dudley Shapere, "Notes Toward a Post-Postivist Interpretation of Science," in Peter Achinstein and Steven Barker (eds.), *The Legacy of Logical Positivism* Baltimore: Johns Hopkins Press, 1969).

7. The longer the hypothesis has been in existence, the more it should have been modified so as to predict well. Accordingly, if a "young hypothesis" and an "old hypothesis" predict equally well, one would prefer to work on the "young hypothesis" because one can anticipate that further modification of it will rapidly enhance its predictive accuracy. See for example, Thomas Kuhn, "The Structure of Scientific Revolutions," *International Encyclopedia of Unified Science*, vol. II, number 2. (University of Chicago, 1970), pp. 144-160.

8. The credibility of a hypothesis will be adversely affected if it conflicts with hypotheses currently accepted as well confirmed. Hempel gives a humorous but telling example. In the New York medical records for 1877, a physician reporting on an exhumation claimed that the hair of the man had burst through the coffin. Although presented by a presumptive eye witness, the claim is rejected--the prior probability is reduced to zero--"because it conflicts with well established findings about the extent to which human hair continues to grow after death." Carl G. Hempel, *Philosophy of Natural Science* (New Jersey: Prentice Hall, 1966), pp. 38-40. As Hempel points out, however, this prior probability principle must be applied with caution: otherwise it could prevent any currently accepted hypothesis from being overthrown. See also Wesley C. Salmon, *The Foundations of Scientific Inference* (Pittsburgh: University of Pittsburgh Press 1967), p.125.

9. For instance the predictionist Wesley C. Salmon offers a series of other criteria for determining the antecedent probability of a hypothesis. See Salmon, *op. cit.*, pp. 118 and 125-127.

10. Specifically, the alternative is that either unemployment and/or the real wage differential have an infleunce on migration. The hypotheses are only precise when we have specified the functional forms, but the example is to aid in understanding the role of antecedent probability, not of functional forms, in testing a hypothesis.

11. A partial regression coefficient represents the measured effect on the endogenous variable (here, migration) resulting from a unit change in the exogenous variable (here, unemployment or real wages) whilst holding the influence of the *other* exogenous variable constant.

12. In absolute values.

13. The *level of significance* is the risk of wrongly rejecting the null hypothesis when the null is in fact true. See also our comments at the end of this paper.

14. This gives the alternative hypothesis, in which we place a high prior degree of confidence, a greater chance of being accepted. See Ronald J. Wonnacott and Thomas H. Wonnacott, *Econometrics* (New York: Wiley, 1970), pp. 66-67.
Bayesian methods are a more formal means of incorporating prior probabilities. Partly because in general they require complete specification of the prior probability density functions (and also more computer time), they are not currently in wide use by economists. See for instance, D.G. Champernowne, *Uncertainty and Estimation in Economics* (San Francisco: Oliver and Boyd, 1969), Vol. 1, pp. 219-273, and Arnold Zellner, *Introduction to Bayesian Inference* (New York: Wiley, 1972).

15. See, for example, Michael D. Resnik, *Elementary Logic* (U.S.A.: McGraw-Hill, 1970), p. 177.

16. Rivett, *op. cit.,* p. 141.

17. The reason for this characteristic of hypotheses is that we can never know that the correlations are not accidental; there is always, to quote Rivett in his "Comment," "the possibility of future disconfirming evidence." This possibility pertains even if the assumption (a hypothesis) is narrowed from, say, "all firms maximise profits" to "all firms *in a particular industry* maximise profits." Contrast, "'Suggest' or 'Entail'-," p. 141.

18. See Rivett's observation following his citation of Johnson on the aims and rationality of economic agents: Rivett, "'Suggest' or 'Entail'," p. 134.

19. But this use of assumptions in determining prior probabilities is greatly weakened by the fact that almost no economic theory has been properly axiomatised. It is not yet the "set of analytical propositions" to which Rivett refers ("'Suggest' or 'Entail'," p. 128), where the assumptions logically imply the hypotheses. In short, economic hypotheses are not in general logically linked to their assumptions. This is considered by Karl Brunner, "'Assumptions' and the Cognitive Quality of Theories," *Synthese: An International Journal for Epistemology, Methodology and Philosophy of Science,* vol. 20, 1969, pp. 519-520.

20. However, if Rivett had said that the antecedent probability of the hypothesis is low when one set of assumptions has been

disconfirmed and the plausibility of alternative sets of assumptions is small, we would have agreed.

21. Rivett, "'Suggest' or 'Entail'," pp. 127-128.

22. The level of significance is also a variable with respect to other criteria, *e.g.*, the loss functions associated with wrongly rejecting hypotheses.

23. The most general tests have been proferred by D.R. Cox, "Tests of Separate Families of Hypotheses," *Fourth Berkeley Symposium*, vol. 1, pp. 105-123. His method avoids formulating a maintained hypothesis that will incorporate both competing families of hypotheses--such a maintained hypothesis has often proved unmanageably comprehensive. He offers a general method based on the Neyman Pearson Likelihood ratio.

    With all due respect for his innumerable contributions, the Frisch statement that a higher test *cannot* be mathematical is wrong. If a test exists, there is no reason why it cannot be expressed using *symbolic* language (i.e., mathematics) (rather than *ordinary* language, even though to do so may be totally undesirable for some reason.

24. See, for example, footnotes 7, 8 and 9 above and also the final paragraph of our comment on "Entailment" and the Relevance of Assumptions.

25. For some suggestions on how weights might be chosen, see D.G. Champernowne, *op. cit.*, p. 242.

26. Marshall Spector, "Theory and Observation," *British Journal for the Philosophy of Science*, vol. 17, 1966, no. 1, pp. 1-20, and no. 2, pp. 89-104.

27. Contrast Rivett, "'Suggest' or 'Entail'," p. 141. For such developments in the meanings of words initially related to "outside objects," see Willard van Orman Quine, *Word and Object* (U.S.A.: Massachusetts Institute of Technology Press, 1968).

7 A Critique of Friedman's Critics

Lawrence A. Boland*

Milton Friedman's essay, "Methodology of Positive Economics" [4, 1953], is considered authoritative by almost every textbook writer who wishes to discuss the methodology of economics. Nevertheless, virtually all the journal articles that have been written about that essay have been very critical. This is a rather unusual situation. The critics condemn Friedman's essay, but virtually all the textbooks praise it. Why should honest textbook writers ignore the critics? It will be argued here that the reason is quite clear. Every critic of Friedman's essay has been wrong. The fundamental reason why all of the critics are wrong is that their criticisms are not based on a clear, correct, or even fair understanding of his essay. Friedman simply does not make the mistakes he is accused of making. His methodological position is both logically sound and unambiguously based on a coherent philosophy of science--Instrumentalism.

In order to defend Friedman from his critics, I shall outline some necessary background knowledge--a clear understanding of the nature of logic and the philosophy of Instrumentalism--and then present a reader's guide to his essay. Based on this background knowledge and the reader's guide, I shall survey and comment upon the major critics of Friedman's methodology. I shall conclude with a suggestion as to how a fair criticism would proceed.

1. The Usefulness of Logic

1.1 Modus ponens: *Logic's Only Useful Property*

Aristotle was probably the first to systemize the principles of logic; most of them were common knowledge in his time. Logic has not changed much since then, although some presentations lead one to think that our logic is different. Modern writers too often discuss logic as if it had nothing to do with truth. But such a view of logic is an error. In Aristotle's view logic was the study of the principles of true and *successful* argument.[1]

Reprinted by permission from the American Economic Association. The article appeared in the *Journal of Economic Literature*, 17 (1979), 503-22.

Recognizing that arguments consist only of individual statements joined together with an "and" or an "or," Aristotle was concerned with determining what kinds of statements are admissible into logical arguments. He posited some rules that are in effect necessary conditions for the admissibility of statements into a logical argument. These rules, which later became known as the axioms or cannons of logic, cannot be used to justify an argument; they can only be used to criticize or reject an argument on the grounds of inadmissibility.[2]

The only purpose for requiring arguments to be logical is to connect the truth of the premises or assumptions to the truth of the conclusions. Merely joining together a set of admissible statements does not necessarily form a logical argument; the only criterion for whether an admissible argument is logical is whether it is a sufficient argument in favor of its conclusions in the following sense. If your argument is logical, then whenever *all* of your assumptions (or premises) are true *all* of your conclusions will be true as well.

To prove that an argument is logical, one must be able to demonstrate its sufficiency. Whenever one establishes the logical sufficiency of a formal (or abstract) argument, one can use that formal argument as a part of a larger empirical (or contingent) argument that is in favor of the truth of any particular conclusion of the formal argument.[3] That is to say, whenever you offer an empirical argument *in favor* of some proposition, you are purporting both that the form of the argument is logically valid *and* that your assumptions are true. In this sense, logical validity is a necessary (but not sufficient) condition for an empirical argument to be true.

Using a formal argument in favor of the truth of any of its conclusions by arguing from the truth of its assumptions is said to be using the argument in the affirmative mode--or more formally, in *modus ponens*. The ability to use any argument successfully in *modus ponens* is the primary necessary condition for the argument's logical validity or consistency (or for short, its "logicality"). However, this is not the only necessary condition for an argument's logicality. Whenever *modus ponens* is assured for a given argument, that argument can always be used in a denial or criticism of the truth of its assumptions. Specifically, if your argument is logical, then any time *any one* conclusion is false *not all* of your assumptions can be true (i.e., at least one assumption must be false).[4] Using this mode of argument against the truth of one's assumptions by arguing from the falsity of a conclusion is called *modus tollens*. Whenever one successfully criticizes an argument by using *modus tollens,* one can conclude that either an assumption is false or the argument is not logical (or both).

1.2 Beyond modus ponens

In order to distinguish *modus ponens* from its corollary *modus tollens*, not only must we explicitly refer to truth and falsity, but we must also specify the *direction* of the argument. Heuristically speaking, *modus ponens* "passes" the truth *forward* from the assumptions to the conclusions.[5] *Modus tollens*, on the other hand, "passes" the falsity *backward* from the conclusions to one or more of the assumptions.[6] The important point here, which I shall argue is implicitly recognized by Friedman in his essay, is that if one changes the direction (forward or backward) of either valid mode of using a logical argument, then the logicality of one's argument ceases to be useful or methodologically signifiClant. Specifically, any use of *modus ponens* in *reverse* is an example of what logic textbooks call "the Fallacy of Affirming the Consequent." Similarly, any use of *modus tollens* in *reverse* is an example of what is called "the Fallacy of Denying the Antecedent." It is especially important to note that truth cannot be "passed" backward nor can falsity be "passed" forward.[7]

The major point to be emphasized here is that while the truth of assumptions and conclusions is connected in the use of a logical argument in *modus ponens*, the truth of the same assumptions and conclusions is not connected if they are used in *reverse modus ponens*. Similarly, their falsity is not connected when used in *reverse modus tollens*.

I think an explicit recognition of the two *reverse* modes of argument is essential for a clear understanding of Friedman's essay. Any methodological criticism which presumes that any formal argument that can be used in *modus tollens* can also be validly used in *reverse modus ponens* is a serious methodological error. Recognition of this methodological error, an error which Friedman successfully avoids, is essential for an appreciation of his rejection of the necessity of testing (as I will show in *Section 3*).

1.3 Objectives of an Argument: Necessity vs. Sufficiency

Finally, there is another aspect of the logicality of an argument that is reflected in Friedman's essay. It has to do with the "necessity" and the "sufficiency" of statements or groups of statements. In some cases one is more concerned with the sufficiency of an argument; in other cases one is more concerned with the necessity of its assumptions. To illustrate, consider the following *extreme* dichotomization. There are basically two different affirmative types of argument: the conjunctive and the disjunctive.

103

Conjunctive type of argument: Because statement A_1 is true, and A_2 is true, and A_3 is true, and ..., one can conclude that the statement C_1 is true.

Axiomatic consumer theory might be an example of such an argument where the A's include statements about the utility function and the existence of maximization is the conclusion. On the other hand,

Disjunctive type of argument: Because statement R_1 is true, R_2 is true, or R_3 is true, or ..., one can conclude that the statement C_2 is true.

A politician's reasons for why he is the best candidate might be an example of this type of argument. These two ways of arguing can be most clearly distinguished in terms of what is required for a *successful refutation* of each type of argument. The conjunctive type of argument is the easiest to refute or criticize. Ideally, a pure conjunctive argument consists of assumptions *each of which is offered as a necessary condition.* It is the conjunction of all of them that is *just* sufficient for the conclusion to follow. If any one of the assumptions were false, then the sufficiency of the argument would be lost. To refute a pure conjunctive argument, one needs only to refute *one* assumption. The disjunctive argument, on the other hand, is very difficult to refute. Because in the extreme case such an argument, in effect, offers every assumption as a *solitarily sufficient condition* for the conclusion to follow, none of the assumptions are necessary. If someone were to refute only one of the assumptions, the argument is not lost. In order to defeat a pure disjunctive argument, one must refute *every* assumption--clearly a monumental task.[8]

2. "Instrumentalism" and Relationship between Logic, Truth, and Theories

2.1 *The Problem of Induction*

The discussion so far has not worried about how one knows the truth of the assumptions (or conclusions). Unfortunately, logic is of little help in determining the truth of a statement. Logic can only help by "passing" along known truths. This limitation of traditional logic leads to a consideration of the so-called *problem of induction:* the problem of finding a form of logical argument where (a) its conclusion is a general statement, such as one of the true "laws" of economics (or nature), or its conclusion is the choice of the true theory (or model) from among various competitors; and (b) its assumptions include *only* singular statements of *particulars* (such as observation reports).

104

With an argument of this form one is said to be arguing inductively from the truth of particulars to the truth of generals. (On
the other hand, a deductive form of argument proceeds from the
truth of generals to the truth of particulars). If one could solve
the problem of induction, the true "laws" or general theories of
economics could then be said to be induced logically from the
particulars. But not only must one solve the problem of induction
one must also acquire access to all the particulars needed for the
application of the solution. Any "solution" that requires an infinity of particulars is at best impractical and at worst an illusion. The requirement of an infinity of true particulars in order
to provide the needed true assumptions for the application of
modus ponens means in effect that such an inductive argument
would not carry the force of *modus ponens*.

One might ask, just what determines whether or not a form of
argument is logical? But I have already discussed this question
above. Recall from *Section* 1.1 that the criterion for
necessary condition for any logical argument is that it must be
capable of fulfilling the promise of *modus ponens*. However, as far as anyone knows modus ponens is assured only by a
"deductive" form of argument.

2.2 *"Inductivism"*

One can identify (at least) three different views of the relationship between logic, truth, and theories. The "inductivists" say
that theories can be true and all true theories (or assumptions)
are the result of applying inductive logic to observations. "Conventionalists" deny that a theory can be inductively proven, and
they furthermore consider it improper to discuss the truth status
of a theory. "Instrumentalists," such as Friedman, are only concerned with the usefulness of the conclusions derived from any
theory. Unlike conventionalists, instrumentalists may allow that
theories or assumptions can be true but argue that it does not
matter with regard to the usefulness of the conclusions. A clear
understanding of inductivism, I think, is essential for the
appreciation of every modern methodological point of view. Even
when economists only argue deductively (that is, by using
modus ponens and including assumptions that are necessarily
in the form of general statements), it might still be asked, how do
they know that the "laws" or other general statements used are
true? The inductivist philosophers have always taken the position
that there is a way to prove the truth of the needed general
statements (as conclusions) using only assumptions of the form of
singular statements (*e.g.*, observations). Such inductivists often think the only problem is to specify which kinds of
singular statements will do the job, *i.e.*, those which are
unambiguously true and capable of forming a sufficient argument
for the truth of a given statement or conclusion.

105

What kinds of statements must economists rely on? Clearly, biased personal reports will not do even if their conjunction could be made to be sufficient. For this reason inductivist philosophers and many well known economists (following John Neville Keynes) distinguish between "positive" statements, which can be unambiguously true, and "normative" ones, which cannot. Singular positive statements would supposedly work because they can be objectively true. But, normative statements are necessarily subjective, hence they would not carry the same logical guarantee of unambiguous truth.

Contrary to the hopes of the inductivists, even though one can distinguish between positive and normative statements, there is no inductive logic that will guarantee the sufficiency of any finite set of singular statements. There is no type of argument that will validly proceed from assumptions that are singular to conclusions that are general statements. Specifically, there is no conjunction of a *finite* number of true singular statements from which unambiguously true general statements will validly follow with the asssurance of *modus ponens*. Thus, distinguishing between positive and normative statements (as most economists do today) will not by itself solve the problem of induction;[9] and for this reason Friedman tries to go *beyond* this distinction.

2.3 *The "Conventionalist" Alternative to Inductivism*

Since no one has yet solved the problem of induction, one is always required to assume the truth of his premises or assumptions. In response to the failure to solve the problem of induction, some philosophers and economists go as far as to avoid using the word "truth" at all. They may, however, attempt to determine the "validity" of a theory or argument, since logic can (at least) help in that determination. Too often, many economists who are unaware of these methodological problems create much confusion by using the word "validity" when they mean "truth" (*e.g.*, see Friedman [4, 1953, pp. 10*ff*]). Their formal alternative to avoiding the word "truth" is to take the position that "truth" is a matter of convention; philosophers who take such a position are thus called "conventionalists." They view theories as being convenient catalogues of "filing systems" for positive reports. Of course, catalogues cannot be properly called true or false. They are to be judged or compared only by criteria of convenience such as simplicity or degrees of approximation or closeness of "fit," etc.

Conventionalism forms the foundation for most methodological discussions in economics today (e.g., which criterion is best, simplicity or generality?). It is also the primary source of methodological problems because its usual application is built upon a fundamental contradiction. Conventionalists presume that it is possible to discuss logical validity without reference to truth or falsity. Yet, as noted above, the fundamental aspect of logic that defines "validity" (namely, the assurance of *modus ponens* or *modus tollens*) requires an explicit recognition of (a concept of) truth or falsity.[10] Conventionalism does not offer a solution to the problem of induction; it only offers a way to avoid discussing such philosophical obstacles. Although Friedman accepts and employs several conventionalist concepts, to his credit he constructs a methodological approach that goes beyond the sterile philosophy of conventionalism.

2.4 *Instrumentalism and the Usefulness of Logic*

For the purposes of discussing Friedman's point of view, one can consider any theory to be an argument in favor of some given propositions or towards specific predictions. As such a theory can be considered to consist only of a conjunction or assumption statements, i.e., statements each of which is *assumed* (or asserted) to be true. In order for the argument to be sufficient it must be a deductive argument, which means that at least some of the assumptions must be in the form of general statements. But, without an inductive logic, this latter requirement seems to raise in a modified form the methodological problems discussed above. When can one assume a theory is true? It is such difficulties that Friedman's essay attempts to overcome [4, 1953].

So long as a theory does its intended job, there is no apparent need to argue in its favor (or in favor of any of its constituent parts). For some policy-oriented economists, the intended job is the generation of true or successful predictions. In this case a theory's predictive success is always a sufficient argument in its favor. This view of the *role* of theories is called "instrumentalism." It says that theories are convenient and useful ways of (logically) generating what have turned out to be true (or successful) predictions or conclusions. Instrumentalism is the primary methodological point of view expressed in Friedman's essay.

For those economists who see the object of science as finding the *one* true theory of the economy, their task cannot be simple. However, if the object of building or choosing theories (or models of theories) is only to have a theory or model that provides true predictions or conclusions, a priori truth of the assumptions is not required if it is already known that the conclusions are true or acceptable by some conventionalist criterion.[11] Thus, theories do not have to be considered true statements about the nature of the world but only convenient ways of systematically generating the already known "true" conclusions.

In this manner instrumentalists offer an alternative to the conventionalist's response to the problem of induction. Instrumentalists consider the truth status of theories, hypotheses, or assumptions to be irrelevant for any practical purposes so long as the conclusions logically derived from them are successful. Although conventionalists may argue about the nature or the possibility of determining the truth status of theories, instrumentalists simply do not care. Some instrumentalists may personally care or even believe in the powers of induction, but such concern or belief is considered to be separate from their view of the role of theories in science.

For the instrumentalists, who think they have solved the problem of induction by ignoring truth, *modus ponens* will necessarily be seen to be irrelevant. This is because they do not begin their analysis with a search for the true assumptions but rather for true or useful (*i.e.,* successful) conclusions. *Modus tollens* is likewise irrelevant because its use can only begin with false conclusions. This also means that like the pure disjunctive argument, the instrumentalist's argument is concerned more with the sufficiency of any assumptions than with their necessity. This is because any analysis of the sufficiency of a set of assumptions begins by assuming the conclusion is true and then asks what set of assumptions will do the logical job of yielding that conclusion. Furthermore, any valid or fair criticism of an instrumentalist can only be about the sufficiency of his argument. The only direct refutation allowable is one that shows that a theory is insufficient, *i.e.,* inapplicable. Failing that, the critic must alternatively provide his own sufficient argument, which does the same job.

By identifying three distinct philosophical views of theories, I am not trying to suggest that one must choose one (that would merely be reintroducing the problem of induction at a new level). Few writers have ever thought it necessary to adhere to just one view. Most writers on methodology in economics make some use of each view. For this reason it is sometimes necessary to sort out these views in order to make sense of methodological essays. I hope to show that even a superficial understanding of these philosophical views will help form a clear understanding of Friedman's essay [4, 1953].

3. A Reader's Guide to Friedman's Essay

3.1 *An Overview*

Friedman's essay is rather long and rambling [4, 1953]. However, he does manage to state his position regarding all of the issues I have discussed so far. Because the essay is long, it is hard to focus on its exact purpose, but I think it can best be understood as an instrumentalist's argument for instrumentalism. As such it tries to give a series of sufficient reasons for the acceptance of instrumentalism. And furthermore, it can be fairly judged only on the basis of the adequacy or sufficiency of each reason for the purpose. We are told that the essay's motivation is to give us a way to overcome obstacles to the construction of a "distinct positive science" centering on the problem of "how to decide whether a suggested hypothesis or theory should be tentatively accepted as part of the 'body of systemized knowledge [of] ... what is'" [4, p. 3]. The "distinct positive science," we are told, is essential for a policy science [4, pp. 5, 6-7]. This methodological decision problem is, in fact, an inductivist's problem.[12] Implicitly, Friedman recognizes that we do not have an inductive logic [4, p. 9], and he offers what he considers to be an acceptable alternative. Basically Friedman's solution (to the problem of induction) is that our acceptance of a hypothesis for the purposes of policy application should be made a matter of "judgement." Judgements, he says, cannot be made a priori in the absence of a true inductive science.

3.2 *"Positive vs. Normative Economics": The Problem of Induction in Instrumentalist Terms*

In the introduction Friedman expresses his interest in the problem of induction and then, in Section I, he restates the problem in instrumentalist terms [4, p. 4]. He says the task of positive economics is to

> provide a system of generalizations that can be used
> to make correct predictions about the consequences of
> any change in circumstances. Its performance is to be
> judged by the precision, scope, and conformity with
> experience of the predictions it yields [4, p. 4].

The inductivist's distinction between positive and normative statements is the most important part of inductivism that is retained by Friedman. And he brings with that distinction the inductivist's claim that normative economics depends on positive economics, but positive economics does not necessarily depend on the normative [4, p. 5]. In this light he notes that even methodological judgements about policy are also positive statements to be accepted on the basis of empirical evidence [4, pp. 6-7].

3.3 *"Positive Economics": Conventionalist Criteria Used with an Instrumentalist Purpose*

Friedman begins Section II with a mild version of conventionalism by saying that a theory (*i.e.*, a set of assumptions) can be viewed as a language whose function is to serve as a filing system for organizing empirical material ... and the criteria by which it is to be judged are those appropriate to a filing system [4, p. 7].

But his viewing a theory as a language has its limitations. I would think that a distinguishing feature of all languages is that they are intended to be both consistent and complete (*e.g.*, there should be nothing that cannot be named or completely described); and this would preclude empirical applications as the theory would, in effect yield only tautologies. To avoid this he adopts the now popular opinion that we must add "substantive hypotheses" [4, p. 8]. But here he again raises an inductivist's problem: how do we choose the substantive hypotheses? Friedman answers that positive statements ("factual evidence") can determine acceptance. He clearly indicates that he does understand the fundamentals of logic by implicitly using *modus tollens*. He says that a

hypothesis is rejected if its predictions are contra-icted... [4, p. 9].

But what about *modus ponens?* Well, that is considered inapplicable because there is no inductive logic. Friedman, using the word "validity" when he means "not inconsistent with facts" (which happens to be a necessary condition of true hypotheses), says

The validity of a hypothesis in this sense is not by itself a sufficient criterion for choosing among alternative hypotheses. Observed facts are necessarily finite in number; possible hypotheses, infinite [4, p. 9].

In other words, one cannot directly solve the problem of induction.

All this means that the main task of a positive economics is left unfulfilled. At this point Friedman says that we need additional criteria (beyond consistency with the facts) if we are going to be able to choose [4, p. 9]. Here he poses the problem of choosing between *competing* hypotheses or theories, *all* of which have already been shown to be consistent with available positive evidence (that is, none of them have been shown to be false using *modus tollens*). The criteria with which he claims there is "general agreement" are the "simplicity" and the "fruitfulness" of the substantive hypotheses [4, p. 10].[13] However, these are not considered to be abstract philosophical (*i.e.*, conventionalist) criteria but rather they, too, are empirically based, hence can be expressed in instrumentalist terms: "Simpler" means requires less empirical "initial knowledge" (the word "initial" refers here to the process of generating predictions with something like *modus ponens*). "More fruitful" means more applicable and more precise [4, p. 10]. The possibility of a tradeoff is not discussed.

Friedman explicitly rejects the necessity of requiring the "testing" of substantive hypotheses before they are used simply because it is not possible. But here is should be noted that his rejection of testing is partly a consequence of his use of the word "testing." Throughout his essay "testing" always means "testing for truth (in some sense)." It never means "testing in order to reject" as most of his critics seem to presume. That is, for Friedman a *successful* test is one which shows a statement (e.g., an assumption, hypothesis, or theory) to be true; and, of course, a minimum condition for a successful test is that the statement not be inconsistent with empirical evidence (see [4, pp. 33-34]).[14]

Appreciating the success of orientation of Friedman's view is essential to an understanding of his methodological judgements. For Friedman, an instrumentalist, hypotheses are chosen because they are successful in yielding true predictions. In other words, hypotheses and theories are viewed as instruments for successful predictions. It is his assumption that there has been a prior application of *modus tollens* (by evolution, see [4, p. 22]), which eliminates unsuccessful hypotheses (ones that yield false predictions), and which allows one to face only the problem of choosing between successful hypotheses. *In this sense,* his concentrating on successful predictions precludes any further application of *modus tollens.* And similarly, any possible falsity of the assumptions is thereby considered irrelevant. Such a consideration is merely an appreciation of the logical limitations of what I called *reverse modus tollens* (above, *Section* 1.2). And since he has thus assumed that we are dealing exclusively with successful predictions (i.e., true conclusions), nothing would be gained by applying *modus ponens* either. This is a straightforward appreciation of the limitations of what I called *reverse modus ponens.* Knowing for sure that the hypotheses (or assumptions) are true is essential for a practical application of *modus ponens,* but such knowledge, he implies, is precluded by the absence of an inductive logic [4, pp. 12-14].

By focusing only on successful hypotheses, Friedman correctly reaches the conclusion that the application of the cirterion of "simplicity" is relevant. He says there is virtue in a simple hypothesis *if* its application requires less empirical information. One reason a simple hypothesis can require less information, Friedman says, is that it is descriptively false [4, pp. 14-15]. (For example, a linear function requires fewer observa-

111

tions for a fit than does a quadratic function.) This raises the question of "unrealistic" descriptions versus "necessary" abstractions. Friedman explicitly recognizes that some economists (presumably, followers of Lionel Robbins) hold a view contrary to his. For them the "significance" of a theory is considered to be a direct result of the descriptive "realism" of the assumptions. But Friedman claims

> the relation between the significance of a theory and the "realism" of its "assumptions" is almost the opposite.... Truly important and significant hypotheses will be found to have "assumptions" that are wildly inaccurate descriptive representations of reality, and, in general, the more significant the theory, the more unrealistic the assumptions (in this sense)....[4, p. 14].

Clearly, this latter judgement is based on the additional criteria of importance and significance that presume a purpose for theorizing. Namely, that theories are only constructed to be instruments of policy. Those economists who do not see policy application as the only purpose of theorizing can clearly argue with that judgement. But nevertheless, in terms of the economy of information, his conclusion is still correct with respect to choosing between *successful* hypotheses that are used as policy instruments.

3.4 *"Realism of Assumptions" vs. the Convenience of Instrumentalist Methodology*

In this Section III, Friedman continues to view successful "testing" to be "confirming," and for this reason he concludes that testing of assumptions is irrelevant for true conclusions (since *modus ponens* cannot be used in reverse). Having rejected the necessity of testing for the truth of assumptions, Friedman examines the question of the relevance of the falsity of assumptions for the various uses of theories. That is, what if one could show that an assumption is false? Does it matter? Friedman argues again [4, p. 18] that the falsity of the assumptions does not matter if *the conclusions are true*. He correctly says: one can say there must be an assumption that is false *whenever* some particular conclusion is false (*modus tollens*), but one cannot say any assumptions are true because any conclusion is true (*reverse modus ponens,* again) [4, p. 19].

This leads Friedman to discuss the possibility that a false assumption might be applied as part of an explanation of some observed phenomenon. Here he introduces his famous version of the "as if" theory of explanation. He says that as long as the observed phenomenon can be considered to be a logical conclusion from the argument containing the false assumption in question, the use of that assumption should be acceptable. In particular, if we are trying to explain the *effect* of the assumed behavior of some individuals (*e.g.*, the demand curve derived with the assumption of maximizing behavior), *so long as the effect is in fact observed and it would be the effect if they were in fact to behave as we assume,* we can use our behavioral assumption even when the assumption is false. That is, we can continue to claim the observed effect of the individual's (unknown but assumed) behavior is as if they behaved as we assume. Note carefully, the individuals' *behavior* is not claimed to be as if they behaved as we assume, but rather it is the *effect* of their behavior that is claimed to be *as if* they behave according to our assumption. Failure to distinguish between the effect and the behavior itself has led many critics to misread Friedman's view. His view does not violate any logical principles in this matter.

So far the choice between competing hypotheses or assumptions has been discussed with regard to currently available observations, *i.e.*, to existing evidence. But a more interesting question is the usefulness of any hypothesis in the future; past success will not guarantee future success. This presents a problem for the methodological conclusions that Friedman has, for the most part, presented correctly up to this point. He offers some weak arguments to deal with this problem. The first is an adaptation of a Social-Darwinist view that repeated success in the face of competition temporarily implies satisfaction of "the conditions for survival" [4, p. 22]. Unfortunately, he does not indicate whether these are necessary conditions, which they must be if his argument is to be complete. He adopts another Social-Darwinist view, which claims that past success of our theory is relative to other competitors, thereby claiming a revealed superiority of our theory. This unfortunately presumes either that the other theories have not survived as well or that the comparative advantage cannot change. The former presupposition, however, would be ruled out by his prior commitment to discussing the problem of choosing between successful theories [4, p. 23]. The latter merely begs the question. Finally he unnecessarily adds the false conventionalist theory of confirmation that says the absence of refutation supports the (future) truth of a statement [4, pp. 22-23].

3.5 *"The Positive Aspects of Assumptions" Are Positive Aspects of Instrumentalist Methodology*

If assumptions do not need to be true, why would one bother worrying about them? Or, in other words, what role do assumptions play? Friedman says their role is positive [4, p. 23]. Assumptions: (a) are useful as an "economical mode" of expressing and determining the state of the "givens" of a theory; that is, the relevant facts in order to provide an empirical basis for the predictions; (b) "facilitate an indirect test" of a hypothesis of a theory by consideration of other hypotheses that are also implied; and (c) are a "convenient means of specifying the condition under which the theory is expected" to be applicable.

Friedman is not very careful about distinguishing between assumptions, hypotheses, or theories, and to make matters worse, in his Section IV he introduces the concept of a model. This can present some difficulty for the careful reader. Inductivist methodology posits significant differences between assumptions, hypotheses, theories, and some other things that are called "laws." The inductivist's distinctions are based on an alleged difference in the levels of inductive proofs of their truth. Assumptions are the least established and laws are the most. Without committing oneself to this inductivist tradition, one can easily see hypotheses as intermediate conjunctions formed by using only part of the assumptions of a theory. For example, the theory of the consumer entails certain hypotheses about the slope of the demand curve, but the assumptions of the theory of the consumer are only part of our market theory of prices. Moreover, the assumptions and hypotheses of consumer theory are independent of the theory of the firm.

Discussing models raises totally new issues. A model of a theory is a conventionalist concept. As Friedman correctly puts it, "the model is the logical embodiment of the half-truth" [4, p. 25]. Models in his sense correspond to the concept of models used in engineering. When one builds a model of something, one must simplify in order to emphasize the essential or significant features. Such implication can always be seen to involve extra assumptions about the irrelevance of certain empirical considerations. These extra assumptions are usually descriptively false.

Most simplifying assumptions are designed to exclude certain real world complications or variables. Such exclusion also reduces the need for information concerning those variables when one wishes to apply the model. In this sense, assumptions are economical in terms of the amount of prior information required for empirical application.

Friedman notes that the problem of choosing models can be seen as a problem of explaining when the model is applicable. To solve the latter version of this problem, he says that to any model of a theory or hypothesis one must add "rules for using the model" [4, p. 25]. These required rules, however, are not mechanical. He says that "no matter how successful [one is in explicitly stating the rules]... there inevitably will remain room for judgement in applying the rules" [4, p. 25]. Unfortunately, the "capacity to judge" cannot be *taught*, as each case is different (another instance of the problem of induction). However, it can be *learned*, "but only by experience and exposure in the 'right' scientific atmosphere" [4, p. 25] (this is a version of conventionalism). This seems to bring us back to the inductive problem that his version of instrumentalism was intended to solve.

In spite of all the discussion about "assumptions," Friedman cautions us not to put too much emphasis on that word. By saying there are problems concerning judgements about the applicability of certain assumptions of particular hypotheses or theories, we are not to be misled into thinking there is some special meaning to the term "assumption." The assumptions of one hypothesis may be the conclusions of a (logically) prior set of assumptions. In other words, when one says a statement is an assumption, one is not referring to any intrinsic property. A statement is called an assumption because that is how one chooses to use it. There is nothing that prevents one from attempting to explain the assumed "truth" of one's assumption by considering it to be a conclusion of another argument, which consists of yet another set of assumptions.[15] Moreover, the popular notion of a "crucial assumption" is likewise relative to the particular model in which it is being used.

In the last part of his Section IV, Friedman faces an alleged problem that may be created by the dismissal of the testability (*i.e.*, confirmability) of assumptions. The set of conclusions of any argument must contain the assumptions themselves. In some cases, within some subsets of assumptions and conclusions of a given theory there is interchangability. In these cases dismissing testability of assumptions can seem to mean that the testability of some conclusions has been dismissed as well. Recall, however, that testing for Friedman still means confirming. Thus, if one considers the testing of an assumption one can, in effect, be seen to be considering merely the confirming of one of the conclusions. Friedman's emphasis on true (successful) conclusions is seen to be playing a role here, too. Of course, there are other conclusions besides the assumptions themselves. However, someone may propose a set of assumptions only because *one* of the (true or observed) conclusions of interest is a logical consequence of that set. If one bothers to use the proposed assumptions to derive other conclusions from these assumptions, one can try to confirm the additional conclusions. In this sense, the assumptions used to derive one conclusion or hypothesis can be used to "indirectly test" the conclusion of interest. Nevertheless, logic does not permit one to see the confirmation of the secondary conclusion as a direct confirmation

115

of the conclusion of interest. The significance of such an indirect test is also a matter of judgement [4, p. 28].

3.6 "Economic Issues" or Some Examples of Instrumentalist Successes

Finally, in his Section V, Friedman applies his methodological judgements to some specific examples, but here he does not raise any new questions of methodology. His objective seems merely to provide a demonstration of the success of instrumentalist methodology with several illustrations. Note that such a line of argument is quite consistent with instrumentalism and its compatibility with the disjunctive form of argument.

4. The Critics

Friedman's paper elicited a long series of critiques, none of which dealt with every aspect of his essay. The primary motivation for all of the critics seems to be that they disagree with particular things Friedman said. I will argue here that the basis for each of the critiques is a misunderstanding and hence a false accusation.

4.1 Testability vs. Refutability: Koopmans

Most misunderstandings are the result of Friedman's "Introduction," where he seems to be saying that he is about to give another contribution to the traditional discussion about methodology of inductivism and conventionalism. Such a discussion would usually be about issues, such as the verifiability or refutability of truely scientific theories. What Friedman actually gives is an alternative to that type of discussion. Unfortunately, most critics miss this point.

In regard to the traditional discussion, Tjalling Koopmans says that the object of our attempts to develop or analyze the "postulational structure of economic theory" is to obtain "... those implications that are verifiable or otherwise interesting" [5, 1957, p. 133]. In this light, Koopmans says that one must distinguish between the logical structure of a theory and the "interpretation" of its terms. He says that the logical structure's validity is considered to be independent of the interpretations (Koopmans is using the term "validity" correctly, but it does not correspond to Friedman's usage). He says, "... from the point of view of the logic of reasoning, the interpretations are detachable. Only the logical contents of the postulates matter" [5, p. 133]. When any argument is logically valid, no interpretation can lead to a contradiction. (This is one interpretation of *modus ponens*). One way to view the testing of an argument is to see

116

a test as one interpretation of the terms such that a conjunction of the argument and the specific interpretation in question forms an empirical proposition about the real world, which does or does not correspond to our observations.

Koopmans also says a "distinction needs to be made here between *explanatory* and *normative* analysis" [5, p. 134]. Here Koopmans explicitly equates *positive* with *explanatory*. He adds that

> these two types of analysis do not necessarily differ in the interpretations placed on the terms. They differ *only* in the motivation of the search for conclusions.... In explanatory analysis, what one looks for in a conclusion or prediction is the possibility of testing, that is, of verification or refutation by observation. Of course, the interpretations of the terms used in the postulates form the connecting link through which observation is brought to bear on the statements that represent conclusions. Verification, or absence of refutation, lends support to the set of postulates taken as a whole (5, p. 134, emphasis added].

Now Friedman clearly does not agree with this distinction since he argues that how one views the parts of a theory depends on its use and that a theory cannot be analyzed independently of its use. Also, Koopmans's statement seems to suggest that priority should be given to testing conclusions. Friedman need not agree. Since Friedman's analysis begins with *successful* conclusions, testing is precluded because it is automatically implied by the usefulness and the logicality of the explanation.

Starting with a different concept of theorizing-- that is, that theories are directly analyzable independently of their uses-- Koopmans proceeds to criticize Friedman by restating Lionel Robbins's methodological position [8, 1935]. The basic concern for Koopmans (but not Friedman) is the sources of the basic premises of assumptions of economic theory. For the followers of Robbins, the assumptions of economic analysis are promulgated and used *because* they are (obviously) true. The truth of the assumptions is never in doubt. The only complaint Koopmans brings against Robbins is that his assumptions were a bit vague - a problem that Koopmans thinks can be solved with the use of sophisticated mathematics. The primary virtue of Koopmans's work is that it does try to solve that problem. Implicitly, both Robbins and Koopmans see the process of economic theorizing as merely the task of applying exclusively *modus ponens* and *modus tollens*. In particular, the sole purpose of developing a theory is so that one can "pass" the obvious truth of the assumptions on to some conclusions.

117

Koopmans seems to object to Friedman's dismissal of the problem of clarifying the truth of the premises-- the problem that Koopmans wishes to solve. Friedman's view is that (*a priori*) "realism" of assumptions does not matter (*i.e.*, *modus ponens* is not applicable). The source of the disagreement is Koopmans's confusion of *explanatory* with positive. Koopmans is an inductivist, who defines successful explanation as being logically based on observably true premises, that is, ones that are in turn (inductively) based on observation. Friedman does not consider assumptions or theories to be the embodiment of truth but only as instruments for the generation of useful (because successful) predictions. Thus, for Friedman *positive* is not equivalent to *explanatory* because he does not use *modus ponens*. Explanation in Koopmans's sense is irrelevant in Friedman's instrumentalism.

In order to criticize Friedman's argument against the concern for the "realism" of assumptions, Koopmans offers an *interpretation* of his own theory of the logical structure of Friedman's view. Koopmans says,

> Since any statement is implied by itself, one *could* interpret Professor Friedman's position to mean that the validity or usefulness of any set of postulates depends on observations that confirm or at least fail to contradict (although they could have) *all* their implications, immediate and derived [5, 1957, p. 138, first emphasis added].

He then goes on to claim that this interpretation of Friedman's argument leads to some objectionable conclusions and thus claims to destroy Friedman's argument. The details of this line of argument do not matter here, since Koopmans's argument itself can be shown to be irrelevant and thus of no logical value.

Koopmans's interpretation contradicts Friedman's purpose (that *some* conclusions be successful--not necessarily *all*). Remember that Friedman is only concerned with the *sufficiency* of a theory or set of assumptions. He would allow any theory to be even more than "just" sufficient[16] so long as it is sufficient for the successful predictions at issue. On the other hand, Koopmans's interpretation falsely presumes a concern for *necessity*. In other words, Koopmans's theory of Friedman's view is itself void because (by his own rules) at least one of its assumptions is false. Or, also by Koopmans's own rules (*modus tollens*) his own theory of Friedman's view must be considered refuted, since the false assumption is also one of the conclusions. His theory is not "realistic" even though some of his conclusions may be. There is nothing in the application of *modus tollens* to a specific interpretation (which necessarily involves additional assumptions--*e.g.*, rule of correspondence) that would require the rejection of Friedman's view itself.[17]

4.2 *Necessity of Verifying Assumptions: Rotwein*

Some economists would accept the obviousness of the premises of economic theory. In this group would fall the self-proclaimed "empiricists." The basis of their philosophy is the view that the truth of one's conclusions (or predictions) rests *solely* (and firmly) on the demonstrable truth of the premises; and the prescription that one *must* so justify every claim for the truth of one's conclusions or predictions. Needless to say, empiricists do not see a problem of induction. Friedman clearly does, and in this sense he is not an orthodox empiricist (even though the term "positive" usually means "empirical"). According to Eugene Rotwein, Friedman criticizes their view by claiming that it represents "a form of naive and misguided empiricism" [9, 1959, p. 555]. Actually, Rotwein sees Friedman's criticism as a naive family dispute among empiricists. What is specifically questioned is

> Friedman's contention ... that the "validity" of a "theory" is to be tested *solely* by its "predictions" with respect to a given class of phenomena, or that the question of whether or to what extent the assumptions of the "theory" are "unreal" (i.e., falsify reality) is of no relevance to such a test [9, p. 556].

(Note that Friedman was not discussing the "validity of theories" but rather the validity of "hypotheses" used in a model of a theory.[18])

Now it seems to me there is "good" and "bad" naivety. Good naivety is exemplified by the little boy in Andersen's story "The Emperor's New Clothes." Good naivety exposes the dishonesty or ignorance of others. Friedman simply refuses to join in the pretense that there is an inductive logic that will serve as a foundation for Rotwein's verificationist-empiricism. Rotwein attempts to twist the meaning of "validity" into a matter of probabilities so that he can use something like *modus ponens* [9, p. 558]. But *modus ponens* will not work with statements whose truth status is a matter of probabilities, and thus Friedman is correct in rejecting this approach to empiricism. Rotwein's arguments are on a far weaker foundation than are Friedman's. It is, in fact, Rotwein's view that is naive, since it is based on an unfounded belief that science is the embodiment of truths based (inductively) on true observations, which are beyond doubt, or on true hypotheses, which can be inductively proven.

119

Some sophisticated and friendly critics of Friedman choose to
criticize only certain aspects while accepting others. This can
lead to criticisms that are necessarily invalid. For example,
Donald Bear and Daniel Orr dismiss Friedman's instrumentalism,
yet they recommend what they call his "as if" principle [1, 1967].
They recommend "as if" because they too accept the view that the
problem of induction is still unsolved. They are correct in appreciating that the principle is an adequate means of dealing with
the problem of induction.

That it is possible to accept one part of Friedman's methodology while rejecting another does not necessarily create a contradiction. The appreciation of such a possibility is facilitated by
recalling that each part of Friedman's argument is designed to be
sufficient. In this vein, Bear and Orr claim that Friedman's
arguments against the necessity of testing and against the necessity of "realism" of assumptions are both wrong. Bear and Orr
(agreeing with Jack Melitz) say that Friedman erred by "... confounding ... abstractness and unrealism" [1, p. 188, *fn.*3].
And they further claim "all commentators except Friedman seem to
agree that the testing of the whole theory (and not just the predictions of theory) is a constructive activity" [1, p. 194,
fn. 15].

*These criticisms are somewhat misleading because Friedman's
concept of testing (sc.* verifying) does not correspond to
theirs. It is not always clear what various writers mean by
"testing," mostly because its meaning is too often taken for
granted. One can identify implicitly three distinct meanings as
used by the authors under consideration. Where Friedman sees
testing only in terms of verification or "confirmation," Bear and
Orr adopt Karl Popper's view that a successful test is a refutation
[1, 1967, pp. 189*ff*]. But Melitz sees testing as confirmation or disconfirmation [6, 1965, pp. 48*ff*]. Unfortunately,
one can only arrive at these distinctions by inference. Bear and
Orr present, in one section, the logic of refuting theories, followed by a lengthy discussion of tests and the logic of testing.
Melitz is more difficult to read. The word "testing," which figures prominently in the article's title, never appears anywhere in
the introduction. Melitz never does directly discuss his own
concept of testing.

In both critiques, the logic of their criticisms is an allegation
of an inconsistency between *their* concepts of testing and
Friedman's rejection of the necessity of testing assumptions. The
logic of their critiques may be valid, but in each case it presumes
a rejection of instrumentalism. But instrumentalism, I argue, is
an absolutely essential part of Friedman's point of view. Conse-

quently, contrary to the critics' views, the alleged inconsistency does not exist *within* Friedman's instrumentalist methodology.

As was argued above (*Sections* 2.4, 3.3 and 3.4), Friedman's concept of testing is quite consistent with *his* instrumentalism and his judgements about testing. Viewed from the standpoint of Friedman's concept of testing, Melitz and Bear and Orr present criticisms that are thus logically inadequate. This situation shows, I think, that one cannot understand the particular methodological judgements of Friedman unless one accepts or at least understands his instrumentalism.

Their suggestion that Friedman's view is based on an error of logic is simply wrong. And furthermore, it is unfair to make that suggestion only on the basis of inconsistency between *their* concept of testing and *his* judgements, which were based on *his* concept. There is no reason why Friedman's view should be expected to be consistent with their view of what constitutes science or of what others think testability or testing really is.

4.4 *Errors of Omission: De Alessi*

Another even more friendly criticism offered by Louis De Alessi. He meekly criticizes Friedman for seeing only two attributes of theories--namely, a theory can be viewed as a language and as a set of substantive hypotheses. On the other hand, De Alessi seems to think Friedman should have included a set of rules of correspondence or rules of interpretation. His criticism of Friedman is in the spirit that such rules of interpretation are necessary for a positive theory. He says, "... Unfortunately, Friedman's analysis has proved to be amenable to quite contradictory interpretations" [2, 1965, p. 477]. But, as I said before, this is not necessarily a criticism for an instrumentalist who has rejected further applications of *modus tollens*.

De Alessi later raises another minor criticism [3, 1971]. He says Friedman leaves room for error by telling us that some assumptions and conclusions are "interchangeable." De Alessi correctly notes that such "reversability" of an argument may imply that the argument is tautological. When an argument is tautological, it cannot also be empirical, *i.e.*, positive. The logic of De Alessi's argument is correct. However, it is not clear that with Friedman's use of "interchangable" he was indicating "reversability" of (entire) arguments. The only point Friedman was attempting to make was that the status of being an "assumption" is not necessarily automatic. In any case, just because some of the conditions and assumptions are interchangable does not necessarily mean that the theory as a whole is tautological. If Friedman were viewing assumptions as "necessary" conditions, then the problem that De Alessi raises would be more serious. But Friedman's instrumentalism does not require such a role for assumptions.

Both De Alessi's criticisms are founded on the view that *modus tollens* can be applied to Friedman's view. In particular, it is the view that was asserted by Koopmans, namely that *if any interpretation* of a view (or argument) is considered false then the view itself must be false. But this presumes that the assumptions were necessary conditions. As I have said, that is not the case with instrumentalism. Hence De Alessi's criticisms are irrelevant, even though one might find merit in the details of his argument.

4.5 *The "F-Twist": Samuelson*

The most celebrated criticism of Friedman's methodology was presented by Paul Samuelson [10, 1963] in his discussion of a paper by Ernest Nagel.[19] Samuelson explicitly attributes the followng proposition to Friedman.

> A theory is vindicable if (some of) its consequences are empirically valid to a useful degree of approximation; the (empirical) unrealism of the theory "itself," or of its "assumptions," is quite irrelevant to its validity and worth [10, 1963, p. 232].

Samuelson calls this the "F-Twist." And about this he says it is

> fundamentally wrong in thinking that unrealism in the sense of factual inaccuracy even to a tolerable degree of approximation is anything but a demerit for a theory or hypothesis (or set of hypotheses) [10, 1963, p. 233].

However, Samuelson admits that his representation of Friedman's view may be "inaccurate" (that is supposedly why he called it the "F-Twist" rather than the "Friedman-Twist"). Nevertheless, Samuelson is willing to apply his potentially false assumption about Friedman to explain (should one say describe?) Friedman's view. His justification for using a false assumption is Friedman's own allegedly valid "as if" principle. Samuelson argues in this way on the basis of the theory that if he can discredit or otherwise refute Freidman's view by using Friedman's view, then followers of Friedman's methodology must concede defeat.

Samuelson's argument goes as follows. First he says:

The motivation for the F-Twist, critics say, is to help
the case for (1) the perfectly competitive laissez faire
model of economics, ... and (2), but of lesser moment, the "maximization-of-profit" hypotheses [10,
1963, p. 233].

Then he says,

If Dr. Friedman tells us this was not so; if his psy-
choanalyst assures us that his testimony in this case
is not vitiated by subconscious motivations, ...--still
it would seem a fair use of the F-Twist itself to say:
"Our theory about the origin and purpose of the F-
Twist may be 'unrealistic' ... but what of that? The
consequence of our theory agrees with the fact that
Chicagoans use the methodology to explain away objections to their assertions" [10, 1963, p. 233].

Samuelson admits that there is an element of "cheap humor" in
this line of argument. But nevertheless, it is an attempt to criticize Friedman by using Friedman's own methodology.

I will argue here that Samuelson does not appear to understand the "as if" principle. In *Section* 3.4 above I argued
that when using the "as if" principle, one must distinguish
between the empirical *truth* of a behavioral assumption and
the *validity of using* that assumption, and I noted that the
latter does not imply the former.

Perhaps Samuelson is correct in attributing a pattern of
behavior to the followers of Friedman and that such a pattern can
be shown to follow logically from his assumption concerning their
motivation, but the "as if" principle still does not warrant the
empirical claim that his assumption about Friedman's or his followers' motivation is true. More important, the "as if" principle is
validly used *only* when explaining *true* conclusions.
That is, one cannot validly use such an "as if" argument as a
critical device similar to *modus tollens*. If the implications
of using Samuelson's false assumption are undesirable, one cannot
pass the undesirableness back to the assumption. Furthermore,
there are infinitely many false arguments that can imply any given
(true) conclusion. The question is whether Samuelson's
assumption is necessary for his conclusion. Of course, it is not,
and that is because Samuelson is imitating Friedman's mode of
argument using sufficient assumptions.

The mode of argument in which Friedman accepts the "as if"
principle is neither a case of *modus ponens* nor *modus
tollens*. Yet when Samuelson proceeds to give a serious cri-

123

ticism of the "as if" principle, he assumes that both of them apply. But even worse, by Samuelson's own mode of argument, his assumption that attributes the F-Twist to Friedman is false and his attempts to apply this by means of *modus ponens* are thus invalid.

5. On Criticizing Instrumentalism

It would seem to me that it is pointless (and illogical) to criticize someone's view with an argument that gives different meanings to the essential terms.[20] Yet this is just what most of the critics do. Similarly, using assumptions that are allowed to be false while relying on *modus ponens*, as Samuelson does, is also pointless. Any effective criticism must deal properly with Friedman's instrumentalism. Presenting a criticism that ignores his instrumentalism will always lead to irrelevant critiques such as those as Koopmans, Rotwein, and De Alessi. None of these critics seems willing to straightforwardly criticize instrumentalism.

Instrumentalism presents certain obstacles to every critic. When instrumentalists argue by offering a long series of reasons, each of which is sufficient for their conclusions, it puts the entire onus on the critic to refute each and every reason. Friedman makes this all the more difficult by giving us, likewise, an instrumentalist argument in support of instrumentalism itself. Thus, refuting or otherwise successfully criticizing only some of Friedman's reasons will never defeat his view. Since Friedman never explicitly claims that his argument is intended to be a logically sufficient defense of instrumentalism, one cannot expect to gain even by refuting its "sufficiency." Yet it would be fair to do so, since "sufficiency" is the only logical idea that instrumentalism uses. Such a refutation, however, is unlikely, since it would seem to require a solution to the problem of induction.

Finally, and most importantly, I think it essential to realize that instrumentalism is solely concerned with (immediate) practical success. In this light, one should ask, "What are the criteria of success? Who decides what they are?" Questions of this type, I think, must also be dealt with before one can ever begin-- constructively or destructively--to criticize effectively the instrumentalism that constitutes the foundation of Friedman's methodology.

What then must one do to form an effective but fair and logical critique of Friedman's methodology? Whatever one does, one cannot violate the axioms of logic. It does not matter to instrumentalists if others have different definitions of the words "testing," "validity," "assumptions," "hypothesis," *etc.* When criticizing an argument in which reasons are offered as sufficient conditions, it should be recognized that *modus tollens* is useless. And when *modus tollens* is useless, there is no way one can directly criticize.

Since, as I have argued here, the internal construction of Friedman's instrumentalism is logically sound, in any effective criticism of his view the only issue possibly at stake is the truth or falsity of instrumentalism itself. But no one has been able to criticize or refute instrumentalism. That no one has yet refuted it does not prove that instrumentalism is universally correct. To claim that it does is to argue from *reverse modus ponens*. Again, this is a matter of logic.

Any effective criticism of instrumentalism must at least explain the absence of refutations. There are, I think, three possible ways any given argument may avoid refutations. First, as a matter of logical form, an argument may merely be irrefutable.[21] Second, if an argument is of a logical form that is conceivably refutable, it may simply be that it is true, hence no one will ever find refutations because they will never exist. Third, the absence of refutations may not be the result of an intrinsic property of the argument itself, but the consequence of how one deals with all potential refutations. That is, the defense may be either circular or infinitely regressive.[22]

As a matter of logic alone, instrumentalism need not be irrefutable. So, as an argument about how one should treat economic analysis, instrumentalism is either true or its proponents have been supporting it with a circularity or an infinite regress. And thus the first question is, is instrumentalism true? Repeated successes (or failed refutations) of instrumentalism is logically equivalent to repeated successful predictions or true conclusions. We still cannot conclude logically that the assumptions, i.e., the bases of instrumentalism itself, are true. They could very well be false, and in the future, someone may be able to find a refutation.

It has been argued in this paper that Friedman's essay is an instrumentalist defense of instrumentalism. That may be interpreted to mean that Friedman's methodology is based on an infinite regress, but if it is then at least it is not internally inconsistent or otherwise illogical. His success is still open to question. The repeated attempts to refute Friedman's methodology have failed, I think, because instrumentalism is its own defense and its *only* defense.

Footnotes

*   I wish to thank Milton Friedman, Mark Blaug, David Laidler, Roger Ransom, and my colleagues Terence Brown, Steve Easton, Zane Spindler, and Herb Grubel for suggestions and criticisms of an earlier draft. I am particularly grateful to Allan Sleeman of Western Washington University and Donna Wilson of Simon Fraser University for their editorial assistance.

1. However, he also explained how one can win an argument by cheating--for example, by concealing the direction of the argument.

2. Specifically, Aristotle said that in order for an argument to be logical, *the premises must not violate any of the following axioms:* First is the *axiom of identity,* *viz.,* different statements cannot use different definitions of the same words; second is the *axiom of the excluded-middle,* *viz.,* statements that cannot be true or false, or can be something else, are prohibited; and finally, the *axiom of non-contradiction,* *viz.,* statements cannot be allowed to be both true and false. Thus, any argument that contains such prohibited statements cannot qualify as a *logical* argument.

3. Previously proven mathematical theorems are the major source of the formal proofs used in economics.

4. These logical conditions are not independent of the axioms of logic. Each condition presumes that the statements of the argument are admissible. For example, each condition presumes that if a statement is not true it must be false.

5. I say "heuristically" because otherwise it is quite incorrect to consider "truth" to be some*thing* that can be passed around. Properly speaking, "truth" is a property of statements only; that is, there is no "truth" without a statement that is true. And, the verb "to pass" suggests the passage of time as well as the involvement of direction, but the intention is to avoid the time aspects. The verb "to connect" preserves the timelessness, but it does not suggest direction.

6. But usually when there are many assumptions, one does not know which assumption "caused" the false conclusion.

7. To illustrate, since this may seem counterintuitive to someone unfamiliar with formal logic, let us consider a simple example of an argument, the statements of which individually do not violate the axioms of logic. Let the assumptions be:

A_1: "All males have negatively sloped demand curves."

A_2: "Only males have negatively sloped demand curves."

A_3: "All my demand curves are negatively sloped."

And let the conclusion that would follow as a matter of logic alone be:

C: "I am a male."

Now let us say we do not know whether the assumptions are true or false. But, let us say we know that the conclusion is true. Does knowing that the conclusion of a logical argument is true enable us to say that we also know that any of the assumptions are true? Unfortunately not. As the above illustrative argument demonstrates, even if the conclusion is true all the assumptions can be false! In other words, although one's argument is logical, one still cannot use its logicality to assert that the assumptions are true on the basis of a known true conclusion. Note also that this example shows that the falsity of any assumption is not necessarily "passed" on to the individual conclusions.

8. This is even more important if we distinguish between the two different purposes for building arguments. A disjunctive argument might be used by a pure politician who wishes to convince us to vote for him or his policy. A conjunctive argument might be the objective of a pure theorist who offers his argument as a test of his understanding of the world or the economy. If the theorist's understanding of the world is correct, he should be able to explain or predict certain relevant phenomena; the assumptions used will represent his understanding (for example, the so-called "laws" of economics, physics, *etc.*). If a prediction turns out wrong, with the use of *modus tollens* one can say there is something wrong with the understanding of the world. A pure politician, contrarily, may not care *why* someone votes for him or his policy so long as the vote is in his favor. *Success* is the politician's primary objective.

9. Few economists today are serious inductivists; yet most follow Friedman's lead by stressing importance of distinguishing between normative and positive statements. It might be argued that for some economists the use of this distinction is merely an unexamined inductivist ritual.

127

10. Truth substitutes, such as probabilities, will not do. Stochastic models, in which the assumptions are in the form of probability distribution statements, usually cannot provide the logical force of either *modus ponens or modus tollens*. This point was stressed by early econometricians, but is usually ignored in most econometrics textbooks.

11. This was seen above as the limitation of *reverse modus ponens* in the illustrative argument about males and negatively sloped demand curves.

12. Which would easily be solved if we only had an inductive logic.

13. Note here, although Friedman uses conventionalist criteria, it is for a different purpose. For a conventionalist the criteria are used as truth status substitutes; in conventionalism one finds that theories are either better or worse. In this sense, Friedman can be seen to pose the problem of choosing among theories already classified as "better" in his sense (successful predictions).

14. I stress, this is the view Friedman uses *in his essay*. In recent correspondence Professor Friedman has indicated to me his more general views of testing in which success might be either a confirmation or a disconfirmation. But he still would question the meaningfulness of "testing in order to reject."

Although Friedman seldom uses the word "truth," it should be noted that throughout he consistently uses the word "validity" (by which he always means at least "not inconsistent with the available facts") in the same sense that "truth" plays in *modus ponens* seemingly while also recognizing that *modus ponens* is assured only when applied to "truth" in the absolute or universal sense (i.e., without exceptions). Technically speaking his use of the word "validity" may lead one to the incorrect identification of "truth" with "logical validity." In this regard, applications of Friedman's methodology are often confused with orthodox conventionalism. This confusion can be avoided by remembering that "validity" is a necessary (but not sufficient) condition of empirical "truth"--hence, validity and truth are not identical--and by recognizing that someone can believe his theory is true, even though he knows he cannot prove that it is true.

15. For example, the assumption of a negatively sloped demand curve may be an assumption for the market determination of price, but it is the conclusion of the theory of the consumer.

16. That is, Friedman might argue that "Occam's Razor" need not be used, as it is a pure intellectual exercise, which serves no useful purpose.

17. Specifically, with an argument consisting of a conjunction of many interdependent assumptions, a false conclusion does not necessarily implicate any particular assumption but only the conjunction of all of them.

18. Nor does he say "solely."

19. Nagel's paper [7, 1963] is often alleged to be a criticism of Friedman's essay. But Nagel's paper only tries to show that some of Friedman's definitions may not be universally accepted. Furthermore, a close reading will show that Nagel explicitly agrees with Friedman's methodological position. It is for this latter reason that Samuelson responds *to Nagel* by offering a criticism of Friedman's position. Also, it might be noted that Stanley Wong's paper [11, 1973] is likewise not very critical of Friedman's methodology, although Wong, like Nagel, does note that Friedman's methodology is an example of instrumentalism.

20. Such an argument would at least involve a violation of the axiom of identity.

21. Statements of the form "there will be a revolution" can never be proven false *even if they are false*. And tautological statements are true by virtue of the logical form alone, hence they cannot be refuted simply because one cannot conceive how they might be false.

22. For example, if one were to argue that revolutions are never successful, and one supports this with the evidence that every revolution has failed, the revolutionary may respond by saying that those were not "genuine" revolutions.

References

[1] Bear, Donald V.T. and Orr, Daniel. "Logic and Expediency in Economic Theorizing," *Journal of Political Economy*, April 1967, 75, pp. 188-96.

[2] De Alessi, Louis. "Economic Theory as a Language," *Quarterly Journal of Economics*, August 1965, 79, pp. 472-77.

[3] _____"Reversals of Assumptions and Implications," *Journal of Political Economy,* July-August 1971, 79 (4), pp. 867-77.

[4] Friedman, Milton. "The Methodology of Positive Economics," in *Essays in positive economics.* Chicago: University of Chicago Press, 1953, pp. 3-43.

[5] Koopmans, Tjalling. *Three essays on the state of economic science.* New York: McGraw-Hill, 1957.

[6] Melitz, Jack. "Friedman and Machlup on the Significance of Testing Economic Assumptions," *Journal of Political Economy,* Feb. 1965, 73, pp. 37-60.

[7] Nagel, Ernest. "Assumptions in Economic Theory," *American Economic Review,* May 1963, 53, pp. 211-19.

[8] Robbins, Lionel. *An essay on the nature and significance of economic science.* London: Macmillan, 1935.

[9] Rotwein, Eugene. "On 'The Methodology of Positive Economics,'" *Quarterly Journal of Economics,* Nov. 1959, 73, pp. 554-75.

[10] Samuelson, Paul. "Problems of Methodology: Discussion," *American Economic Review,* May 1963, 53, pp. 231-36.

[11] Wong, Stanley. "The 'F-Twist' and the Methodology of Paul Samuelson," *American Economic Review,* June 1973, 63 (3), pp. 313-25.

Part Five   The Role of Empiricism in Economics

In Part Four the reader was introduced to the topic or methodology of positive economics which stressed predictions and the importance of their verification in economics. Part Five is a continuation of Part Four and looks at the other end, so to speak, of the methodological spectrum by suggesting that assumptions made in model building or in the setting up of hypotheses cannot be ignored. Before noting what Eugene Rotwein covers in his article, a brief explanation of the two viewpoints which form part of the empiricist school of economics, namely the analytical school of moderate empiricism (to use Ian Stewart's terms) would be useful.

What seems to distinguish the analytical school is that its adherents accept common sense observations and introspection as acceptable ways of verifying economic and other theory. In other words, theory propositions (for example, the quantity demanded is inversely related to the product's price) are obvious from commonsense and testing by inductive--statistical procedures are unnecessary. Because economists of the analytical school believe that many hypotheses are true from common sense, these people are mainly concerned with whether or not a hypothesis applies to a certain real world situation, and whether this is true or not depends on how correctly a hypothesis' assumptions fit the real world situation that is being explained. For further details, readers should consult Lionel Robbins' *An Essay on the Nature and Significance of Economic Science.*

The hallmark of the moderate empiricist is that the assumptions as well as the predictions of economic theory must be tested against reality. Such economists believe that we must show that assumptions reflect the real world or otherwise the predictions themselves from the theory tell us little about the explanation of events. The interested reader should consult the article by D.P. O'Brien which is noted in this part's suggested readings; it presents the moderate empiricist position.

The central point of empiricism according to Eugene Rotwein is the need for repeated testing of all empirical generalizations by reference to experience and the continual modification of theory in light of these tests. Empiricists recognize that realistic assumptions are essential to the validity of any economic theory. Rotwein contrasts this approach with the one which Milton Friedman espoused in his famous *Essays in Positive Economics*. Rotwein devotes most of his article to a criticism of works by Martin Bronfenbrenner, Fritz Machlup, and D.V.T. Bear and Daniel Orr, who to a greater or lesser extent accept the fact that assumptions may not need to be tested and may not be realistic. Rotwein argues that their arguments are faulty, and he still remains convinced that in a scientific methodology the assumptions must be tested and, for explanation, they must reflect important aspects of the real world.

Boland (1982) argues that the question of realism of assumptions should be viewed in the light of one's objective. For short-run practical problem-solving the truth of one's assumptions is logically unnecessary. To illustrate this point he uses the story of the television repairman (p. 145), which goes like this. 'When we take our television set to the repairman, we do not usually think it is necessary to quiz the repairman about his understanding of electromagnetics or quantum physics'. For most practical purposes, we find it quite adequate to believe that the tube or transistor or whatever in the television needs repairing, and afterwards all is well with the television--it works beautifully. Thus for positive economics the instrumentalism, which puts premium on simplicity, is all that is necessary.

8 Empiricism and Economic Method: Several Views Considered

Eugene Rotwein*

In the present period with its unparalleled emphasis on the empirical testing of hypotheses, the demands that the standards of science impose on economics are of obvious moment. Accordingly, it might be expected that writings on the methodology of economics generally would reflect these standards. This, however, is not the case. Insofar as economics is regarded as a "science," no one, of course, is flatly opposed to empiricism. Yet, the constructions of empiricism or of its application to economics vary considerably and in ways which significantly affect both general perspectives and the treatment of important controversial questions within the field.

Some time ago, procedures employed in the empirical testing of economic hypotheses were attacked severely by Milton Friedman in his essay "The Methodology of Positive Economics,"[1] Friedman's position, which branded much such empirical testing as a misguided use of scientific method, has been criticized in some detail by myself and others.[2] It is the principal purpose of this article to examine several more recent writings which deal with questions of a general methodological character within the context of economics. Either explicitly or otherwise these raise the same issue considered by Friedman, and, as I shall seek to show, they contribute in various ways to a perpetuation of error regarding the application of empirical principles to the area of economics.

Empiricism and the Background Controversy in Economics

Before considering these writings it will be helpful if brief attention is given to two questions: What are the foundations of empiricism and, in light of this, the shortcomings of Friedman's position? What is the nature of the general methodological background, historically speaking, in which the issue raised by Friedman is to be viewed?

To turn to the first question, empiricism rests on an analysis of the manner in which human "belief" is formed. Since this is

Reprinted from the *Journal of Economic Issues* by special permission of the copyright holder, the Association for Evolutionary Economics. The article originally appeared in the *Journal of Economic Issues*, 7 (1973), 361-82.

133

fundamental, it is ultimately on the acceptability of this analysis that the empirical method stands or falls. There is, of course, no single ground on which belief rests. Man has been transported to a state of belief on the basis of pure emotion, astrology, palmistry, and messages from crystal balls. He confuses dreams with reality, and he hallucinates. Were there nothing beyond such diversity, however, "science" would be impossible; for it is the hallmark of science that its methods of verification can *compel* general agreement. It is the kind of thinking that underlies science - but which in everyday affairs is far more common - that the empiricist takes as the basis for his position on the requirements for establishing belief. Needless to say, although it may have uncomfortable consequences, one may persistently reject even the most compelling empirical evidence. But insofar as the procedures employed in testing any view depart from the testing procedures of science, that view must be acknowledged to remain (more or less) private. It manifestly cannot be argued on scientific grounds that the view should be accepted as valid.

Science seeks general relations between matters of fact, or those general empirical relations that can be couched in the hypothetical form "if A then B," where A is the event denoted by the assumption (or antecedent) of the hypothesis, and B is the prediction (or consequent). When we speak of establishing belief in the context of science, we are then speaking of the method of validating or gaining acceptance of such propositions. In dealing with the question of validation, a basic premise of the empirical position is that it is not permissible to assert that, in the nature of things, relations conflicting with those observed *cannot* occur. If we could make such an assertion, this would imply that relations between matters of fact were logical, which is to say that the opposite of any such relation would violate the principle of noncontradiction (that is, the principle that nothing can be in and out of existence at the same time) and for this reason would be inconceivable or impossible. The opposite of any statement concerning matter-of-fact relations, however, is always conceivable simply because the entities or events related are conceptually separable and therefore can be imagined to assume any form we may choose. This, and only this, is the reason why--as distinct from propositions that are logically related--no proposition concerning empirical relations can be treated as "certain."

Rejecting certainty within the world of empirical relations, the empiricist concerns himself with the probable and argues that, for purposes of ascertaining this, there is ample evidence to be drawn from experience. Here the empiricist accepts the view (which must be treated as a faith) that it is through an understanding of the past that the future may be foreseen. If empirical predictions cannot be made with certainty, what is most likely to occur, in a word, is a repetition of the regularities between events already observed. In other words, our confidence in the occurrence of any prediction B is contingent on the occurrence of another event A, where evidence indicates that the two are invariably related. Our ability to foresee the future, or the transformation of the chaos of "possibility" into the more orderly stuff of "probability" --thus rests on a continuing refinement and improvement in the procedures for ascertaining such regularities.

To consider Friedman's central thesis, this arose out of criticism of certain doctrines fundamental to orthodox economic analysis, specifically, the theory of perfect competition and, more broadly, the principle of marginalism. The criticism centered on the realism of the assumptions underlying these doctrines. Seeking to rebut this attack, Friedman argued that the concern with assumptions represented a total misdirection of effort since, properly construing scientific method, the validity of a theory depended solely on the accuracy of its predictions and not on the realism of its assumptions. For example, the validity of the theory of perfect competition, Friedman contended, did not depend at all on the nature of the markets in which the theory was used for predictive purposes.[3]

As is clear, this argument totally brushes aside the rationale for empirical modes of testing in science. On probability grounds, the belief that any prediction will occur depends on the occurrence of another event (denoted by the assumption) which evidence indicates is invariably related to the prediction. Validity is an index of the confidence we may repose in the belief, and its test involves assertions with respect to the "realism" of both the assumption and the prediction. Friedman thus ignored the essential condition in science for establishing the validity of a probability statement: he was asserting that confidence in a theory for predictive purposes was unaffected by an *observed absence* of association between the conditions specified by its assumptions and the event predicted.[4] The point may be stated in terms of the requirements for scientific explanation. Although there may be substantial variation in the explanatory content of accepted hypotheses, evidence of a constancy of association between the events related in the hypothesis is likewise essential (as it is for prediction) to the explanation of one of the events by the other.[5] It manifestly cannot be said that the conditions unique to a perfectly competitive market "explain" some given price or output phenomenon in cases where the market is monopolistic. Although Friedman applied the term *"explanation"* to cases of this latter nature, in arguing that the realism of the assumptions of a theory was irrelevent to its validity his analysis disregarded the requirements for *"explanation"* as this term is used in science and, commonly, outside the context of science as well.[6]

It should be noted that nothing in the foregoing implies that a prediction drawn from assumptions that are erroneous may not prove accurate. In the realm of relations between matters of fact anything is conceivable; it might turn out that the predicted phenomenon, to use Friedman's phrase, behaved "as if" the assumptions were true when they were, in fact, false. What is implied, rather, is that, to the degree that the prediction depends on the use of erroneous assumptions (which is, of course, what necessitates the employment of the "as if" formulation), it loses plausibility. Accordingly, the evidence concerning the prediction which is required to gain acceptance of its own probability will grow, which is but another way of saying that falsity in any assumption (even if it should, by chance, lead to a true prediction) is an "invalid" element in the hypothesis.[7]

We have been dealing with the foundations of empiricism. But this leads directly to our second question, which concerns the general background of contemporary methodological discussion. For since the principles considered are of general applicability, they are fundamental to the empirical tradition in economics and also go far toward setting the scene for current debate over economic methodology. This is not to say, of course, that in the past the practices of economists typically have been thoroughly empirical. Nor is it to say that formal methodological theory in economics traditionally has taken full account of the central implication of empiricism, that is, the need for repeated testing of all empirical generalizations by reference to experience and the progressive modification of the theoretical apparatus of the discipline in the light of such tests. However, in one basic sense which is of special relevance here--the recognition in principle that realistic assumptions are essential to the validity of theory-- the empirical tradition in economics has a venerable lineage. The major classical economists, for example, relied heavily on deduction and argued that this was indispensable to the development of economics as a science. With an eye toward this, it has indeed been asserted--and approvingly--that various nineteenth-century classical economists believed, as does Friedman, that the realism of their premises was irrelevant to the validity of their theories.[8] The evidence is entirely to the contrary. Representing the more general view of the period, not a single classical economist who dealt extensively with methodological theory (for example, Nassau Senior, or J.S. Mill, or J.E. Cairnes) ever doubted that unrealistic assumptions would impair the validity of their theoretical analysis.[9]

This empirical standard, however, has been a constant source of difficulty. For the failure to meet the standard has been one of the most important general grounds on which both the classical and neoclassical economists have been criticized. And owing to its importance, both schools of economists have themselves given

136

much attention to this issue. Considering all views, however, the positions taken have differed. Some of the classical economists, among others, acknowledged the lack of realism in the basic premises and the subsidiary assumptions they employed for deductive purposes and, in conformity with their methodological theory, stressed the need to keep these departures from realism in mind when applying the conclusions of their deductive analysis to experience.[10] Although similarly recognizing the pervasive importance of realism, others stressing the importance of deduction in economics have slighted or subjected the need for repeated and careful testing of the basic premises of their analysis on the grounds that experience already had established their universal and immutable truth.[11] A third and quite different position – stated in its most extreme form by Ludwig von Mises and representing an outgrowth of the Austrian approach--has posited a separate deductive world of "pure theory" in which the basic assumptions of economics, although regarded as fundamental to an understanding of the real world, are held to be apprehended *a priori* and are hence alleged to be true independently of any empirical tests.[12]

The requirement that assumptions be "realistic" has indeed long been a heavy cross for the economic theorist to bear. And in propounding his new version of empiricism (a form of "demi-empiricism" which acknowledges the empirical nature of theoretical assumptions but denies the relevance of tests of their realism for "validity") Friedman was seeking to cast off this burden once and for all. In doing so, Friedman was concerned to defend his own brand of theory. Nonetheless, his position has had a broader appeal. It stressed tests of predictions. But pending such tests, it afforded *carte blanche* for the disregard of any and all varieties of "unrealism" in theoretical model-building and so appeared to provide a new and sweeping warrant for a practice which theortical economists of many persuasions have not found uncongenial to their inclinations. To many (although clearly not all) it seemed that Friedman had made the breakthrough: In boldly proclaiming the "irrelevance" of the long gnawing criticisms of traditional empiricists, he had at one stroke gained for unrealistic economic theorizing a measure of scientific respectability that it previously had not enjoyed. It is scarcely surprising then that others dealing with economic methodology subsequently should have used his analysis, in one fashion or another, to defend the extensive use of "theory" in empirical inquiry.

An Eclectic View

To turn to these post-Friedman writings, let us consider first an essay by Martin Bronfenbrenner which, among other things, is pointedly concerned with the "Friedman controversy," or "the battle of the assumptions."[13] Notwithstanding his own deep in-

137

terest in economic theory, Bronfenbrenner is an eclectic--in practice as well as in principle. Much of his essay reflects his open-mindedness and his unwillingness to bind himself to any orthodoxy. But in his treatment of the controversy it is largely this eclecticism that leads him astray.

Specifically, Bronfenbrenner contends that in their selection of hypotheses theorists are willing to sacrifice predictive efficiency and explanatory power for simplicity, whereas institutionalists are willing to sacrifice these same objectives for realistic assumptions. In his view both these approaches are legitimate. The particular approach which one adopts, he argues, is wholly a matter of personal preference. The Friedman controversy is thus to be regarded essentially as one concerning personal tastes, and it is misleading to suppose that the issues raised can properly be treated in terms of general methodological standards.[14] This position may appear to afford an inviting way out of the controversy touched off by Friedman's view since it offers something to everyone. But it should be apparent that this overextends eclecticism.

For the hallmark of science lies precisely in its employment of procedures which are based on general methodological principles. The objectives of these procedures consist in nothing other than the discovery of propositions with predictive efficiency and explanatory power. Once attained, these are never sacrificed for anything else. As noted, it is likewise a characteristic of science that the evidence which its procedures yield (that is, evidence indicating a constancy of association between events) is capable of compelling general agreement. Were this not the case, science typically would have yielded little beyond the cacophony of interminable squabbles between rival personalities. Properly altered, there is manifest truth in Bronfenbrenner's view. Purely personal preference (depending on the character and background of the investigator) certainly will influence the choice among alternative hypotheses when the evidence for any one of the alternatives is not considered satisfactory. However, in treating predictive efficiency and explanatory power as matters subordinate to the indulgence of personal preferences, Bronfenbrenner not only misstates the ultimate objectives of scientific inquiry, but also, through this misstatement, neglects the basic issue in the controversy. That the issue is the evidentiary requirements for achieving predictive efficiency and explanatory power themselves. In substance this central question is not discussed.[15]

In his general statement Bronfenbrenner also misrepresents the essential methodological difference between the approaches of the theorists and the institutionalists. This flows from a misidentification of the issue of "simplicity versus realism" as it arises in Friedman's analysis with the issue as it arises in the

138

context of disagreement between theorists and institutionalists. In the latter context the distinction between *"simplicity"* and *"realism"* refers to the degree and pattern of abstraction involved in the statement of a hypothesis. Theorists differ from institutionalists in the sense that, when treating the same problem area, they generally are disposed to "simplify" by rejecting as irrelevant various "realistic" considerations concerning institutions which the institutionalists regard as crucial. Nonetheless, they both agree insofar as they accept as essential the process of abstraction itself--or the omission from the assumptions of a hypothesis of factors considered irrelevant to the problem under analysis. Were this not recognized, one would be obliged, in treating any problem, to deal with everything in the universe at once (something which no institutionalist, however comprehensive and scrupulous his eye for detail, has yet undertaken or ever deemed necessary). Although differing in the character of their abstractions, both institutionalists and theorists can likewise agree--and as scientists are indeed constrained to agree--that the resolution of their differences regarding these assumptions depends ultimately on evidence concerning the extent to which the conditions specified in the rival assumptions do *in reality* form parts of regularly recurring relationships within the problem area under study. In this sense there is no methodological controversy between the two at all.

When considered in the context of Friedman's central argument, the distinction between simplicity and realism has a very different meaning. Although he was speaking of theory, Friedman's main point did not involve the question of abstraction or the legitimacy of confining theoretical assumptions to a relatively small number of facts surrounding a problem while *excluding* large numbers of others. As Bronfenbrenner recognizes, Friedman was arguing that it was legitimate (or did not affect validity) to *include* specifications in theoretical assumptions which contradicted or falsified the circumstances surrounding a problem.[16] The assumption (for the sake of "simplicity") that a given case was perfectly competitive when it was, in fact, monopolistic would, in his view, have no bearing on its validity either for purposes of prediction or explanation. This is a quite special view. In its disregard of the nature and test of a probability statement it sets Friedman methodologically in opposition to theorists and institutionalists alike insofar as both the latter pursue the objectives of science.

Science as Preeminently "Pure Theory"

A second view which warrants attention is the position taken by Fritz Machlup. Although Machlup has long been a defender of theoretical economic analysis, the nature of his defense has undergone change. In his well-known debate with R.A. Lester concerning the validity of the principle of marginalism, Machlup recognized that the realism of theoretical assumptions was a matter of central significance in evaluating economic theory.[17] But since that time, and specifically since the appearance of Friedman's essay on methodology, he has drawn away from his earlier concession to catholicity. In the treatment of the routes to the understanding of economic experience, Machlup's more recent methodological tracts (more fully reflecting the Austrian influence) increasingly have emphasized the difference between the world of "exact laws" or "pure theory" and the world of empirical generalization--to the advantage of the former and the disadvantage of the latter. His methodological theory, however, is not entirely in the Austrian mold but represents an attempt to amalgamate aspects of the Austrian position with the position taken by Friedman. Through portions of his treatment, moreover, there runs an empirical element that Machlup never attempts, much less manages, to harness to the rest of his analysis. His latest general methodological essay, in which his position appears in its fullest form, is of special interest because it well serves to highlight the difficulties inevitably encountered by anyone seeking to preserve a place of superiority for pure theory in the world of science.[18]

In Machlup's view, *"theory"* consists of the pure constructs of human reason; and, while such constructs bear a relationship to reality, the distinguishing characteristic of pure theory is said to lie in its reliance on "idealization, hypothecation and heuristic fictions" which are introduced for purposes of "analytical convenience." This is contrasted with "inductive generalizations," which are based on operational (empirical) constructs. If theoretical generalizations are regarded as fictitious or "ideal," Machlup has recognized that they are drawn from experience. Nonetheless, like von Mises, he sees pure theory as something basically different from inductive generalization. Despite any similarities, they differ "in kind." As such, the superiority of theoretical over inductive generalization is to be found in the logical relations within theoretical systems. For these enable us, through deduction from broad generalizations, to explain and interpret wide ranges of empirical phenomena. Theoretical systems make it possible for us to move from "causes to consequences" so that theoretical conclusions are "logically necessary." Inductive generalizations, on the other hand, are only "correlation statements." As such they are usually "narrow" and yield only "some more or less definite probability value."[19]

In its treatment of the relation between theoretical (or logical) systems and inductive generalizations, this statement is internally inconsistent and misleading. On the one hand, theoretical systems yield cause and effect relations, which means that they yield statements concerning matters of fact. On the other hand, theo-

140

retical generalizations--the basis of the logical systems--are sharply distinguished from "correlation statements." This implies that the theoretical generalizations do not themselves take the form of matter-of-fact statements, which leads us to wonder how these generalizations can form part of, or explain, any causal relation. Manifestly, if the material of logical sequences is to form part of a causal relation, the major premises of these sequences must contain the basis for establishing the relationship; and these premises (as in the theoretical proposition: "Entrepreneurs maximize profit") reduce to nothing other than "correlation statements" or statements of association between events or entities. A related difficulty is found in Machlup's treatment of the conclusions of logical systems. If these conclusions are statements of causal relations, they are probability statements, as are the matter-of-fact propositions that comprise the premises. No amount of deductive reasoning can alter this (although the showing that an empirical statement is deducible from more general and true premises enhances its own probability value). Yet, contrasting these conclusions with the probabilistic nature of inductive statements, Machlup treats the former as "logically necessary."

Also indefensible is Machlup's contention that empirical propositions are generally "narrow" and therefore cannot be employed as the major premises of logical systems. An empirical proposition, in Machlup's definition, is one that does not contain fictitious or ideal elements, but this has no bearing on the breadth or the degree of generality of the proposition. Is the empirical proposition: "All living things are mortal" narrower than the theoretical proposition: "All entrepreneurs maximize profit"? Propositions may be narrow and fictitious or broad and realistic and vice versa; and it is precisely the breadth of the empirical generalizations and the extent of their logical interrelations with lower order propositions that constitute the distinguishing characteristic of the most advanced sciences. Machlup argues that, owing to errors of observation and measurement alone, empirical propositions generally cannot, in fact, be logically interrelated. "The impurities and inaccuracies inherent in most or all practicable operations with sensory observations and recorded data," he states, "destroy the logical links between different concepts."[20]

The implication is that the "laws" of science, taken as statements which do not include error terms, contain fiction and presumably, therefore, must be classified as theories. Even allowing for the many relatively unrefined empirical generalizations (where there are no errors of observation), this would indeed entail an extensive reclassification. However, the errors in question are designated "errors of observation and measurement" precisely because the evidence (including evidence concerning the nature of measuring instruments, and so forth) creates a strong presumption that they spring from imperfections in experimental tech-

141

niques. In other words, it may be presumed that, were it not for such imperfections, the laws would be seen to operate as stated, or that for purposes of the general analysis of experience they confidently can be used as they stand. This is quite different from Machlup's theories which contain "real fiction," or misrepresentations of experience which, for the sake of analytical convenience are introduced deliberately. It may be added that when the laws are corrected to allow for observational errors the magnitude of the errors is small enough to permit for reliable predictions covering wide ranges of events, including events involving relatively precise measurement.

It has been observed that Machlup's analysis raises serious questions concerning the place of his theoretical systems in the (empirical) area of science because he treats the premises and conclusions of these systems as statements which differ from probability statements. Machlup's essay, however, throws further light on the issue, for it also deals explicitly with the test of theoretical propositions within the context of science. Since theory is said to contain fiction, here one encounters the crucial question: How can a proposition that is fictitious (and we are speaking of "real fiction") be regarded as valid either for purposes of prediction or explanation in the world of real experience? It is possible to argue--and indeed often has been argued--that fictitious theory, although invalid, is useful as a first approximation to experience because it simplifies complex phenomena and thus renders them more tractable to analytical treatment. A progressive rectification of the fictions and the conclusions drawn from them may then provide a fruitful basis for developing more satisfactory hypotheses. So viewed, the value of the first approximation would vary with the extent of its falsifications and with the difficulty, accordingly, in progressing through successive approximations to the real dimensions of the problem without substantially sacrificing the analytical advantages of the initial theoretical framework.[21]

Machlup, however, does not consider pure theory in its role as a first approximation; his statements imply that, as it stands, it has considerable scientific value.[22] But his treatment of the test by which its value is established is curious. Speaking generally, he points out that the constructs of a theory cannot be too fictitious because this would impair their value in explaining real phenomena.[23] This appears to be a recognition that theoretical generalizations *are* matter-of-fact statements and are so to be judged. The implication then, clearly, is that in appraising the validity of a theory it is appropriate to consider whether and to what extent its assumptions are fictitious, or to treat the realism of its assumptions as essential in evaluating both its predictive reliability and explanatory value.[24] In pointedly considering the test of a theory, Machlup, however, retreats from this implication. He contends, rather, that in testing a theory attention need only be given the realism of the initiating change in the problem under study (such as the imposition of an excise tax on an industry) and the accuracy of the consequences (with respect, say, to commodity price) which flow from the theoretical apparatus employed to analyze the effects of the change.[25]

An examination then of the realism of the theoretical assumptions themselves (in the above case those regarding the structure of the industry in question) is not, in fact, to form part of the test by which we judge the validity of a theory.[26] This turns out to be the same as Friedman's test of a theory, although the approach to it is somewhat different. Seeking to establish the validity of theory despite the falsity of its assumptions, Friedman spoke as though the fictions of theory did not at all impair its explanatory value. In contrast, Machlup acknowledges the functional relationship between the realism of theoretical assumptions and their value in explaining experience. But--persuaded nonetheless that theoretical generalizations somehow differ "in kind" from correlation statements and that a substantial measure of self-sufficiency can be claimed for theoretical systems solely on the basis of their "logic"--he then proceeds as though tests of theoretical hypotheses can disregard this critical relationship between "realism" and "explanation."[27] A final accent on this note of self-sufficiency appears in Machlup's concluding comments on the test of a theory. Disregarding the role of "repetition" in the testing process, he here contends that only "occasional" verification of its hypotheses suffices to establish confidence in the whole theoretical system.[28]

Accepting Questionable Assumptions as "Expedients"

A methodological position which differs from those already considered is that of D.V.T. Bear and Daniel Orr; for in this case it is argued unqualifiedly that tests of assumptions are relevant in testing hypotheses.[29] The analysis here, however, is also concerned with a special problem, namely, the testing of hypotheses when the realism of assumptions is difficult to ascertain; and it is this portion of their treatment that is open to criticism.

The authors argue that this problem is generally a vexing one because the testing of assumptions is always "hard" and typically far more difficult than the testing of predictions. However, where the assumptions "do not flatly contradict anything observable," it is legitimate, they point out, to treat their specifications as correct and proceed directly to a test of the predictions. In their view, on grounds of "expediency" there is a "powerful justification" for employing this method in economics, as elsewhere, because it enables us to "get on with the generation of testable prediction statements." Adducing the model of perfect

143

competition as an illustrative case, the authors contend that "it is wrong categorically to disregard predictions from a perfectly competitive model on the grounds that any of the four to five inadequately rationalized intermediate theory textbook conditions of perfect competition do not hold. Such a rejection is erroneous because of the difficulty in establishing how widely or how significantly the actual situation varies from perfect competition."[30] Although the rationale for the approach is basically different from Friedman's, and the scope and pattern of its application likewise would differ, Bear and Orr thus advocate a testing procedure which, presumably over a large range of cases in economics, is the same as that supported by Friedman. In these cases (where it is difficult to test certain assumptions relevant to particular hypotheses) our choice among existing hypotheses should depend wholly on the predictive findings; and (until the assumptions are tested) the theory with the greatest predictive success is to be given preference over the rest.

Setting aside the issue of its applicability to economics and considering the question on general methodological grounds, there is nothing objectionable in this mode of testing hypotheses when assumptions are unobservable. While the test is not as complete as one which also covers the assumptions, favorable findings on the observable implications of the assumptions support a presumption that these assumptions are correct and thus enhance our confidence in them.[31] Employed commonly on the frontiers of natural science (where it is especially likely that the hypotheses will contain unobservable assumptions), this method of testing may provide a basis for assessing rival theories (for example, different theories of light) and for the selection of a single theory as preeminent in explaining the class of phenomena involved.

In the natural sciences the procedure has indeed proved powerful. But is it likely to prove generally powerful in economics? To begin with, when certain assumptions of a hypothesis are unobservable the acceptance of the hypothesis on the basis of observable predictions requires highly imposing evidence of success in prediction simply because the experimental evidence must be drawn *wholly* from such findings. The importance of this consideration in a nonlaboratory field such as economics—where serious problems often are encountered in performing crucial experiments on predictions—should be apparent.

The authors' case for concentrating attention on predictions, moreover, is scarcely strengthened by their arguments concerning assumptions. There is no foundation for their view that assumptions (the specifications of the "if" clause of hypotheses) are generally more difficult to test than predictions (the specifications of the "then" clause). The nature of the assumption and the prediction (and hence the relative difficulty of testing each)

144

varies with the particular analysis; moreover, the assumption of one hypothesis may serve as the prediction of another.

Similarly, Bear and Orr present no substantial argument to support their view that economic assumptions in particular are commonly unobservable. The case drawn from the nature of market structure assumptions in the area of price theory, if anything, constitutes evidence of a contrary nature. On the basis of such considerations as the number of firms in the industry, the importance of product differentiation, and the conditions of entry into the industry (as affected by product differentiation and other factors), there are numerous departures from the assumption of perfect competition that--given the whole spectrum of theoretical departures--would be regarded as "wide" by virtually everybody.[32] There are also numerous cases where the nature of the market is difficult to ascertain in the sense that the question evokes disagreement. But here, contrary to the view of the authors, the relevant circumstances cannot simply be treated as "unobservable," since many observers believe that the cases in fact reveal a considerable measure of noncompetition.

There also is reason to believe that this kind of case is not at all atypical in economics. In a large proportion of the instances, statements appearing as assumptions in economic hypotheses are at least partially observable, or are commonly believed to be so. Included would be assumptions of a "subjective" character (for example, the profit maximization assumption) since these are to some degree testable by introspection and communication. Under these circumstances an evaluation of the plausibility of predictive findings on the basis of the "realism" of the assumptions is frequently unavoidable. In the area specifically of industrial organization (where there is abundant ground for doubting that any *one* existing model, or therefore its predictions, can be applied to all cases), the task of gaining acceptance of the general applicability of the perfectly competitive predictions would indeed require successful predictive evidence of monumental proportions. When consideration, furthermore, is given the difficulty in economics of conducting controlled experiments on predictions which are free of ambiguous results, the procedure urged by Bear and Orr is seen in a very different light. Economics is not physics, much less physics on the frontiers; and while evidence on predictions is basic to progress in any area of science, there is little reason to expect that in economics broadscale progress can be made without a continued and concomitant examination of the assumptions which are germane to the predictions.

Concluding Comments

Among the deficiencies in formal treatments of economic methodology, the most general and significant (as revealed over a considerable time span) has been the uncritical acceptance of procedures that do not meet the stringent empirical standards of science. This shortcoming may be attributed to a tendency to view methodology within the context of the difficulties encountered in the area of economics, a pattern clearly apparent in the writings discussed. All deal with the role of deductive process in economics which, typically based on "analytically convenient" oversimplifications of reality, has been the principal mode of accommodation to the methodological difficulties of the discipline. Although this procedure has been of value within limits (and the limitations have not gone unrecognized), in practice the extensive dependence on the method has engendered a disposition to treat economic theory as though its validity could be established without full and repeated reference to experience. Again, as on occasions in the past, this perspective has prompted an attempt at justification through the use of formal methodological theory. On the contemporary scene the principal new attempt of this nature--Friedman's--has taken the form of a claim that the deductive process need only be opened to empirical test at the "prediction" end, but in one fashion or another the influence of his position is evident in the other writings considered.

Observing the difficulty in resolving controversy in economics, Bronfenbrenner accepts as correct methodology the unrestrained indulgence of personal proclivities in the choice of assumptions and hypotheses. (One wonders whether this is not an archly disguised statement of resignation to an unpalatable and presumably unalterable reality, or a wry way of saying that, given the nature of the field, an interminable clash between subjectively inspired views is *for economics* "scientific method.") Machlup--arguing for the superiority of unrealistic theoretical analysis while seeking to make allowance for empirical considerations--is led into a maze of insupportable and internally conflicting views (including the Friedman position) only to withdraw eventually into a substantially self-justifying deductive world of "pure theory." Bear and Orr explore the requirements of empiricism more thoroughly, but, similarly confronting the issue of conflict concerning "assumptions," they transform this into a demi-blessing by consigning the realism of a wide range of economic assumptions to the domain of the "unknown" and by supposing that, as such, they can be handled as science handles "unobservables." For an extensive variety of cases the way is thus to be opened for shifting emphasis to the process of deducing predictions at the expense of a concern with the realism of the assumptions employed.

The formal methodological analysis developed within a discipline affords one kind of overview of the discipline itself. Such an overview may be misleading, since methodological prescriptions

146

may be honored in the breach--and often by their own authors. But is also may be significantly illuminating since (as one among several forces) persuasions of a methodological nature may lend momentum to intellectual movements by endowing them with a highly general rationale. The heavy reliance on deductive analysis in economics was the outgrowth of many influences, not the least of which were the vexing investigatory problems encountered in the field, but the sanction provided by methodological argument has helped perpetuate this type of approach. The more recent concern with the empirical testing of hypotheses, whatever its variants, is likewise the product of many forces, but it owes some of its momentum to persistent methodological criticism of the weight traditionally given deduction.

No science progresses in an "ever onward and upward" fashion. In the social sciences, where the subject matter is highly complex and the discipline of the laboratory is wanting, movements both backward and downward are particularly likely to occur, and perhaps especially so in the area of formal methodology. The standards of science in social fields are so difficult to meet that in these realms there is an ever-present susceptibility to more permissive versions of "science." Formal views on methodology thus generally are vulnerable to the winds of controversy over substantive doctrine, the prevailing climate of opinion, and the professional fashions of the period, all of which shape the special permissiveness that is legitimized. It is not at all paradoxical, then, that contemporary methodological tracts should contain errors that writers of a much earlier period--including the classical economists--would not have made.

Methodological theorizing that loses an eye for the full demands of empiricism may succeed in affording some sort of sanction for virtually any practice. Even inadequately justified lines of analysis and inquiry may not prove entirely sterile. But, in affording them sanction, methodological theory abets the perpetuation of practices whose costs are not small. These entail the continuing diversion of intellectual effort into channels that produce little of importance for new knowledge and the impairment of perspective and judgment in making use of knowledge we already possess.

Footnotes

*   The author is Professor of Economics, Queens College of the City University of New York, Flushing.

1. See Friedman's *Essays in Positive Economics* (Chicago: University of Chicago Press, 1953), pp. 3 ff.

2. My criticism is contained in my article "On 'The Methodology of Positive Economics'," *Quarterly Journal of Economics* 73 (November 1959): 552-75. For other criticisms of Friedman's position, see Ernest Nagel, "Assumptions in Economic Theory," and Paul Samuelson, "Problems of Methodology - Discussion," *American Economic Review* 53 (May 1963): 211-19 and 231-36, respectively; and Jack Melitz, "Friedman and Machlup on the Significance of Testing Economic Assumptions," *Journal of Political Economy* 82 (February 1965): 37-60.

3. See Friedman, *Essays,* pp. 8-9, 14, 16-18.

4. Friedman argues that it is not the realism of all but only of "theoretical" assumptions that is irrelevant in testing hypotheses. He states, in fact, that in testing the predictions of a theory it is essential to observe and specify the conditions under which these predictions occur (see ibid., p. 19). Indeed, the predictions of science, as conditional general statements, always contain "assumptions," so that realistic assumptions are essential to valid scientific predictions themselves. A recognition of all this, however, is inconsistent with Friedman's position regarding the test of a theory. In stressing the necessity for observing and specifying the conditions under which a prediction occurs, Friedman is implicitly recognizing that in the future we will look for the reoccurrence of these latter real conditions to tell us when the event predicted will reoccur, which is to say that, insofar as they are unrealistic, the assumptions of the theory lack validity for purposes of prediction. To argue that it is the unrealistic assumptions of the theory that are valid whenever its predictions are accurate while stressing the importance of ascertaining the actual conditions under which the predictions occur is much akin to asserting that "in curing disease it is but necessary to rub a rabbit's foot, provided one takes the proper drugs." Cf. Rotwein, "On 'The Methodology,'" pp. 560-61.

5. Although typically there would be agreement on whether a particular association of events had explanatory content, the explanation afforded is a matter of degree; for it depends on the degree to which the conditions contained in the assumption can be related to other experience. The prediction: "Aspirin will alleviate headaches" would gain explanatory content if it were related to a broader condition which specified the manner in which the chemical properties of aspirin affected the brain. In turn this would become more explanatory if the chemical properties of aspirin were shown to have

similar effects on other parts of the body, or if aspirin were shown to be a subgroup of chemicals having such effects, and so forth. For a discussion of the relationship between prediction and explanation and the range of variation between the two, see Carl G. Hempel, *Aspects of Scientific Explanation* (New York: Free Press, 1965), especially pp. 364-74.

6. Cf. Friedman, *Essays*, pp. 8, 12-15, 20, 41.

7. Sometimes in support of the Friedman view that the realism of theoretical assumptions does not matter, cases are cited in which there is already abundant evidence for belief in the prediction itself. This plainly begs the question since, for purposes of drawing the prediction or establishing belief in it, there is no dependence on the assumption whose falsity is said to be of no significance. For example, one can introduce any one of an indefinite number of false assumptions into an hypothesis whose prediction is that man is mortal without affecting our belief in the latter. Needless to say, however, as soon as we wish to explain man's mortality in terms of broader considerations, the realism of the assumption employed becomes crucial. Moreover, although we may believe that man is mortal independently of any explanation, such explanation--in principle--enhances the probability value of the belief.

8. Cf. below pp. 371-72 and n. 26. It should perhaps be pointed out that nothing in our argument implies that deduction is not important in the process of empirical inquiry. The question at issue concerns the significance of the realism of any proposition employed--whether deductively or otherwise--in exploring experience.

9. In the detailed attention given the realism of economic assumptions, the writers mentioned make unequivocally clear their belief that unrealistic assumptions would adversely affect the accuracy of their predictions. To cite but one of many of Mill's coments (which appear in his treatment of the "Logic of the Moral Sciences"):

> All the general propositions which can be framed by the deductive science, are therefore, in the strictest sense of the word, hypothetical. They are grounded on some supposititious set of circumstances, and declare how some given cause would operate in those circumstances, supposing that no others were combined with them. If the set of circumstances supposed have been copied from those of any existing society, the conclusions will be

true of that society, provided, and in as far as, the effect of those circumstances shall not be modified by others which have not been taken into the account. If we desire a nearer approach to concrete truth, we can only aim at it by taking, or endeavoring to take, a greater number individualizing circumstances into the computation.

System of Logic (London: Longmans, 1865), pp. 489-90. See also chap. 5 in Mill's *Essays on Some Unsettled Questions of Political Economy* (London: London School of Economics and Political Science, 1948); and J.E. Cairnes *The Character and Logical Method of Political Economy* (London: Macmillan, 1878), especially pp. 45-57. In his treatment Senior raises objections to the use of unrealistic assumptions which are worth repeating on the present scene. He points out that such assumptions are objectionable because (1) their use renders a science "unattractive" since it renders it irrelevant to "what is actually taking place"; (2) anyone starting from arbitrarily assumed premises is "in danger of forgetting, from time to time, their unsubstantitated foundation, and of arguing as if they were true"; and (3) reasoning on the basis of unreal assumptions is especially susceptible to logical error since anyone dealing with an imaginary world is less likely to be startled by strange conclusions which might have alerted him to his mistakes. See N.W. Senior, *Four Introductory Lectures in Political Economy* (London: Longmans, 1852), pp. 63-65. For a general treatment of the economic methodology of the period, see J.N. Keynes *The Scope and Method of Political Economy* (London: Macmillan, 1917), especially pp. 11-20, 211-20.

10. Among the classical economists Mill and Cairnes best represent this point of view. It is for this reason that both--anticipating the later position taken by Alfred Marshall and others--emphasized that the conclusions of economic reasoning constituted only statements of "tendencies" subject to correction for errors of omission and commission in the treatment of reality in the reasoning process. Cf. Mill, *System of Logic,* pp. 487ff; and Cairnes, *Character and Logical Method,* pp. 48ff. This view is an early statement of the position that the deductive analysis of economic theory represents but the first stage in a process of successive approximations. See below p. 371.

11. Senior's comments on the basic premises of economics are of this character. See his *Political Economy* (London: Griffin, 1873), p. 3. Among neo-orthodox economists, several statements of Lionel Robbins are of a similar nature. See

his *An Essay on the Nature and Significance of Economic Science* (London: Macmillan, 1932), especially pp. 78-92, and 83-86.

12. See Ludwig von Mises, *Human Action, A Treatise on Economics* (New Haven: Yale University Press, 1963), pp. 7-8, 32-41, 64, 351, 868.

13. See his "A 'Middlebrow' Introduction to Economic Methodology" in *The Structure of Economic Science,* ed. Sherman R. Krupp (Englewood Cliffs, N.J.: Prentice-Hall, 1966), pp. 5-24.

14. See Bronfenbrenner, "A 'Middlebrow' Introduction," pp. 17-18.

15. Although he does not amplify or seek to support his statement, Bronfenbrenner asserts that he does not agree with the view that a preference for realistic assumptions is "inherent in normal human nature" or that such realism is essential either to prediction or explanation (ibid., p. 18). With respect to human nature, as has been noted there is no single basis on which human belief is formed. The main issue here, however, concerns the procedures for validating propositions *within the context of science.* The "realism" which is essential to establishing the regularity of association between events on which scientific belief is based is, of course, also found to a substantial degree in "normal" human behavior. Otherwise, science itself would have little or no place in human affairs.

16. Notwithstanding the basic difference between these two positions, Friedman draws on the argument for the necessity of abstraction in support of his main thesis concerning the irrelevance of falsity in assumptions. Cf. Rotwein, "On 'The Methodology,'" pp. 564-65.

17. See his "Marginal Analysis and Empirical Research," reprinted from *American Economic Review* 36 (September 1946), in *Essays on Economic Semantics* (Englewood Cliffs, N.J.: Prentice-Hall, 1963), pp. 147-90. The acceptance of the importance of the realism of assumptions is evident throughout the article. Speaking of all aspects of theory, Machlup concludes that "the correctness, applicability and relevance of economic theory constantly needs testing through empirical research" (p. 190).

18. See his article, "Operationalism and Pure Theory in Economics," in *Structure,* ed. Krupp, pp. 53-67.

19. Ibid., pp. 57-58, 67.

20. Ibid., p. 61.

21. What is sought in the first and simplified approximation is a determinate solution, and the more this approximation falsifies experience the more difficult is it to preserve the elements of determinacy as the unrealistic assumptions are modified in successive approximations. It can be argued that first approximations themselves may afford valuable insights into experience. Insights, however, are not validated hypotheses and are usually the subjects of considerable controversy. See Rotwein, "Mathematical Economics: The Empirical View and an Appeal for Pluralism," in *Structure,* ed. Krupp, pp. 111-12.

22. Machlup, "Operationalism and Pure Theory in Economics," in *Structure,* ed. Krupp, p. 66.

23. Ibid., pp. 57-58.

24. In addition to assumptions whose specifications are demonstrably false, Machlup (in opposing the position of those who insist on operational definitions of theoretical constructs) argues for the legitimacy of using theoretical assumptions whose specifications are either unobservable or very difficult to observe. In these latter cases, the degree of falsification involved, if any, cannot, of course, be ascertained, or, if so, only imperfectly at best. This raises special questions which are considered below. See pp. 143-144.

25. Ibid., p. 65.

26. In an earlier article Machlup asserts that this was the position of Mill, Senior, and Cairnes and credits Mill with its original formulation. "The point to emphasize is that Mill does not propose to put the *assumptions* of economic theory to empirical tests, but only *the predicted results that are deduced from them.*" See his "The Problem of Verification in Economics," *Southern Economic Journal* 22 (July 1955): 7. Cf. the treatment of this question above on pp. 134-136 and n. 9. In light of the full nature of the evidence on the issue (Machlup cites but one statement by Mill taken out of context), his interpretation must be regarded as an instance of the not uncommon practice of misreading the past out of a zealous desire to discover support for the views of the present.

27. In view of the central significance of this inconsistency in Machlup's argument, it is not surprising to find that it should

lead to vagueness and ambiguity elsewhere in his analysis. For example, while Machlup's test of a theory makes no place for an examination of the realism of theoretical assumptions, he subsequently states that it is necessary that there be "links" between empirical data and "*some* of the crucial theoretical constructs." Ibid., p. 66. [Italics mine.] This same difficulty appears in even more striking form in Machlup's Presidential Address before the American Economic Association. Here he states: "The model of the firm in traditional price theory is not, as so many writers believe, designed to serve to explain and predict changes in the behavior of real firms; instead, it is designed to explain and predict changes in observed prices (quoted, paid, received) as effects of particular changes in conditions (wage rates, interest rates, import duties, excise taxes, technology, etc.). In this causal connection the firm is only a theoretical link, a mental construct to explain how one gets from the cause to the effect. This is altogether different from explaining the behavior of a firm." "Theories of the Firm: Marginalist, Behavioral, Managerial," *American Economic Review* 57 (March 1967): 9.

The inescapable difficulty which the question of "explanation" poses for the Machlup-Freidman approach is conspicuously apparent in this struggle with ambiguity. The theorist's reference to any fictitious constructs he may have used of course "explains" what *he* did--or his own mental processes--in relating the variables here described as "cause and effect." But Machlup's view that these mental processes, insofar as they deal with constructs that falsify what we know about firms, can serve to explain *actual relations involving firms* (that is, relations between cost and price) is something which itself defies explanation. It is precisely because this procedure is "altogether different from an explanation of the behavior of the firm" that it *cannot* explain such price-cost relationships. If the "false" is to be regarded as in any sense explanatory of reality, then plainly a new term is needed to denote what is usually meant by "explanation".

It is noteworthy that Machlup himself considers the behavior of *real* firms in a competitive industry and argues that, with respect to its impact on the direction of market changes, it does not significantly depart from what would be expected of the fictitious firm, that is, one that single-mindedly pursued maximum profits. (Cf. Machlup, p. 12 ff.) This of course is to descend from the level of pure theory to an attempt at genuine explanation. But then what purpose is served by treating industry behavior as the product of single-minded maximizing agents? One can simply replace

153

this with the statement: *"Some* firms in a competitive industry maximize profit" (while others, of course, do not seek losses). Or, probably more realistically, one can abandon reference to profit maximization altogether. With respect to the prediction of the *mere direction* of market changes, there is no inference that can be drawn from the maximization assumption (whether applied to some or all firms) that cannot be drawn from the assumption that competitive firms simply seek to "make money"--meaning that they exploit advantages to increase their profit in degrees unspecified. Nonetheless, with respect to the prediction as stated, Machlup not only insists on the retention of the concept of the maximizing firm as "a postulate in a web of logical connections" but also seeks to preserve the notion that mental processes employing such fictitious constructs "explain" experience.

28. Machlup, "Operationalism and Pure Theory in Economics," in *Structure,* ed. Krupp, p. 66.

29. D.V.T. Bear and Daniel Orr, "Logic and Expediency in Economic Theorizing," *Journal of Political Economy,* 75 (April 1967): 188-96. The argument considered below is found on pp. 194-96.

30. Ibid., p. 195.

31. I discussed this point in my article "On 'The Methodology,'" pp. 570-73. In the literature of the philosophy of science the term "theory" often is reserved exclusively for the hypothesis with unobservable assumptions. This contrasts with a "law", where all elements of the hypothesis are observable.

32. Bear and Orr give no justification for their assertion that the conditions of perfect competition are "inadequately rationalized" or, more precisely, for the view that the model is so inadequately rationalized that no standards are afforded for determining when significant departures from the model exist. This extraordinary view is indeed contradicted by their own phraseology, that is, their reference to "the predictions from a perfectly competitive model." If the model were as inadequately rationalized as their treatment implied, there would be little or no basis for drawing predictions from the model.

Part Six   How Theories are Verified

The two readings in this part deal with the important issue of whether or not assumptions need to be "testable" and "tested" in the field of economics. Both Fritz Machlup and Chris Archibald outline the history of this debate which began in the nineteenth century with Senior, J.S. Mill, and Cairnes, and (in one sense) reached a watershed with Milton Friedman's famous essay, "The Methodology of Positive Economics," noted in Part Four of this reader.

Archibald's paper reviews three essays on the state of economic science written by T.C. Koopmans in 1957. Koopmans is critical of Friedman's views that the test of the theory be based on predictions of the theory and not the assumptions; in the process Koopmans agrees with economists like T.W. Hutchison who support the verification of at least some assumptions or postulates. One useful feature of Archibald's paper is his history of four uses or definitions of "assumptions" in economics. Many other writers fail to make such a distinction and as a result their arguments often apply only if a certain definition is used. As he points out some classes of assumptions may need verification, while others may not.

Along these lines of investigation, Machlup differentiates among fundamental assumptions such as people act rationally, specific assumptions such as expenditures for table salt are a small portion of most households' annual budgets, and deduced low-level hypotheses such as a reduction in the price of table salt will not result in a proportionate increase in salt consumption. Fundamental assumptions, he argues, do not require independent empirical tests but specific assumptions and deduced hypotheses should be empirically testable. When his article first appeared, it led to a literary debate between himself and T.W. Hutchison.

The reader wanting to examine further the evolution of the debate over verification of assumptions, predictions, or both, should refer to the discussion in the texts by M. Blaug or H. Katouzian. There, in footnotes and the body of the books, the reader will find references which are too numerous to re-list here.

Statistical testing of a model and its assumption are mostly based either on the Likelihood Ratio (LR), Wald, or Lagrange Multiplier (LM) principle. The LR approach directly compares the null and alternative hypothesis on an equal basis. The Wald testing method starts at the alternative hypothesis and examines the movement toward the null hypothesis. Finally, the LM principle begins at the null hypothesis and examines whether the movement toward the alternative hypothesis would lead to an improvement. The LM test is generally computationally simpler and more convenient to apply than either the Wald or Likelihood Ratio test, especially when the model to be tested is complex. A review of the potential use of the LM principle to a wide range of econometric problems can be found in Engle (1982). All these testing procedures cannot always be applied when testing two alternative (non-nested) models neither of which is a special case of the other. A survey of alternative non-nested tests can be found in James MacKinnon (1982).

9 The Problem of Verification in Economics

Fritz Machlup*

I

It will be well for us first to clear the ground lest we get lost in the rubble of past discussions. To clear the ground is, above all, to come to a decision as to what we mean by verification and what it can and cannot do for our research and analysis.

The Meaning of Verification

A good book of synonyms will have the verb "verify" associated with the more pretentious verbs "prove," "demonstrate," "establish," "ascertain," "confirm," and with the more modest verbs "check" and "test." The verbs in the former group would usually be followed by "that"--"we shall prove that..."--the verbs in the latter group by a "whether"--"we shall check whether...." Besides this difference between "verify that" and "verify whether," there is the difference between verification as a process and verification as an affirmative result of that process. By using *"test"* for the former and *"confirmation"* for the latter we may avoid confusion. Where the distinction is not necessary, "verification" is an appropriate weasel-word, meaning both test and confirmation.

Verification in research and analysis may refer to many things including the correctness of mathematical and logical arguments, the applicability of formulas and equations, the trustworthiness of reports, the authenticity of documents, the genuineness of artifacts or relics, the adequacy of reproductions, translations and paraphrases, the accuracy of historical and statistical accounts, the corroboration of reported events, the completeness in the enumeration of circumstances in a concrete situation, the reliability and exactness of observations, the reproducibility of experiments, the explanatory of predictive value of· generalizations. For each of these pursuits, the term verification is used in various disciplines. But we intend to confine ourselves to the last one mentioned: the verification of the explanatory or predictive value of hypothetical generalizations.

Although definitions are sometimes a nuisance rather than an

Reprinted by permission from the *Southern Economic Journal*, 22 (1955), 1-21.

aid, I shall try my hand at one, and say that verification in the sense most relevant to us--the testing of generalizations--is *a procedure designed to find out whether a set of data of observation about a class of phenomena is obtainable and can be reconciled with a particular set of hypothetical generalizations about this class of phenomena.*

Truth and Reality

I have carefully avoided the words "truth" and "reality," although the Latin *veritas* forms the root of the term defined. I eschewed references to truth and reality in order to stay out of strictly epistemological and ontological controversies. Not that such discussions would be uninteresting or unimportant; he who never studies metaphysical questions, and even prides himself on his unconcern with metaphysics, often does not know how much in fact he talks about it. To stay away from metaphysics one has to know a good bit about it.

The function of words chosen--testing, checking, confirming--is precisely to enable us to leave the concepts of truth and reality in the background. If I should slip occasionally and say that a proposition is "true" or a phenomenon is "real," this should be taken merely as an unguarded way of speaking; for I mean to say only that there seems to be considerable "support" or "evidence" for the proposition in view of a marked *correspondence* or consistency between that proposition and statements about particular observations.

Special and General Hypotheses

My definition of verification related only to hypothetical generalizations. But the status of *special hypotheses about single events or unique situations* (and their causes, effects, and interrelations) also calls for examination, for it is with these that economic history and most of applied economics are concerned. Such special hypotheses--to establish the "facts"--are of course also subject to verification, but the rules and techniques are somewhat different from those of the verification of general hypotheses.

In a murder case we ask "who done it?" and the answer requires the weighing of several alternative special hypotheses. Such special hypotheses may be mental constructions of unobserved occurrences which could have taken place in conjunction with occurrences observed or conclusively inferred. It is an accepted rule that a special hypothesis will be rejected if it is contradicted by a single inconsistency between a firmly established observation and any of the things that follow logically from the combination of the special hypothesis and the factual assumptions of the argument.

158

But this weighing and testing of special hypotheses in the light of the known circumstances of the case always involves numerous *general* hypotheses. For example, the generalization that "if a man is at one place he cannot at the same time be at another place" may be of utmost importance in verifying a suspicion that Mr. X was the murderer. And whenever observations have to be interpreted and special hypotheses applied to reach a conclusion about what are the "concrete facts," the argument will presuppose the acceptance of numerous general theories or hypotheses linking two or more (observed or inferred) "facts" as possible (or probable) causes and effects. This is the reason why it has to be said over and over again that most of the facts of history are based on previously formed general hypotheses or theories. Although this has been an important theme in the discussion of the relation between theory and history, and one of the central issues in the *Methodenstreit* in economics, it is not an issue in our discussion today. At the moment we are concerned with the verification of general hypotheses and theories, not of propositions concerning individual events or conditions at a particular time and place. But this much ought to be said here: to establish or verify "historical facts," we must rely on the acceptance of numerous general hypotheses (theories); and to verify general hypotheses we must rely on the acceptance of numerous data representing "facts" observed or inferred at various times and places. We always must take something for granted, no matter how averse we are to "preconceptions."

Theories, Hypotheses, Hunches, Assumptions, Postulates

No fixed lines can be drawn between theories, hypotheses, and mere hunches, the differences being at best those of degree. There are degrees of vagueness in formulation, degrees of confidence or strength of belief in what is posed or stated, degrees of acceptance among experts, and degrees of comprehensiveness or range of applicability.[1]

A hunch is usually vague, sometimes novel, original, often incompletely formulated; perhaps more tentative than a hypothesis, although the difference may lie just in the modesty of the analyst. A hypothesis may likewise be very tentative; indeed, some hypotheses are introduced only for didactic purposes, as provisional steps in an argument, in full knowledge of their inapplicability to any concrete situation and perhaps in preparation for a preferred hypothesis. Distinctions between hypotheses and theories have been suggested in terms of the strength of belief in their applicability or of the comprehensiveness (range) of their applicability.[2] But so often are the words theory and hypothesis used interchangeably that there is not much point in laboring any distinguishing criteria.

159

Perhaps it should be stressed that every hypothesis may have the status of an "assumption" in a logical argument. An assumption of a rather general nature which is posited as a "principle" for an argument or for a whole system of thought, but is neither self-evident nor proved, is often called a "postulate." Just as there may be a connotation of tentativeness in the word "hypothesis," there may be a connotation of arbitrariness in the word "postulate."[3] But since no fundamental assumption in an empirical discipline is definitive, and since all are more or less arbitrary, it is useless to insist on subtle distinctions which are (for good reasons) disregarded by most participants in the discussion.[4]

Confirmation versus Non-Disconfirmation

How is a hypothesis verified? The hypothesis is *tested* by a two-step procedure: first deducing from it and the factual assumptions with which it is combined all the conclusions that can be inferred, and second, confronting these conclusions with data obtained from observation of the phenomena concerned. The hypothesis is *confirmed* if reasonable correspondence is found between the deduced and the observed, or more correctly, if no irreconcilable contradiction is found between the deduced and the observed. Absence of contradictory evidence, a finding of non-contradiction, is really a negation of a negation: indeed, one calls a hypothesis "confirmed" when it is merely *not* disconfirmed.

Thus, the procedure of verification may yield findings compelling the rejection of the tested hypothesis, but never findings that can "prove" its correctness, adequacy or applicability.[5] As in a continuing sports championship conducted by elimination rules, where the winner stays in the game as long as he is not defeated but can always be challenged for another contest, no empirical hypothesis is safe forever; it can always be challenged for another test and may be knocked out at any time. The test results, at best, in a "confirmation till next time."

Several logicians use the word "falsification" for a finding of irreconcilable contradiction; and since a hypothesis can be definitely refuted or "falsified," but not definitely confirmed or "verified," some logicians have urged that we speak only of "falsifiable," not of verifiable propositions. Because the word "falsification" has a double meaning, I prefer to speak of refutation or disconfirmation. But the dictim is surely right: testing an empirical hypothesis results either in its diconfirmation or its non-disconfirmation, never in its definitive confirmation.

Even if a definitive confirmation is never possible, the number of tests which a hypothesis has survived in good shape

160

will have a bearing on the confidence people have in its "correctness." A hypothesis confirmed and re-confirmed any number of times will have a more loyal following than one only rarely exposed to the test of experience. But the strength of belief in a hypothesis depends, even more than on any direct empirical tests that it may have survived, on the place it holds within a hierarchical system of inter-related hypotheses. But this is another matter, to be discussed a little later.

Nothing that I have said thus far would, I believe, be objected to by any modern logician, philosopher of science, or scientist. While all points mentioned were once controversial, the combat has moved on to other issues, and only a few stragglers and latecomers on the battlefield of methodology mistake the rubble left from long ago for the marks of present fighting. So we shall move on to issues on which controversy continues.

II

Which kinds of propositions can be verified, and which cannot? May unverified and unverifiable propositions be legitimately retained in a scientific system? Or should all scientific propositions be verified or at least verifiable? These are among the controversial issues--though my own views are so decided that I cannot see how intelligent people can still quarrel about them, and I have come to believe that all good men think as I do, and only a few misguided creatures think otherwise. But I shall restrain my convictions for a while.

Criticizing extreme positions is a safe pastime because one may be sure of the support of a majority. But it is not for this reason but for the sake of a clear exposition that I begin with the presentation of the positions which *extreme apriorism,* on the one side, and *ultra-empiricism,* on the other side, take concerning the problem of verification in economics.

Pure, Exact, and Aprioristic Economics

Writers on the one side of this issue contend that economic science is a system of *a priori* truths, a product of pure reason,[6] an exact science reaching laws as universal as those of mathematics,[7] a purely axiomatic discipline,[8] a system of pure deductions from a series of postulates,[9] not open to any verification or refutation on the ground of experience.[10]

We must not attribute to all writers whose statements were here quoted or paraphrased the same epistemological views. While for Mises, for example, even the fundamental postulates are *a priori* truths, necessities of thinking,[11] for Robbins they are "assumptions involving in some way simple and indisputable facts

of experience."[12]   But most of the experience in point is not
capable of being recorded from external (objective) observation;
instead, it is immediate, inner experience. Hence, if verification
is recognized only where the test involves objective sense-exper-
ience, the chief assumptions of economics, even if "empirical,"
are not independently verifiable propostions.

This methodological position, either asserting an *a priori*
character of all propositions of economic theory or at least denying the independent objective verifiability of the fundamental
assumptions, had been vigorously stated in the last century by
Senior[13] and Cairnes,[14] but in essential respects it goes back to
John Stuart Mill.

Mill, the great master and expositor of inductive logic, had
this to say on the method of investigation in political economy:

> Since... it is vain to hope that truth can be arrived at,
> either in Political Economy or in any other department of
> the social science, while we look at the facts in the con-
> crete, clothed in all the complexity with which nature has
> surrounded them, and endeavour to elicit a general law by a
> process of induction from a comparison of details; there re-
> mains no other method than the *a priori* one, or that
> of 'abstract speculation.'[15]

> By the method *a priori* we mean ... reasoning from
> an assumed hypothesis; which is not a practice confined to
> mathematics, but is of the essence of all science which ad-
> mits of general reasoning at all. To verify the hypothesis
> itself *a posteriori,* that is, to examine whether the
> facts of any actual case are in accordance with it, is no
> part of the business of science at all but of the *appli-
> cation* of science.[16]

This does not mean that Mill rejects attempts to verify the
results of economic analysis; on the contrary,

> We cannot ... too carefully endeavor to verify our theory,
> by comparing, in the particular cases to which we have
> access, the results which it would have led us to predict,
> with the most trustworthy accounts we can obtain of those
> which have been actually realized.[17]

The point to emphasize is that Mill does not propose to put
the *assumptions* of economic theory to empirical tests, but
only the *predicted results that are deduced from them*. And
this, I submit, is what all the proponents of pure, exact, or
aprioristic economic theory had in mind, however provocative
their contentions sounded.[18] Their objection was to verifying the
basic assumptions in isolation.

162

Opposed to these tenets are the ultra-empiricists. "Empiricist" is a word of praise to some, a word of abuse to others. This is due to the fact that there are many degrees of empiricism. Some economists regard themselves as "empiricists" merely because they oppose radical apriorism and stress the dependence of theory on experience (in the widest sense of the word); others, because they demand that the results deduced with the aid of theory be compared with observational data whenever possible; others, because they are themselves chiefly concerned with the interpretation of data, with the testing of hypotheses and with the estimates of factual relationships; others, because they are themselves engaged in the collection of data or perhaps even in "field" work designed to produce "raw" data; others, because they refuse to recognize the legitimacy of employing at any level of analysis propositions not independently verifiable. It is the last group which I call the ultra-empiricists.[19] Then there are the ultra-ultra-empiricists who go even further and insist on independent verification of all assumptions by objective data obtained through sense observation.

The ultra-empiricist position is most sharply reflected in the many attacks on the "assumptions" of economic theory. These assumptions are decried as unverified, unverifiable, imaginary, unrealistic. And the hypothetico-deductive system built upon the realistic or unverifiable assumptions is condemned either as deceptive or as devoid of empirical content,[20] without predictive or explanatory significance,[21] without application to problems or data of the real world.[22] Why deceptive? Because from wrong assumptions only wrong conclusions follow. Why without empirical significance? Because, in the words of the logician Wittgenstein, "from a tautology only tautologies follow."[23]

If the ultra-empiricists reject the basic assumptions of economic theory because they are not independently verified, and reject any theoretical system that is built on unverified or unverifiable assumptions, what is the alternative they offer? A program that begins with facts rather than assumptions.[24] What facts? Those obtained "by statistical investigations, questionnaires to consumers and entrepreneurs, the examination of family budgets and the like."[25] It is in research of this sort that the ultra-empiricists see "the only possible scientific method open" to the economist.[26]

This, again, is the essence of the ultra-empiricist position on verification: the ultra-empiricist is so distrustful of deductive systems of thought that he is not satisfied with the indirect verification of hypotheses, that is, with tests showing that the results deduced (from these hypotheses and certain factual assumptions) are in approximate correspondence with reliable observational data; instead, he insists on the independent verification of all the assumptions, hypothetical as well as factual, perhaps even of each intermediate step in the analysis. To him "testable" means "directly testable by objective data obtained by sense observation," and propositions which are in this sense "non-testable" are detestable to him.

The Testability of Fundamental Assumptions

The error in the antitheoretical empiricist position lies in the failure to see the difference between *fundamental* (heuristic) hypotheses, which are not independently testable, and *specific* (factual) assumptions, which are supposed to correspond to observed facts or conditions; or the differences between hypotheses on different levels of generality and, hence, of different degrees of testability.

The fundamental hypotheses are also called by several other names, some of which convey a better idea of their methodological status: "heuristic principles" (because they serve as useful guides in the analysis), "basic postulates" (because they are not to be challenged for the time being), "useful fictions" (because they need not conform to "facts" but only be useful in "as if" reasoning), "procedural rules" (because they are resolutions about the analytical procedure to be followed), "definitional assumptions" (because they are treated like purely analytical conventions).

A fundamental hypothesis serves to bring together under a common principle of explanation vast numbers of very diverse observations, masses of data of apparently very different sort, phenomena that would otherwise seem to have nothing in common. Problems like the explanation of the movements in wages in 13th and 14th century Europe, of the prices of spices in 16th century Venice, of the effects of the capital flows to Argentina in the 19th century, of the consequences of German reparation payments and of the devaluation of the dollar in the 1930s; problems like the prediction of effects of the new American quota on Swiss watches, of the new tax laws, of the increase in minimum wage rates, and so forth--problems of such dissimilarity can all be tackled by the use of the same fundamental hypotheses. If these hypotheses are successful in this task and give more satisfactory results than other modes of treatment could, then we accept them and stick by them as long as there is nothing better--which my be forever.

That there is no way of subjecting fundamental assumptions to independent verification should be no cause of disturbance. It does not disturb the workers in the discipline which most social scientists so greatly respect and envy for its opportunities of

164

verification: physical science. The whole system of physical mechanics rests on such fundamental assumptions: Newton's three laws of motion are postulates or procedural rules for which no experimental verification is possible or required; and, as Einstein put it, "No one of the assumptions can be isolated for separate testing." For, he went on to say, "physical concepts are free creations of the human mind, and are not, however it may seem, uniquely determined by the external world."[27]

Much has been written about the meaning of "explanation." Some have said that the mere *description* of regularities in the co-existence and co-variation of observed phenomena is all we can do and will be accepted as an *explanation* when we are sufficiently used to the regularities described.[28] There is something to this view; but mere resignation to the fact that "it always has been so" will not for long pass as explanation for searching minds. The feeling of relief and satisfied curiosity--often expressed in the joyous exclamation "ah haahh!"--comes to most analysts only when the observed regularities can be deduced from general principles which are also the starting point--foundation or apex, as you like--of many other chains of causal derivation. This is why Margenau, another physicist, said that an explanation involves a "progression into the constructional domain. We explain by going 'beyond phenomena.'"[29] But this clearly implies that the explanatory general assumptions cannot be empirically verifiable in isolation.

Logicians and philosophers of science have long tried to make this perfectly clear. Although appeals to authority are ordinarily resorted to only where an expositor has failed to convince his audience, I cannot resist the temptation to quote two authorities on my subject. Here is how the American philosopher Josiah Royce put it:

One often meets with the remark that a scientific hypothesis must be such as to be more or less completely capable of verification or of refutation by experience. The remark is sound. But equally sound it is to say that a hypothesis which, just as it is made, is, without further deductive reasoning, capable of receiving direct refutation or verification, *is not nearly as valuable to any science as is a hypothesis whose verification, so far as they occur at all, are only possible indirectly, and through the mediation of a considerable deductive theory,* whereby the consequences of the hypothesis are first worked out, and then submitted to test.[30]

And here is the same idea in the words of the British philosopher of science, Richard B. Braithwaite:

For science, as it advances, does not rest content with establishing simple generalizations from observable facts. It tries to explain these lowest-level generalizations by deducing them from more general hypotheses at a higher level... As the hierarchy of hypotheses of increasing generality rises, the concepts with which the hypotheses are concerned cease to be properties of things which are directly observable, and instead become 'theoretical' concepts--atoms, electrons, fields of force, genes, unconscious mental processes--which are connected to the observable facts by complicated logical relationships.[31]

And he states that "the empirical testing of the deductive system is effected by testing the lowest-level hypotheses in the system."[32]

Assumptions in Economics, Pure and Applied

Examples of *fundamental assumptions* or "high-level generalizations" in economic theory are that people act rationally, try to make the most of their opportunities, and are able to arrange their preferences in a consistent order; that entrepreneurs prefer more profit to less profit with equal risk.[33] These are assumptions which, though empirically meaningful, require no independent empirical tests but may be significant steps in arguments reaching conclusions which are empirically testable.

Examples of *specific assumptions* are that the expenditures for table salt are a small portion of most households' annual budgets; that the member banks are holding very large excess reserves with the Federal Reserve Banks; that there is a quota for the importation of sugar which is fully utilized. Examples of *deduced "low-level hypotheses"* are that a reduction in the price of table salt will not result in a proportionate increase in salt consumption; that a reduction in the discount rates of the Federal Reserve Banks will at such times not result in an increase in the member banks' lending activities; that a reduction in sugar prices abroad will not result in a reduction of domestic sugar prices. All these and similar specific assumptions and low-level hypotheses are empirically testable.

Perhaps a few additional comments should be made concerning the fundamental assumptions, particularly the postulate of rational action, the "economic principle" of aiming at the attainment of a maximum given ends. Any independent test of this assumption by reference to objective *sense*-experience is obviously impossible. Those who accept findings of introspection as sufficient evidence may contend that the fundamental assumption can be, and constantly is, verified. Those who accept findings of interrogation (that is, replies to questions put to large numbers of introspectors) as "objective" evidence may content that the assumption of "maximizing behavior" is independently testable. But such a test would be gratuitous, if not misleading. For the fundamental assumption may be understood as an idealization with constructs so far removed from operational concepts that contradiction by testimony is ruled out; or even as a complete fiction with only one claim: that reasoning *as if* it were realized is helpful in the interpretation of observations.[34]

Economists who are still suspicious of non-verifiable assumptions, and worry about the legitimacy of using them, may be reassured by this admission: The fact that fundamental assumptions are not directly testable and cannot be refuted by empirical investigation does not mean that they are beyond the pale of the so-called "principle of permanent control," that is, beyond possible challenge, modification or rejection. These assumptions may well be rejected, but only together with the theoretical system of which they are a part, and only when a more satisfactory system is put in its place; in Conant's words, "a theory is only overthrown by a better theory, never merely by contradictory facts."[35]

III

What I have said and quoted about assumptions and hypotheses on various "levels" of abstraction may itself be too abstract, too remote from our ordinary terms of discourse, to be meaningful to many of us. Perhaps it will be helpful to try a graphical presentation of a simple model of an analytical system combining assumptions of various types.

A Model of an Analytical Apparatus

The design for the model was suggested by the usual metaphors about an analytical "apparatus," "machine," or "engine of pure theory." Something goes into a machine and something comes out. In this case the input is an assumption concerning some "change" occurring and causing other things to happen, and the output is the "Deduced Change," the conclusion of the (mental) operation. The machine with all its parts furnishes the connection between the "assumed cause," the input, and the "deduced effect," the outcome. The main point of this model is that *the machine is a construction of our mind, while the assumed and deduced changes should correspond to observed phenomena, to data of observation, if the machine is to serve as an instrument of explanation or prediction.* In explantions the analytical machine helps select an adequate "cause" for an observed change; in predictions it helps find a probable "effect" of an observed change.[36]

The machine consists of many parts, all of which represent

167

assumptions or hypotheses of different degrees of generality. The so-called *fundamental assumptions* are a fixed part of the machine; they make the machine what it is; they cannot be changed without changing the character of the entire machine. All other parts are exchangeable, like coils, relays, spools, wires, tapes, cylinders, records, or mats, something that can be selected and put in, and again taken out to be replaced by a different piece of the set. These exchangeable parts represent *assumptions about the conditions* under which the Assumed Change must operate. Some of the parts are exchanged all the time, some less frequently, some only seldom. Parts of type A, the Assumed Conditions as to "type of case," are most frequently exchanged. Parts of type B, the Assumed Conditions as to "type of setting," will stay in the machine for a longer time and there need be less variety in the set from which they are selected. Parts of type C, the Assumed Conditions as to "type of economy," are least exchangeable, and there will be only a small assortment of alternative pieces to choose from.

Now we shall leave the engineering analogies aside and discuss the status of all these assumptions regarding the operational and observational possibilities and the requirements of verification.

Verified Changes under Unverified Conditions

Both the Assumed Change and the Deduced Change should be empirically verifiable through correspondence with data of observation. At least one of the two has to be verifiable if the analysis is to be applied to concrete cases. Hence the concepts employed to describe the changes should, if possible, be operational. This raises no difficulty in the case of most kinds of *Assumed Change* in whose effects we are interested, for example: changes in tax rates, customs duties, foreign-exchange rates, wage rates, price supports, price ceilings, discount rates, open-market policies, credit lines, government expenditures, agricultural crops—matters covered in reports and records. There are difficulties concerning some other kinds of Assumed Change, such as improvements in technology, greater optimism, changed tastes for particular goods—things for which recorded data are often unavailable. As regards the *Deduced Change* the requirement that it be operational will usually be met, because we are interested chiefly in effects upon prices, output, income, employment, etc.,—magnitudes reported in statistical series of some sort. To be sure, the figures may be unreliable and the statistical concepts may not be exact counterparts to the analytical concepts, but we cannot be too fussy and must be satisfied with what we can get.

In principle we want both Assumed Change and Deduced Change to be capable of being compared with recorded data so that the correspondence between the theory and the data can be checked. The analysis would be neither wrong nor invalid, but it would not be very useful if it were never possible to identify the concrete phenomena, events, and situations, to which it is supposed to apply. Once we have confidence in the whole theoretical system, we are willing to apply it to concrete cases even where only one of the two "changes," either the "cause" or the "effect," is identifiable in practice, rather than both. For example, we are

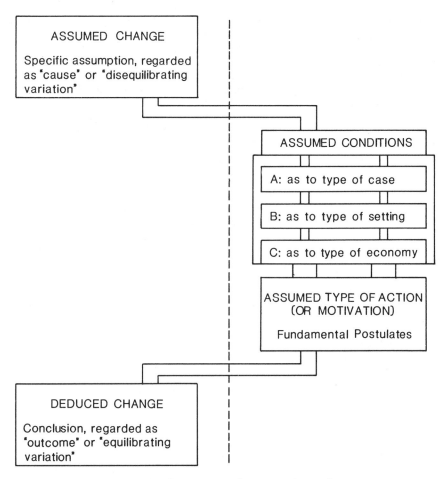

Fig. 1 A Model of the Use of An Analytical Apparatus

Note: On the right side is the "machine of pure theory," a mental *construction* for heuristic purposes; on the left side are assumptions of independent and dependent variables whose *correspondence* with data of observation may be tested.

169

prepared to base policy decisions on explanations or predictions where one of the phenomena cannot be isolated in observation from the complex of simultaneous variations. For purposes of verification of the entire theory, however, we shall have to identify both the phenomena represented by the Assumed Change and the Deduced Change--although such verification may be practical only on rare occasions.

We need not be particularly strict concerning the verification of the *Assumed Conditions*. Regarding them, a casual, perhaps even impressionistic empiricism will do, at least for most types of problems. The Assumed Conditions refer to personal characteristics, technological or organizational circumstances, market forms, enduring institutions--things of rather varied nature. Few of the Conditions are observable, except through communication of interpretations involving a good deal of theorizing by the parties concerned. Often the Conditions are not even specified in detail, but somehow taken for granted by analysts working a familiar milieu. All of the Conditions are hypothetical parameters, assumed to prevail at least for the duration of the process comprising all the actions, interactions and repercussions through which the Assumed Change is supposed to cause the Deduced Change.

Assumed Conditions of Type A, that is, as to *"type of case,"* refer to conditions which may vary from case to case and influence the outcome significantly, but are sufficiently common to justify the construction of "types" for theoretical analysis. Here is a list of examples: type of goods involved (durable, non-durable, perishable; inferior, non-inferior; taking up substantial or negligible parts of buyer's budget; substitutable, complementary; etc.); cost conditions (marginal cost decreasing, constant, increasing; joint costs, etc.); elasticity of supply or demand (positive, negative, relatively large, unity, less than unity); market position (perfect, imperfect polypoly; collusive, uncoordinated oligopoly; perfect, imperfect monopoly); entry (perfect, imperfect pliopoly); expectations (elastic, inelastic; bullish, bearish; certain, uncertain); consumption propensity (greater, smaller than unity); elasticity of liquidity preference (infinite, less than infinite, zero).

Assumed Conditions of Type B, that is, as to "type of setting," refer to conditions which may change over brief periods of time--say, with a change of government or of the political situation, or during the business cycle--and are apt to influence the outcome in definite directions. A list of examples will indicate what is meant by conditions prevailing under the current "setting"; general business outlook (boom spirit, depression pessimism); bank credit availability (banks loaned up, large excess reserves); central bank policy (ready to monetize government securities, determined to maintain easy money policy, willing to let interest rates rise); fiscal policy (expenditures fixed, adjusted to tax revenues, geared to unemployment figures; tax rates fixed, adjusted to maintain revenue, etc.); farm program (support prices fixed, flexible within limits, etc.); antitrust policy (vigorous prosecution of cartelization, etc.); foreign aid program; stabilization fund rules; trade union policies.

Assumed Conditions of Type C, that is, as to "*type of economy*," refer to conditions which may vary from country to country and over larger periods of time, but may be assumed to be "settled" for a sufficiently large number of cases to justify taking these conditions as constant. Examples include legal and social institutions; private property; freedom of contract; corporation law; patent system; transportation system; enforcement of contracts; ethics of law violations; social customs and usages; monetary system (gold standard, check system, cash holding habits).

Assumed Conditions are exchangeable because the effects of an Assumed Change may have to be analysed under a variety of conditions: for example, with different degrees or forms of competition, different credit policies, different tax structures, different trade union policies, etc. But it may also be expedient, depending on the problem at hand, to regard a variation of an Assumed Condition as an Assumed Change, and *vice versa*. For example, the problem may concern the effects of a wage rate increase under various market conditions or, instead, the effects of a change in market position under conditions of automatic wage escalation; the effects of a change in monetary policy with different tax structure, or the effects of a change in the tax structure under different monetary policies.

After listing the many examples of the various types of Assumed Conditions it will probably be agreed that a rigid verification requirement would be out of place. Usually the judgment of the analyst will suffice even if he cannot support it with more than the most circumstantial evidence or mere "impressions." Suppose he deals with a simple cost-price-output problem in a large industry, how will the analyst determine what "type of case" it is with regard to "market position?" Lacking the relevant information, he may first try to work with a model of perfect polypoly[37]--although he knows well that this cannot fit the real situation--and will note whether his deduced results will be far off the mark. He may find the results reasonably close to the observed data and may leave it at that. For to work with a more "realistic" assumption may call for so many additional assumptions for which no relevant information is available that it is preferable and unobjectionable to continue with a hypothesis contrary to fact. When a simpler hypothesis, though obviously unrealistic,

gives consistently satisfactory results, one need not bother with
more complicated, more realistic hypotheses.

Ideal Type of Action, Unverified but Understood

While solid empirical verification is indicated for the Assumed
Change, and casual empirical judgments are indicated for the
Assumed Conditions, the *Assumed Type of Action* forms
the fundamental postulates of economic analysis and thus is not
subject to a requirement of independent verification.

Various names have been suggested for the fundamental postulates of economic theory: "economic principle," "maximization
principle," "assumption of rationality," "law of motivation," and
others. And their logical nature has been characterized in various ways: they are regarded as "self-evident propositions,"
"axioms," "*a priori* truths," "truisms," "tautologies," "definitions," "rigid laws," "rules of procedure," "resolutions,"
"working hypotheses," "useful fictions," "ideal types," "heuristic
mental constructs," indisputable facts of experience," "facts of
immediate experience," "data of introspective observation," "private empirical data," "typical behavior patterns," and so forth.

Some of these characteristics are equivalent to or consistent
with each other, but some are not. How can a proposition be both
a priori and empirical, both a definition and a fact of experience? While this cannot be, the distinctions in this particular
instance are so fine that conflicts of interpretation seem unavoidable. Logicians have long debated the possibility of propositions
being synthetic and yet *a priori*, and physicists are still
not quite agreed whether the "laws" of mechanics are analytical
definitions or empirical facts. The late philosopher Felix
Kaufmann introduced as a middle category the so-called "rules of
procedure," which are neither synthetic in the sense that they
are falsifiable by contravening observations nor *a priori* in
the sense that they are independent of experience;[38] they are
and remain accepted as long as they have heuristic value, but
will be rejected in favor of other rules (assumptions) which seem
to serve their explanatory functions more successfully.

If this debate has been going on in the natural sciences, how
could it be avoided in the social sciences? If issues about "self-
evident," "inescapable," or "indisputable" insights arose concerning the physical world, how much more pertinent are such
issues in the explanation of human action, where man is both
observer and subject of observation! This, indeed, is the essential difference between the natural and the social sciences: that
in the latter the facts, the data of "observation," are themselves
results of interpretations of human actions by human actors.[39]
And this imposes on the social sciences a requirement which does

172

not exist in the natural sciences: that all types of action that are used in the abstract models constructed for purposes of analysis be "understandable" to most of us in the sense that we could conceive of sensible men acting (sometimes at least) in the way postulated by the ideal type in question. This is the crux of Max Weber's methodology of the social sciences, and was recently given a refined and most convincing formulation of Alfred Schuetz.[40]

Schuetz promulgates three postulates guiding model construction in the social sciences: the postulates of "logical consistency," of "subjective interpretation," and of "adequacy." The second and third of these postulates are particularly relevant here:

> In order to explain human actions the scientist has to ask what model of an individual mind can be constructed and what typical contents must be attributed to it in order to explain the observed facts as the result of the activity of such a mind in an understandable relation. The compliance with this postulate warrants the possibility of referring all kinds of human action or their result to the subjective meaning such action or result of an action had for the actor.

> Each term in a scientific model of human action must be constructed in such a way that a human act performed within the life world by an individual actor in the way indicated by the typical construct would be understandable for the actor himself as well as for his fellowmen in terms of common-sense interpretation of everyday life. Compliance with this postulate warrants the consistency of the constructs of the social scientist with the constructs of common-sense experience of the social reality.[41]

Thus, the fundamental assumptions of economic theory are not subject to a requirement of independent empirical verification, but instead to a requirement of understandability in the sense in which man can understand the actions of fellowmen.[42]

IV

We are ready to summarize our conclusions concerning verification of the assumptions of economic theory. Then we shall briefly comment on the verification of particular economic theories applied to predict future events, and on the verification of strictly empirical hypotheses.

Verifying the Assumptions

First to summarize: We need not worry about independent verifications of the fundamental assumptions, the Assumed Type of

Action; we need not be very particular about the independent verifications of the other intervening assumptions, the Assumed Conditions, because judgment based on casual empiricism will suffice for them; we should insist on strict independent verifications of the assumption selected as Assumed Change and of the conclusion derived as Deduced Change; not that the theory would be wrong otherwise, but it cannot be applied unless the phenomena to which it is supposed to apply are identifiable. *Simultaneous verifications of Assumed Change and Deduced Change count as verification--in the sense of non-disconfirmation--of the theory as a whole.*

Now it is clear why some writers insisted on the *a priori* nature of the theory and at the same time on its empirical value for the area of Applied Economics; for one may, if one wishes, regard the theory, or model, as a construction *a priori,* and the directions for its use, the instructions for its applications,[43] as an empirical appendage in need of verification. Returning to the analogy of the analytical machine, one may say that the machine and its parts are always "correct," regardless of what goes on around us, whereas the *choice* of the exchangeable parts and the *identification* of the events corresponding to the Assumed and Deduced changes may be wrong.

Testing the Predictive Values of Theories

We have examined the empiricists' charges against the theorists--charges of contemptuous neglect of the requirement of verification--and have concluded that these charges must be dismissed insofar as they refer to a failure to verify all assumptions directly and in isolation from the rest of the theory. We must yet examine another count of the charge of insufficient attention to verification: an alleged failure to test the correspondence between Deduced (predicted) and Observed outcomes. These kinds of tests are obligatory.

If verification of a theory takes the form of testing whether predictions based on that theory actually come true, one might think that this can be done in economics no less than in the physical sciences. It cannot, alas, because of the non-reproducibility of the "experiments" or observed situations and courses of events in the economy. For, while certain types of events, or "changes," recur in the economy often enough, they recur rarely under the same conditions. If some significant circumstances are different whenever a phenomenon of the same class recurs, each recurrence is virtually a "single occurrence." Economic theory applied to single events, or to situations significantly different from one another, cannot be tested as conclusively as can physical theory applied to reproducible occurrences and conditions.

174

Not long ago I was challenged to admit that my theories, even though applied to ever-changing circumstances, could be tested provided I were prepared to make unconditional predictions which could be compared with actual outcomes. Of course, I could only dare make unconditional predictions--without hedging about probability and confidence limits--where I was absolutely certain that my diagnosis of the situation (i.e., of *all* relevant circumstances) *and* my foreknowledge of government and power group actions *and* the theory on which the prediction rests were all perfectly correct. Suppose that I was so foolhardy as to be sure of all this and that I did make a number of unconditional predictions. Still, unless reliable checks were possible to verify separately every part of my diagnosis and of my anticipations regarding government and power group actions, my theory could not be tested. There could be lucky "hits" where wrong diagnoses would compensate for mistakes due to bad theories; there could be unlucky "misses" where wrong diagnoses spoiled the results of good theorizing. Despite a large number of good hits the theories in question could not be regarded as confirmed, even in the modest sense of not being disconfirmed, because a joint and inseparable test of diagnosis, anticipations, and theory says nothing about the theory itself.

Where the economist's prediction is *conditional*, that is, based upon specified conditions, but where it is not possible to check the fulfillment of all the conditions stipulated, the underlying theory cannot be disconfirmed whatever the outcome observed. Nor is it possible to disconfirm a theory where the prediction is made with a stated *probability* value of less than 100 percent; for if an event is predicted with, say, 70 percent probability, any kind of outcome is consistent with the prediction.[44] Only if the same "case" were to occur hundreds of times could we verify the state probability by the frequency of "hits" and "misses."

This does not mean complete frustration of all attempts to verify our economic theories. But it does mean that the test of most of our theories will be more nearly of the character of *illustrations* than of verifications of the kind possible in relation with repeatable controlled experiments or with recurring fully-identified situations. And this implies that our tests cannot be convincing enough to compel acceptance, even when a majority of reasonable men in the field should be prepared to accept them as conclusive, and to approve the theories so tested as "not disconfirmed," that is, as "O.K."

Strictly Empirical Hypotheses

All this seems to circumscribe rather narrowly the scope of empirical verification, if not empirical research, in economics. But to draw such a conclusion would be rash. For there is a large body of economics apart from its theoretical or "hypothetico-deductive" system: namely, the empirical relationships obtained through correlation of observations, but not derivable, or at least not yet derived, from higher-level generalizations. Every science has such a body of strictly empirical hypotheses, no matter how fully developed or undeveloped its theoretical system may be.

I define a strictly empirical hypothesis as a proposition predicating a regular relationship between two or more sets of data of observation that cannot be deduced from the general hypotheses which control the network of interrelated inferences forming the body of theory of the discipline in question. The distinction is made in almost all disciplines; it is best known as the distinction between "empirical laws" and "theoretical laws," though several other names have been used to denote the two types of scientific propositions. The philosopher Morris Cohen spoke of "concrete laws" in contrast to "abstract laws." Felix Kaufmann, though using the terms empirical and theoretical laws, characterized the former as "strict laws," the latter as "rigid laws." The physicist Henry Margenau contrasted "epistemic" or "correlation laws" with "constitutive," "exact," or "theoretical" laws. And Carl Menger, the founder of the Austrian School and protagonist in the *Methodenstreit,* distinguished "empirical laws" from "exact laws," the latter dealing with idealized connections between pure constructs, the former with "the sequences and coexistences of real phenomena."[45]

The study of the "sequences and coexistences" of the real phenomena depicted in statistical records yields correlational and other empirical findings which have to be tested and modified whenever new data on the same class of phenomena become available. While the constructs and deductions of the theoretical systems will influence the selection, collection and organization of empirical data, the particular relationships established between these data by means of correlation analysis and other statistical techniques are not deducible from high-level assumptions and can neither confirm nor disconfirm such assumptions. But these relationships, especially the numerical estimates of parameters, coefficients, or constants, are themselves subject to verification by new observations.

Verification of Empirical Hypotheses

Every one of us has lately been so much concerned with statistical demand curves, saving and consumption functions, investment functions, import elasticities and import propensities that a description of these and similar research activities is not necessary. The trouble with the verification of the empirical hypotheses derived by means of statistical and econometric analysis is that

176

successive estimates on the basis of new data have usually been seriously divergent. Of course, such variations over time in the numerical relationships measured are not really surprising: few of us have expected these relationships to be constant or even approximately stable. Thus when new data and new computations yield revised estimates of economic parameters, there is no way of telling whether the previous hypotheses were wrong or whether things have changed.

That the numerical relationships described by these empirical hypotheses may be subject to change--to unpredictable change--alters their character in an essential respect. Hypotheses which are strictly limited as to time and space are not "general" but "special" hypotheses, or *historical propositions*. If the relationships measured or estimated in our empirical research are not universal but historical propositions, the problem of verification is altogether different--so different that according to intentions expressed in the introduction we should not be concerned with it. For we set out to discuss verification of *generalizations*, not of events or circumstances confined to particular times and places. If all propositions of economics were of this sort, the dictum of the older historical school, that economics cannot have "general laws" or a "general theory," would be fully vindicated.

If a hypothesis about the numerical relationship between two or more variables was formulated on the basis of statistical data covering a particular period, and is later compared with the data of *another period*, such a comparison would be in the nature of a verification only if the hypothesis had been asserted or expected to be a universal one, that is, if the measured or estimated relationships had been expected to be constant. In the absence of such expectations the test of a continuing "fit" (between hypothesis and new data) is just a comparison between two historical situations, an attempt to find out whether particular relationships were stable or changing. A genuine verification of a previously formulated hypothesis about a given period calls for comparisons with additional data relating to the *same period*, to check whether the previous observations and their previous numerical description had been accurate. In brief, a historical proposition can only be verified by new data about the historical situation to which it refers. This holds also for geographic propositions and comparisons between different areas.

However, although the changeable "structures"[46] estimated by statistical and econometric researchers are nothing but historical propositions, there are probably limits to their variations. For example, we may safely generalize that the marginal propensity to consume cannot in the long run be greater than unity; or that the elasticity of demand for certain types of exports of certain types of countries will not in the long run be smaller than

177

unity. Statements about definite limits to variations of special or historical propositions are again general hypotheses; they are not strictly empirical but universal in that they are deducible from higher-level generalizations in the theoretical system of economics. The various successive estimates of changeable structures may then be regarded as verifications of general hypotheses according to which certain parameters or coefficients must fall within definite limits. Since these limits are usually rather wide, verification will of course not be the rigorous kind of thing it is in the physical sciences with its numerical constants and narrow margins of error.

But neither this nor anything else that has been said in this article should be interpreted as intending to discourage empirical testing in economics. On the contrary, awareness of the limits of verification should prevent disappointments and present challenges to the empirical worker. May he rise to these challenges and proceed with intelligence and fervor by whatever techniques he may choose.

Footnotes

* A paper presented at the Annual Conference of the Southern Economic Association in Biloxi, Mississippi, on November 19, 1954. The author is indebted to several of his colleagues, but chiefly to Dr. Edith Penrose, for criticism and suggestions leading to improvements of style and exposition.

1. The belief that a "hunch" is something fundamentally different from a "theory" may be responsible for certain antitheoretical positions of some historians and statisticians. Those who claimed the priority and supremacy of fact-finding over "theoretical speculation" might have accepted the contention that you cannot find facts without having some hunch. But this is practically all that the theorists meant when they claimed that theory must precede fact-finding, whether historical or statistical, and that history without theory, and measurement without theory are *impossible*. There are kinds of fact-finding which pre-suppose full-fledged theories; some simpler kinds may start with vague hunches.

2. "A hypothesis is an assumption ... tentatively suggested as an explanation of a phenomenon." Morris R. Cohen and Ernest Nagel, *An Introduction to Logic and Scientific Method* (New York: Harcourt, Brace, 1938), p. 205. - "A hypothesis ... is ... a theory which has, at present at least,

a limited range of application. It is promoted to the status of a theory if and when its range is deemed sufficiently large to justify this more commendatory appelation." Henry Margenau, "Methodology of Modern Physics," *Philosophy of Science*, Vol. II (January 1935), p. 67.

3. Cf. Wayne A. Leeman, "The Status of Facts in Economic Thought," *The Journal of Philosophy*, Vol. XLVII (June 1951), p. 408. - Leeman suggests that economists prefer the term "assumption" because it "escapes ... the undesirable connotations" of the terms "hypothesis" and "postulate."

4. "So far as our present argument is concerned, the things (propositions) that we take for granted may be called indiscriminately either hypotheses or axioms or postulates or assumptions or even principles, and the things (propositions) that we think we have established by admissable procedure are called theorems." Joseph A. Schumpeter, *History of Economic Analysis* (New York: Oxford University Press, 1954), p. 15.

5. There are no rules of verification "that can be relied on in the last resort. Take the most important rules of experimental verification: reproducibility of results; agreement between determinations made by different and independent methods; fulfillment of predictions. These are powerful criteria, but I could give you examples in which they were all fulfilled and yet the statement which they seemed to confirm later turned out to be false. The most striking agreement with experiment may occasionally be revealed later to be based on mere coincidence...." Michael Polanyi, *Science, Faith and Society* (London: Cumberlege, 1946), p. 13.

6. "The ultimate yardstick of an economic theorem's correctness or incorrectness is solely reason unaided by experience." Ludwig von Mises, *Human Action: A Treatise on Economics* (New Haven: Yale University Press, 1949), p. 858.

7. "There is a science of economics, a true and even exact science, which reaches laws as universal as those of mathematics and mechanics." Frank H. Knight, "The Limitations of Scientific Method in Economics," in R.G. Tugwell, ed., *The Trend of Economics* (New York: Crofts, 1930), p. 256.

8. "Economic theory is an axiomatic discipline...." Max Weber, *On the Methodology of the Social Sciences* (Glencoe, Ill.: Free Press, 1949), p. 43.

9. "Economic analysis ... consists of deductions from a series of postulates ...." Lionel Robbins, *An Essay on the Nature and Significance of Economic Science* (London: Macmillan, 2nd ed., 1935), p. 99.

10. "What assigns economics its peculiar and unique position in the orbit of pure knowledge and of the practical utilization of knowledge is the fact that its particular theorems are not open to any verification or falsification on the ground of experience." Ludwig von Mises, op. cit., p. 858.

11. Ludwig von Mises, op. cit., p. 33.

12. Lionel Robbins, op. cit., p. 78, also pp. 99-100.

13. Nassau William Senior, *Political Economy* (London: Griffin, 3rd ed., 1854), pp. 5, 26-29.

14. John E. Cairnes, *The Character and Logical Method of Political Economy* (London: Macmillan, 1875), especially pp. 74-85, 99-100.

15. John Stuart Mill, "On the Definition of Political Economy; and on the Method of Investigation Proper to It" in *Essays on Some Unsettled Questions of Political Economy* (London, 1844, reprinted London School of Economics, 1948), pp. 148-49.

16. Ibid., p. 143.

17. Ibid., p. 154.

18. "Aprioristic reasoning is purely conceptual and deductive. It cannot produce anything else but tautologies and analytic judgments." While this sounds like and "empiricist's" criticism of the aprioristic position, it is in fact a statement by Mises. (Op. cit., p. 38) Mises emphasizes that "the end of science is to know reality," and that "in introducing assumptions into its reasoning, it satisfies itself that the treatment of the assumptions concerned can render useful services for the comprehension of reality." (Ibid., pp. 65-66.) And he stresses that the choice of assumptions is directed by experience.

19. It is in this last meaning that empiricisms has usually been discussed and criticized in philosophy. In the words of William James, radical empiricism "must neither admit into its constructions any element that is not directly experienced, nor exclude from them any element that is directly experienced. For such a philosophy, *the relations that connect experiences must themselves be experienced relations, and any kind of relation experienced must be accounted as 'real'*

as *anything else in the system*." William James, *Essays in Radical Empiricism* (New York: Longmans, Green, 1912), pp. 42-43.

20. "That 'propositions of pure theory' is a name for ... propositions not conceivably falsifiable empirically and which do not exclude ... any conceivable occurrence, and which are therefore devoid of empirical content...." T.W. Hutchison, *The Significance and Basic Postulates of Economic Theory* (London: Macmillan, 1938), p. 162.

21. "... that propositions of pure theory, by themselves, have no prognostic value or 'causal significance.'" T.W. Hutchison, op. cit., p. 162.--The clause "by themselves" makes Hutchison's statement unassailable, because nothing at all has causal significance by itself; only in conjunction with other things can anything have causal significance. But if Hutchison's statement means anything, it means an attack against the use of empirically unverifiable propositions in economic theory, regardless of their conjunction with other propositions. Indeed, he states that "a proposition which can never conceivably be shown to be true or false ... can *never* be of any use to a scientist" (ibid., pp. 152-53).

22. With regard to the "fundamental assumption" of economic theory concerning "subjectively rational" and "maximizing" behavior, Hutchison states that "the empirical content of the assumption and all the conclusions will be the same--that is, nothing." Ibid., p. 116.

23. Ludwig Wittgenstein, *Tractatus Logico-Philosophicus* (London: Routledge & Kegan Paul, 1951), p. 167.

24. "... if one wants to get beyond a certain high level of abstraction one has to begin more or less from the beginning with extensive empirical investigation." T.W. Hutchison, op. cit., p. 166.

25. Ibid., p. 120. This does not answer the question: "what facts?" Precisely what data should be obtained and statistically investigated? What questions asked of consumers and entrepreneurs?

26. Ibid., p. 120. I could have quoted from dozens of critics of economic theory, from adherents of the historical, institutional, quantitative schools, and these quotations might be even more aggressive. I have selected Hutchison because he is the critic best informed about logic and scientific method.

27. Albert Einstein and Leopold Infeld, *The Evolution of Physics* (New York: Simon and Schuster, 1938), p. 33.

28. Cf. P.W. Bridgman, *The Logic of Modern Physics* (New York: Macmillan, 1927), p. 43.

29. Henry Margenau, *The Nature of Physical Reality* (New York: McGraw-Hill, 1950), p. 169.

30. Josiah Royce, "The Principles of Logic," in *Logic, Encyclopaedia of the Philosophical Sciences,* Vol. 1 (London: Macmillan, 1913), pp. 88-89.

31. Richard Bevan Braithwaite, *Scientific Explanation: A Study of the Function of Theory, Probability and Law in Science* (Cambridge: University Press, 1953), p. ix.

32. Ibid., p. 13.

33. For most problems of an enterprise economy no exact specifications about "profit" (whose? for what period? how uncertain? etc.) will be needed. There are some special problems for which "specific assumptions" concerning profit are needed. Needless to say, the assumption about entrepreneurs will be irrelevant for problems of centrally directed economies.

34. Or, again in a different formulation: the fundamental assumption is a resolution to proceed in the interpretation of all data of observation as if they were the result of the postulated type of behavior.

35. James B. Conant, *On Understanding Science* (New Haven: Yale University Press, 1947), p. 36.

36. On the problem of prediction versus explanation see the chapter on "Economic Fact and Theory" in my book *The Political Economy of Monopoly* (Baltimore: Johns Hopkins Press, 1952), pp. 455 ff.

37. Under perfect polypoly the individual seller assumes that his own supply will not affect any other seller or the market as a whole and, thus, that he could easily sell more at the same price and terms. This condition was also called "pure competition," "perfect competition," or "perfect market" (although it has little to do with any effort of "competing" or with any property of the "market"). See Fritz Machlup, *The Economics of Sellers' Competition* (Baltimore: Johns Hopkins Press, 1952), pp. 85-91, and pp. 116 ff.

38. Felix Kaufmann, *Methodology of the Social Sciences* (New York: Oxford University Press, 1944), pp. 77 ff, especially pp. 87-88.

39. "... the object, the 'facts' of the social sciences are also opinions--not opinions of the student of the social phenomena, of course, but opinions of those whose actions produce his object.... They [the facts] differ from the facts of the physical sciences in being ... beliefs which are as such our data ... and which, moreover, we cannot directly observe in the minds of the people but recognize from what they do and say merely because we have ourselves a mind similar to theirs." F.A. v. Hayek, "Scientism and the Study of "Soc-" "iety," *Economica, New Series,* Vol. V (August 1942), p. 279. Reprinted F.A. v. Hayek, *The Counter-Revolution of Science* (Glencoe, Ill.: Free Press, 1952).

40. Alfred Schuetz, "Common-Sense and Scientific Interpretation of Human Action," *Philosophy and Phenomenological Research,* Vol. XIV (September 1953), pp. 1-38. Idem., "Concept and Theory Formation in the Social Sciences," *The Journal of Philosophy,* Vol. LI (April 1954), pp. 257-273.

41. Schuetz, "Common-Sense, etc., " p. 34.

42. Disregard of this requirement is, in my view, the only serious flaw in the otherwise excellent essay on "The Methodology of Positive Economics" by Milton Friedman, *Essays in Positive Economics* (Chicago: University of Chicago Press, 1953), pp. 3-43.

43. Cf. Milton Friedman, op. cit., pp. 24-25.

44. This statement, it should be noted, refers to *general* theories which are part of a hypothetico-deductive system, not to strictly empirical hypotheses obtained by statistical inference. The predictions in question can never be in precise numerical terms, because no numerical magnitudes can be deduced from the assumptions of the type used in "general theory."

45. Carl Menger, *Untersuchungen uber die Methode der Social-wissenschaften und der Politischen Oekonomie insbesondere* (Leipzig: Duncker & Humblot, 1883), pp. 28, 36.

46. In the sense used by Tjallong Koopmans and other econometricians.

10   The State of Economic Science[1]

G.C. Archibald

In these three essays[2] Professor Koopmans offers what he calls
'... one man's explanations of some recent developments in economic theory, his comments and perplexities about the character
and basis of economic knowledge, and his intuitions about possible directions of future work in theory and in empirical investigations.' The first essay, on 'Allocation of Resources and
the Price System,' is the explanation; Professor Koopmans provides a short course in set theory in order to exhibit some new
work. This is fun; one may doubt if the re-working of a very
familiar field with the new tools has yielded much of importance,
but the tools are most attractive and are clearly displayed. The
second essay, on 'The Construction of Economic Knowledge,'
raises problems of methodology which will be the main subject of
this review. In the third essay, on 'The Interaction of Tools and
Problems in Economics,' Professor Koopmans uses his tremendous
knowledge of recent developments in mathematical economics and
econometrics in the U.S.A. to write a fascinating account of the
new problems and opportunities. We shall quote one of his examples later, and we may find in it a clue to an obscurity in the
second essay.

Koopmans' essay on methodology is, if I understand it correctly, open to two main criticisms. The first is that, compared
with the position reached by an earlier writer on the methodology
of economics, Koopmans appears to take a step backwards. The
second is that he does little to clear up our outstanding difficulties. These criticisms depend upon a view of the methodological
debate in economics: the discussion of Koopmans must therefore
be prefaced by a brief history of this debate.

Lionel Robbins' classic *Nature and Significance*[3] may con-
veniently be taken as a starting point. His methodology may be
exhibited by quotation:

> The propositions of economic theory, like all scientific the-
> ory, are obviously deductions from a series of postulates.
> And the chief of these postulates are all assumptions involv-
> ing in some way simple and *indisputable* facts of ex-
> perience relating to the way in which the scarcity of goods

Reprinted by permission from *The British Journal of Philosophy
of Science*, 10 (1959), 58-69.

which is the subject-matter of our science actually shows itself in the world of reality. The main postulate of the theory of value is the fact that individuals can arrange their preferences in an order, and in fact do so. The main postulate of the theory of production is the fact that there are more than one factor of production. The main postulate of the theory of dynamics is the fact that we are not certain regarding future scarcities. *These are not postulates the existence of whose counterpart in reality admits of extensive dispute once their nature is fully realised. We do not need controlled experiments to establish their validity: they are so much the stuff of our everyday experience that they have only to be stated to be recognised as obvious.* Indeed, the danger is that they may be thought to be so obvious that nothing significant can be derived from their further examination. Yet in fact it is on postulates of this sort that the complicated theorems of advanced analysis ultimately depend. And it is from the existence of the conditions they assume that the general applicability of the broader propositions of economic science is derived.[4]

On the problem of explaining consumers' behaviour, and the circumstance that their valuations of goods are subjective, he writes:

... we do in fact *understand* such terms as choice, indifference, preference, and the like in terms of inner experience.[5]

And, on 'Economic Generalisations and Reality':

In Economics, as we have seen, the ultimate constituents of our fundamental generalisations are known to us by immediate acquaintance. In the natural sciences they are known only inferentially. There is much less reason to doubt the counterpart in reality of individual preferences than that of the assumption of the electron. *It is true that we deduce much from definitions.* But it is not true that the definitions are arbitrary.[6]

It appears now that the propositions of economics are deducible from 'obvious and indisputable' postulates (or definitions). Hence we are not concerned with their testability, much less with their testing. Experiment is not merely difficult: it is irrelevant, unnecessary. Consider this passage:

According to pure monetary theory, if the quantity of money in circulation is increased and other things remain the same, the value of money must fall. This proposition is deducible from the most elementary facts of experience of the science, and its truth is independent of further inductive test.[7]

186

After the 'Nature and Significance', the next major contribution was Hutchison's. He insisted that the criterion of testability be rigorously applied to existing economic thought, and that there must be more room in economics than Robbins and others had allowed for looking at the facts in relation to theories. This was an advance; but Hutchison was unfortunately vague on the question of what we tested. He appears to have thought that it was in testing the assumptions of economic theory that empirical work was required.[8] At about the same time, a group of Oxford economists, conscious of the need for more facts, were acting on it: they were endeavouring to test the realism of such assumptions as that businessmen endeavour to set price and output so as to maximise their immediate, short-run profits.[9] Their method, roughly speaking, was to ask businessmen what they did, and why.[10] The answers they got were, roughly speaking, that businessmen did not try to maximise profits: they sought a 'fair profit' or a 'normal profit'; they determined price by adding to the cost of raw materials and labour a mark-up to 'cover overheads and a reasonable profit'--except when market conditions prevented them.

The results were widely interpreted as meaning that prices were formed by adding a pre-determined mark-up to the prime costs of manufacturing. All the loose ends and loop-holes were pointed out (the frequent alibis in the form of reservations about 'market conditions', the indeterminacy of 'normal' or 'fair' profit, the indeterminacy of the mark-up to cover overheads unless expected sales at the given price had already been calculated), but still 'this is what businessmen say they do'. In the debate that followed some people argued that businessmen could not maximise profits because they had never heard of marginal cost and marginal revenue (terms used in the economist's verbal translation of the mathematical solution of a simple maximisation problem); others, that since profit maximisation was the only 'rational' thing to do, businessmen 'must' maximise profits. The attempt to check the realism of the postulates led only to a methodological schism in economics: on the one hand we had those who paraded their 'realism'--'this is how businesses actually work'--and were indifferent to the arguments that their theory was indeterminate and therefore irrefutable; on the other hand we had those who stuck to 'rational' theory, and appeared more and more indifferent to reality (as understood by the first group). We still suffer from this sterile and muddle-headed dispute.

It was left to Professor Friedman[11] to tell economists that the proof of the pudding is in the eating, that a hypothesis is to be tested by comparison of its implications with observation, and that descriptive unreality in the assumptions is not a defect but a necessity. Friedman's revolutionary essay (1953) was an attempt to state, in the context of economics, some principles of scientific method which have been current in the natural sciences since, I

187

understand, Galileo. But economics is difficult, and there are difficulties in Friedman's essay, so we still have plenty of problems. The most serious ones are the problems of how we test, and what criteria we have for a good test. It is here that Friedman is most disturbing in his apparent complacency over what has already been done. The example is again the theory of the firm, the subject of much of the Oxford enquiry discussed above. It is extremely doubtful, in my opinion, if the theory of the firm has *ever* been the subject of really serious testing.[12] There are two common problems Friedman ignores. First, how is any theory which is purely static to be tested at all? The hypothesis, strictly interpreted, says that adjustments take place with zero time-lag, which we know is false. How 'unstrictly' can we interpret it, and still have a refutable hypothesis? Second, there is the problem of the ubiquitous *ceteris paribus* clause. If the 'other things' are not specified in advance,[13] there is an alibi for any refutation. If they are, we at least have a chance of learning from a refutation that the hypothesis must be widened to include some 'other things' as variables.[14]

On the testing of the theory of the firm, Friedman writes:[15]

An even more important body of evidence for the maximization-of-returns hypothesis is experience from countless applications of the hypothesis to specific problems and the repeated failure of its implications to be contradicted. This evidence is extremely hard to document; it is scattered in numerous memorandums, articles, and monographs concerned primarily with specific concrete problems *rather than with submitting the hypothesis to test. Yet the continued use and acceptance of the hypothesis over a long period, and the failure of any coherent, self-consistent alternative to be developed and be widely accepted, is strong indirect testimony to its worth.* The evidence for a hypothesis always consists of its repeated failure to be contradicted, continues to accumulate so long as the hypothesis is used, and by its very nature is difficult to document at all comprehensively. It tends to become part of the *tradition and folklore* of a science revealed in the tenacity with which hypotheses are held rather than in any textbook list of instances in which the hypothesis has failed to be contradicted.

The question is whether this is good enough. My own opinion is that it is not. Consider:

(i) The age of a hypothesis, and the absence of a 'widely accepted rival', are arguments that have been advanced in defence of practically every serious error ever made.

(ii) Is it not precisely those hypotheses which are wrapped in the cotton wool and authority of 'tradition and folklore' that most urgently require testing?

(iii) Whether or not an economist *intended* to test a hypothesis is certainly irrelevant if, when he 'used' it, he *in fact* did so in such a way as to expose it to test. But 'use' alone proves nothing, and we may suspect that an investigator who is trying to refute a hypothesis is more likely to expose it to a serious test than one who is not. And, after all, for every test that would refute a hypothesis, there may be several that would not. We might suspect that Friedman is here looking for 'confirmation' rather than refutation. Some documentation of serious tests conducted by accident would be really useful.

This passage I take seriously because its purport is to encourage complacency and to discourage that sceptical re-examination of the allegedly obvious that is the prerequisite of progress. In the preceding passage on the theory of the firm, Friedman is also, I think, mistaken, but the mistake here is less dangerous. He says, in effect, that we have the following evidence for profit maximisation: let businesses behave in any way at all; those which do maximise profits will flourish and those which do not will not; hence we know from 'natural selection' that profit maximisation is a good hypothesis. Consider:

(i) Profit maximisation is consistent with losses (i.e., loss minimisation). The profit maximising hypothesis says nothing about capital structure, technical innovation, or, in fact, about survival at all.

(ii) To survive it is only necessary to be as well adapted as your rivals; it is not necessary to be perfect.[16]

The main criticisms of Friedman are, then, (a) an omission-- he says nothing about the criteria for a good test, and (b) complacency--in consequence, perhaps, of (a), he far too readily accepts hypotheses as tested. One would feel better had he, if only once, said something to indicate that he thought that testing in economics was very difficult, and that it was hard to say what hypotheses, if any, had really been exposed to a critical test. There are other difficulties, but we may leave these for the moment.

It is against this background that I propose to discuss Koopmans' contribution, which means taking his argument quite out of the order in which he develops it, and fitting it into my own scheme (to which I add the warning that I find parts of his essay obscure: my interpretation may well be mistaken). My two main criticisms, that he takes a step backwards, and that he does nothing to clear up our difficulties, can now be reformulated: where Friedman made an advance, Koopmans ignores him; where Friedman was wrong or inadequate, Koopmans gives little help.

Koopmans' complaint against Robbins is that Robbins believed the major propositions of economics to depend on well-tested premises when, in fact, these premises are inadequate; he criticises Robbins, not for failing to state that the conclusions required testing, but for wrongly believing that the premises were adequate. His complaint is, therefore, of 'casual empiricism', which should now be replaced with '... direct or indirect testing of postulates'. Thus he refers with approval to Hutchison '... who sees in the recognition of uncertainty the turning point beyond which *empirical verification of postulates should become the main preoccupation of economists.*[17] This appears to throw the whole business back where it was before Friedman, and to re-open the door to the debate which followed the Oxford enquiry. (There is, however, another interpretation of Koopmans which will be suggested below.) We must now consider two respects in which Friedman left things unclear. He was concerned to show that descriptive unreality in the assumptions is both necessary and a virtue: the object of science is to predict from incomplete knowledge of the state of the world, and we can only discover what we can leave out of the hypothesis by our experience with its implications. It might have helped had he added that, even if assumptions were testable in any sense, and had been tested, and our deductions were logically correct, this would be no guarantee of the usefulness of the conclusions. It is not even a guarantee that the conclusions have testable content, much less that they will survive testing, because, obviously, we may have omitted important variables; the only way to find out is to test the implications. Friedman might also have avoided the confusion caused by the word 'assumptions' in economics. In a passage which Koopmans criticises, Friedman writes[18] that the difficulty of testing in economics leads people '... to suppose that hypotheses have not only "implications" but also "assumptions" and that the conformity of these "assumptions" to "reality" is a test of the validity of the hypothesis *different from* or *additional to* the test by implications. This widely held view is fundamentally wrong...'. Friedman is right to put the word 'assumptions' in quotation marks, but it is a pity that he did not explain why. Economists use the word without the slightest regard for the logical status of the 'assumption'. Consider some examples:

(1) 'Assumptions' about motivation, of which we have two important cases:

(a) Profit Maximisation. The alternative to testing implications here is, presumably, the notoriously unreliable method of asking people about their motives. Businessmen commonly reply that profit maximisation is not their motive. Friedman tells us to test implications, and believes, on what I think is insufficient evidence, that the implications of profit maximisation have stood up well to test. Koopmans, apparently believes that we should enquire further into the 'descriptive accuracy' of the assumption, but does not tell us how to improve on the Oxford method.

(b) Utility Maximisation. Perhaps introspection convinces some people that they endeavour to select those purchases, among all those their incomes make possible, which will yield them the greatest utility; but such introspection does not convince everyone, its results not being interpersonally testable. It is hard to see what those who want to 'test postulates' can do in this case except explain their intuitions and invite others to do likewise.

(2) Empirical 'assumptions' of the existence and stability of functional relations, which we do want to test and measure directly. This testing is no guarantee that later conclusions are correct; but it may serve to remove an avoidable error (compare the discussion of input-output models below, and Koopmans' suggestions for improving them).

(3) The 'assumption' that certain things are constant, or 'may be neglected' for the moment. This may be a case of (2) above; but it may also be a device for temporarily limiting the field of an analytical study, e.g. 'I shall discuss the effect of a customs union on the terms of trade, *assuming* that the union is accompanied by no changes in technique, monetary policy, fiscal policy, ...'.

(4) 'Assumptions' may also be used to explain the problem to which the hypothesis is meant to refer. New 'testing assumptions' may mean asking if the case at hand is one the hypothesis was designed for.

The many uses to which the word 'assumption' is put in economics have obscured the debate over whether we can 'test' them, or, if we can, if it establishes anything. Koopmans does nothing to clear this up. In spite of the care and rigour of his earlier analysis he appears, in his discussion of Friedman, simply to substitute the term 'postulate' for 'assumption' without any clarification whatever.

This interpretation of Koopmans, then, is that he follows Hutchison in calling for 'empirical verification of postulates' (or assumptions), and that he has done nothing to clear up the ambiguity of the terms. This interpretation gains support from the passages in which he criticises Friedman.[19] He points out that every statement implies itself, and that, in any case, '... in many systems of related propositions, one has a certain freedom of choice as to which statements one wishes to regard as premisses, and which ones as derived implications.' Hence, he appears to argue, the 'assumptions' which, according to Friedman, cannot provide an alternative test, can be turned into implications which, according to Friedman, we must test. Thus it is suggested that we have 'direct' implications and 'direct' tests of the postulates--'their accuracy in describing directly observed individual behaviour'; and that there is no reason for exempting some implications from test. Later on,[20] when Koopmans speaks of '... the intentional ignoring of obviously important aspects of reality...', there is no direct reference to Friedman, but we may conclude that Friedman is his target. Later, too, he writes of '... exhibiting the postulational basis, *and thereby the ultimate observational evidence,* on which our statements rest.'[21]

There are some rather obvious comments.

(1) We always, necessarily, 'ignore aspects of reality'. Our object, I take it, is to discover what aspects we can afford to ignore, or, better, what aspects we cannot ignore for a given purpose.

(2) Both Friedman and Koopmans point out that we have some 'freedom of choice' as to which statements are to be regarded as premisses and which as conclusions. What neither of them points out is that the choice is dictated by the problem at hand. If we want a hypothesis to predict prices, we require an implication about prices, which we shall test against our observation of prices. Perhaps Koopmans is thinking only of the second type of 'assumption' discussed above, that of a stable functional reltionship between variables, which we do require to test. Such a relationship may well be the 'conclusion' of one part of our theory, and the 'assumption' of another part.

(3) 'There are fairies' implies 'there are fairies'. What of it? The trivial circumstance that a statement implies itself does not of itself make anything testable. Some 'assumptions' are empirical, and may be 'wrong' (although probably the best way to find out how much and for what their 'wrongness' matters is to test predictions based on them); some assumptions are non-empirical, i.e., non-testable in any terminology one chooses to employ, and will not in this respect be altered by their being made implications of some other statement. What 'direct implication' of utility maximisation is testable? (Intuition provides no inter-personal test.)

192

(4) It is not clear what 'direct' and 'indirect' tests mean in Koopmans' usage. Does Koopmans mean that 'profit maximisation' is a 'direct' implication of profit maximisation, which is to be 'directly' tested by asking businessmen if this is their motive? When they deny that this is their motive, does Koopmans regard this as a refutation of the hypothesis? He gives us no help. (In this connection it is startling to find that Koopmans approves Friedman's 'natural selection' argument that we criticised above.[22])

There is one other puzzling aspect of Koopmans' writing which we may notice here. He appears to see a conflict between rigour and realism[23] which I find hard to understand. The apparent realism, achieved at the expense of rigour, by the 'inextricable intermingling of facts and reasoning', is a harmful illusion against which Koopmans has warned us.[24] It appears that he is again worrying about the descriptive unreality of postulates which are framed with sufficient precision to permit rigorous analysis. Thus in his discussion of the theory of choice in conditions of uncertainty of von Neumann and Morgenstern,[25] he writes: '... the situations described in the model are, at least in their most direct interpretation, still so far removed from those met with in reality that verification by observation of actual economic decisions appears difficult, whereas verification in experimentally created conditions may well be of limited relevance for explanatory theory'.[26] He overlooks the fact the Friedman and Savage,[27] and Markowitz,[28] have treated the von Neumann–Morgenstern theory as a positive hypothesis about behaviour, and compared its implications with observations about the purchase of insurance and lottery tickets. That I think there are implications they overlooked, and that these implications will lead to a refutation, is beside the point: the point is that the implications of the theory can be tested whether its formulation is rigorous (and postulates 'unreal') or nonrigorous ('realistic'?); if it is rigorously formulated it is, of course, likely to be easier to discover just what it does imply.

It was suggested above that there was another possible interpretation of Koopmans' essay. To find this we must turn to the sections in the third essay on 'Computing and Predictions of Production Potential' and on 'Statistical Inference and the Measurement of Economic Behaviour'. We shall find here, too, what Friedman omitted entirely, and what Koopmans omitted from his essay on methodology--some discussion of the criteria of a good or a critical test. Here, in fact, he shows us a fascinating example of some old problems in testing. It will be most convenient to set out the problem, and Koopmans' discussion, first, and then to see if his discussion suggests a reinterpretation of his earlier remarks on methodology.

The problem is to find a decisive test for an input-output

model. This model is constructed, very roughly, in the following way. The industries of the economy are grouped into a number of 'sectors', the output of each of which is treated as homogeneous. Each sector purchases materials from some others, and the ratios between these inputs, and the output of that section, in the base year, are then taken as fixed coefficients. If the desired composition of final output (i.e., investment, exports, personal consumption, defence, etc.) is specified, it is now possible to obtain from the model the output level required in each sector. The use of the model, then, is to answer such a question as 'is this rate of re-armament technically possible?' But before it can be used, the model must be tested. The obvious test is to compare the predictions for a given year derived from the model with observations for that year. With no standards of comparison, however, it is impossible to assess the significance of a given error. Hence 'naive models' are constructed, the predictions from which can be used for comparison. With a naive model, for example, we might simply extrapolate on the assumption that the ratio of each sector's output to total output is a constant. A 'semi-naive' model has been constructed with which we predict each sector's output from multiple regression of that output on total output and on time. The results of comparison are, apparently, that the semi-naive model leads to the best predictions, and that the input-output model is no better than the naive model. This is disappointing; but Koopmans does not think that it is decisive. A decisive test, he suggests, would only be afforded by a major upheaval, such as war or serious depression, which drastically altered the composition of total output. So long as this changes slowly, he does not find it surprising that naive extrapolation yields quite good predictions. The situation seems to be, however, that both the input-output model and the 'naive' model constructed for comparison depend on naive extrapolation, the former of constancy in the coefficients, the latter of constancy in the composition of final output. Which yields the worse predictions depends on which extrapolation is worse. The problem, which Koopmans does not discuss, is therefore to *predict which* extrapolation will be worse. This is not a problem that can be solved within the framework of either model. Koopmans goes on to suggest a way in which the input-output model might be improved. Its use involves treating as homogeneous commodities that are not, and all the different production processes that go on within each sector as though they were identical, which they are not. These are 'unrealistic assumptions'. Hence he suggests that the sectors be 'taken to bits' in order that information available at the engineering level can be used to check the coefficients that are 'assumed'. Work on these lines is apparently going on.

We now come to the second possible interpretation of Koopmans. If, by testing assumptions, and not 'ignoring obviously important aspects of reality', he meant such activities as improving estimates of coefficients, we might reinterpret much of what he says on methodology that was criticised above. A difficulty remains, however: there are several different uses of the word 'assumptions', and this interpretation will not fit all of them. We should therefore suggest that Koopmans, thinking of a particular, and useful, case of 'testing assumptions', had been led to a generalisation which does not fit the other cases, and is therefore misleading. If this is the case, then the difficulty lies in his having confused the point, overlooked by Friedman, that *some* assumptions need testing, with the general argument of 'descriptive accuracy' versus 'testing implications'. Had Koopmans attempted some taxonomy of assumptions, we might have been saved both this confusion and our difficulty in interpreting his intention.

Footnotes

1. Many of the arguments of this review I owe to the current school of thought among some of my colleagues at the London School of Economics. I am particularly indebted to Dr. J. Agassi, Mr. K. Klappholz, and Dr. R.G. Lipsey.

2. Tjalling C. Koopmans, *Three Essays on the State of Economic Science,* McGraw-Hill, 1957, pp. xi + 231, $6.50.

3. Lionel Robbins, *An Essay on the Nature and Significance of Economic Science,* London, 1932, 2nd edn. 1935. All references here are to the 2nd edn.

4. Lionel Robbins, *An Essay on the Nature and Significance of Economic Science,* London, 1932, 2nd edn., 1935, pp. 78-79. [Italics mine.] T.W. Hutchison, *The Significance and Basic Postulates of Economic Theory,* London, 1938, p. 131, quotes other economists to much the same effect, and deals thoroughly with them. Koopmans quotes the same passage from Robbins, and offers, as we shall see below, an interpretation slightly different from that suggested here.

5. Ibid, p. 88. Italics in original.

6. Ibid, p. 105. Italics mine. The individual preferences in question, incidentially, mean not just that individuals prefer some things to others, but that they have a complete and consistent ordering of all conceivable bundles of (completely divisible) goods, which ordering is independent of prices and of the preferences of others.

7. Ibid, p. 117. Robbins continues that the correct application of the propostion depends on correctly perceiving what is to be regarded as money.

8. There is little discussion in Hutchison's book of what and how we test, but what he does say lends itself to this interpretation. He writes of the need for '... assumptions more nearly descriptive of the economic life of a contemporary community...', and of finding out, '... by the most extensive statistical investigation, precisely what these assumptions are...' (p.74); of '... empirical verification...' of the 'fundamental assumption' (of maximising behaviour) (p.83); he argues that, because existing value theory ignores uncertainty, it is 'inapplicable' when individuals are uncertain what behaviour would maximise their returns (p.89); and he concludes that, for a more 'realistic' analysis, we require more 'realistic assumptions' (pp.119-120). Hutchison's intention may have been to urge us to compare predictions with observation; but, if so, he did not make himself sufficiently clear.

9. See particularly the paper by Hall and Hitch reprinted in *Oxford Studies in the Price Mechanism,* ed. Wilson and Andrews, Oxford, 1951. The Oxford work was, I think, undertaken before the publication of Hutchison's book; but it is convenient to take them together because they are alike in insisting, both that facts and theories be studied in close relation to one another, and, as I interpret them, that the role of the factual study is in checking the descriptive reality of the assumptions of the theory. Some of the Oxford studies, however, were concerned with testing or measuring functional relationships such as the interest-elasticity of investment. The criticisms made here of the 'Hutchison-Oxford' position are not meant to apply to these studies.

10. There have been many criticisms of their technique, e.g., of the sample chosen, with which we are not concerned here.

11. Milton Friedman, 'The Methodology of Positive Economics', in his *Essays in Positive Economics,* Chicago, 1953. Since I criticise Friedman below, I should like to acknowledge now the great debt I owe to his writings on methodology.

12. I except the work of the late L. Rostas on the 'cost-plus' hypothesis (*Productivity, Prices and Distribution in Selected British Industries,* National Institute of Economic and Social Research, Cambridge, 1948), at least one version of which he appears to have refuted decisively; but his work on the profit-maximising hypothesis is less satisfactory.

13. The list of 'other things' is obviously infinite. The point is to specify which of them in particular are constants in the hypothesis in question, *and to ensure that they are observables.* 'Other things' which are to be held constant in economics commonly include such non-observables as 'tastes', 'expectations', or 'the state of business confidence'. A hypothesis constructed like this can never be refuted. Cf. Hutchison's discussion of the *ceteris paribus* clause, op. cit., pp. 40-46.

14. This point is made by Hutchison, p. 44.

15. Ibid, p. 22. Italics mine except *for*.

16. Darwin seems to have anticipated this sort of misuse of his argument. He wrote: 'Natural selection tends only to make each organic being as perfect as, or slightly more perfect than, the other inhabitants of the same country with which it comes into competition ... *Natural selection will not produce absolute perfection,* nor do we always meet, so far as we can judge, with this high standard under nature.' (*The Origin of Species,* Everyman edition, p. 187, italics mine). I am indebted to Dr. Lipsey for pointing this out to me.

17. Ibid, p. 150. Italics mine. The difference, if any, between Koopmans' interpretation of Robbins and mine is not important. The important difference is over what we think should be done about it. Koopmans' agreement with Hutchison is also expressed in a footnote, p. 132.

18. Op. cit., p. 14. [Italics in original.] See Koopmans, pp. 137-142.

19. pp. 138-140.

20. p. 143.

21. p. 144. Italics mine.

22. p. 140. It is only fair to point out, however, that he suggests other implications and other evidence, and concludes that the profit maximisation postulate should be replaced with an appropriate postulate about survival policies.

23. See, e.g., pp. 142-143.

24. p. 144. Koopmans writes an excellent warning against false optimism based on the apparent realism of non-rigorous intuitive argument.

25. J. von Neumann and O. Morgenstern, *Theory of Games and Economic Behaviour,* Princeton, 1947.

26. p. 159. I think we might substitute 'testing' for 'verification' in this passage without making too much fuss.

27. Milton Friedman and L.J. Savage, 'The Utility Analysis of Choices Involving Risk', *Journal of Political Economy,* 1948, reprinted in *Readings in Price Theory,* American Economic Association, 1953.

28. Harry Markowitz, 'The Utility of Wealth', *Journal of Political Economy,* 1952.

Part Seven   Some Aspects of Model Building and Policy Making Role

Alan Coddington, in his article, "Economists and Policy," examines what is perhaps the most important role that the economist can play, namely as an advisor to some government, business, or institution, especially in the eye of the public. Coddington does not question the fact that such a role is appropriate for an economist; in fact he would argue that it is. Instead, he wonders how this role can be improved. Given that economists will act as advisors, what can be done to improve the type of advice which they might provide?

Coddington, in turn, studies five suggestions to improve this task: (1) economic data (or statistics) should be made reliable or more detailed or available more quickly; (2) there should be more statistical testing of economic theories (i.e. a greater use of econometrics); (3) people formulating and implementing policies should be exposed to more economic theory while those formulating theory should become more aware of actual policy problems; (4) economic theory should be more rigorously articulated (i.e., more mathematical, more formalized, more deductive), and (5) policy advice should be based more on common sense and less on the application of particular economic theories. Coddington concludes that economic theory and statistics can serve to discipline the judgments which pass as policy advice; theory and data impose system, coherence, and explicitness to policy judgments.

Stewart writes that the job of the applied economists is to give advice on the economic consequences of aiming for one goal rather than another or on the alternative means of reaching a given goal. This problem-solving process can be broken down into four phases: (1) problem formulation; (2) data collection; (3) analysis; and (4) recommendation. As Stewart notes, each phase has its special problems and solutions which he describes in some detail; this is a good guide to anyone interested in how the advisor should approach his job in a general manner.

As Kenneth Boulding points out in his article "Economics as A Political Science," issues of economic policy are also issues of politics. Ely Devons takes up this theme in his two papers which are noted in the suggested readings. Of particular interest here is his discussion of the types of knowledge which economists bring to this economic-political policy process: (1) economic theories, (2) common-sense maxims about economic behavior, and (3) knowledge and statistics describing the main features of the economy. Each kind of knowledge has a contribution to make in the policy advisory role, but that one should not overestimate the usefulness of economists to policy making. For some policy issues, economics may not be able to provide answers to the policy maker's questions; for example, the economist may be able to tell only the direction of change of some variable whereas the policy maker wants also to know the magnitude of the change. For other policy issues, Devons notes correctly that economists themselves may be in disagreement on the fundamental forces in operation; the policy maker is then faced with a range of views which may be contradictory.

A different perspective for a proper role for economists in macroeconomic policy making is provided by Robert Lucas who has argued that as advice-giving professors, we are way over our heads! He goes on to say that: "Economists who pose this 'what is to be done today?' question as though it were somehow the acid test of economic competence are culture-bound (or institution-bound) to an extent they are probably not aware of. They are accepting as given the entirely unproven hypothesis that the fine-tuning exercise called for by the Employment Act is a desirable and feasible one." The Robert Lucas article provides a fresh argument for fixed rule policy proposals advanced by Milton Friedman in 1948 and 1959. In other words, economists may serve as advisors but should not become involved in day to day fine tuning of the economy.

In many cases economists advising the government or private sector would construct a model, derive predictions from that model, test these predictions with real-world data, and then base his or her conclusions on the test. The reading by L. McClements takes up several aspects of this model-building experience which has become a large part of contemporary economics. An economic model is a simplification of some complex economic phenomena which are pertinent to the analysis of the problem under investigation. McClements notes that model building (i.e., the theoretical and empirical process of constructing quantitative representations of economic phenomena) requires the economist to utilize four disciplines or branches of knowledge: (1) economic theory, (2) the technical and institutional apparatus of the topic or area which is under investigation, (3) econometric theory (see Part Three of this reader), and (4) computer science. This is not an easy task as anyone who has built models can attest.

With these aspects as background, McClements comes to the

heart of the matter, namely the four strategies involved in the construction and use of economic models. He describes and explains the following stages in this process: (1) the model must be specified based on theory, (2) the necessary data must be collected and prepared in a form which is suitable for the model, (3) appropriate econometric and computational methods are applied to the problem which is being studied. His approach is excellent in that it emphasizes the theoretical aspects and the empirical aspects as one process; it is too easy to fall into the problem of dealing with these as separate and distinct aspects of modelling. The reader would benefit additionally by reading Jan Tinbergen's lecture, "The Use of Models: Experience and Prospects" delivered in Stockholm, Sweden, December 1969 when he received the Nobel Prize in Economic Science. This lecture is reprinted in the *American Economic Review*, December 1981. The macroeconometric methodology as outlined in this part has been under attack by critics who are dissatisfied with the existing methodology. E. Malinvaud in his article, "Econometrics Faced With the Needs of Macroeconomic Policy," provides a synthesis of the criticism and attempts to answer the question: "What contribution must econometricians bring in response to the present critics and in search of an improved methodology?" This article should bring the reader up-to-date on the position of the skeptics on the current state of the macroeconometric methodology and a description of a new research program.

An extensive literature exists on the problems which must be faced and maybe overcome in each of the stages of model building which McClements describes. Some of these are addressed in other parts of this reader. For example, Part Three looks at econometrics and computational methods in economics and Part Nine questions some of the assumptions upon which model building is based. Besides these references a few other points should be noted just in passing. For several economists, mathematics has become an important part of the specification of any model. The articles by William Baumol and Eugene Rotwein in Krupp's *The Studies of Economic Science* explain the uses and abuses of mathematics in economics in general and in model building in particular. See also Chapter 7 in Katouzian's *Ideology and Method in Economics*. Although some writers seem to use the words model and theory almost interchangeably, others go out of their way to try to show that they are different. For a discussion of this distinction, see the discussion by Ian Stewart in his *Reasoning and Method in Economics*. For the data collection phase of McClement's model-building exercise, the abstract concepts must be "operationalized" or defined in such a way as to allow their measurement. For a discussion of this, see Fritz Machlup's "Operational Concepts and Mental Constructs in Model and Theory Formulation."

11 Some Aspects of Model Building

L.D. McClements*

Introduction

Models are appearing with increasing frequency in the literature.
Some applaud these trends; others condemn them. Whether the
growth of model building[1] is approved of or lamented, its import-
ance--if only in terms of its share of the literature--cannot be
denied. Given the diffusion of the subject, those who question
its utility cannot simply be ignored. Nor can the construction of
models be dismissed as irrelevant. Those who commend the
quantification of economic phenomena are under some obligation to
justify the activity. Can the potential usefulness of models be
determined in advance? Can the utility of models be assessed at
all? Alternatively, those who decry the construction of models
require an understanding of the process in order to pin-point its
weaknesses. Why should model building be dismissed? In what
respects are models wrong, unhelpful, or misleading? Or, should
we prefer to sit astride the ideological fence then both aspects of
the problem need to be considered. What are the strengths and
weaknesses of model building? Are some models more useful in
certain situations and others of no assistance on other occasions?
And if so, why?

Some Terms

Before proceeding further, it will be helpful to clarify some concepts. The term 'model' denotes a simplification of some complex
economic phenomena. This abstraction retains all the features of
reality which are pertinent to the analysis of the problem under
consideration: it focuses attention on these at the expense of
less important factors. Thus different models of the same events
may be appropriate for the analysis of various facets of these
phenomena. The combined theoretical and empirical process of
constructing quantitative representations of economic phenomena
will be termed 'model building'. Models may be framed in verbal,
geometric, or mathematical terms. For model building purposes
the abstractions are usually developed in mathematical form, this
being better suited for the articulation and analysis of complex
relationships. However, the basic concepts incorporated in most

Reprinted with revisions by permission from the *Journal of Agricultural Economics*, 24 (1973), 103-20.

models can usually be readily interpreted in geometric and verbal terms. Indeed the presentation of most models in the literature involves a considerable amount of verbal description. Thus access to them does not necessarily require mathematical knowledge for they can be appraised in less formal terms: indeed models have been described as 'quantitative common sense' [35].

Very broadly, a twofold classification can be made of the models in the literature. First, there are models based on mathematical programming methods which are usually used for planning purposes [9]. Typically, mathematical programming models involve the maximisation (or minimisation) of some objective such as profits (or costs) subject to a number of limiting factors or constraints. Probably the most frequent application of mathematical (or linear) programming methods by agricultural economists in this country is in the maximisation of farm gross margins subject to the resources available, and thus recommending an optimal combination of enterprises. However, the basic prototype is very flexible and can be adapted for numerous applications; information theory, systems analysis, inventory analysis, simulation, gaming, input-output analysis, and so on [10,14]. While the modifications and applications are complex, the prototype is relatively straightforward. Furthermore, there is a *tendency* for the applications to be highly specific in that they are formulated for the solution of a narrowly defined problem. The first characteristic accounts in part for the analytical power of the mathematical programming method, and the second stems to some extent from its logical precision.

Econometric models constitute the second broad classification. They are based on the linear regression method and extensions thereof as found in the standard texts on econometric theory [12, 16]. The basic methods tend to be more involved,[2] and the models rather less specific and equally flexible, compared with mathematical programming methods. While much of this paper is relevant to models centred on mathematical programming techniques, it is largely written with econometric models in mind. This approach reflects the interests of the author rather than any more fundamental distinction.

Disciplines

What disciplines are involved in the construction of economic models of the agricultural sector? The number is in part semantic, depending on the demarcation of the various subject areas, but at least four categories can be identified. First, the term 'econometric' suggests that economic theory will play an important part in model building. Second, most models of the agricultural sector will have some technical content derived from the agricultural sciences. They will also involve institutional detail of the industry--the province of the more general agriculturalist. Thus technical and institutional information constitutes the second discipline. The techniques of measurement--also suggested by 'econometric'--form the third category. The branch of mathe matical statistics which has developed into econometric theory provides the means of quantifying and testing the relationships between economic variables. Finally, the mechanics of estimation and testing draw on a fourth discipline--computational methods and computer science. The contribution of these various disciplines can be seen from a more detailed description of each subject area.

Economic theory provides the abstract framework for economic models of the agricultural sector.[3] On the basis of simple, but approximate, assumptions (sometimes referred to as basic or primary hypotheses or axioms) about economic behaviour a series of qualitative statements (secondary hypotheses or predictions) can be derived. The profit maximising firm of the theories of supply and derived demand, and the rational or utility maximising consumer of demand theory, represent such behavioural assumptions or axioms. From these behavioural assumptions can be deduced, usually with the aid of mathematics, various statements about the firm's supply or demand function or the consumer's demand function. The theory indicates the variables which enter these functions, and the signs of their coefficients. Thus the prices of complements and substitutes in production enter a firm's supply function for a commodity in addition to the commodity's price and the price of inputs. Furthermore, the coefficients of these variables will be alternatively positive and negative in sign. The theory may, in addition, give some indication of the absolute or relative magnitudes of coefficients. For the single product firm Mosak [27] indicates that the (negative) elasticities of output with respect to the n input prices, e_{oi}, sum to minus the (positive) supply elasticity, e_{oo}.

$$- e_{oo} = \sum_i e_{oi} \quad (i=1,\ldots\ldots,n) \tag{1}$$

A one per cent increase in product price will lead to the same increase in supply as a one per cent decline in all input prices.

In practice, it may be difficult to obtain an index of all input prices and the supply function may exclude the price of some less important inputs. Nevertheless, we would expect (1) to approximately hold, and the exclusion of some input prices would mean that if anything the input elasticities should sum to rather less than the product price elasticities in absolute terms. For example, pigmeat can be considered as a single product industry in the U.K. If the long-run supply elasticity is known to be about

+1.6, then the input elasticities should sum to about -1.6. Feed accounts for at least two-thirds of the costs of production, so the feed elasticity should be greater than -1.6. Indeed, with various not unrealistic assumptions about the possibilities for substitution between feed and other inputs, the relative magnitude of these coefficients can be related to production costs. For a profit maximising firm in long-run equilibrium with limited scope for substitution between inputs, the elasticities of output with respect to input prices should be approximately proportional to the input share of total revenue. Thus with a supply elasticity of +1.6 for pigmeat and little substitution between feed and other inputs in production, the elasticity of supply with respect to feed and other input prices should be about -1.1 and -0.5 respectively.

But, many would argue, firms do no maximise profits, consumers do not act rationally. Friedman [11] holds that these behavioural assumptions do not need to be descriptively realistic. The real test of theory is the usefulness and validity of the statements or predictions derived from the behavioural assumptions. Nagel [29] has some sympathy with this empiricist viewpoint, but suggests that behavioural assumptions need to have an element of realism in order to produce useful statements.[4] Firms and consumers may not consciously seek to maximise profits or act rationally, but they do tend to behave in this way. Divergence from these norms which is prolonged or substantial in magnitude is unlikely. Thus these simple, but approximate, behavioural assumptions are very useful in empirical work.[5]

Alternatively, Leontief [22] argues that the behavioural assumptions are often too restrictive to allow the resulting statements to be useful in practice. Thus classical supply theory may be inadequate for the analysis of short-run adjustments of output. This shortcoming stems in part from the device of fixed inputs in the short-run theory of the firm. Alchian [1] suggests that in practice all inputs are variable in the short-run: they appear fixed because they are costly to adjust. Hence adjustment costs are the cause; and resource inflexibility the manifestation. The introduction of adjustment costs which increase at an increasing rate with the rate of change of output enables the derivation of a dynamic theory of supply and derived demand [38].[6] The partial adjustment rule introduced by Nerlove as an empirical expedient can, under certain conditions, be rationalised in terms of adjustment costs. In this way more realistic behavioural assumptions can result in statements or predictions which are more useful in practice. Frequently, however, the price of realism is some loss of analytical power. The gain in descriptive accuracy has to be weighed against the difficulty of deriving statements or predictions about economic relationships which are widely applicable, which can be tested in a meaningful way, and which serve analytical as well as predictive purposes. The balance between descriptive accuracy and analytically useful models is a sensitive one, and the derivation of statements is usually a difficult task: for these reasons the existing body of theory should not be abandoned lightly.

To summarise, economic theory provides a set of statements about economic relationships on the basis of simple, but approximate, behavioural assumptions. These assumptions may be unrealistic and require replacement or elaboration[7] - for example, the replacement of the concept of fixed inputs by the idea of adjustment costs in the theory of the firm. The application of the body of logical constructs which constitute economic theory enables us to focus on the important features of a particular economic question. Theory therefore has an important part to play in the analysis and modelling of economic systems which are typically intricate and complex.

Technical and institutional factors are also important in the construction of models of the agricultural sector. The biological basis of agricultural production is complex, and some understanding of its involved nature is necessary for the construction of sufficiently realistic models. At a simple level, factors such as the gestation and growing period of commodities determine the minimum lag with which supply can respond to revised output decisions. Yield per unit of a commodity may be influenced by the stage at which it is harvested or slaughtered. Output will be a function not only of the quantity of inputs but of their quality. Probably the most difficult technical questions relate to involved problems such as rotational constraints, and are not purely technical in nature. For example, a part of what are referred to as rotational constraints can be subsumed under adjustment costs--the cost of output foregone in moving from one rotational sequence to another. Technical information enables questions of the following kind to be answered. To what extent is it feasible to vary output by influencing yield? Do variations in yield influence quality? Are seasonal variations in output due to technical considerations such as day length and temperature, or to economic factors? To what extent do input quality changes influence output, and how far is the input quality mix influenced by the relative prices of quality attributes? How binding are purely technical rotational considerations? Can such constraints be relaxed by technical developments, and if so, how rapidly will such innovations diffuse through the agricultural sector? Even the best scientific opinion will differ on the more involved questions and the model builder may have no alternative but to resort to his own judgement. However, it should be clear from the above discussion that there is no rigid demarcation between technical and economic factors. Thus the best judgement on these matters is likely to be based on both a technical and an economic appreciation of the situation.

Institutional detail of the sector is also important. The various institutions and their rules form the framework within which economic activity in the agricultural sector operates. The structure and pricing policy of input suppliers may influence production in an important way. If the production of livestock is specialised into breeding and fattening functions, as it is to a considerable extent with sheep and pigs, then the supply decision will be based on store stock prices. Store prices will in turn be influenced by considerations such as weather conditions, feed supplies and prices, and the availability of store stock, in addition to the price of fatstock. Thus a model would need to explain the suppy of and the demand for store stock as well as the supply of and demand for fatstock. For many agricultural products in the U.K. price formation at the first hand marketing level is influenced to a considerable extent by arrangements for the administration of price guarantees, and by statutory marketing institutions. A knowledge of these arrangements and of their operation is essential if a model is to be a good analogy of the system which it claims to represent.

Econometric theory. The construction of models involves the joint process of determining the magnitudes of the coefficients of the various relationships of the system and testing whether all the factors do belong to the relationships.[8] To this end the methods of statistical inference are employed in the construction process. A stochastic error term is added to each of the relationships of the system to account for excluded variables, incorrect functional form, and measurement error in the data.

$$Q = P + U \qquad\qquad (2)$$

Q and U are (nx1) column vectors of observations and error terms respectively, P is a (nxm) matrix of observations, and   is a (mx1), column vector of coefficients to be determined. If some restrictive assumptions are made about the error term in (2)—that it is normally distributed with zero expected value and that its expected variance and covariance are a constant and zero respectively—then the relationship can be estimated by Ordinary Least Squares (O.L.S). In the experimental sciences these assumptions are ensured by the adoption of the appropriate experimental design, sampling, and so on—and the estimator is unbiased and efficient.[9] Experimentation is usually impossible in the social sciences so that the assumptions of O.L.S. are frequently violated, estimates are biased, and have larger variances than can be obtained by other methods, i.e. they are inefficient. Econometric theory has evolved tests for the violation of these assumptions, methods for analysing the effects where the assumptions are not satisfied, and more satisfactory alternative estimators for situations where the assumptions cannot be met. Autocorrelation, heteroskedasticity, simultaneous bias, specification bias, and measurement error are all problems of economic relation-ships which violate the assumptions of O.L.S. Often the constituent members of economic relationships are moving so closely together (multicollinear) that it is impossible to identify their separate influences. Or there may be insufficient information for a particular relationship to be identified. For example, supply fluctuations as a result of climatic variations may allow a demand relationship to be estimated, but insufficient shifting of demand may preclude the identification of a supply function--Figure 1.

Lagged variables of the type which result from the partial adjustment model create special problems of estimation and testing. In this situation O.L.S. estimates are biased and only consistent[10] in the absence of autocorrelation, and the standard test for autocorrelation is no longer appropriate. It is essential that all these problems are taken into account during estimation and testing of a model. One difficulty of econometrics is that while analytical methods can indicate the direction or magnitude of problems such as bias when one assumption is violated, it is difficult or impossible to do so when more than one condition is not met. Monte Carlo studies can provide some insights into difficulties of this kind: thus Waud [40] and Morrison [28] examine the effect of estimating distributed lag models when various complications are present.

Figure 1. Supply fluctuations enable the identification of a demand curve although the supply curve may not be identified.

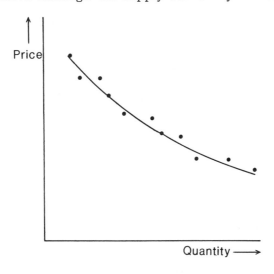

The problems of estimation and testing of economic relationships are involved, and are pursued in depth in the textbooks on econometric theory. It is sufficient to note that econometric theory is a vital input in the model building process: without due regard for the problems of estimation and testing the quantification of economic relations cannot proceed on a sound basis.

Computer science and its rapid development has been one of the most important factors influencing the increase in model building. Yet the part played by computational techniques in the construction of a model is frequently overlooked: it is just as important as econometric theory. The highly collinear nature of many economic series was noted earlier, and this can lead to excessive rounding error in matrix inversion. Furthermore, some numerical methods are more accurate than others, and use of the best procedures is of the greatest importance. Longley [24] investigated why some standard regression packages gave wildly different estimates for one set of data, and found that different computational methods were largely responsible. Table 1 shows the estimates obtained from these data using a standard regression program which is widely available in this country. The coefficients are seldom of the correct sign, let alone of the right order of magnitude.

While these estimates are based on an especially difficult set of data, multicollinear situations often arise in empirical work and create enough problems without having the added difficulties of computational errors. One wonders about the proportion of estimated models in the literature which contain errors of this kind – and the possibly higher proportion which have not been considered worthy of publication for this reason!

Table 1. Estimates of regression coefficients by a standard regression program compared with accurate values calculated on a desk calculator

Coefficient	Desk Calculator*		Regression Program	
Intercept		−3482258.6330		−295298.0000
X_1	+	15.0619	−	43.0130
X_2	−	0.0358	+	0.0615
X_3	−	2.0202	−	0.5639
X_4	−	1.0332	−	0.6156
X_5	−	0.0511	−	0.3816
X_6	+	1829.1515	+	199.2170

* as given in Longley [24].

Special regression programs are therefore essential for econometric work. Stewart [37] has developed a regression program which takes account of problems of this kind. The most accurate computational methods are used and checking procedures are included so that if problems such as rounding error become excessive computation ceases.[11] Similarly, many of the other complications which arise in econometric work require specialised programming and computational facilities. Computer science is thus an essential ingredient in the construction of econometric models.

To summarise, four disciplines have been identified. Each has a distinctive part to play, and each is essential for the construction of models of the agricultural sector. The role played by these disciplines and other factors will be considered in more detail by looking at the stages in the construction process.

Stages

If the justification for building a model--be it a problem to be solved or a need to acquire knowledge--is taken as given, four stages can be delineated. First, the model must be specified on the basis of the relevant theoretical, technical and institutional information. Second, the necessary data must be collected and prepared in a form suitable for the model. Third, estimation and testing involves the specification of a stochastic or random error term as part of the various relationships of the model and proceeds by applying the appropriate econometric models and computational methods to the data. Finally, the estimated model is applied in the analysis of the problem in hand. Very broadly, application may involve forecasting or 'policy' analysis. In both cases an explanation and understanding of historical phenomena is required: historical relationships are then used to forecast future events or to analyse the implications of alternative future courses of action.[12]

Model specification draws heavily on all the disciplines outlined in the previous section. First, it requires the selection of the most suitable logical constructs of economic theory for the analysis of the problem in hand. This selection is less straightforward than it might appear at first sight. In studying the demand for agricultural products the theory of consumer demand will be appropriate. However 'demand theory' covers a range of possibilities. From an additive utility function the Linear Expenditure System of demand relationships can be derived [13]. However, while direct additivity (or no specific substitution or complementary relationships among commodities) may be acceptable at the level of analysis which considers broad categories like food, durables, clothing, and so on, it is unlikely to be suitable where interest lies in the extent to which butter will be substituted for margarine with changing relative prices. The almost

211

direct additivity of utility is more appropriate even when commodities are quite widely defined,(2) and this requires different demand formulations. For a durable commodity like wool a model which takes account of its durability would be preferred, while for others such as tobacco yet a different theoretical model which allows for habit formation may be considered appropriate.

What part does the relevant theory or analytical framework, once selected, play in model building? To begin with, it indicates the variables which enter a relationship. It may also give some guidance on the functional form of the relationship. Since economic systems are typically complex, and the number of possible functional forms is usually large, the selective role of theory is very important. Equally important is the *a priori* specification of coefficient signs and the kind of relationships among variables shown in equation (1). Theory also provides a logical framework within which new variables can be considered. If X is thought to be important on intuitive grounds then in what way must the behavioural assumptions be modified or extended in order to incorporate X in a particular relationship? The answer to this question may facilitate both the estimation and interpretation of the eventual model in addition to enabling the specification of the relationship.

Economic theory provides relationships of two kinds: behavioural functions derived from behavioural assumptions, and accounting or definitional identities. The demand or supply function is an example of the first category, while the equality of supply and demand in the form of a market clearing identity is an example of the second kind.

A realistic model must also take account of technical and institutional factors. Technical considerations may range from the simple specification of a minimum lag between output decisions and eventual supply, to much more complex formulations which require considerable thought and ingenuity. Variations in pig slaughterings due to differing seasonal proportions of pork and bacon production provides a good illustration of technical considerations in model specification. Slaughterings will not simply be related to previous levels of the breeding herd: an increase in pork production in any quarter leads to a reduction in average slaughter weight and age. As a result slaughterings increase in that quarter and decline in the subsequent quarter since fewer pigs are available for slaughter at (older) bacon weights. Hence a knowledge of the slaughter age of pork and bacon pigs can enable, with the aid of a pork or bacon slaughter series, the construction of a relationship which allows for variations in supplies due to fluctuating slaughter weights.

Institutional factors are also important. The existence of

contracts may preclude the immediate response of market shares to relative prices, or the introduction of contracts may alter an existing relationship. The method of paying price guarantees can influence the specification of a model. If paid at about the same time as market returns reach producers then a total returns variable will enter a supply function. Payment in arrear may, depending on the time period of the analysis, justify the inclusion of market returns and price guarantees as separate variables. Alternatively, production decisions may be based on guaranteed prices rather than total returns and this variable would be specified as the decision variable in a supply function.

Familiarity with both technical and institutional features of the system is important in the specification of models of the agricultural sector. As with theory, the information thus gained need not only relate to the variables and signs of coefficients entering a relationship. It may also be possible to specify the absolute or relative magnitude of coefficients the higher litter size of sows compared with gilts can be specified as a restriction of this kind in a model. Indeed, the functional nature of technical relationships may be derived from technical considerations. The number of store or fat pigs may be linearly related to the number of sows in pig: further, in the absence of other variables in the relationship, if there are no sows there will be no store or fat pigs so an intercept term is unnecessary (Figure 2). Technical or institutional information may also contribute definitional identities. Thus total returns are defined as the sum of market prices and guarantee payments (there would be no point in estimating this identity--although estimates exist in the literature--for it already

Figure 2. A technical relationship between sow and store pig numbers

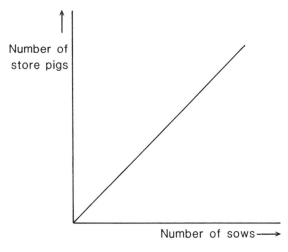

Number of store pigs

Number of sows⟶

indicates, in effect, that the 'coefficients' are unity). A model specified in this way will be *structural*: that is, it will show all the relationships between all the variables in the system. As such it will incorporate a wealth of theoretical, technical and institutional information about the economic system being modelled.

The variables in the system may be endogenous or exogenous --determined within or outside the system being considered respectively. And endogenous variables can relate to either the current period or some previous period or periods: if lagged, together with exogenous variables they are predetermined in that they affect the system in any time period but are not influenced by it in that period. If a relationship of the model contains more than one endogenous variable they will be simultaneously determined. And if simultaneous, it must be checked that the relationship is identified--otherwise the estimation of coefficients will not be possible as is the case with the supply curve in Figure 1. Alternatively, the system may be recursive--the matrix of current endogenous variables can be arranged in lower triangular form. Or, the system may be made up of relationships containing one endogenous variable: each can be considered as a complete model. Finally, the system can be composed of a combination of simultaneous recursive or single equation blocks of equations.

Having specified the model on the basis of theoretical technical and institutional considerations, it will be useful to take account of another question before proceeding further. Can the model, as specified, answer the problems which were the original justification for its construction? These objectives may have become confused, or indeed lost, in the intricacies of the specification stage and some reorientation or shift in emphasis may be required. The re-examination of objectives in the context of the specified model has the advantage that the problem can be formalised and articulated within this framework. Indeed as a result some aspects of the problem may already be resolved. Attention can therefore be focussed on the critical aspects of the model and on areas of difficulty where possibly value judgements have to be made or further work is required. In order to quantify and test the specified model observation of the system is necessary.

Data collection and preparation should require little comment although it is frequently overlooked in empirical work. While it may, on occasion, be useful to specify a model in terms of the variables we ideally require, in practice we are limited to those data that are available, can be collected, or can be derived from existing statistics. To this extent the available data influence the specification of the model. In terms of accuracy British agricultural statistics are amongst the best in the world. They are also amongst the most comprehensive, although not always

214

readily available in published form. These features are due to both historical factors and the deep government involvement in pricing in the industry.

Some of the available series are more accurate than others, and the method of collection may give some guidance in this respect. Measurement error may be systematic, for example seasonal, or it may result from another factor such as the introduction of a new policy instrument. Regular or permanent shifts of this kind can usually be accommodated in a model given a knowledge of the periods to which they relate. Thus the introduction of the Bacon Curing Industry Stabilisation Scheme at the end of 1966 led to an apparent increase in curers' returns of bacon into cure. As fresh pork production is estimated as a residual after deducting bacon pigmeat from total pigmeat this suggests that a shift would occur in both series. In this way a knowledge of the data and how they are collected can be useful at the specification stage.

However, data are frequently unavailable in the form required for a model. They may be collected on a weekly or annual basis for policy purposes and so require manipulation for a quarterly model, or ignore quality changes in the good to which they relate.[13] Similarly, geographic coverage may differ as may the categories to which the information relates. Thus some manipulation of the existing data base is usually necessary. While collection and manipulation may appear a mundane and uninteresting task it it critical for the construction process: a model can be no better than the information on which it is based.

Estimation and testing follows logically from, and draws heavily on, the first two stages. First a stochastic error term is specified in addition to the variables and functional form of the various behavioural and technical relationships of the model. Second, the appropriate estimator is selected. The specification stage will help in that it will indicate whether the system is simultaneous, recursive or a set of single equations. If simultaneous the equations of the model will need to be identified or over-identified and this will influence the estimator which is used. Or, a model nonlinear in the parameters may require a nonlinear estimating technique. Third, the appropriate estimator is applied to estimate and test the specified relationships. The first tests to be considered will be those which relate to the violation of the assumptions of the estimator--for example, the Durbin-Watson test for first order autocorrelation in O.L.S.

Given the correct estimator the actual model testing process is involved: there is no single criterion for assessing the estimates. The goodness of fit as represented by $\bar{R}^2$, and the t ratios of coefficients (or equivalent tests of significance), are standard tests. If we have two specifications of a relationship, one true and the other false, then by applying the O.L.S. the true specification will give the maximum fit [39]. Unfortunately we do not know that any specified relationship is true--all may be false. However, careful specification will increase the likelihood that a relationship is true and this adds weight to the importance of the specification stage. Furthermore, the *a priori* determination of coefficient signs enables one-tailed tests of significance rather than the more usual two-tailed tests of experimental work. We test either the hypothesis that is significantly greater than zero or alternatively that it is less than zero rather than the more usual hypothesis that it is greater or less than zero. The gain in efficiency is considerable: with twenty degrees of freedom the t ratios are 2.1 and 1.7 respectively at the 95 per cent level of significance.[14] Specification therefore plays an important part at the testing stage in that it can lead to a more efficient estimator.

Where the absolute or relative magnitudes of coefficients are specified the estimated coefficients can be checked against them or restricted accordingly. The latter process is widely used in empirical work - for example, the deflation of prices and incomes by an index of consumer prices restricts demand functions to be homogenous of degree zero in prices and incomes so that changes in the general price level do not affect consumption. The advantage of restrictions is a gain in efficiency [12]. Alternatively, estimated coefficients can be compared with specified values and this can provide a criterion for the selection of the 'best' estimates. Where specified and estimated coefficients are in conflict, confidence in the correctness of the prior information must be balanced against the conditional probability that the data would occur if the information was correct [7] p. 289. A knowledge of how the data are collected, and of the reliability of technical and institutional information, can be invaluable in making this appraisal.

Specification is also important at the estimation stage because it determines the factors which are tested as important in a relationship. The theorem on specification bias indicates that the coefficients of the included explanatory variables in an equation will be biased to the extent that these variables are related to an important excluded variable. Careful specification is more likely to lead to the inclusion of the important variables in a relationship.

To summarise, the specification stage is extremely important when it comes to estimation and testing for several reasons. It can lead to reduced bias and increased efficiency in an estimator --two basic and desirable properties--in addition to providing an additional criterion for the selection of the best estimates. These three considerations suggest that there is no single index of the quality of an econometric relationship. Measures such as R^2 and t ratios must be taken into account together with more subjective criteria like conformity with prior information which are less easy to calibrate. This approach highlights the importance of developing structural models which incorporate the maximum amount of *a priori* and other information about the system to supplement the information content of the data. It also suggests the unsuitability of certain estimating procedures which are widely used in scientific work. Stepwise regression excludes variables which do not attain a predetermined significance level. Yet the significance 'level' will depend on the specification of coefficient signs (which may not be possible for all variables in a relationship) and there are other important tests of a model which this approach overlooks. For example, a variable may be important but for the period of the analysis it may have undergone relatively little variation. In graphical terms we would be trying to fit a straight line to a tight cluster of observations--or in the extreme case trying to fit a straight line to a point. A stepwise regression program or the blind use of significance tests would immediately reject such a variable. Knowledge of its importance from prior information would lead to its inclusion at low significance levels. Clearly such a model would be better suited for both forecasting and policy analysis--unless we could be certain that for both purposes the important variable in question would undergo little variation.

Application provides the most powerful test of a model. The best model should give the most accurate forecasts and the most precise policy analysis. Thus a carefully specified *structural* model, which incorporates the maximum amount of information about the system, will give the most accurate estimates and be of greatest utility. However, its usefulness stems not only from its historical descriptive accuracy, but from its flexibility. Changes in the structure of an economic system can be envisaged in both forecasting and policy analysis. These changes can be more readily incorporated in a structural model: indeed it will usually be impossible to incorporate them in a 'reduced form' model which has not been specified in structural form. The adaptation of British agricultural policy from a system of input subsidies and guaranteed prices to the import levies of the Common Agricultural Policy (C.A.P.) is a good example of such structural change. Many relationships between key economic variables will be radically altered as a result, and historic relationships are unlikely to give either good forecasts or analyses. Thus the feed formula in the guaranteed price for pigs means that feed prices have had little impact on U.K. supply in the past, but this certainly will not continue with the adoption of the C.A.P. for pigmeat. The relationship shown in equation (1) above, and the subsequent discussion on the relative magnitude of the supply and feed price elasticity, gives one estimate of the likely impact of feed price changes on pig production. Similarly, naive price expectations may have been acceptable in the past in view of the stability of many agricultural commodity prices, but this will not necessarily be the case in the future under the C.A.P.

A major difficulty of testing a model in terms of its utility in application is the length and difficulty of the process. A few forecasts can be good or bad by chance so that a number of forecasts are required for sound conclusions. Policy analyses may be even more difficult to assess. A development suggested by the model may lead to countervailing policy action which invalidates the initial analysis based on the model, this being conditional upon unchanged policies. Thus any straightforward comparison between the model and the actual outcome is an invalid criterion of the model's utility so that while application is the acid test of a model it is a difficult and lengthy test to perform. This explains the emphasis on statistical testing of models and reinforces the need for tests derived from the specification stage.

The various tests may lead to the rejection of the specified model in which case each stage in the construction process will need to be re-examined. It may be necessary to reject the original behavioural assumptions and begin afresh with more realistic assumptions. An important technical or institutional factor may have been overlooked, there may be data errors, or estimation and testing may be at fault. While the stages outlined above are highly stylised and idealised they are not necessarily consecutive. Their inter-related nature means that the stages can proceed together to some extent, and the lengthy process of specifying, testing, applying, then re-specifying, re-testing, and re-applying may permit an omission of some of the stages.

Some Implications

The stages outlined above have some important implications. First, they suggest some very broad and general criteria for the very broad and general criteria for the appraisal of models.[15] These criteria can be applied to some specific formulations. Second, this approach to the construction of models of the agricultural sector has implications not only for research, but for the teaching of agricultural economics in this country.

The stages of the preceding section reflect an approach to model construction which emphasises the importance of specification for statistical inference in economic systems. In practice it may be tempting to collect some data, obtain a regression program (preferably stepwise), and retain the 'significant' variables. If the results are 'bad', specification is redundant; if 'good', they can usually be rationalised. It should be clear that this approach is unlikely to provide useful models. By trying enough variables significant coefficients can always be obtained as many economic series tend to move together. But the data usually do not contain sufficient information for this indiscriminate approach to succeed, and in any case econometric methods are not suited to this use. Thus, Ramsey [30] concludes that econometric techniques are most powerful in discriminating among a small number of well defined alternatives: their usefulness rapidly diminishes with the increasing number of possibilities which are considered. Detailed specification is therefore desirable for the estimation and testing of economic relationships, and economic theory is an important input in the specification process. Failure to spend enough time on specification has led to comments such as 'measurement without theory' [21], 'regress now and think later'[17] 'forty equations in forty minutes', 'data mining' [19], and 'the game of maximising $\bar{R}^2$ ... should not be employed in serious work' [8].

The effort devoted to specification therefore provides a very useful rule of thumb for the appraisal of models. This will generally be apparent from the proportion of a paper devoted to this topic, or from references to other articles where the model is specified. If the specificiation stage is not spelled out, it will be useful to consider the implications of the eventual model. What rationale underlies the estimated model? Is it plausible?

Consider, for illustrative purposes, an industry supply function for a commodity of the form

$$Q_t = a + bGM_{t-1} \qquad (3)$$

where Q_t is supply in year t and GM_{t-1} gross margin in the previous year. On the face of it, this might appear quite a reasonable specification. However a look at national statistics reveals that some 'fixed' inputs like labour and machinery do vary from year to year. Equation [3] can also be rewritten, since gross margin is total revenue TR less variable costs VC

$$Q_t = a + bTR_{t-1} - bVC_{t-1} \qquad (4)$$

Turning to farm management handbooks we find that variable costs account for anything from 20 to 80 per cent of total revenue. Theoretical considerations suggest that all input prices enter the long-run supply function. Thus estimates of (3) will suffer from specification bias to the extent that the excluded 'fixed' input prices are related to the included gross margin variable. As higher fixed input prices will tend to be associated with higher gross margins, the estimate of b,$\hat{b}$, will be biased downward. Moreover, from (4) it is clear that (3) involves the impli-

219

cit restriction that a unit increase in variable costs leads to the same change in supply as a unit decrease in total revenue. To take some extreme possibilities, fixed costs can double, or decline to zero, but supply will be unaffected. Even if variable costs only account for one (or ten or twenty) per cent of total revenue fixed costs will not influence supply. This suggests that the bias in (3) could be especially large for these products, and b will differ from the true supply and variable input price elasticities--for example, for b = +1.0 the actual supply and variable input price elasticities might be +1.25 and -0.75 respectively rather than +1.0 and -1.0 as estimated. Clearly the bias due to specification error, in addition to that due to a restriction which is theoretically implausible, could lead to very serious errors in estimates of (3).

The relationship between wholesale price WP and retail price RP might be specified as

$$RP_t = a + bWP_t \qquad\qquad (5)$$

This formulation reflects the belief that retailers operate a simple pricing rule of thumb and take fixed proportional margins (a = o,b>1), although it includes the possibility that retail prices are fixed (a>0,b = o) regardless of wholesale prices. However, it is difficult to derive (5) within the perfectly competitive paradigm. Equation (5) asserts that changes in labour costs, for example, do not influence retail margins. Only if the costs of retailing increase at the same rate as wholesale prices would (5) include competitive behaviour, and the volatile wholesale prices of most agricultural commodities makes this unlikely. There is a lot of general evidence [33] that cost factors are important in retailing. In order to test whether costs influence retail margins (5) could be respecified as

$$RM_t = a + bP_t \qquad\qquad (6)$$

where RM is the retail margin (RP-WP), and P the cost of inputs in retailing. A model of this kind for carcase meats, which also allowed for the possibility of price levelling, suggests that input prices are an important determinant of retail meat margins [26].

Thus by considering some of the implications of a specified model an insight can be gained into its limitations. Deficiencies due to data errors and inappropriate estimators and tests may be less easy to identify, but often it would appear that estimators and tests have been misused. There may be no alternative but to use a method the assumptions of which are violated, but at least this factor must be kept in mind in the presentation and interpretation of results. Often the direction, if not the magnitude, of bias can be determined analytically. The results of Table 1 suggest care in the use of regression programs: these need to be specifically developed for econometric work rather than adapted from more general scientific uses. Finally, models can be assessed in terms of their usefulness when applied in the analysis of problems.

The basis of model building is essentially economic and econometric, and it is important that a sound training be given in these rapidly developing disciplines.[16] Supplemented by technical and institutional information, and drawing on data of the agricultural sector, they should enable the construction of *useful* models.

Summary

Model building has the advantage that it organises and quantifies--however imperfectly--economic phenomena. Models can also deal with multi-dimensional situations, unlike most human minds which can only operate in a few dimensions. More complex situations can therefore be formulated and articulated within the formal framework of a model. Moreover the assumptions and judgments embodied in an empirical model can be made more explicit than in other approaches. Conclusions will be more scientific being based on observation of and inferences drawn from the economic system: they will tend to be more impersonal and less influenced by the individual's value judgements or at least the extent to which conclusions are the result of personal considerations should be more readily apparent. Furthermore, models can be less restrictive than other modes of analysis in that a wider range of alternative possibilities can be considered within them. However, it was demonstrated above that some very limited formulations were also possible. A major theme of this paper is that careful specification is most likely to lead to flexible and useful models.

The disadvantage of the approach is that models may not be sufficiently realistic analogies of the systems which they purport to represent. As such their usefulness may be limited. However, models are by definition simplistic and therefore unrealistic. So they must be judged in terms of the problem which they are designed to solve. A further disadvantage of empirical models is that estimated relationships may be in error, and the second major theme of this paper is that there exist a number of tests in addition to formal tests of significance which can be applied to reduce the likelihood of error.

Some of the disillusionment with model building may have arisen from the over-ambitious claims of the proponents of the approach. Professor Johnston suggests that 'As with most religions it was, perhaps the minor prophets who did most damage with their extravagant claims for the benefits to flow from the new approach...' [19]. Certainly there is an element of truth in the definition of quantitative methods as giving 'the right answer to the wrong question' [5]. But equally, there is some substance in the description 'the art of giving bad answers to problems to which otherwise worse answers are given' [35]. Both the right and the bad answers are based on the intricate and sophisticated technology of model building. The third theme stemming from this paper is that the answers can only be made more relevant and more accurate by getting to know the technology of model building: doctrine and ideology serve neither the proponents nor the opponents of the approach.

Footnotes

*   The author gratefully acknowledges the constructive comments of B.E. Hill, J. Lingard, S.O. Matthews, A.J. Rayner, T.D. Sparrow and E.M. Wilkinson on a draft of this paper. This is an abridged version of his article. The deletions have been made with the permission of the author.

1.   For a fascinating discussion of the factors which lead to rapid changes of this kind in the social sciences, see Johnson [15].

2.   In support of this assertion, there exists a guide to mathematical programming in one lesson [3], but not, so far as I am aware, a similar exposition of econometric model building.

3.   For an excellent review of developments in microeconomic theory as they relate to mathematical programming models, see Shubik [36].

4.   For a more recent discussion of this dilemma, see Rivett [34].

5.   Loasby[23] emphasises that some economic 'hypotheses' are in fact paradigms. Within a give problem area a paradigm defines the relationships to be examined and the appropriate methods and abstractions. This conceptual framework enables a range of hypotheses or statements to be generated about economic relationships. For example, perfectly competitive and behavioural theories of the firm constitute different paradigms, and both may be 'correct' in that they are useful for the examination and analysis of different problems.

6.   It is interesting that the concept of adjustment costs is also playing an important part in the development of macroeconomics. Brunner[6] cites information and adjustment costs as

having a central role in the monetarist counter-revolution to Keynesian orthodoxy.

7. Since models are by definition simplifications it follows that they are also unrealistic: they should be *sufficiently* good approximations to reality for the analysis of the problem in hand.

8. Hypothesis testing is appropriate for discriminating between alternatives derived within a single paradigm but is not suited for deciding between paradigms, or for validating a paradigm [23] p. 867.

9. For a good introduction to the concepts of statistical inference, and the desirable properties such as unbiasedness, efficiency and consistency of estimators, see [41] Chapters 1 and 2.

10. A consistent estimator is one in which the estimated coefficient approaches the actual value of the parameter as the sample size becomes infinite. This large sample property is of limited value in many economic applications as they relate to small samples.

11. The author once had difficulty reproducing some published results. It was found that the relationship in question contained four quarterly intercept dummy variables in addition to an intercept term--equivalent to perfect multicollinearity. Estimates which were 'plausible' had been obtained by trying enough variables and combinations of variables. In fact they were simply rounding error generated by the computer.

12. This being so there is little justification for the frequent distinction between forecasting and 'other' types of model. Both applications require the best possible explanation of existing phenomena and this will be obtained from the best estimate of the structure of the economic system--see Klein [20], pp. 251-255.

13. For example, Rayner [31] has shown that about two-thirds of the increase in farm tractor prices between 1948 and 1965 could be accounted for by quality changes, while in the case of fertiliser the quality effect was even greater (32).

14. Note that the specification of the technical relationship in Figure 2 leads to the exclusion of an intercept term and thus conserves one degree of freedom.

15. Christ [7] suggests that models should be relevant to the problem under analysis, they should be simple, theoretically

plausible, possess high explanatory ability, accurate coefficients, and forecasting precision.

16. The rapidity of these developments is reflected by the large number of new journals which are appearing in these areas: it is estimated that more new economics journals have been established since 1959 than existed prior to that year [4]. Some idea of the changes in econometric theory can be obtained from a comparison of three textbooks of econometric theory [20], [16], and [18] which have been published in the last twenty years.

References

[1] Alchian, A.: 'Costs and Outputs' in *The Allocation of Economic Resources*, Abramovitz, M. (ed.), Stanford, Stanford University Press, 1959.

[2] Barten, A.P.: 'Consumer Demand Functions under Conditions of Almost Additive Preferences', *Econometrica*, 32, pp. 1-38, 1964.

[3] Baumol, W.J.: 'Activity Analysis in one Lesson'. *American Economic Review*, 48, pp. 837-873, 1958.

[4] Berg, S.V.: 'Increasing the Efficiency of the Economic Journal Market'. *Journal of Economic Literature*, 9, No. 3, pp. 798-813, 1971.

[5] Borch, K.H.: *The Economics of Uncertainty*. Princeton, New Jersey, Princeton University Press, 1968.

[6] Brunner, K.: 'The Monetarist View of Keynesian Ideas'. *Lloyds Bank Review*, No. 102, October, 1971.

[7] Christ, C.F.: *Econometric Models and Methods*, New York, Wiley, 1966.

[8] Dhrymes, P.J.: 'On the Game of Maximising $\bar{R}^2$'. *Austridlian Economic Papers*, 9, No. 15, pp. 177-185, 1970.

[9] Dorfman, R.: '"Mathematical" or "Linear" Programming: A Non-mathematical Exposition'. *American Economic Review*, 43, pp. 797-825, 1953.

[10] Dorfman, R.: 'Operations Research'. *Surveys of Economic Theory Volume III: Resource Allocation.* London, Macmillan, 1967.

[11] Friedman, M.: 'The Methodology of Positive Economics' in *Essays in Positive Economics,* University of Chicago Press, 1953.

[12] Goldberger, A.S.: *Econometric Theory,* New York, Wiley, 1964.

[13] Goldberger, A.S. and Gamaletos, T.: 'A Cross-Country Comparison of Consumer Expenditure Patterns'. *European Economic Review,* 1, No. 3, pp. 357-400, 1970.

[14] Hicks, J.R.: 'Linear Theory' in *Surveys of Economic Theory Volume III: Resource Allocation,* London, Macmillan, 1967.

[15] Johnson, H.G.: 'The Keynesian Revolution and Monetarist Counter-Revolution'. *American Economic Review,* 61, No. 2, pp. 1-14, 1971.

[16] Johnston, J.: *Econometric Methods,* New York, McGraw-Hill, 1963.

[17] Johnston, J.: Review of 'Specification and Uses of Econometric Models'. *The Manchester School,* 38, pp. 369-370, 1970.

[18] Johnston, J.: *Econometric Methods,* Second edition, New York, McGraw-Hill, 1971.

[19] Johnston, J.: Review of 'The Econometric Study of the United Kingdom'. *Economica,* 38, pp. 444-446, 1971.

[20] Klein, L.R.: *Textbook of Econometrics,* Evanston, Row Peterson and Co., 1953.

[21] Koopmans, T.C.: 'Measurement Without Theory'. *Review of Economic Statistics,* 29, 1947.

[22] Leontief, W.: 'Theoretical Assumptions and Non-observed Facts'. *American Economic Review,* 61, No. 1, pp. 1-7, 1971.

[23] Loasby, B.J.: 'Hypothesis and Paradigm in the Theory of the Firm'. *Economic Journal,* 81, pp. 863-885, 1971.

[24] Longley, J.W.: 'An Appraisal of Least Squares Programs for the Electronic Computer from the Point of View of the User'. *Journal of American Statistical Association*, 62, pp. 819-840, 1967.

[25] Malinvaud, E.: *Statistical Methods of Econometrics*, Amsterdam, North-Holland Publishing Co., 1966.

[26] McClements, L.D.: 'An Analysis of Retail Meat Pricing Behaviour in Britain'. In preparation.

[27] Mosak, J.L.: 'Interrelations of Production Price and Derived Demand'. *Journal of Political Economy*, 46, pp. 761-787, 1938.

[28] Morrison, J.L.: 'Small Sample Properties of Selected Distributed Lag Estimates'. *International Economic Review*, 11, pp. 13-23, 1970.

[29] Nagel, E.: 'Assumptions in Economic Theory'. *American Economic Review*, 53, pp. 211-219, 1963.

[30] Ramsey, J.B.: 'Models, Specification Error, and Inference: A Discussion of some Problems in Econometric Methodology'. *Bulletin Ox. Univ. Inst. Econ. Stats.* 32, No. 4, pp. 301-318, 1970.

[31] Rayner, A.J.: 'Price-Quality Relationships in a Durable Asset: Estimation of a Constant Quality Price Index for New Farm Tractors 1948-1965'. *Journal of Agricultural Economics*, 19, pp. 231-249, 1968.

[32] Rayner, A.J. and Lingard, J.: 'Fertiliser Prices and Quality Change'. *Journal of Agricultural Economics*, 22, pp. 149-162, 1971.

[33] Reddaway, W.B.: *Effects of the Selective Employment Tax: First Report.* London, H.M.S.O., 1970.

[34] Rivett, K.: 'Suggest or Entail?: The Derivation and Confirmation of Economic Hypotheses'. *Australian Economic Papers*, 9, No. 15, pp. 127-148, 1970.

[35] Saaty, T.L.: *Mathematical Methods of Operations Research*, New York, McGraw-Hill, 1959.

[36] Shubik, M.: 'A Curmudgeon's Guide to Microeconomics'. *Journal of Economic Literature*, 8, No. 2, pp. 405-434, 1970.

[37] Stewart, J. *Computational Aspects of Multiple Regression*, M.A. (Econ) Dissertation, University of Manchester, 1968.

[38] Strotz, R. and Eisner, R.: 'Determinants of Business Investment' in *Impacts of Monetary Policy*. Commission on Money and Credit, Englewood Cliffs, Prentice-Hall, 1963.

[39] Theil, H.: *Economic Forecasts and Policy*, Second Edition, Amsterdam, North-Holland Publishing Co., 1965.

[40] Waud, R.N.: 'Misspecification in the Partial Adjustment and Adaptive Expectations Model'. *International Economic Review*, 9, pp. 204-217, 1968.

[41] Wonnacott, R.J. and Wonnacott, T.H.: *Econometrics*, New York, Wiley, 1970.

12 Economists and Policy

Alan Coddington*

Control of the economy is often presented in dramatic terms. It has been likened to driving a car with no front window but only a rear mirror, to catching trains using last year's Bradshaw and to navigating a ship with every possibility, indeed likelihood, of being blown off course. To remember that what is actually happening is that decisions are being made about taxation, government spending and financial arrangements, requires a decisive triumph of mind over metaphor.

The way economists have approached the problems of controlling the economy is hardly as dramatic or colourful as the political imagery might lead one to expect. They have frequently been blamed for the dismalness, narrowness or base materialism of their outlook. 'The age of chivalry is gone,' it was announced, 'that of sophisters, economists and calculators has succeeded'. (This remark is not taken from a *Times* leader, a Noel Coward play, nor even from Mr. Malcolm Muggeridge's reflections, but from Burke's thoughts on the French revolution.)

Similar sentiments have been widely expressed since Burke's day, and stem partly from the mistaken impression that economics is both a celebration of acquisitiveness and an intellectual underwriting of the existing order. But, of course, 'economic man' stands or falls by his explanatory value for economic phenomena, not the attractiveness of his alleged character. At a more down to earth level, economists have been criticized for their tendency to take a two-handed approach to policy questions, that is to say, to make liberal use of the phrases, 'on the one hand... but on the other hand...'. But, to be charitable, such an approach can often be useful in analyzing and clarifying the issues--in simply mapping out the various possibilities.

Role of Economists

Indeed, I believe that charity is not entirely out of place in one's view of the economic profession, if not of its individual members. For, unlike any other profession one can think of, it is widely expected both to maintain standards of scholarship and to produce national policies that are administratively workable and

Reprinted by permission from the *National Westminster Bank Quarterly Review* (February 1973), 59-68.

politically acceptable. It should be noticed that this is the role expected of the *profession*: very few economists would seriously attempt to encompass, at any point in time, the whole spectrum of endeavour from pure theory to practical politics, although they might traverse the spectrum during the course of their careers as they move from the university to Whitehall, and sometimes back again.

It is, however, an exaggeration to talk of economists 'producing' policies, for in truth their role is, at best, limited to advising on policy. In other words, they are one link only in the chain that produces economic policy. Also involved are the statistics on which diagnoses and forecasts are based, the ministers who take responsibility for the decisions which are made, and the administrators who put the decisions into effect. One might like to think of the policy advice as being the crucial link in the chain, but if the chain analogy is sound, how can one link be more crucial than another? One cannot, on the face of it, give credit solely to the economic advisers when things go well, nor make them the sole objects of blame when things go badly.

What I want to consider here are the possibilities for improving economic policy. And since the implementation of policies involves the decisions of ministers, the skills of administrators and the availability of economic statistics as well as theory-based advice, there are all kinds of possibilities. Leaving aside the manner in which policy is implemented by ministers and administrators, many ways have been suggested for improving the information and advice on which policy is based. It has been urged that economic statistics should be made more reliable, or more detailed, or more comprehensive, or more quickly available; that there should be more statistical testing of economic theories; that there should be more 'contact' between economic theorizing and actual policy problems; that economic theory should be more rigorously articulated; that policy advice should be more 'open-minded' rather than an attempt to apply particular economic theories; and so on.

This could, perhaps, be presented as an investment problem, along these lines: given certain limited resources to employ, how would one allocate them between these various possibilities, with the object of improving policy advice? Those who have felt impelled to pronounce on this matter have usually been of the view that the current allocation of effort between these possibilities is so unbalanced that any reasonable increment should all go to one of them--a favourite item being the first one (the improvement, or increased production, of economic statistics--or 'facts' as they are rather question-beggingly called by those, such as Worswick[1] and Leontief[2], who advocate this line of action). Let us take the possibilities one by one, starting with that involving economic statistics.

Economic Statistics

The results of measuring anything are subject to a range of uncertainty, and economic magnitudes are obviously no exception. In fact the term 'exact science' is a contradiction in terms: arithmetic is exact in the abstract, but it only becomes science when it represents calculation about something which is measured with some degree of accuracy. That statistics are uncertain to some degree does not, accordingly, mean that they are worthless, since there is no alternative to uncertain statistics except, presumably, uncertain guesses. Indeed, if we know the degree to which economic statistics are uncertain this is in itself a valuable piece of information, for without it we cannot make the division between what we really know and what we think we know, but don't.

The first problem, then, is creating an appreciation of the degree of reliability of the various statistical aggregates we deal with. For example, national income is quoted to five digits, even though, on the CSO's own estimate that the figure is good to about 3 per cent, only the first two of the digits are significant. It would have to be good to about 1 per cent or better for the third digit to be significant. Thus, the 1966 estimate of 1964's national income was quoted as £26,593 million, rather than, as it should have been, £27,000 million. The other three digits do not embody information: they waste the time of type-setters and proof-readers, and give a misleading impression to all those--in industry, government and the universities--who make use of the statistics. Oskar Morgenstern wrote a whole book making and substantiating this point, as long ago as 1950[3], but matters have, if anything, deteriorated since then, probably because the widespread availability of computing facilities has taken the effort out of spuriously precise calculations, so that the insignificant digits can reproduce themselves without limit.

In the summer of 1967, a drop in unemployment of 468 persons was recorded and widely reported and commented upon; although, at the same time, it could seriously be argued that the unemployment figures underestimated the situation by something of the order of a million people, because of various forms of 'disguised unemployment'. Of course, once the figures are 'seasonally adjusted', they no longer refer to a number of actual persons anyway. As another example, the 'uncooking' or 'recooking' of the balance-of-payments statistics in the summer of 1969 is also worth recalling. Judicious re-working of the figures managed all but to abolish a recorded deficit of some £500 million per year.

Sources of Uncertainty

One could easily multiply examples, but the point should be clear enough. In any case, the issue we are concerned with is how to make improvement; and in order to answer that one, we must take some view as to the sources of uncertainty in economic statistics. It will make a difference to the possible methods of improving matters whether one regards the major source of error as the incorrect initial recording of information (for example on tax returns), the administrative processes of gathering, class- ifying and processing the information or the inherent fuzziness of the economic concepts in terms of which classification and aggre- gation of the information take place. If the raw data themselves are mis-recorded one may attempt to improve things by expanding the monitoring efforts of the agency concerned--HM Inspector of Taxes in the example cited. How one improves administrative pro- cesses of collection and compilation is now always obvious, but there are clear cases where improvement is simply held up by lack of resources.

The problem of the fuzziness of economic concepts is trickier still, and it would seem that this is something which sets a def- inite limit on the value of the other types of improvement; it is something we just have to live with. What is or is not a part of the nation's capital stock, and its total, cannot be entirely settled by reflecting on the concept of 'capital'. The concept may be standardized in practice by adopting one or another of various possible sets of conventions. Although such sets of conventions are a practical necessity in making any accounting system work- able, it remains the case that the precision of the quantities does not entail a corresponding precision with regard to what they are quantities of.

Thus, in regard to economic statistics, tentative conclusions might be that it is not at all obvious that the quality could be much improved; that, in some cases, an improvement could be achieved by putting more resources into administration; but that, in any event, there are limits to the accuracy or reliability of the statistics, arising from the inherent fuzziness of the economic concepts in terms of which they are gathered and expressed. Such a conclusion would not, of course, apply to the claim that what we need are statistics of a different type, rather than simply better statistics--for example, data on the intentions or expecta- tions of traders rather than the usual ex post data relating to realized transactions.

The Bradshaw Lag

One of the major determinants of the value of economic statistics for the guidance of policy is something we have not yet consid- ered: how up to date they are when they become available. The fact that there is a lag, due to administrative processes, between information being recorded, and aggregate statistics being available, has obvious implications; it means that one never knows where the economy is, only where it was some time ago (a few months or a few quarters, depending on the statistics involved). This lag is esoterically known as 'the Bradshaw lag' in honour of Harold Macmillan's remark, while Chancellor, about using published economic statistics.

The existence of this lag makes counter-cyclical policy particularly tricky. For it means that even our knowledge of the current state of the economy is a matter for forecasting, so that if the economy has in fact reached the peak or trough of the cycle during the Bradshaw lag, a projection of the most recent data could be quite misleading. It could happen that, projecting forward from the most recent information, we appear to be in the downswing, while in fact the trough has been reached and an upswing has begun. In such circumstances the expansionary policy that appears to be called for to counteract what is mistakenly believed to be a continuing downswing would reinforce the upswing which is actually taking place. What this means is that stabilization policy must attempt to anticipate the economy's movement during the period of the Bradshaw lag.

The problem is further complicated by the fact that expansionary or contractionary measures take time to have effect and, furthermore, do not have their effects uniformly, but in a gradually increasing manner as they begin to 'bite'. This forward lag has also to be anticipated in carrying out a stabilization policy which is not to be self-defeating.

These possibilities were first dicussed in the 1950s by Milton Friedman[4] and later in a brilliant pioneering article by Phillips[5], the originator of the Phillips curve. The difference between the two was that Friedman was trying to show that discretionary stabilization is so prone to perverse results that we should shun it, whereas Phillips was trying to find out if more sophisticated forms of discretionary policy rules would be likely to perform better, in the face of the various lags and uncertainties. Phillips essentially took an engineering approach to the problem and asked, given that the economy involves processes in which production reacts gradually, and with an unknown lag, to aggregate demand, what kinds of measures will best stabilize production and employment? That is to say, given some underlying, but unknown, relationships between demand (including government spending), production and employment, how should government spending be made to vary in the light of recorded variations in production or employment, in order that these should be stabilized? Detailed work in the spirit of Phillips' pioneering results is being carried out in the Economics Department at Queen Mary College.

Econometrics

The second of the possibilities that I outlined earlier was the suggestion that there should be more statistical testing of theories --that is to say, that we should do more econometrics. Now the testing of theories is like virtue: everyone is in favor of it. But in order to set up an econometric test one has to make a number of assumptions about what depends on what, what is independent of what, what form the dependencies take, the effect of neglected factors, the lags involved in the relationships, and so on. What is evidently tested, then, is the theory together with all the auxiliary assumptions that have made the test possible. To regard the result as a test of the theory alone, one must maintain the truth of the auxiliary assumptions on a priori grounds or attempt to test them independently, which would require the making of further assumptions. And so it would go on. There are good reasons for regarding econometric work as *consequential*, but in no instance can it be *decisive*.

Econometric work seems to have taught us something--although it is hard to think of a single surprising result from it. In the field of monetary economics, for example, it seems fairly well established that the demand for money is sensitive to the rate of interest, but that there is no clear indication of the existence of a Keynesian 'liquidity trap': a floor below which the rate of interest cannot be driven by speculative activities.

Contact Between Theory and Policy

The third of the suggested possibilities was the proposal that there should be more 'contact' between economic theorizing and actual policy problems. One's initial reaction to this proposal is: 'Of course, but how?' The Fulton Report favoured the forced feeding of civil servants on certain allegedly key parts of economic theory. In the event, however, such moves have taken the form of courses in 'Basic Numeracy' in which the would-be numerates spend their time, for example, dividing hypothetical cash flows by $(1 + r)^n$ in the light of the instructions that r, which represents the discount rate, is to be taken as 10 per cent, and n is the hypothetical futurity of the hypothetical cash flow in question. A comparable exercise in basic literacy might be to make a list of all the subordinate clauses in the Fulton Report.

But contact between theory and practice could be made by a movement from either side. So perhaps students should learn their economics in sandwich courses or on day release from the Treasury or the Milk Marketing Board. Or, perhaps, like students of modern languages, economists should spend a year in the trenches, using the rather specialized and artificial modern language they have been learning, before taking their degree. My own solution would be to refuse to accept economics students straight from school. This would make some minimum 'real world' (or 'outside world' as some of my students call it) experience part of the entry requirements for reading for an economics degree.

Danger in Formalization

What of the fourth suggestion, that economic theory should be more rigorously articulated? There are many who would claim that greater rigor is needed in the interests of the development of economic theory, although it might seem farfetched to claim that this would also contribute materially to the improvement of policy advice.

Now, no one is opposed to rigor of argument; one simply raises the questions: how does one achieve it, and at what cost? When economists talk about the increased rigor of their theorizing, what they invariably mean is its formalization in mathematical terms. But it is far from established that a mathematically formalized version of a theory is, in any important sense, more rigorous than it would otherwise have been. Whereas formalization may force us to be grammatical in our theorizing (so to speak) it offers no help in pinning down the meaning of what is being said.

It is, of course, the formalization of ideas that allows economic theorizing to be converted into *deductive* processes-- the drawing of necessary inferences from postulated assumptions. And once theorizing has been converted into deductive processes it can be carried on without regard to the truth of either the postulates or their implications, or indeed, even the meaning of the propositions involved. This being the case, it could be seriously argued that the lack of contact between theory and actual problems, referred to earlier, may in fact be widened by the over-reliance on deductive processes.

More Open-Minded Advice

The final suggestion for improvement was that policy advice should be more 'open-minded', and less of an attempt to apply particular economic theories. This, I believe, is a favourite among administrators who are on the receiving end of economic policy advice. Be that as it may, the suggestion is clearly a plea for scepticism and eclecticism, and, as such, deserves to be considered seriously. Now, the trouble with being sceptical about economic theory, keeping an open mind, and approaching problems on their own merits, is that one is invariably driven back to a reliance on common sense; and common sense is widely regarded not only as common, but also as sensible. So this seems a very good insurance against half-baked schemes stemming from speculative theorizing. But the trouble with common sense in economic affairs is that it is usually not an alternative to applying economic theories, but rather a case of applying extremely primitive (and often demonstrably misguided) economic theories. Try getting someone to use open-minded common sense to think about the burden of the national debt, the effects of a general increase in thriftiness, or the employment-effects of increasing the size of a balanced budget. One is liable to end up with some uncommon nonsense, even by the standards of logical consistency and general coherence.

For example, many of those who rely on 'common sense' to think about balance-of-payments problems come up with variations on the theme of "Britain Must Pay Its Way'--meaning, presumably, that Britain must generate a surplus on its balance of payments at existing parities--a view which probably has more to do with the interpretation of the sterling exchange rate as a virility symbol, and international indebtedness as a violation of the protestant ethic, than with the realities of international monetary problems.

The question of whether or not to engage in economic theory, in the knowledge that it might even be wrong and misleading, is rather like that of whether to sell arms to repressive regimes, in that if you don't do it somebody else will. Common sense, insofar as it says anything on the matter, is not an alternative to economic theory, but a special case of it.

Ministerial Responsibility

We turn finally to the most difficult of all aspects of economic policy, ministerial responsibility for policy decisions and the execution of policy by the administrative arm of government. To comment on how these could be improved is to expound a political philosophy. Even to attempt practical suggestions in the absence of practical experience would denote a lack of common sense. All one can do is warn against a self-defeating imbalance of effort in the attempts to improve economic policy. In short, it is no use drawing up fancy policies for which no minister would want to be held responsible or that would be impossible to administer.

It is also at the ministerial level that the inescapable conflict between the various goals of economic policy must be resolved. The fact that a government is committed to pursue the goals of growth, full employment, price stability, not to mention the more detailed objectives of regional, urban and environmental policies, itself gives no indication of how much one of these goals should be sacrificed in the interests of another. Of course, in public, ministers talk as if, after the coming breakthrough at any rate, all good things will come together. In practice, however, they

236

must, and do, face up to trade-offs, and are prepared to sacrifice full-employment for a balance-of-payments surplus or the hope of a lower rate of inflation. Not unnaturally, ministers try to present such actions as having been forced upon them or as 'the only way out' rather than as calculated choices. But presumably no one is taken in by such rhetoric.

It is also as well to realize that each ministry is not just an indifferentiated hierarchy of civil servants. The economic advisers in the civil service are distinct from the administrators proper; and each group has its own norms, traditions, aspirations and vested interests in the use of its skills. That is to say, there is the question of the internal politics of the ministries themselves. Economic advisers can decide what advice to give; but administrators and ministers can decide on what matters to request advice, and furthermore, whether or not to take the advice that is offered.

What follows from all this? We know that the economic theory on which policy advice is based is in a state of flux, and we have seen that the statistics by means of which the state of the economy is assessed are incomplete and uncertain to a degree which is itself uncertain. It follows that the proffering of advice on policy in such circumstances must involve a considerable exercise of judgment. One might even go to the extreme and claim that such advice is *all* judgment, and that economic policy is an art, quite separate from and independent of, the science of economics. But even if economic policy were an art, it would still have to be based on some practical precepts. In which case, we may ask what the relation of these precepts is to the propositions of economic theory. In light of the discussion, it should be clear that the relation is not one of entailment or logical necessity, for there is a logical gulf between theory and policy which it is the task of judgment to bridge. On the other hand, it is hard, especially for an economist, to believe that the precepts are totally independent of the propositions of economic theory. The fact that economists make use of some of their theoretical ideas as more than window dressing in attacking or advocating particular policies helps to establish this point. So the relation between theoretical propositions and practical precepts would appear to be neither entailment nor independence, but the logically much more troublesome relation of suggestion.

Conclusions

What, I think, follows from this discussion is that although economic theory and statistics cannot lead to policy advice without the application of judgment, they can serve to *discipline* that judgment: they can impose system, coherence and explicitness on it. Setting up an ideal of disciplined judgment for policy advice means, in these terms, there are two ways in which advice can be deficient. It can consist of undisciplined judgment, or it can consist of discipline for its own sake. In practice, of course, politicians and administrators have tended to err in the former way, and professional economists in the latter.

The ideal lies, not in a compromise between the theoretical and the practical, but in a combination of two quite distinct types of skills. But how are these skills to be combined? My discussion has shown, I think, why the solution offered by Worswick involves a misconception. He sees the failure of economics to grapple usefully with real problems as requiring the redress of an imbalance of specialisms within the profession. I have presented it as requiring the redress of an imbalance of skills within each economist.

Footnotes

*   Alan Coddington has a D.Phil. in Economics from the University of York, and is a lecturer in Economics at Queen Mary College, University of London. He has taught at the Centre for Administrative Studies and has been a consultant to the O.E.C.D.

1.   G.D.N. Worswick, "Is Progress in Economic Science Possible?" *Economic Journal,* March 1972.

2.   W. Leontief, "Theoretical Assumptions and Nonobserved Facts", *American Economic Review*, March 1971.

3.   O. Morgenstern, *On the Accuracy of Economic Observations*, Princeton University Press, 1950.

4.   M. Friedman, "The Effects of a Full Employment Policy on Economic Stability: A Formal Analysis" in *Essays in Positive Economics*, University of Chicago Press, 1953.

5.   A.W. Phillips, "Stabilization Policy in a Closed Economy," *Economic Journal*, June 1954.

Part Eight   Pattern Modelling, Storytelling, Holism, and Behavioral Requirements

The article by Charles Wilber and Robert Harrison enunciates the model of explanation which is implicit in the methodology of economics called institutionalism. Institutional economics has a relatively long history among economists since it goes back to the writings of Thorstein Veblen and John R. Commons, but has more recently undergone a re-birth as a counter methodology to the logical positivism of I.M.D. Little and Milton Friedman (see Part Four of this reader). As a background to their discussion of institutionalism, Wilber and Harrison outline the development of formal laws and logical positivism within economics; they note that "the philosophical idea behind these developments is the belief that order and rationality in the world can be understood by making use of reason alone; truth about this world lies in the logic of the economic theory." Wilber and Harrison describe why unrealistic assumptions have not harmed positive economics, and why they survived even in the face of predictions which fail to fit the facts. They note that some economists would now argue that modern economic theory is to be regarded as prescriptive, or as an ideal, rather than as descriptive of the economic world as it really exists. In fact, the perceived failures of positive economics have led some economists to adopt the methodology of "storytelling." This involves analyzing descriptively a problem with a broader based approach encompasing, besides economics, other disciplines such as psychology and political science.

With this as a comparison, Wilber and Harrison present the versions of institutionalism: holistic (focuses on the pattern of relations among parts and the whole), systematic (the parts can only be understood in terms of the whole), the evolutionary (changes in the pattern of relations are seen as the essence of social reality). One implication of these characteristics is that institutionalism has no body of integrated theory. If they do not apply a body of theory to explain situations, what approach is used to explain reality? Wilber and Harrison describe the participant-observer method as the most common means among institutionalists with their stress on holistic explanation. This method is used to construct a pattern model of explanation; this model is complex in that it captures the interactive relationships between the parts and the whole. Wilber and Harrison end their article with a brief discussion of a few problems which the institutional methodology encounters.

The literature of and about institutional economics is large and far ranging. The interested reader should consult almost any issue of *The Journal of Economic Issues* for one to several articles on the topic. To be more specific, the aspects of pattern modelling are set out in Abraham Kaplan's *The Conduct of Inquiry* (Chapter 9) and in Paul Diesing's *Patterns of Discovery in the Social Sciences* (Part III). The methodology is used in the works of J.K. Galbraith, Warren Samuels, Willard Mueller, and Charles C. Craypo, to note only a few. Gunnar Myrdal, another institutionalist, compares it to "conventional" economics and makes a case for the continued importance of institutionalism in the future. Allan Gruchy, in the article noted in the suggested readings, divides institutional economists into four groups: the post-1939 mainstream, the general, the radical, and the applied; he provides some examples of each, compares their ideas and impact, and suggests that they will have to pay more attention to institutionalism's theoretical underpinnings and policy position.

Herbert Simon's article presents a brief history of one aspect of the ongoing struggle between institutionalism and neoclassical theory. He surveys some of the literature on the behavior of firms. More specifically, Simon places the advances in what he calls behavioral theory or bounded rationality in the context of the more widely used and accepted view of the firm as a perfect rationalizer. He brings to the reader's attention the relatively new ideas of satisficing, X-efficiency, adaptive learning, and sales maximization. This article is provided as a sort of case study of one field in economics where the debate over institutionalism has been active.

In 1962, Thomas Kuhn published his famous *The Structure of Scientific Revolutions* which has changed the way in which many scientists view the formation of thought within their discipline. While there is perhaps no good substitute for reading this book, the article by A.W. Coats in this part of the reader does present Kuhn's main ideas and attempts briefly to apply them to the field of economics. It is not hard to draw a parallel between his displacement of paradigms and the movement within economics from general acceptance of neoclassical to Keynesian general theory. As one paradigm (the knowledge and techniques accepted by the dominant groups of members of a science) replaces another due to the appearance of contradictions to the old paradigm, a revolution occurs in the methods, theories, and techniques of the discipline.

240

Needless to say, there has been some debate about whether the idea of paradigms has any usefulness in a social science like economics. Martin Bronfenbrenner argues that neither Kuhn's "catastrophic" theory nor "incrementalism" (a science which developed from one experiment to the next) describe economics' evolution very well; he believes that a dialectic of thesis--anti-thesis--synthesis does a better job of explaining how ideas change over time in that discipline. George Stigler raises the important point that Kuhn fails to describe in sufficient detail the nature of a paradigm (he fails to operationalize that concept); as a result, it is impossible to test his ideas empirically. G.E. Peabody's article provides a good summary of Kuhn's ideas which relate to paradigms and investigates the usefulness of that concept within the broader framework of a more general criticism of contemporary economics as practised by "most" economists.

For the reader who is interested, the entire field of the history of economic thought can be studied in order to evaluate the place of Kuhn's paradigms within the changing ideas of economists. The suggested readings include two interpretative essays by T.W. Hutchison. The evolution of economic thought can of course be put into the paradigm mold, but on the other hand, K.R. Popper and I. Lakatos have suggested other frameworks for the development of social sciences; these ideas are compared and contrasted by Blaug, Katouzian, and in several of the articles in the book which is edited by S. Latsis.

In the 1960s and 1970s several of the methodological issues, which have been discussed in this reader, spread to the sub-discipline of economic history. In particular a group of economic historians applied the tools of logical positivism, econometrics and mathematical economics to the study of the past. These efforts met with strong and concerted criticism from several economic historians with qualitative, institutional, holistic view of economic history. The study of the past often assigned a secondary position in training of economists. Some economists even argued that the past had no useful economics. The issue then is whether anything useful can be learned by economists in studying economic history. These topics are discussed in detail by D. McCloskey and D. North.

13 The Methodological Basis of Institutional Economics: Pattern Model, Storytelling, and Holism

Charles K. Wilber with Robert S. Harrison

> *Between elephantine profundity and sprightly persiflage,*
> *between the Scylla of spurious precision and the*
> *Charybdis of vacuous innuendo, the Institutionalist*
> *navigates as best he/she can.**

What can be said about the truth value of explanations found in institutional economics? Consideration of the question requires a review of a number of other issues. To discuss the truth value of propositions requires a consideration of models of explanation. Since institutionalism's mode of explanation has developed, at least in part, in reaction to standard economics, the models of explanation underlying both standard and institutional economics must be analyzed and compared.

This essay seeks to discover the model of explanation *implicit* in institutionalist writings. It does not prescribe what that method *should* be. Over the years and again in preparation for the writing of this essay, I have read widely in institutional economics,[1] from the classics of Thorstein Veblen and John R. Commons to the contemporary masters, J.K. Galbraith and Gunnar Myrdal, through the interpretation of Allan Gruchy, K. William, Kapp, and Warren Samuels, concluding with every volume and issue of the *Journal of Economic Issues*. Because of space limitations it is impossible to provide documentary evidence for every contention. Rather, illustrative citations will be provided.

Contemporary philosophy of science has been drawn upon to understand institutionalist methodology and how it differs from that of standard economics.[2] The principal task of modern scientists has been to understand, interpret, and explain the reality which surrounds them. However unified this purpose may appear, the question of how to go about this process of explanation has been the source of great controversy. At the heart of it is the issue that modern sciences are differentiated only by differences in subject matter, not in method. Formalism, including logical

Reprinted from the *Journal of Economic Issues* by special permission of the copyright holder, The Association for Evolutionary Economics. The article appeared in the *Journal of Economic Issues*, 12 (1978), 61-90.

positivism and *a priori* rationalism, expresses this view. Most of standard economics falls into this category. *Holism,* including pattern models and storytelling,[3] expresses the belief that a change in subject matter requires a change in method. Institutional economics, radical political economy, and Marxism fall into this category.

Formalism and Standard Economics

Formalism is a method that consists of a formal system of logical relationships abstracted from any empirical content it might have in the real world. For example, the theory of the firm in standard economics deals with the behavior of the firm involved in any process of production using any inputs at any set of relative prices with any technology. It is characterized by the use of mathematics (at least implicitly) and by the development of an axiomatic, deductive structure.

The beginning point in a formal method is the construction of a model of a system or process. A set of postulates and definitions is derived by separating an empirical process into its obvious divisions and specifying the necessary or possible relations among them. Sometimes a pre-existing logical model will be imported and used, such as set theoretic models in microeconomics.

Once the definitions and postulates are established, the next step is to deduce the inherent dynamics of the system. Since the microeconomics of standard theory is an equilibrium system, the inherent dynamics lead to a steady state. In growth theory this is modified by the use of difference equations, "Berlitz" methods, and the like.

At this point in the formal method, the abstract model must be interpreted by providing a set of correspondence rules that relate formal terms of the theory to empirical concepts. For example, first derivatives are interpreted as marginal products, marginal utilities, and so on. In this way the theory attains empirical content. A theory, therefore, is merely an abstract model that has one or more interpretations. "Rules of Interpretation do make a truth claim; they claim that the structure of relations in a calculus is the same structure that exists in some part or aspect of the empirical world."[4] Thus it is assumed that the structure of reality is approximated by the logical structure of the calculus, or set theory, or difference equations.

Formal methods produce models that are capable of yielding lawlike statements. These formal laws are not empirical generalizations but are logical deductions that make *a priori* statements about necessary connections between abstract entities. For example, the beginning postulates of the standard theory of the firm define the firm as a rational decision maker that attempts to maximize expected returns and has the information and ability to do so. Lawlike statements that can be deduced from this include the proposition that firms will continue buying inputs and producing and selling outputs up to the point where expected returns are maximized--where marginal cost equals marginal revenue. This statement does not describe how actual firms behave, but how an ideally rational firm would behave. And this is determined not from observation but from logical deduction. These types of law-like statements are difficult to falsify empirically because of changing *ceteris paribus* conditions.

Most of standard microeconomics has consisted of this type of formal model. Until the development of econometrics in the 1950s, little attempt was made to test empirically the propositions of economic theory. In reality most standard economists were descendants not of Isaac Newton,[5] but of Rene Descartes, who argued that we can know the world through reason alone. For Descartes, the real world is characterized by order and rationality and thus is best apprehended through an appeal to human reason alone. Implicit in standard theory, therefore, was the position that truth about reality lies in the logic of the theory. This is the nature of the economic theory from which Veblen, Commons, and Wesley Mitchell dissented. The focus on the logic of the formal model meant that rational behavior was emphasized and custom and habit ignored; competition was glorified, and the changing nature of technology, business organization, and the role of the state totally omitted; and the presence of unemployment was dismissed as a disequilibrium condition.

Beginning in the 1940s, economists such as Paul Samuelson attempted to reconstruct economic theory in a way that would make it empirically testable.[6] They drew upon physics as the paradigm science and on logical positivism, which was then at its peak. The latter, in turn, had constructed its model of explanation by observing the practice of physicists. Logical positivism attempted to show that empirically falsifiable propositions could be derived from formal models. The development of the computer and of statistical techniques has reshaped standard economics in the past 25 years. Some economists still deal with purely formal models, for example, the application of set theory to consumer demand theory. But most economists have become positivists, that is, they see empirical verification as the key to economic science.

Institutionalists, however, still see much of modern economics as incapable of explaining the real world. An analysis of why is necessary.

The classical modern version of logical positivism is found in

the work of Carl Hempel and Paul Oppenheim.[7]   The now famous
"covering law model of explanation" purports to schematize the
"function and essential characteristics of scientific explanation."
Although originally intended to codify the structure of explanation
in the physical sciences, it was adopted by economists due to the
belief that sciences are differentiated by subject matter, not
method.   Hempel and Oppenheim argue that scientific explanation
is always characterized by general laws which, in effect, cover or
subsume the event under scrutiny.   Thus, for logical positivists
the difference between a scientific explanation and a merely ad hoc
one is that every explanation is subsumed or covered by one or
more of the general laws.   The diagram below will help clarify
their model.

Covering Law Model of Explanation

L_1, L_2, L_3 ... L_n General Laws   Explanans
C_1, C_2, C_3 ... C_n Antecedent conditions

Logical   E Description of the empirical
deduction →   phenomenon to be explained   Explanandum
                 (hypothesis)

The explanans, which include antecedent conditions and general
laws are a class of propositions which account for the observed
phenomenon that is, the things that do the explaining.   The C_n's
are statements of antecedent conditions which are observed facts
relevant to the phenomenon to be explained and which provide the
empirical content for the theory.   The L_n's are general laws generated by the particular science (for example, in economics, maximizing behavior) which refer particular instances to general
principles.   Using the laws of logical deduction, a logical positivist is able to generate an explanandum or hypothesis from the explanans.   This explanandum, the event to be explained, acts as a
prediction of a correlational relationship in the real world.   It is
then subjected to empirical testing such as statistical inference or
direct observation in order to assess the truth of the hypothesis.
The hypothesis and hence the explanation are tentatively held as
true and accepted if the hypothesis is not disconfirmed; likewise,
if the hypothesis is disconfirmed, it is rejected as false.   Since
logical positivists maintain that we cannot *know* the truth,
they argue that the best one can do is to put forward hypotheses
and subject them to rigorous tests.   Within this framework, positivists assert that science proceeds by accumulating *potentially
falsifiable, but nonfalsified (confirmed) propositions about the
subject matter.*   As we shall subsequently demonstrate, this
assertion is an ideal that is observed more in rhetoric than in
practice.

The logical positivists' formal model requires that explanation and prediction be symmetrical. That is, explanation occurs when the explanandum is derived after the event, whereas prediction occurs when the explanandum is derived before the event takes place. Due to the ahistorical and universal nature of positivists' general laws, there is a *logical necessity* that explanation and prediction be symmetrical. Moreoever, it is critical to the viability of this symmetric relation that tentatively held hypotheses, in practice, be potentially falsifiable, but as yet nonfalsified. Indeed, explanation is not considered adequate unless it could have served as the basis of prediction.

Modern economics has been given its most explicit espousal of logical positivism in the works of I.M.D. Little[8] and especially in Milton Friedman's *Essays in Positive Economics*.[9] In search of a legitimate methodology, Friedman's work can be seen as an attempt to counter the charges leveled at standard economics by both institutionalists and Marxists. Principally, these charges centered on the neoclassical theory of the firm.[10] The institutionalists claimed that standard assumptions concerning the behavior of entrepreneurs were contradicted by empirical evidence and therefore unrealistic. Friedman's now classic chapter 1 of his Essays was an attempt to show the irrelevance of this charge and thereby restructure economic theory into a logical positivist form. Friedman's argument has become so pervasive (despite disagreement over details) that the positivist method is found in one form or another in most of the leading introductory economics texts.[11]

The goal of positive economics "is to provide a system of generalizations that can be used to make correct predictions about the consequences of any change in circumstances. Its performance is to be judged by the precision, scope, and confirmity with experience of the predictions its yields."[12] Predictability, then, is the crucial element in positive economics. Insofar as prediction and explanation are symmetrical in all positive sciences, explanation in standard economic theory takes the form of logically deducing an explanandum (hypothesis/prediction) from the explanans (general laws and antecedent conditions).

Since correct predictions imply correct explanations, scientific explanation in economics, proceeds by tentatively accepting those theories which yield hypotheses (or predictions) that when tested exhibit a high degree of correspondence to the real world. A low level or lack of correspondence indicates a flaw in the theory, and it is rejected as disconfirmed. As positivists, then, it is by testing that economists resolve disputes and assess competing theories. Testing the models' predictions against experience serves to validate or verify the "system of generalizations" and leads to the accumulation of laws that constitute general theory. However, the key feature of positive theory, in economics, is the claim to prediction. Thus, economists will seek those theories which best explain/predict the empirical phenomena of the economic world.

Since the validity of a model is to be judged by its predictive ability, the realism of its assumptions or the static nature of its structure become irrelevant issues. In a formal model, all assumptions are more or less abstract and unrealistic because it cannot, by definition, capture or reproduce the whole of reality. Consequently, assumptions facilitate abstraction, and this enables the economist to explain the underlying order of things.

Since standard economists place so much weight on the ability to predict as the means of verifying the truth of a theory, it is necessary to explore the success of such an endeavor in economics. Successful prediction of economic phenomena has been consistently lacking over past years. This failure is highlighted by the nation's recent experience with unemployment, inflation, and the energy crisis. Insofar as positive economic theories are to be "judged solely by [their] predictive ability," why is it that, in practice, when economists' theories fail to fit the facts, they are not rejected? In order to clarify this difficulty, two related issues need to be addressed. The first is concerned with the efficacy of applying logical positivism to economics. In other words, is the subject matter of economics amenable to ahistorical universal generalization which can form the basis for successful prediction? A second related issue involves the problem of positivist insularity from theory rejection. That is, how is it possible that orthodox economic theory remains intact despite the repeated failure of its hypotheses to yield accurate factual predictions?

With respect to the first issue, the position of positive economics is that knowledge, whether in the physical or social sciences, is to be distinguished solely on the basis of the empirical subject matter and not by methodology. An implicit assumption is that the subject matter of economics is comparable to that of the physical sicneces, where the subject matter and its response to external factors is characterized by its high degree of stability over time. For example, a falling object with a certain mass has accelerated and will always accelerate at a rate fixed by the law of gravity. Thus, the successful application of the theoretical methods used in the physical sciences the subject matter of economics is contingent upon the stability of the data generated by the economic agents.

Robert Heilbroner argues that certain types of economic data are highly unstable. He classifies economic data into two different categories: The first relates to "the physical nature of the

248

production process," whereas the second relates to "the behavioral response to economic stimuli."[13] Heilbroner further argues
that although behavioral data tend to exhibit a high degree of
long-run stability due to the influence of "habits, customs, traditions and usages of society," technical data such as long-run
production functions are highly unstable and impossible to predict.[14] On the other hand, whereas it may be possible to predict
"with a fair degree of accuracy the actual production possibilities
open to society in the short-run," short-run behavioral responses
tend to be highly unpredictable.[15] Consequently, the instability
of economic data makes ahistorical generalizations exceedingly
problematic and severely limits the ability of economists to predict
successfully.

Another characteristic difference between the subject matter
of the social and physical sciences is the inherently poor experimental quality of social phenomena. Unlike the physical sciences,
the social sciences must attempt to generalize from open rather
than closed systems. In the physical sciences, researchers can
artifically construct an experimental design which enables them to
control some variables while allowing others to vary. Because the
subject matter of economics is not amenable to controlled experiments, "economics has resorted to the use of partial equilibrium
analysis in an attempt to reduce the complexity of economic
phenomena to manageable proportions."[16] Since all factors vary
at once in economic phenomena, the positive economist utilizes the
ceteris paribus technique in order to control artificially the potentially random behavior of certain factors. This technique
serves to give the model, although not the subject matter itself, a
degree of determinedness. Therefore, due to the nature of the
subject matter and to the inherently poor experimental design
found in economic phenomena, we conclude that successful prediction is extremely difficult to achieve in economics. As such,
the applicability of positive methodology to the task of explaining
economic phenomena is seriously compromised. This conclusion
leads us to the second issue.

Despite the difficulty of obtaining successful prediction,
positive economists have achieved a high degree of insulation from
the failure of their predictions. Why is this so? It is Thomas
Kuhn's concept of a paradigm which lies behind economists' resistance to acknowledging the failure of their predictions as evidence
of an incorrect theory. In the pursuit of "normal science" the
economist is guided by the dictates of his own paradigm. Behind
this paradigm lie the economist's general theory and doctrine
which determine his choice of relevant problems, provide the
analytical tools, and supply a general vision of how reality is
structured. Kuhn argues that this paradigm, together with its
basic hypotheses, once established in the very thought processes
of its members is rarely, if ever, shaken by empirical discon-

firmation. Consequently, for the positive economist, hypotheses are seldom disconfirmed and general theory rarely or never disproved. However, the crucial issue is: What are the mechanisms which allow economists to rationalize the failure of their predictions and thereby protect both their methodology and their paradigm? The high degree of insulation afforded to standard theory arises because of the highly conditional nature of its predictions, which are dependent upon the *ceteris paribus* clauses holding and upon the data being representative of economic reality. In the physical sciences, when the researcher's model repeatedly fails to predict correctly, he blames his model. The economist is able to rationalize the failure of his prediction by blaming the *ceteris paribus* clauses, the data, or the specific testing procedure itself. These three mechanisms, examined below, make it easy for economists to reject a disconfirmation as invalid and, thus, insulate their theory from refutation.

First is the *ceteris paribus* problem. As mentioned briefly above, economists rely heavily upon *ceteris paribus* clauses when constructing their hypotheses in order to "control" their subject matter. Such hypotheses in economics are typically stated in the form of "if ... then" propositions. Since the "ifs" do change, an econometric test that disconfirms the theory can always be rejected as "misspecified."

Second is the difficulty of constructing a clear-cut test of an hypothesis in economics. Most of the traditional statistical tests, such as null hypotheses, are very weak ones which a large number of different theories are capable of passing. Thus, when empirical tests fail to discriminate adequately among competing theories, economists tend to assess theories on the basis of desirable logical qualities such as simplicity and generality, all qualities inherent in formal models.

Third, both the methods of collection and construction of economic data are unreliable. Typically, economic data are statistically constructed and are not conceptually the same as the corresponding variables in the theory. Therefore, econometricians and statisticians engage in data "massaging." If a test disconfirms an hypothesis, the investigator can always blame the data--they have been "massaged" either too much or not enough.

Positive economics thus becomes perfectly insulated from refutation. It cannot be harmed by demonstrating that the assumptions and laws of the formal model are abstract and unrealistic, and the model is not rejected when its predictions fail to fit the facts. What is left of "normal economic science"? When a theory is able to obtain such a high level of insulation that its substantive hypotheses are, in practice, nonfalsifiable, we contend that the theory collapses into an *a priori* formal model that compels assent by its logic, not by its conformity with empirical reality. As such, economic theory functions more as a prescriptive than descriptive device. That is, theory functions as a parable to elucidate the ideal toward which we should strive.

For economists such as Paul Samuelson, Robert Solow, and Wassily Leontief, neoclassical economic theory has become the "grand parable" that is still defended against nonbelievers but is not taken too seriously as a scientific explanation of "what is." Rather, attention is focused on the development of a set of "engineering tools"--linear programming, input-output analysis, cost-benefit analysis, and so on. Economics has come to be conceived in engineering terms: How do you maximize some objective function in the face of various constraints?

Where does all this leave standard economics? In microeconomics, economists seeking to explain events have ended up as *a priori* rationalists by insulating their theories from empirical falsifications. Others have dropped the problem of explanation and concentrate on using economic theory as a guide to action. When empirical reality diverges from the model, they recommend changes in the reality. Macroeconomists have generated various forecasting models that concentrate on prediction. They have been adjusted so often to attain better predictions that little coherent theory remains. At best, ad hoc explanations are developed to support the predictions--predictions that have been notoriously inaccurate.

The final outcome of the use of formal methods in economics is that those methods fail to generate the hoped for results, and the investigators end up engaging in what Ben Ward calls "storytelling." Instead of explaining something by logically deducing an hypothesis as a specific instance of a more general law and then subjecting it to empirical verification, economists tell a variety of stories--some more plausible than others. Some take their logical models and tell a story about a world of perfect competition: Institutions are characterized by smallness, everyone has the same motive, and all problems are frictions, externalities, and other "sociological penumbra." Other economists prepare econometric studies, "massage" the data on the basis of other information, vary the auxiliary hypotheses to *paribus the ceteris*, develop *ad hoc* explanations and thus make up a story about what happened.

The use of the term *storytelling* is not meant pejoratively. Rather, it is an accurate description of most work in the social sciences. To recognize that fact should be helpful to economics.

It is indeed ironic that one of the great benefits formalism has conferred on economics is not the formalism itself but the pressure toward systematic storytelling. One remembers once again the reaction to programming studies in which the benefit they produce is appraised not so much in terms of the formal results as of the pressure toward systematic, goal-oriented collection of facts. A linear programming formulation then becomes essentially no more than the outline of a story one wants to tell. Best results are achieved when that is exactly the way in which one looks at the formalism, retaining perfect freedom to resort to information which will not fit the programming framework if it will help tell the story better.

The point is that the basic methodological element in economics, and all social science, is not the study but the story.

The main point is not really that this is how economists ought to behave. It is rather that this is how they do in fact behave; this is, roughly speaking, the methodology that we actually use in establishing our professional beliefs. Perhaps the science could be improved if we were more honest about this matter, for practitioners might then feel under less pressure to transform their studies into models of a procedure that has not worked and which really is not even believed. The result of that practice has been to sweep under the table some of the most important and profound issues that economics faces, as well as substantially to distort much potentially useful work.[17]

Institutionalism, Holism, and Pattern Models

Since at least Veblen's time, institutionalists have recognized that formal methods--whether of the *a priori* rationalist type or of the logical positivist covering law model--fail to explain the nature of social reality. Thus, institutionalism has been engaged in a twofold task over the years. One, detailed above, has been a critique of standard theory; the other, the positive task of developing its own explanations of social phenomena.

The holistic nature of institutionalism has ruled out other than incidental use of formal methods. Instead, institutionalists have engaged in a systematic form of storytelling that Abraham Kaplan calls a "pattern model."[18]

At the most general level, institutional economics can be characterized as holistic, systemic, and evolutionary.[19] Social reality is seen as more than a specified set of relations; it is the process of change inherent in a set of social institutions which we call an economic system. The process of social change is not purely mechanical; it is the product of human action, but action which is definitely shaped and limited by the society in which it has its roots. Thus, institutionalism is holistic because it focuses on the pattern of relations among parts and the whole. It is systemic because it believes that those parts make up a coherent whole and can be understood only in terms of the whole. It is evolutionary because changes in the pattern of relations are seen as the very essence of social reality.

At a more concrete level, institutional economics has had an appreciation for the centrality of power and conflict in the economic process.

> The preoccupation with the role of conflict, power and coercion is an intellectual heritage which ... early American institutionalists like Veblen and Commons have reformulated and integrated ... into their analysis of "vested interests," absentee ownership, the economic role of the state, the legal foundations of capitalism, the importance of collective and political bargaining, public utility regulations and the analysis of collusion between financial, industrial and political power.[20]

This heritage is carried on today by John Kenneth Galbraith's work on the "planning system,"[21] Warren Samuels on law and economics,[22] Willard Mueller on antitrust,[23] and Charles Craypo on the impact of conglomerate mergers on collective bargaining;[24] the list could go on and on. Conflict is generated by changes in technology, social institutions, and distributions of power and thus is an inherent part of the economic process.

At the motivational level, institutional economics always has recognized the importance of "nonrational" human behavior in economic decision making.[25] A thirst for power and adventure, a sense of independence, altruism, idle curiosity, custom, and habit may all be powerful motivations of economic behavior. Thus, institutionalists have been particularly critical of the economic man assumption of neoclassical economics.[26]

These characteristics of institutionalism--holistic, systemic, evolutionary--combined with the appreciation for the centrality of power and conflict and the recognition of the importance of nonrational human behavior, differentiate instituionalism from standard economics. Formal models simply cannot handle the range of variables, the specificity of institutions, and the nongenerality of behavior.

Partly because of these characteristics, institutionalism has "no body of integrated theory such as characterizes neoclassical and Marxian economics."[27]

Institutionalist-heterodox economists have a truly wide range of interests and competing emphases: technology, power, institutions, the state of the working class, in strumentalism, pragmatism, conflict and its resolution, social forces, distribution, evolution, philosophical-ethical relativism or absolutism, progress, contextualism, economic organization and control ... deliberative social control and/or social change, institutional design and performance, socialization of the corporate system, economic planning, the economic role of government, the logic of reform and/or industrialization, humanism, and, *inter alia*, economic development and growth. There are alternative formulations of problems and issues, different visions of holism and evolution, different areas of specialized interests, and reformist urges without agreement as to agenda.[28]

Instituionalism includes Mueller's antitrust and Galbraith's national planning, Clarence Ayres's theoretical musings, and Harry Trebings's case studies of public regulation, to name but a few of the better-known incongruous bedfellows.[29] What ties these economists together is not a shared body of theory but a common model of explanation. In his perceptive essay entitled "*The Journal of Economic Issues* and the Present State of Heterodox Economics," Samuels admits that "institutionalism may have no elaborate corpus of analysis, rather only a way of investigation with some important guides to inquiry." He goes on to say: "I think that institutional economics does involve more than this but am prepared to recognize that substantively it may be closer to an investigatory mode than a corpus of knowledge comparable to other schools of thought."[30]

We do not want to argue whether or not there is an institutionalist economic theory. Our argument is that implicit in the work of institutionalists is a common "investigatory mode" or model of explanation that conforms to what philosophers of science call a pattern model. Institutionalism's investigatory mode is holistic, systemic, and evolutionary.

Holism is a term originally coined by the South African scholar Jan Christiaan Smuts from the Greek world *holos,* which means whole. He applied the term in categorizing the new type of theories in the physical sciences that were gaining widespread recognition in his time.[31] These new evolutionary or dynamic theories (Charles Darwin's theory of evolution, 1859; Henri Becquerel's theory of radioactivity, 1895; Albert Einstein's theory of relativity, 1915) had finally displaced the old inherited mechanistic scientific theories of Newton and the pre-Darwin world. This post-Darwinian type of scientific thought which Smuts describes as "holistic" conceived of the physical word as an evolving dynamic whole, as opposed to the "atomistic" theories, which held a static or deterministic view of the world. These holistic theories are essentially couched in the belief that the whole is not only greater than the sum of its parts, "but that the parts are so related that their functioning is conditioned by their interrelations."[32]

For the holist, then, explanation of reality cannot be had through the application of universal laws, with successful predictions the only form of verification. Rather, an event or action is explained by identifying its place in a pattern that characterizes the ongoing processes of change in the whole system. As the philosopher Michael Scriven has said: "In place of the social scientists' favorite myth of the Second Coming (of Newton), we should recognize the Reality of the Already-Arrived (Darwin); the paradigm of the explanatory but non-predictive scientist."[33]

Thorstein Veblen, the recognized founder of the institutionalist tradition, brought this holist philosophical orientation to the study of the U.S. economy. Veblen conceived of the economic order as an evolving scheme of things or cultural process. His construction of a "systems economics" was to remain the point of reference from which later institutionalists were to criticize the narrow "market economics of choice" espoused by standard economics. In Samuels's summary he remarks: "The institutionalist paradigm focuses upon ... an holistic and evolutionary view of the structure-behavior-performance of the economy ... in a system of general interdependence or cumulative causation."[34] This could also serve as a summary of holism.

> The picture of the economy which is incorporated within or emerges from the institutionalist paradigm is that of a system of power, with elements of both conflict and harmony, and with conflict as both causes and consequences of economic evolution. It is, even more fundamentally, a picture of deep cumulative causation between market forces and institutions; of profound impacts of organizations and control forces; of existential systemic diversity and openendedness; of multiple social valuational processes, including the market; of inevitable and deep legal foundations; and of individual and collective action. The allocation of resources is seen to be a result of decisional forces and institutions which operate through and indeed form market supply and demand and which are subject to deliberate and nondeliberative re formation. It is a conception of the economy with respect to which the conditions of market equilibrium and the attainment of optimal solutions are but narrow, albeit important, slices.[35]

This picture of the economy could only have been derived from a holist methodology. Formalist methods could not have created this pattern or story.

Although the holistic intellectual orientation has been a part of the thought process of both social and physical scientists since the middle of the nineteenth century, recent attention to holism by philosophers of sciences has led to a coherent expression of its methodology. Most notably, the works of Abraham Kaplan and Paul Diesing each contain explicit presentations of the holist model of explanation. These authors seek to uncover the implicit structural framework which facilitates holist theorists' explanations of reality. In Diesing's outstanding work, *Pattern of Discovery in the Social Sciences*, he generalizes across all social sciences in order to explicate the characteristics common to all holist-type theories. Diesing finds a commonality among such theories which includes their conception of reality, the structure of their explanations, the primacy of their subject matter, and their particular form of logic. We shall examine these characteristics below, but first let us turn to the procedure frequently used for deriving holistic explanations.

In Diesing's view, the approach which has achieved the greatest success in constructing holistic explanations in the social sciences is what he terms the participant-observer method. When using this method, the primary subject matter for the researcher is a single, self-maintaining social system. Although holists have varying conceptions of how whole the system needs to be, one thing is clear. It is not the sheer magnitude of the whole that is important, but that the particular system under investigation constitute a *unified* whole. The magnitude of the selected system may vary from a single family to a larger society with its culture, or perhaps from a formal organization or institution to a whole historical epoch. In any case, the emphasis is upon the individuality or uniqueness of the particular system.

The first step toward constructing a holist model via the participant-observer method is the "socialization" of the theorist. As participants, investigators allow the subject matter to impress upon them its norms and to instill within them its categories. Unlike positivists, who impose external formulas upon the subject matter, the participant-observer attempts to remain close to the concrete form of the system.

Despite Veblen's self-proclaimed disinterest, institutionalists ranging from Richard Ely and John R. Commons through Gardiner Means, John Kenneth Galbraith, John Blair, and Gunnar Myrdal have been participants as well as observers. Most of the best-known institutionalists have developed their ideas while being "socialized" in a system - public utility regulation, price control, economic planning, antitrust, small business. In the first issue of the *Journal of Economic Issues*, the editor, Forest G. Hill, stated: "The title of this *Journal* may suggest its main emphasis. It will be broadly concerned with major issues of public policy."[36] Clearly, institutionalists have been participant-observers in the sense used by Diesing.

In remaining close to the concrete reality of the system studied, the theorist is in a unique position to perceive a wide variety of recurrent themes (importance of ceremony, target profits/markup pricing) that appear in a variety of contexts. A theme is more important the more links it has with other themes, because the holist wants to construct a model which emphasizes the interconnectedness or unity of the system. These recurrent themes may take the form of an accepted practice (ceremonies), a cultural norm (conspicuous consumption), or a particular mode of production (competitive capitalism) which more or less conditions everything else, or some recognized social objective (social status). As an observer, the researcher looks for themes which illuminate the system's wholeness, that is, which contribute to its individuality or oneness. It is in this sense that holists find general laws (law of demand) and universal categories (utility) especially unsuited to the task of describing the unity of the particular system.

The next step of the procedure is to make explicit this information which, as a participant, the researcher is now able to perceive. Initially, this process is rather haphazard. The researcher constructs tentative hypotheses about parts of the system out of the recurrent themes that become obvious to him or her in the course of the socialization process. These hypotheses or interpretations of themes are tested by consulting a wide variety of data (previous case studies, survey data, personal observations, and so forth). Evidence in support of an hypothesis or interpretation is evaluated by means of contextual validation. This technique is a process of cross-checking different kinds and sources of evidence, and it serves as an indirect means of evaluating the plausibility of one's initial interpretations. The validity of a piece of evidence in support of a particular statement can be assessed by "comparing it with other kinds of evidence on the same point" or by "evaluating the source of the evidence by locating other kinds of evidence about that source."[37] If the researcher is unable to secure evidence in support of earlier hypotheses or if the validity of the evidence or its source proves to be questionable, the interpretations and/or hypotheses are revised or discarded. Gradually, as socialization proceeds, the researcher becomes increasingly attuned to accurate perception and interpretation of the recurrent themes and formulation of validated hypotheses. The holist uses this experience and the various pieces of evidence to build up a many-sided, complex picture of the subject matter. Unfortunately, this technique of contextual validation can never produce the rigorous certainty espoused by logical positivists; it can only indicate varying

257

degrees of plausibility. However, a test of a particular theme or
hypothesis at this level of development need never be conclusive
in order to have importance for the holist, since later tests are
likely to catch errors that were missed by earlier ones.

Eventually, after several themes have been validated, the
holist proceeds to the last step of the procedure--building a
model. This type of model with its emphasis upon recurrent
themes within or around the individual system is aptly known to
philosophers of science as the pattern model of explanation.[38] It
is constructed by linking validated hypotheses or themes in a
network or pattern. In addition, the pattern model theorist's
account of a particular part should refer to the multiplicity of
connections between that part and the whole system. It is in this
way that the holist attempts to capture the interactive relationship
between part and whole. As the holist constructs the system
model his earlier description of the parts are continually tested by
how well they fit together in a pattern and to what extent new
evidence can be explained within the pattern. The holist is constantly seeking to obtain a finer and finer degree of coherence
between his account of the system as a pattern of interconnections
and the real system. However, since new data are constantly
coming in and since the system itself is evolving, the model is
continually being revised and can neither be completed nor rigorously confirmed. As Diesing points out:

> The nature of human subject matter also produces incomplete-
> ness of pattern. Human systems are always developing and
> always unfinished; they always retain inconsistencies, am-
> biguities, and absurdities. Belief systems never achieve
> complete rationality and consistency; personalities and
> groups are always in the process of resolving old conflicts
> and sharpening new ones; accumulations of power are always
> crumbling and being rebuilt; ceremonies are being elaborated
> or simplifed. Consequently, a faithful model of a particular
> system at a particular time will itself include inconsistencies,
> ambiguities, and exceptions. How many of these are due to
> the inconsistencies of the subject and how many to the loose-
> ness of the method is difficult to say.[39]

Verification of the pattern model as a whole consists of expanding it further and filling in more details. That is, the researcher is reasonably certain that an explanation is a correct one
if new data and different kinds of evidence tend to fall into place
in the pattern. Consequently, verification of the truth of the explanation lies not in any one component but in the whole. This is
due to the low level of reliability the holist attaches to any
particular interpretation of a specific part (since the parts are
only contextually validated). Holists argue that their explanation
is a correct one if, as the pattern becomes more complex and de-

tailed, a greater variety of evidence easily falls into place. At this point, it is more difficult to imagine an alternative pattern or explanation which manages to include the same themes. As a consequence, the explanation of the whole system is tentatively held as true, until an alternative or revised pattern is able to supercede the old model by incorporating an even greater variety of data. In a parallel discussion, Benjamin Ward offers a check-list for verifying a story:

1. Are the facts and theories correctly stated?

2. Are important facts or theories omitted?

3. Can one find other stories which use the facts and theories employed in the given story?

4. Are the facts and theories relevant or essential to the story; that is, can no other hypotheses be used to tell as good a story about the facts?

5. Do experts in the various parts of the story believe the story itself?

6. Are values correctly stated?

7. Are all relevant values included?

The stronger the "Yes" to each of these questions, the stronger is the verification of the story.[40]

From the viewpoint of the holist the primary function of laws and theories (within the pattern model) is to provide *understanding*; from the viewpoint of the logical positivist (within the formal model), it is to allow *predictions*. Within the context of the pattern model, the pattern which provides the explanation does not uniquely determine the parts. Thus, knowledge of the whole pattern and of some of the parts does not necessarily enable the holist to predict any or all unknown parts. "The explanation still explains even though it leaves open a range of possibilities, so that which possibility is actualized is knowable only after the fact ... The theory of evolution explains highly specialized forms as produced by natural selection from a succession of less specialized ones, but the more highly specialized are predictable only in a general way."[41] Thus, the accuracy of predictions cannot be the main form of verification in the pattern model.

Much institutionalist work stops at the level of pattern models based on case studies.[42] A few institutionalists--Veblen, Ayres,

Myrdal, Galbraith--have attempted to construct more general theory from the pattern model approach. All through the process of building up a pattern model the holist is continually comparing his case with others known to him, thereby using one case to suggest things to look for in another. One potential result of such a process of comparison is the development of a typology: Veblen's stage of theory of capitalism, Common's concept of "reasonable capitalism," Galbraith's planning system. Continued study of the type lead to hypotheses about which of its characteristics--technological change, ceremony, industrial goodwill, technostructure--are particularly important in conditioning the others and what are the dynamics of the type. Such a construct as Galbraith's planning system is what Diesing calls a *real type*; "A real type groups a number of cases together because they have many important characteristics in common. It is thus more like a mode than a formal construct. The type has no reality apart from the cases it summarizes, and might have been called a nominal type rather than a real type. The cases, not the type, are real; they are distinct, independent entities and not merely instances or exemplifications of an abstract universal, as cases are in formal typologies."[43]

The use of typologies can guide the researcher in asking relevant questions of a new case. However, there is always the risk of converting this type into a stereotype. This is usually the result of inadequate empiricism. "Types are treated as already completed and verified theories rather than as tentative groupings useful in illuminating particular cases ... a person falls into this misuse of typologies when he has too much theory and not enough experience, and tries to make his theory substitute for the careful empirical study of cases."[44] Some earnest disciples of Marx, Veblen, and Ayres fall into this trap.

Comparison of widely varying types enables one to identify the more general characteristics of many types of human systems - universal or nearly universal values, institutions, system problems, mechanisms, and the like. Needless to say, few have been found. The ceremonial-technological dichotomy may be one. General theorizing of this kind attempts to transcend the relativity inherent in the pattern model approach by seeking general characteristics of human systems.

With few exceptions, modern institutionalism has not created any general theory (Myrdal's theory of circular causation is the exception according to Kapp[45]) and has not even developed existing models and types. In reviewing the state of institutionalism, Samuels, concludes:

The JEI has received and published little creative work directly expanding upon the historic contributions of Thorstein

Veblen, John R. Commons, and Clarence Ayres, among others, and upon the contemporary contributions of John Kenneth Galbraith, Gunner Myrdal, K.W. Kapp, and Kenneth Boulding, among others. There has been some explanation and exegesis, but there have been submitted too many attempts at retrospection and too few at analytical development. The need is to use and transcend and not merely to rehearse the old.[46]

As we have seen, the pattern model is most frequently the procedure one uses when deriving holistic explanations. This specific procedure tends to generate a certain commonality among holistic theories. This commonality is evidenced by their conception of reality, the structure of their explanations, the primacy of their subject matter, and their particular form of logic. We will examine each of these four categories in turn.

First is the holist conception of reality. Holistic social scientists argue that social reality must be studied as a whole human system in its natural setting. Obviously, human wholes will tend to differ greatly with respect to size, complexity, degree of self-sufficiency, and relationships to the larger wholes that include them. However, the crucial element of this view is the concept of interrelationship or unity. That is, according to Diesing, "The holist standpoint includes the belief that human systems tend to develop a characteristic wholeness or integrity."[47] Thus unity may take the form of a set of values that expresses itself throughout the system, or it may be that a particular socioeconomic structure tends to condition everything else. Holists may disagree on whether this unity derives from some basic source (for example, religion, ethics, technology, personality) or from some complex interweaving of a number of factors, but they all agree that the unity is there.

The implication is that the characteristics of a part are largely determined by the whole to which it belongs and by its particular location in the whole system. Thus, if two superficially similar parts of different systems, let us say markets, are compared closely, they will be found to vary in characteristic ways. Robert Heilbroner has given the example of markets in underdeveloped countries.[48] Some economic development experts observed that people spent a large amount of time haggling over prices in local output markets in a particular peasant society. They set up a pilot project wherein a fixed price supermarket replaced the old peasant market. It was a failure because the new market did not satisfy the social intercourse provided by the old market system. Thus superficially similar parts, markets, provided different functions in different systems.

Since holists acknowledge the organic unity of human wholes, they are obligated to study the whole living system rather than one part taken out of context. The context of a particular event is important to the holist because the character of any given part is largely conditioned by the whole to which it belongs and by its particular function and location in the larger whole system. Witness the above example of markets. In addition, holists believe that their account of the particular part under investigation should somehow capture this unity or interconnection between part and whole. For the participant-observer constructing a pattern model this means looking for themes that express themselves throughout the system as a network of interrelations and describing these connections in the pattern.

Moreover, the holist conception of reality includes the belief that the parts are at once conditioning and conditioned by the whole. As such, reality for holists is viewed as a process of evolutionary change driven by the dynamic interaction between the parts and whole. However, this particular conception of reality does not manifest itself necessarily in the *a priori* belief that everything is related to everything else. Rather, according to Diesing, it is "the methodological necessity of pushing on to new aspects and new kinds of evidence in order to make sense of what one has already observed... It is one's inability to develop an intelligible and validated partial model that drives one on."[49] For holist economists, then, this means that an intelligible and relevant model of the economic *system* cannot be obtained by isolating the phenomenon of exchange from its interrelationship with the social whole. Insofar as holists conceive of social reality as an organic unity, any given part of the whole cannot be interpreted or explained without reference to the larger whole which contains it.

Another distinguishing aspect of holist methodology can be found in the structure of their explanations. To use Kaplan's terminology, the structure of holistic theories is concatenated (linked together) rather than hierarchical, as in formal theories. Holistic theories, in contrast to formal ones, are composed by linking together several relatively independent parts, rather than by logically deducing an explanandum from an explanans. Each segment of a concatenated theory is first developed, interpreted, and tested (contextually) independent of the other segments, then each is systematically linked to the other parts in a pattern. Each part is likely to be composed of several relatively independent subsections. As such, a concatenated theory with its several independent sections and subsections provides a many-sided, complex picture of the subject matter. A hierarchical theory, in contrast, is always one-sided. It takes one set of relations, one structure, or a single process and abstracts it out of the coherent whole and subjects it to logical study. For example, standard economists will focus on the process of exchange or resource allocation in abstraction from the society in which the process is imbedded.

The concatenated structure of holist explanations is necessitated in part by holists' conception of reality. Rather than say that we understand or explain something when we can predict it, the holist says that we have an explanation for something when we understand its place in the whole. Thus, in a pattern explanation, according to Kaplan, "something is explained when it is so related to a set of other elements that together they constitute a unified system. We understand something by identifying it as a specific part in an organized whole."[50] Consequently, something cannot be understood simply by exhibiting it as a concrete reflection of some universal principle; instead, the best one can do is identify it as part of an organized whole by constructing a model which links its particular function to the whole network of themes and connections.

Since holists do not attempt to subsume their particular system under general principles applicable to all systems, their concepts are relatively concrete, particularized, and close to the real system being described. The primacy of subject matter over method, then, is a crucial element of holist methodology. Diesing notes: "The holist believes in the primacy of subject matter; he believes that whatever else a method may be, it should at least be adequate to the particular thing described and should not distort it."[51] As we have seen earlier, opposing this view are the logical positivists. They assert that whatever else method is, it should first and foremost be "scientific." For them, if the canons of the scientific method are violated, or worse, if the method is radically altered or a new one adopted to fulfil the specific requirements of the subject matter, then the result cannot be science. On the other hand, holists do not predetermine the appropriate framework in which to explain their subject matter. In fact, they would not object to those who would attempt to recast holistic theories into a more traditionally acceptable form, but they would insist that the end product not distort the uniqueness and individuality of the system.

A final point with respect to the primacy of subject in the pattern model is that both explanandum and explanans are on the same level of generality. Both are equally particularized to the system being described. External formulas such as general laws or other universal categorizations are never imposed on the subject matter *a priori*. No statement within the pattern explanation need be generalized beyond the particular system. In this sense, holists allow the nature of the subject matter to dictate the specific method most appropriate to the task of interpreting, understanding, and explaining it. Kaplan makes the point with his usual clarity and preciseness:

> The point is that the attainment of acceptable explanations is not the accumulation of eternal and absolute truths: we have not, in attaining them, laid another brick on the edifice, not fitted another piece into the mosaic. What has happened is that we have found something which serves the ends of inquiry at a particular time and place; we have gotten hold of an idea which we can do something with--not to set our minds at rest but to turn their restlessness into productive channels. Explanations do not provide us with something over and above what we can put to some use, and this statement is as true of understanding as it is of prediction.[52]

The fourth and final characteristic of holistic concepts is that they are frequently, although not always, related dialectically. "Two concepts are dialectically related when the elaboration of one draws attention to the other as an opposed concept that has been implicitly denied or excluded by the first; when one discovers that the opposite concept is required (presupposed) for the validity or applicability of the first; and when one finds that the real theoretical problem is that of the interrelation between the two concepts, and the real descriptive problem that of determining their interrelations in a particular case."[53] There are many examples of dialectical logic in institutionalist thought: the ceremonial-technological dichotomy, Veblen's pecuniary versus economic values, Common's concepts of the real (going plant) and the financial (going business), Galbraith's countervailing power, and so on.

What explains the frequent occurrence of dialetical concepts in holistic theories? One reason is that they serve to counterbalance the human tendency to be biased, one-sided, abstract. They make thought and theories more concrete. "One begins with some historically or empirically suggested viewpoint and develops it until its shortcomings are clear enough to suggest the outlines of an opposing, formerly excluded viewpoint; then the latter is developed and related back to the first."[54] In effect, dialectic is the logic of the concrete. The fact that dialectic is a correction of one-sidedness also helps explain why many holistic works are not dialectical. There is only so much time, and in many cases the best a single researcher can hope for is a one-sided picture of reality that will be corrected by someone else who has constructed another but different one-sided view. Then others can combine the two.

Another possible reason for the use of dialectical logic is the holist's abhorrence of atomism. A whole cannot be divided into parts and treated independently of the whole and of the internal

264

relations among the constituent parts. Dialectics, as the logic of internal relations, is used to overcome atomism. But as Samuels points out: "Emphasis upon holism, evolution, process, and eclecticism does not save institutionalists from committing the same or similar questionable practice as their neoclassical counterparts, not the least being single-factor explanations."[55]

Problems with Institutionalism's Holistic Methodology

Institutionalists have found holist concepts more useful than formal models for dealing with considerations of power, conflict, distribution, social relations, nonmarket institutions and processes, and the like. However, there are severe limitations to holism. First, because of their lack of precision, the use of holist concepts must be continuously monitored by reference to observation, cases, and examples. Holism separated from its empirical base easily becomes loose, uncontrolled speculation. Institutionalist have not escaped this fate. As Samuels points out: "Institutionalists and heterodox economists have produced bodies of thought which are as relativistic in their development, ambiguous in their central meaning and as much a blend of explanation and rationalization and of narrowness and breadth as neoclassicism." Furthermore, "there is a great deal of so-called analysis which is but a euphemism for the writer's preferences. There is both criticism of others' myths and the promulgation of one's own."[56]

A second problem is that the impreciseness and generality of holist concepts make any definitive verification of hypotheses impossible. Again, Samuels points out that "it is uncertain as to the degree to which the holistic conception of the economy can be (1) specified, (2) separated from the rest of society, and (3) made manageable for analytical purposes, quite aside from its being made operational for testing purposes."[57] As a consequence the institutionalist using holist theories should remember that these theories are always tentative and subject to change.

The precision and rigor that characterize formal theories are not unqualified virtues. If a school of thought, for example, certain traditions within standard economics, begins to overemphasize precision and rigor it will tend to fall into theoretical stagnation and preoccupation with logical and empirical detail. Diesing points out that "every scientific tradition I have examined contains a balance of precision and vagueness, rigor and suggestiveness, but ... different traditions apportion the two elements in different fashions."[58] Balance serves the conflicting scientific needs of creativity and control. Precision and rigor provide empirical or logical control. Vagueness and suggestiveness facilitate creativity.[59] If a school of thought, as have certain traditions within institutionalism, begins to overemphasize vagueness and suggestiveness it will tend to fall into diffuse and uncontrolled speculation. A central problem of any methodology is how to strike a balance between precision and rigor, on the one hand, and vagueness and suggestiveness, on the other, and how to relate the two so that they synergize rather than cancel each other.

Conclusion

Let us conclude this exploration into methodology with a few comments comparing the formal theories of standard economics and the holist theories of institutional economics. In general, the emphasis in formal models is on laws, while in a pattern model it is on facts or on low level empirical generalizations. Empirical facts are included as part of the explanans in a formal model, but only as circumstances that condition the applicability of the general laws. Deductive laws and abstract empirical generalizations are sometimes used in a pattern model, but only as suggestive guides in the search for observable concrete connections or patterns; and these laws and empirical generalizations are open to modification in the process.

In reviewing Lance Davis's and Douglass North's neoclassical explanation for institutional change, Dudley Dillard illustrates the difference between the formal model of neoclassical economics and the pattern model of institutional economics:

> Veblen's institutionalism differs greatly in approach, content, and scope from that of Davis and North. Veblen's is a theory of cumulative economic change based primarily on the dynamics of technology. His theory of business enterprise rests on the concept of process rather than of equilibrating forces or of rational economic individualism. *Veblen attempts to generalize from the facts of experience about the working of the economic system as a whole. Davis and North do not generalize from the facts of experience; rather, they attempt to construct a model based on assumptions about how economic agents would behave if they acted rationally in their self-interest.* In turn, the facts of experience are utilized by them to test the model (theory). If one is interested primarily in how the real world does in fact behave, the Davis-North approach will prove fruitful only if one believes that economic behavior is rational and predictable.[60]

Use of the pattern model appears appropriate when an explanation involves many diverse factors, each of which is important; when the patterns or connections among these factors are important; and when these patterns can be observed in the particular case under study. Use of the covering law model appears more appropriate when one or two factors or laws determine what is to be explained and when these factors or laws are better known and understood than the specific instance. The formal models of standard economics have their use, even by institutionalists, for certain types of problems. Most of the issues institutionalists deal with, however, are better handled by holist methods.

Perhaps the practice of both standard and institutionalist economics could be improved if the proper domain of formal and holist methods were understood and respected. And then, perhaps, institutionalism could stop feeling defensive about its methods as compared to standard economics.

Footnotes

* Slightly altered from Peter McClelland, *Causal Explanation and Model Building in History, Economics, and the New Economic History*. The authors are, respectively, Professor and Chairman, and Graduate Research Assistant, Department of Economics, University of Notre Dame, Notre Dame, Indiana.

1. In addition to the original works, the following interpretive essays were particularly helpful in writing this article. Allan Gruchy, *Modern Economic Thought* (New York: Prentice-Hall, 1947), and *Contemporary Economic Thought* (Clifton, N.J.: Augustus M. Kelley, 1972); Wesley C. Mitchell, *Types of Economic Theory*, Vol. 2 (New York: Augustus M. Kelley, 1969), chapters 20 and 22; K. William Kapp, "The Nature and Significance of Institutional Economics," Kyklos 29, fasc. 2 (1976): 209-30; Warren J. Samuels, "*The Journal of Economic Issues* and the Present State of Heterodox Economics," Report to 1974 and 1976 AFEE Executive Board (mimeo); and the following articles, all from the *Journal of Economic Issues*: Andrew Vayda, "On the Anthropological Study of Economics," 1 (June 1967): 86-90; George Dalton, "Economics, Economic Development, and Economic Anthropology," 2 (June 1968): 173-86; Allan Gruchy, "Neoinstitutionalism and Economics of Dissent," 3 (March 1969): 3-17; Warren Samuels, "On the Future of Institutional Economics," 3 (September 1969): 67-72; Philip Klein, "Economics: Allocation or Valuation?" 8 (December 1974): 785-811; Paul Strassmann, "Technology: a Culture Trait, a Logical Category, or Virtue Itself?" 8 (December 1974): 671-87; James Buchanan and Warren Samuels, "On Some Fundamental Issues in Political

Economy: An Exchange of Correspondence," 9 (March 1975): 15-38; Allan Gruchy, "Institutionalism, Planning, and the Current Crisis," 11 (June 1977): 431-48; and Robert Solo, "The Need for a Theory of the State," 11 (June 1977): 379-85.

2. The following were of particular value: Abraham Kaplan, *The Conduct of Inquiry: Methodology for Behavioral Science* (San Francisco: Chandler Publishing Co., 1964); Paul Diesing, *Patterns of Discovery in the Social Sciences* (Chicago: Aldine-Atherton, 1971); William Dray, *Laws and Explanation in History* (Oxford: The Clarendon Press, 1957); Peter D. McClelland, *Causal Explanation and Model Building in History, Economics, and the New Economic History* (Ithaca: Cornell University Press, 1975); Martin Hollis and Edward Nell, *Rational Economic Man: A Philosophical Critique of Neo-Classical Economics* (London: Cambridge University Press, 1975); and the following articles, all from the *Encyclopedia of Philosophy*: "Empiricism," vol. 2; "History of Epistemology," vol. 3; "Explanation in Science," vol. 3; "Historical Explanation," vol. 4; "Holism and Individualism in History and Social Science," vol. 4; "Logical Positivism," vol. 5; "Rationalism," vol. 7; and "Verifiability Principle," vol. 7.

3. See Benjamin Ward, *What's Wrong with Economics?* (New York: Basic Books, 1972), chapter 12.

4. Diesing, *Patterns of Discovery*, p. 36.

5. See Piero V. Mini, *Philosophy and Economics: The Origin and Development of Economic Theory* (Gainesville: University of Florida Press, 1974).

6. See particularly Paul Samuelson, *Foundations of Economic Analysis* (Cambridge, Mass.: Harvard University Press, 1947).

7. Carl G. Hempel and Paul Oppenheim, "Studies in the Logic of Explanation," *Philosophy of Science* 15 (April 1948): 135-75.

8. I.M.D. Little, *A Critique of Welfare Economics*, 2nd ed. (Oxford: The Clarendon Press, 1957).

9. Milton Friedman, *Essays in Positive Economics* (Chicago: University of Chiago Press, 1953).

10. See Richard A. Lester, "Shortcomings of Marginal Analysis for Wage-Employment Problems," *American Economic Review*, 36 (March 1946): 63-82.

11. See particularly Richard Lipsey and Peter Steiner, *Economics* (New York: Harper & Row, 1966). Lipsey published an earlier version in England under the title *Introduction to Positive Economics*. Oddly, the ascent of positivism in economics has coincided with a decrease in its popularity among professional philosophers.

12. Friedman, "The Methodology of Positive Economics," in *Essays*, p. 4.

13. Robert L. Heilbroner, "On the Limits of Economic Prediction," *Diogenes*, 70 (April 1970): 36.

14. Ibid., p. 37.

15. Ibid., p. 33.

16. Alfred F. Chalk, "Concepts of Change and the Role of Predictability in Economics," *History of Political Economy*, 2 (Spring 1970): 114.

17. Ward, *What's Wrong with Economics*? pp. 188, 190.

18. Kaplan, *Conduct of Inquiry*, chapter 9.

19. See Kapp, "Nature and Significance," p. 214; see also Samuels, "Journal of Economic Issues," p. 12.

20. Kapp, "Nature of Significance," p. 215.

21. See particularly John Kenneth Galbraith, *Economics and the Public Purpose* (Boston: Houghton Mifflin, 1973).

22. See particularly Warren J. Samuels, "Interrelations between Legal and Economic Processes," *Journal of Law and Economics* 14 (October 1971): 435-50, and "The Coase Theorem and the Study of Law and Economics," *Natural Resources Journal*, 14 (January 1974): 1-33.

23. See particularly Willard F. Mueller, "Antitrust in a Planned Economy," *Journal of Economic Issues*, 9 (June 1975): 159-80.

24. See particularly Charles Craypo, "Collective Bargaining in the Multinational, Conglomerate Corporation: Litton's Shutdown of Royal Typewriter," *Industrial and Labor Relations Review*, 29 (October 1975): 3-25.

25. See many of the works by Veblen and Wesley Clair Mitchell.

26. "The hedonistic conception of man is that of a lightning calculator of pleasures and pains, who oscilates like a homogeneous globule of desire of happiness under the impulse of
stimuli that shift him about the area, but leave him intact. He
has neither antecedent nor consequent. He is an isolated,
definitive human datum, in stable equilibrium except for the
buffets of the impinging forces that displace him in one direction or another. Self-imposed in elemental space, he spins
symmetrically about his own spiritual axis until the parallelo-
gram of forces bears down upon him, whereupon he follows
the line of the resultant. When the force of the impact is
spent, he comes to rest, a self-contained globule of desire as
before." Thorstein Veblen, "Why is Economics Not an Evolutionary Science?" in *The Place of Science in Modern
Civilization* (New York: B.W. Huebsch, 1919, Russell &
Russell, 1961), pp. 73-74.

27. Samuels, "Journal of Economic Issues," p. 12.

28. Ibid., pp. 26-27.

29. See ibid., for a recitation of the wide variety of subjects and
approaches appearing in the *Journal of Economic Issues*.

30. Ibid., p. 12.

31. See Gruchy, *Modern Economic Thought*, p. 4.

32. Ibid.

33. Quoted in Kaplan, *Conduct of Inquiry*, p. 349.

34. Samuels, "Journal of Economic Issues," p. 41.

35. Ibid., pp. 41-42.

36. "Editors Notes," *Journal of Economic Issues* 1 (June
1967): 137.

37. Diesing, *Patterns of Discovery*, pp. 147-148. Again,
"taken separately, these bits of evidence mean little; combined, they tell a good deal" (ibid., p. 147).

38. See Kaplan, *Conduct of Inquiry*, chapter 9; and Diesing,
Patterns of Discovery, Part II.

39. Diesing, *Patterns of Discovery*, p. 165. Also, "it is no
shortcoming of the explanation that there is something else to
be explained. On the contrary, finality is a mark of runic

explanations, not scientific ones; the road of inquiry is always open, and it reaches beyond the horizon" (Kaplan, *Conduct of Inquiry*, p. 341).

40. Ward, *What's Wrong with Economics?* p. 189.

41. Kaplan, *Conduct of Inquiry*, p. 347. Also, "one cannot deduce specific predictions of future behavior in novel circumstances from a pattern explanation; the symmetry of prediction and explanation that occurs in a deductive model is not present... In novel circumstances one may be able to say that a certain range of behavior is likely and another range unlikely, but not that any specific thing must occur." Diesing, *Patterns of Discovery*, p. 164.

42. See the following articles in the *Journal of Economic Issues*: Robert Alexander, "The Import Substitution Strategy of Economic Development," 1 (December 1967): 297-308; Jack Barbash, "American Unionism: From Protest to Going Concern," 2 (March 1968): 45-59; Milton Lower, "Institutional Bases of Economic Stagnation in Chile," 2 (September 1968): 283-97; James V. Cornehls and Edward Van Roy, "Economic Development in Mexico and Thailand: An Institutional Analysis (Part One)," 3 (September 1969): 16-32, and Part Two, 3 (December 1969): 21-38; William K. Tabb, "Perspectives on Black Economic Development," 4 (December 1970): 68-81; Irvan Grossack, "Public Regulation of the Indian Steel Industry," 5 (March 1971)" 86-97; A.M. Agapos, "Competition in the Defense Industry: An Economic Paradox," 5 (June 1971): 41-55; Warren Gramm, "Industrial Capitalism and the Breakdown of the Liberal Rule of Law," 7 (December 1973): 577-603; Everett Kassalow, "The Transformation of Christian Trade Unionism in France," 8 (March 1974): 1-39; Manley Irwin and Kenneth Stanley, "Regulatory Circumvention and the Holding Company," 8 (June 1974): 395-411; John Blair, "The Implementation of Oligopolistic Interdependence," 9 (June 1975): 297-318; Richard Chase, "Keynes and U.S. Keynesianism," 9 (September 1975): 441-70; Lewis Hill et. al., "Inflation and the Destruction of Democracy: The Weimar Republic," 11 (June 1977): 299-313; and all of the June 1976 issue (volume 10, number 2).

43. Diesing, *Patterns of Discovery*, p. 198.

44. Ibid., p. 200.

45. See Kapp, "Nature and Significance," pp. 217-28.

46. Samuels, "Journal of Economic Issues," p. 13. In a brief reference to institutionalism Diesing comments that in its

sometimes proclaimed method "the self-maintaining system to be studied is the total set of institutions in which a particular economy functions, seen in historical perspective. I have not succeeded in understanding this method adequately since it seems to have remained a proposal rather than an actuality for over a half century," Diesing, *Patterns of Discovery*, p. 7.

47. Ibid., p. 137.

48. Lecture at The American University, Washington, D.C., 1972.

49. Diesing, *Patterns of Discovery*, p. 167.

50. *Kaplan, Conduct of Inquiry*, p. 333.

51. Diesing, *Patterns of Discovery*, p. 140.

52. Kaplan, *Conduct of Inquiry*, p. 355.

53. Diesing, *Patterns of Discovery*, p. 212.

54. Ibid., p. 218.

55. Samuels, "Journal of Economic Issues," p. 23.

56. Ibid., pp. 23, 29.

57. Ibid., p. 24.

58. Diesing, *Patterns of Discovery*, p. 221.

59. For an example see Abraham Hirsch, "The A Posteriori Method and the Creation of New Theory: W.C. Mitchell as a Case Study," *History of Political Economy*, 8 (Summer 1976): 195-206.

60. Dudley Dillard, "Review of Lance E. Davis and Douglass C. North, "Institutional Change and American Economic Growth," *Journal of Economic Issues*, 8 (December 1974): 917-18 (emphasis added).

14 Is There a "Structure of Scientific Revolutions" in Economics?

A.W. Coats

According to well informed observers, we are now in the midst of a 'revolution' in the historiography of science. The conventional 'uniformitarian' conception of scientific progress as a continuous process of stockpiling facts and techniques is being challenged by a 'catastrophist' view that the process has been subject to periodic breakdowns and changes of direction, discontinuities obscured by historians who have unconsciously interpreted the past in the light of their own epistemological preconceptions. The leading advocate of the catastrophist viewpoint is Thomas S. Kuhn whose brilliant book *The Structure of Scientific Revolutions* (1962), has provoked considerable controversy among historians of science[1]; and this paper is designed to draw the attention of economists to his stimulating central thesis.

It is appropriate to compare the history of economics with the history of the natural sciences, not only because economists have persistently striven to emulate the natural scientists' methods but also because any signs of an antipositivist movement among historians of science are obviously of interest to those engaged in the interminable debate about 'positive' economics, as well as to historians.[2] Moreover, both groups may derive intellectual stimulus from Kuhn's effort to synthesize epistemology, the sociology of knowledge and the study of science as a profession.

From a sociological viewpoint, science may be regarded as 'an institutional mechanism for sifting warranted beliefs', a process controlled by a group of persons known as 'scientists'; and there are obvious reasons why the 'self-corrective mechanisms of science as a social enterprise "have functioned less effectively in economics than, say, in physics"'.[3] It is a field in which the authority of tradition has been strong, well-defined standards of scientific or technical competence have been lacking, and those seeking conclusive empirical tests of hypotheses have encountered serious technical and methodological difficulties.[4] The history of economics has been punctuated by recurrent bitter methodological disputes, disputes influenced by policy issues as well as by purely scientific considerations. Nevertheless it is widely recognized that the differences between economics and the natural sciences are differences of degree rather than kind, and as Kuhn

Reprinted by permission from *Kyklos*, 22 (1969), 289-94.

demonstrates, methdological disputes in any branch of science are often marred by the conspicuous irrationality of the disputants for, as Karl Popper has observed, the 'criterion of demarcation' by which scientific propositions are distinguished from non-scientific propositions is fundamentally based on 'a proposal for agreement or convention--a decision going beyond rational argument'.[5]

Although Kuhn's approach to the history of science was influenced by his awareness of the differences between the social and the natural sciences, any economist who reads his book will be struck by certain marked similarities. Kuhn maintains that 'normal' science is dominated by 'paradigms' which he defines as 'universally recognized scientific achievements that for a time provide model problems and solutions to a community of practitioners'(p. x), and the paradigm's function is regulative (i.e. normative) as well as cognitive since it provides the scientist not only with 'a map, but also with some of the directions essential for map-making' (p. 108). A paradigm is not simply a theory; it incorporates 'accepted examples of scientific practice' which include 'law, theory, application and instrumentation together' (p. 10); and it enables the scientists in that field to take the foundation of their knowledge for granted and concentrate their attention on the solution of more concrete problems, or 'puzzles'. Obviously no paradigm is complete; if it were, 'normal' scientific activity would cease, for there would be no unsolved puzzles'; and as 'normal' research proceeds unexpected or anomalous results appear. For a time these will be ignored, or dismissed as irrelevant or accidental, because 'the scientist who pauses to examine every anomaly he notes will seldom get any significant work done' (p. 82). But as the anomalies grow in number and importance, they eventually become 'critical'; a sense of crisis develops as the inadequacy of the ruling paradigm becomes increasingly apparent, and research is diverted from puzzle-solving to paradigm-testing (pp. 91, 82-4). However, any serious challenge to an established paradigm will provoke a reaction, which is both natural and healthy since the challengers are threatening the established scientific tradition, with its concomitant network of commitments to specific concepts, theories, instruments, and standards of scientific performance (p. 42). In the ensuing debate all the scientific passions are aroused; and if the ruling paradigm is overthrown its defeat will be due to a 'conversion experience', a 'transfer of allegiance', rather than to 'the logical structure of scientific knowledge', for the change is dependent on the possibilities inherent in the new paradigm rather than any demonstrable proof of its superiority (pp. 94, 150, 156-7).

This bald summary does scant justice to Kuhn's cogent and subtle argument, which is buttressed by a wealth of historical illustrations; but it should be enough to suggest its relevance to

274

economics. Have there been phases of crisis and paradigm-change in economics, and if so have they resulted from the failure of crucial experiments or from extra-scientific sources? Kuhn himself doubts whether there have been any paradigms in the social sciences (p.15), but this remark suggests the ambiguity of the paradigm concept, for it may be interpreted as a specific book or style of exposition, a 'basic theory', a *Weltanschauung*, or the entire range of scientific activity.[6] Fortunately this definitional difficulty creates no fundamental problems for the social scientist for he is much less concerned with instruments, apparatus, and applications of theory than the natural scientist, and in the social science context a paradigm may be defined as a 'basic theory'. From this standpoint economics may be regarded as more 'uniformitarian' than the natural sciences, for despite persistent and often penetrating criticism by a stream of heterodox writers (e.g. socialists, evolutionists, institutionalists) it has been dominated throughout its history by a single paradigm--the theory of economic equilibrium via the market mechanism.[7] According to Kuhn's criteria economists may be said to have enjoyed considerable success in two phases of the 'normal' scientific activity of actualizing the promises inherent in their paradigm, i.e. extending the knowledge of 'relevant' facts, and improving the 'articulation' of the paradigm itself (p. 24). However, their efforts to improve the match between the facts and the paradigm's predictions have met with only limited success, although this is understandable in view of the virtual absence of 'instrumental expectations'.[8] Does this not mean that by comparison with the natural sciences economics has not yet passed beyond the 'developmental' or pre-paradigm stage?

The application of Kuhn's approach to economics does not merely involve the translation of a few methodological commonplaces into a new language; it provides a new interpretive framework--a basis from which to re-examine the precise scientific importance of successive theoretical advances. By emphasizing the regulative as well as the cognitive functions of paradigms Kuhn suggests new relationships among the ingredients in familiar debates. The process of paradigm change in the natural sciences may be regarded as an ideal type which may be used to clarify the interrelationships between the terminological, conceptual, personal, ideological and professional (i.e. careerist) elements in the developments of scientific knowledge. This approach provides a framework, not a straitjacket. Kuhn explicitly denies that science is monolithic; and although competing paradigms can co-exist in any given scientific field only during crisis periods, not all theories achieve paradigm status, and there are many specialized overlapping and interpenetrating paradigms (pp. 61, 77, 94, 49-51).

Needless to say, the structure of scientific revolutions is

much less readily discernible in economics than in the natural sciences. Economic theories (whether paradigms or sub-paradigms) are usually less rigid and compelling than their natural science equivalents, hence they rarely represent an obvious challenge to the established scientific tradition. Instead of outright hostility they more often encounter neglect, scepticism, or even anti-intellectual scorn. However, the most striking example of a paradigm-change in economics, the Keynesian revolution of the 1930's, possessed many of the characteristics associated with Kuhn's 'scientific revolutions'. There were unrecognized precursors of Keynes, a growing concern about the inadequacy of existing theory, and a change of psychological outlook on the part of many economists vitually amounting to a 'conversion experience'. The revolution was led by a band of youngsters (apart from the Peter-Pan like figure of Keynes himself) who encountered fierce resistance from their elders; but within a remarkably short time the new paradigm had won an almost complete victory.[9] As with paradigm changes in the natural sciences, the initiative had come from *within* the scientific community--indeed, at its very heart, and its leader knew exactly what he was doing. There was certainly 'no standard higher than the assent of the relevant community' (p.93), but it is now clear that the Keynesian paradigm was not 'incompatible' with its predecessor, and during the subsequent 'mopping-up operations' (p. 24) it proved necessary to devote considerable effort to the task of clarifying and systemizing Keynes's ideas. Yet he had undoubtedly provided his professional colleagues not only with a new 'map, but also with some of the directions essential for map-making' (p.108); and the whole process would repay systematic study in terms of the cognitive and regulative functions attributed to Kuhn's paradigms.

The Keynesian revolution was unique in the history of economics, especially in regard to its regulative impact on the economics profession.[10] However, earlier revolutions have occurred, each of which has exhibited points of similarity with Kuhn's revolutions--much as the victory of classical economics via the Political Economy Club; the *Methodenstreit* between German and Austrian economists; and the more purely cognitive marginal utility revolution. Obviously Kuhn's model will not fit all these cases. But it adds precision to Schumpeter's conception of the 'classical situation', and serves as a healthy corrective to more deterministic sociological models.[11] If there is any discernible pattern in the development of economic science, it is one that combines ideas and events in a flexible manner; and the significance of Kuhn's approach stems from its demonstration of the mediating role played by the scientific community.

Summary

In *The Structure of Scientific Revolutions* T.S. Kuhn argues that the history of the natural sciences has been marked by periodic crises, when the dominant 'paradigm' is challenged, rejected, and displaced by a new paradigm. Since the paradigm's functions are both regulative and cognitive, this process has sociological as well as purely epistemological aspects.

With the exception of the Keynesian revolution of the 1930s, there have been no phases of paradigm change in economics quite like those in the natural sciences. This is due mainly to the nature of economic paradigms (or 'basic' theories) which are less precise and less liable to falsification. 'Critical anomalies' and 'crucial experiments' do not arise in economics, as in the natural sciences; and yet the process of paradigm change may serve as an ideal type, which can be used to clarify the interrelationships between the terminological, conceptual, personal, and professional elements involved in the development of economic ideas, especially in such episodes as the emergence of classical (Ricardian) economics, the *Methodenstreit*, or the marginal utility revolution.

Footnotes

1. Subsequent references to Kuhn will appear as page numbers in the text. For background discussion see Gerd Buchdahl, 'A Revolution in Historiography of Science', *History of Science*, Vol. 4, 1965, pp. 56-69. Also C.C. Gillespie, 'Review of Joseph Agassi', in: *Isis*, Vol. 55, 1964, pp. 97-9; and Walter F. Cannon, 'The Uniformitarian-Catastrophist Debate', *Isis*, Vol. 51, 1960, pp. 38, 55.

2. See, for example, T.W. Hutchison, *'Positive Economics' and Policy Objectives*, 1964, and A.W. Coats, 'Value Judgements in Economics', *Yorkshire Bulletin of Economic and Social Research*, Vol. 16, 1964, pp. 53-67.

3. The quotations are from Ernest Nagel, *The Structure of Science, Problems in the Logic of Scientific Explanation* (1961), p. 490.

4. For some illustrations, see A.W. Coats, 'The Role of Authority in the Development of British Economics,' *Journal of Law and Economics*, Vol. 7, 1964, pp. 88-95.

5. See *The Logic of Scientific Discovery* (1961), pp. 37-8.

6. Cf. Buchdahl's critical comments, *op. cit.*, pp. 58-9. Also the reviews of Kuhn by Dudley Shapere in the *Philosophical Review*, Vol. 73, 1964, pp. 383-94, and H.V. Stropes-Roe, in *The British Journal for the Philosophy of Science*, Vol. XV, 1964, p. 159.

7. Donald Gordon concludes his comments on Kuhn somewhat complacently by claiming that the persistence of this economic paradigm is 'a tribute to the supremacy of purely positivistic forces'. Cf. 'The Role of the History of Economic Thought in the Understanding of Modern Economic Theory', *American Economic Review*, Vol. 55, 1965, p. 124. To my knowledge, this was the first published attempt to relate Kuhn's views to economics. Cf. my unpublished monograph, *The Role of Value Judgements in Economics* (University of Virginia, Thomas Jefferson Center for Studies in Political Economy), Mimeo, May 1964, pp. 56-61.

8. Cf. Kuhn, p. 67, and the comments on econometrics in Henry W. Briefs, *Three Views on Economic Method* (1960), pp. 29-30.

9. For some characteristically penetrating observations on this episode see Joseph A. Schumpeter, *History of Economic Analysis* (1954), pp. 1180-1. The older generation's opposition, Schumpeter noted, did not merely stem from arteriosclerosis, for they were the beneficiaries as well as the victims of their training. They had acquired, among other things, 'analytic experience. And in a field like economics, where training is often defective and where the young scholar very often simply does not know enough, this element in the case counts much more heavily than it does in physics where teaching, even though possibly uninspiring, is always competent'. See also, R.F. Harrod, *The Life of John Maynard Keynes* (1952), pp. 451-467, for valuable personal and methodological insights into the Keynesian Revolution.

10. According to one bitter critic, 'most of the younger sceptics who expressed misgivings about the "new" economics began to be eliminated from academic life. There was no inquisition, no discernible or intentional suppression of academic freedom; but young non-conformists could seldom expect promotion. They appeared rather like young physicists who were arrogant enough to challenge the basic validity of revolutionary developments which they did not properly understand. To suggest that Keynes was all wrong was like questioning the soundness of Einstein or Bohr. The older economists could

declare their doubts without serious loss of prestige, but any dissatisfaction on the part of the younger men seemed to be evidence of intellectual limitations'. W.H. Hutt, 'Critics of the "Classical Tradition"', *South African Journal of Economics*, Vol. 32, 1964, p. 81. For interesting earlier comments see his The Economists and the Public (1936), p. 245.

11. Cf. Schumpeter, op. cit., pp. 51, 87, 143, 380; also W.A. Stark, 'The "Classical Situation" in Political Economy', *Kyklos*, Vol. 12, 1959, pp. 57-63.

15 Rational Decision Making in Business Organizations

Herbert A. Simon*

In the opening words of his *Principles*, Alfred Marshall proclaimed economics to be a psychological science:

> Political Economy or Economics is a study of mankind in the ordinary business of life; it examines that part of individual and social action which is most closely connected with the attainment and with the use of the material requisites of wellbeing.

> Thus it is on the one side a study of wealth; and on the other, and more important side, a part of the study of man. For man's character has been moulded by his every-day work, and the material resources which he thereby procures, more than by any other influence unless it be that of his religious ideals.

In its actual development, however, economic science has focused on just one aspect of man's character, his reason, and particularly on the application of that reason to problems of allocation in the face of scarcity. Still, modern definitions of the economic sciences, whether phrased in terms of allocating scarce resources or in terms of rational decision making, mark out a vast domain for conquest and settlement. In recent years there has been considerable exploration by economists even of parts of this domain that were thought traditionally to belong to the disciplines of political science, sociology, and psychology.

I. Decision Theory as Economic Science

The density of settlement of economists over the whole empire of economic science is very uneven, with a few areas of modest size holding the bulk of the population. The economic Heartland is the normative study of the international and national economies and their markets, with its triple main concerns of full employment of resources, the efficient allocation of resources, and equity in distribution of the economic product. Instead of the ambiguous

Reprinted by permission of The Nobel Foundation, 1978. This article is the lecture Herbert Simon delivered in Stockholm, Sweden, December 8, 1978, when he received the Nobel Prize in Economic Science.

and over-general term "economics," I will use "political economy" to designate this Heartland, and "economic sciences" to denote the whole empire, including its most remote colonies. Our principal concern in this paper will be with the important colonial territory known as decision theory. I will have something to say about its normative and descriptive aspects, and particularly about its applications to the theory of the firm. It is through the latter topic that the discussion will be linked back to the Heartland of political economy.

Underpinning the corpus of policy-oriented normative economics, there is, of course, an impressive body of descriptive or "positive" theory which rivals in its mathematical beauty and elegance some of the finest theories in the physical sciences. As examples I need only remind you of Walrasian general equilibrium theories and their modern descendants in the works of Henry Schultz, Samuelson, Hicks, and others; or the subtle and impressive body of theory created by Arrow, Hurwicz, Debreu, Malinvaud, and their colleagues showing the equivalence, under certain conditions, of competitive equilibrium with Pareto optimality.

The relevance of some of the more refined parts of this work to the real world can be, and has been, questioned. Perhaps some of these intellectual mountains have been climbed simply because they were there--because of the sheer challenge and joy of scaling them. That is as it should be in any human scientific or artistic effort. But regardless of the motives of the climbers, regardless of real world veridicality, there is no question but that positive political economy has been strongly shaped by the demands of economic policy for advice on basic public issues.

This too is as it should be. It is a vulgar fallacy to suppose that scientific inquiry cannot be fundamental if it threatens to become useful, or if it arises in response to problems posed by the everyday world. The real world, in fact, is perhaps the most fertile of all sources of good research questions calling for basic scientific inquiry.

A. *Decision Theory in the Service of Political Economy*

There is, however, a converse fallacy that deserves equal condemnation: the fallacy of supposing that fundamental inquiry is worth pursuing only if its relevance to questions of policy is immediate and obvious. In the contemporary world, this fallacy is perhaps not widely accepted, at least as far as the natural sciences are concerned. We have now lived through three centuries or more of vigorous and highly successful inquiry into the laws of nature. Much of that inquiry has been driven by the simple urge to understand, to find the beauty of order hidden in complexity. Time and again, we have found the "idle" truths arrived at through the process of inquiry to be of the greatest moment for practical human affairs. I need not take time here to argue the point. Scientists know it, engineers and physicians know it, congressmen and members of parliament know it, the man on the street knows it.

But I am not sure that this truth is as widely known in economics as it ought to be. I cannot otherwise explain the rather weak and backward development of the descriptive theory of decision making including the theory of the firm, the sparse and scattered settlement of its terrain, and the fact that many, if not most, of its investigators are drawn from outside economics--from sociology, from psychology, and from political science. Respected and distinguished figures in economics--Edward Mason, Fritz Machlup, and Milton Friedman, for example--have placed it outside the Pale (more accurately, have placed economics outside its Pale), and have offered it full autonomy provided that it did not claim close kinship with genuine economic inquiry.

Thus, Mason, commenting on Papandreou's 1952 survey of research on the behavioral theory of the firm, mused aloud:

...has the contribution of this literature to economic analysis really been a large one?... The writer of this critique must confess a lack of confidence in the marked superiority, *for purposes of economic analysis*, of this newer concept of the firm, over the older conception of the entrepreneur [pp. 221-222].

And, in a similar vein, Friedman sums up his celebrated polemic against realism in theory:

Complete "realism" is clearly unattainable, and the question whether a theory is realistic "enough" can be settled only by seeing whether it yields predictions that are good enough *for the purpose in hand* or that are better than predictions from alternative theories [p. 41, emphasis added].

The "purpose in hand" that is implicit in both of these quotations is providing decision-theoretic foundations for positive, and then for normative, political economy. In the views of Mason and Friedman, fundamental inquiry into rational human behavior in the context of business organizations is simply not (by definition) economics--that is to say, political economy--unless it contributes in a major way to that purpose. This is sometimes even interpreted to mean that economic theories of decision making are not falsified in any interesting or relevant sense when their empirical predictions of *microphenomena* are found to be grossly incompatible with the observed data. Such theories, we are told, are still realistic "enough" provided that they do not contradict aggregate observations of concern to political economy. Thus economists who are zealous in insisting that economic actors maximize turn around and become satisficers when the evaluation of their own theories is concerned. They believe that businessmen maximize, but they know that economic theorists satisfice.

The application of the principle of satisficing to theories is sometimes defended as an application of Occam's Razor: accept the simplest theory that works.[1] But Occam's Razor has a double edge. Succinctness of statement is not the only measure of a theory's simplicity. Occam understood his rule as recommending theories that make no more assumptions than necessary to account for the phenomena (*Essentia non sunt multiplicanda praeter necessitatem*). A theory of profit or utility maximization can be stated more briefly than a satisficing theory of the sort I shall discuss later. But the former makes much stronger assumptions than the latter about the human cognitive system. Hence, in the case before us, the two edges of the razor cut in opposite directions.

In whichever way we interpret Occam's principle, parsimony can be only a secondary consideration in choosing between theories, unless those theories make identical predictions. Hence, we must come back to a consideration of the phenomena that positive decision theory is supposed to handle. These may include both phenomena at the microscopic level of the decision-making agents, or aggregative phenomena of concern to political economy.

B. *Decision Theory Pursued for its Intrinsic Interest*

Of course the definition of the word "economics" is not important. Like Humpty Dumpty, we can make words mean anything we want them to mean. But the professional training and range of concern of economists does have importance. Acceptance of the narrow view that economics is concerned only with the aggregative phenomena of political economy defines away a whole rich domain of rational human behavior as inappropriate for economic research.

I do not wish to appear to be admitting that the behavioral theory of the firm has been irrelevant to the construction of political economy. I will have more to say about its relevance in a moment. My present argument is counterfactual in form: *even if* there were no present evidence of such relevance, human behavior in business firms constitutes a highly interesting body of empirical phenomena that calls out for explanation as do all bodies of phenomena. And if we may extrapolate from the history of the other sciences, there is every reason to expect that as explanations emerge, relevance for important areas of practical application will not be long delayed.

It has sometimes been implied (Friedman, p. 14) that the correctness of the assumptions of rational behavior underlying the classical theory of the firm is not merely irrelevant, but is not even empirically testable in any direct way, the only valid test being whether these assumptions lead to tolerably correct predictions at the macroscopic level. That would be true, of course, if we had no microscopes, so that the micro-level behavior was not directly observable. But we do have microscopes. There are many techniques for observing decision-making behavior, even at second-by-second intervals if that is wanted. In testing our economic theories, we do not have to depend on the rough aggregate time-series that are the main grist for the econometric mill, or even upon company financial statements.

The classical theories of economic decision making and of the business firm make very specific testable predictions about the concrete behavior of decision-making agents. Behavioral theories make quite different predictions. Since these predictions can be tested directly by observation, either theory (or both) may be falsified as readily when such predictions fail as when predictions about aggregate phenomena are in error.

C. Aggregative Tests of Decision Theory: Marginalism

If some economists have erroneously supposed that micro-economic theory can only be tested by its predictions of aggregate phenomena, we should avoid the converse error of supposing that aggregate phenomena are irrelevant to testing decision theory. In particular, are there important, *empirically verified*, aggregate predictions that follow from the theory of perfect rationality but that do not follow from behavioral theories of rationality?

The classical theory of omniscient rationality is strikingly simple and beautiful. Moreover, it allows us to predict (correctly or not) human behavior without stirring out of our armchairs to observe what such behavior is like. All the predictive power comes from characterizing the shape of the environment in which the behavior takes place. The environment, combined with the assumptions of perfect rationality, fully determines the behavior. Behavioral theories of rational choice--theories of bounded rationality--do not have this kind of simplicity. But, by way of compensation, their assumptions about human capabilities are far weaker than those of the classical theory. Thus, they make modest and realistic demands on the knowledge and computational

285

abilities of the human agents, but they also fail to predict that those agents will equate costs and returns at the margin.

D. Have the Marginalist Predictions Been Tested?

A number of empirical phenomena have been cited as providing more or less conclusive support for the classical theory of the firm as against its behavioral competitors (see Dale Jorgensen and Calvin Siebert). But there are no direct observations that individuals or firms do actually equate marginal costs and revenues. The empirically verified consequences of the classical theory are almost always weaker than this. Let us look at four of the most important of them: the fact that demand curves generally have negative slopes; the fact that fitted Cobb-Douglas functions are approximately homogeneous of the first degree; the fact of decreasing returns to scale; and the fact that executive salaries vary with the logarithm of company size. Are these indeed facts? And does the evidence support a maximizing theory against a satisficing theory?

Negatively Sloping Demand Curves. Evidence that consumers actually distribute their purchases in such a way as to maximize their utilities, and hence to equate marginal utilities, is non-existent. What the empirical data do confirm is that demand curves generally have negative slopes. (Even this "obvious" fact is tricky to verify, as Henry Schultz showed long years ago). But negatively sloping demand curves could result from a wide range of behaviors satisfying the assumptions of bounded rationality rather than those of utility maximization. Gary Becker, who can scarcely be regarded as a hostile witness for the classical theory, states the case very well:

> Economists have long been aware that some changes in the feasible or opportunity sets of households would lead to the same response *regardless of the decision rule used.* For example, a decrease in real income necessarily decreases the amount spent on at least one commodity... It has seldom been realized, however, that the change in opportunities resulting from a change in relative prices also tends to produce a systematic response, regardless of the decision rule. In particular, the fundamental theorem of traditional theory-- that demand curves are negatively inclined--largely results from the change in opportunities alone and is largely independent of the decision rule. [p. 4]

Later, Becker is even more explicit, saying, "Not only utility maximization but also many other decision rules, incorporating a wide variety of irrational behavior, lead to negatively inclined demand curves because of the effect of a change in prices on opportunities" (p.5).[2]

First-Degree Homogeneity of Production Functions. Another example of an observed phenomenon for which the classical assumptions provide sufficient, but not necessary, conditions is the equality between labor's shore of product and the exponent of the labor factor in fitted Cobb-Douglas production functions (see Simon and Ferdinand Levy). Fitted Cobb-Douglas functions are homogeneous, generally of degree close to unity and with a labor exponent of about the right magnitude. These findings, however, cannot be taken as strong evidence for the classical theory, for the identical results can readily be produced by mistakenly fitting a Cobb-Douglas function to data that were in fact generated by a linear accounting identity (value of goods equals labor cost plus capital cost), (see E.H. Phelps-Brown). The same comment applies to the SMAC production function (see Richard Cyert and Simon). Hence, the empirical findings do not allow us to draw any particular conclusions about the relative plausibility of classical and behavioral theories, both of which are equally compatible with the data.

The Long-Run Cost Curve. Somewhat different is the case of the firm's long-run cost curve, which classical theory requires to be U shaped if competitive equilibrium is to be stable. Theories of bounded rationality do not predict this--fortunately, for the observed data make it exceedingly doubtful that the cost curves are in fact generally U shaped. The evidence for many industries shows costs at the high-scale ends of the curves to be essentially constant or even declining (see Alan Walters). This finding is compatible with stochastic models of business firm growth and size (see Y. Ijiri and Simon), but not with the static equilibrium model of classical theory.

Executive Salaries. Average salaries of top corporate executives grow with the logarithm of corporate size (see David Roberts). This finding has been derived from the assumptions of the classical theory of profit maximization only with the help of very particular *ad hoc* assumptions about the distribution of managerial ability (see Robert Lucas, 1978). The observed relation is implied by a simple behavioral theory that assumes only that there is a single, culturally determined, parameter which fixes the average ratio of the salaries of managers to the salaries of their immediate subordinates (see Simon, 1957). In the case of the executive salary data, the behavioral model that explains the observations is substantially more parsimonious (in terms of assumptions about exogenous variables) than the classical model that explains the same observations.

Summary: Phenomena that Fail to Discriminate. It would take a much more extensive review than is provided here to establish the point conclusively, but I believe it is the case that specific phenomena requiring a theory of utility or profit maxi-

287

mization for their explanation rather than a theory of bounded rationality simply have not been observed in aggregate data. In fact, as my last two examples indicate, it is the classical rather than the behavioral form of the theory that faces real difficulties in handling some of the empirical observations.

Failures of Classical Theory. It may well be that classical theory can be patched up sufficiently to handle a wide range of situations where uncertainty and outguessing phenomena do not play a central role--that is, to handle the behavior of economies that are relatively stable and not too distant from a competitive equilibrium. However, a strong positive case for replacing the classical theory by a model of bounded rationality begins to emerge when we examine situations involving decision making under uncertainty and imperfect competition. These situations the classical theory was never designed to handle, and has never handled satisfactorily. Statistical decision theory employing the idea of subjective expected utility, on the one hand, and game theory, on the other, have contributed enormous conceptual clarification to these kinds of situations without providing satisfactory descriptions of actual human behavior, or even, for most cases, normative theories that are actually usable in the face of the limited computational powers of men and computers.

I shall have more to say later about the positive case for a descriptive theory of bounded rationality, but I would like to turn first to another territory within economic science that has gained rapidly in population since World War II, the domain of normative decision theory.

E. Normative Decision Theory

Decision theory can be pursued not only for the purposes of building foundations for political economy, or of understanding and explaining phenomena that are in themselves intrinsically interesting, but also for the purpose of offering direct advice to business and governmental decision makers. For reasons not clear to me, this territory was very sparsely settled prior to World War II. Such inhabitants as it had were mainly industrial engineers, students of public administration, and specialists in business functions, none of whom especially identified themselves with the economic sciences. Prominent pioneers included the mathematician, Charles Babbage, inventor of the digital computer, the engineer, Frederick Taylor, and the administrator, Henri Fayol.

During World War II, this territory, almost abandoned, was rediscovered by scientists, mathematicians, and statisticians concerned with military management and logistics, and was renamed "operations research" or "operations analysis." So remote were the operations researchers from the social science community that economists wishing to enter the territory had to establish their own colony, which they called "management science." The two professional organizations thus engendered still retain their separate identities, though they are now amicably federated in a number of common endeavors.

Optimization techniques were transported into management science from economics, and new optimization techniques, notably linear programming, were invented and developed, the names of Dantzig, Kantorovich, and Koopmans being prominent in the early development of that tool.

Now the salient characteristic of the decision tools employed in management science is that they have to be capable of actually making or recommending decisions, taking as their inputs the kinds of empirical data that are available in the real world, and performing only such computations as can reasonably be performed by existing desk calculators or, a little later, electronic computers. For these domains, idealized models of optimizing entrepreneurs, equipped with complete certainty about the world--or, at worst, having full probability distributions for uncertain events--are of little use. Models have to be fashioned with an eye to practical computability, no matter how severe the approximations and simplifications that are thereby imposed on them.

Model construction under these stringent conditions has taken two directions. The first is to retain optimization, but to simplify sufficiently so that the optimum (in the simplifed world!) is computable. The second is to construct satisficing models that provide good enough decisions with reasonable costs of computation. By giving up optimization, a richer set of properties of the real world can be retained in the models. Stated otherwise, decision makers can satisfice either by finding optimum solutions for a simplified world, or by finding satisfactory solutions for a more realistic world. Neither approach, in general, dominates the other, and both have continued to co-exist in the world of management science.

Thus, the body of theory that has developed in management science shares with the body of theory in descriptive decision theory a central concern with the ways in which decisions are made, and not just with the decision outcomes. As I have suggested elsewhere (1978b), these are theories of how to decide rather than theories of *what* to decide.

Let me cite one example, from work in which I participated, of how model building in normative economics is shaped by computational considerations (see Charles Holt, Franco Modigliani, John Muth, and Simon). In face of uncertain and fluctuating production demands, a company can smooth and stabilize its production and employment levels at the cost of holding buffer inventories. What kind of decision rule will secure a reasonable balance of costs? Formally, we are faced with a dynamic programming problem, and these generally pose formidable and often intolerable computational burdens for their solution.

One way out of this difficulty is to seek a special case of the problem that will be computationally tractable. If we assume the cost functions facing the company all to be quadratic in form, the optimal decision rule will then be a linear function of the decision variables, which can readily be computed in terms of the cost parameters. Equally important, under uncertainty about future sales, only the expected values, and not the higher moments, of the probability distributions enter into the decision rule (Simon, 1956b). Hence the assumption of quadratic costs reduces the original problem to one that is readily solved. Of course the solution, though it provides optimal decisions for the simplified world of our assumptions, provides, at best, satisfactory solutions for the real-world decision problem that the quadratic function approximates. In-principle, unattainable optimization is sacrificed for in-practice, attainable satisfaction.

If human decision makers are as rational as their limited computational capabilities and their incomplete information permit them to be, then there will be a close relation between normative and descriptive decision theory. Both areas of inquiry are concerned primarily with procedural rather than substantive rationality (Simon, 1978a). As new mathematical tools for computing optimal and satisfactory decisions are discovered, and as computers become more and more powerful, the recommendations of normative decision theory will change. But as the new recommendations are diffused, the actual, observed, practice of decision making in business firms will change also. And these changes may have macro-economic consequences. For example, there is some agreement that average inventory holdings of American firms have been reduced significantly by the introduction of formal procedures for calculating reorder points and quantities.

II. Characterizing Bounded Rationality

The principal forerunner of a behavioral theory of the firm is the tradition usually called Institutionalism. It is not clear that all of the writings, European and American, usually lumped under this rubric have much in common, or that their authors would agree with each other's views. At best, they share a conviction that economic theory must be reformulated to take account of the social and legal structures amidst which market transactions are carried out. Today, we even find a vigorous development within

290

economics that seeks to achieve institutionalist goals within the context of neoclassical price theory. I will have more to say about that a little later.

The name of John R. Commons is prominent--perhaps the most prominent--among American Institutionalists. Commons' difficult writings (for example, *Institutional Economics*) borrow their language heavily from the law, and seek to use the *transaction* as their basic unit of behavior. I will not undertake to review Commons' ideas here, but simply remark that they provided me with many insights in my initial studies of organizational decision making (see my *Administrative Behavior*, p. 136).

Commons also had a substantial influence on the thinking of Chester I. Barnard, an intellectually curious business executive who distilled from his experience as president of the New Jersey Bell Telephone Company, and as executive of other business, governmental, and nonprofit organizations, a profound book on decision making titled *The Functions of the Executive*. Barnard proposed original theories, which have stood up well under empirical scrutiny, of the nature of the authority mechanism in organizations and of the motivational bases for employee acceptance of organizational goals (the so-called "inducements-contributions" theory); and he provided a realistic description of organizational decison making, which he characterized as "opportunistic." The numerous references to Barnard's work in *Administrative Behavior* attest, though inadequately, to the impact he had on my own thinking about organizations.

A. *In Search of a Descriptive Theory*

In 1934-35, in the course of a field study of the administration of public recreational facilities in Milwaukee, which were managed jointly by the school board and the city public works department, I encountered a puzzling phenomenon. Although the heads of the two agencies appeared to agree as to the objectives of the recreation program, and did not appear to be competing for empire, there was continual disagreement and tension between them with respect to the allocation of funds between physical maintenance, on the one hand, and play supervision on the other. Why did they not, as my economics books suggested, simply balance off the marginal return of the one activity against that of the other?

Further exploration made it apparent that they didn't equate expenditures at the margin because, intellectually, they couldn't. There was no measurable production function from which quantitative inferences about marginal productivities could be drawn; and such qualitative notions of a production function as the two managers possessed were mutually incompatible. To the public works administrator, a playground was a physical facility, serving as a green oasis in the crowded gray city. To the recreation administrator, a playground was a social facility, where children could play together with adult help and guidance.

How can human beings make rational decisions in circumstances like these? How are they to apply the marginal calculus? Or, if it does not apply, what do they substitute for it?

The phenomenon observed in Milwaukee is ubiquitous in human decision making. In organization theory it is usually referred to as *subgoal identification*. When the goals of an organization cannot be connected operationally with actions (when the production function can't be formulated in concrete terms), then decisions will be judged against subordinate goals that can be so connected. There is no unique determination of these subordinate goals. Their formulation will depend on the knowledge, experience, and organizational environment of the decision maker. In the face of this ambiguity, the formulation can also be influenced in subtle, and not so subtle, ways by his self-interest and power drives.

The phenomenon arises as frequently in individual as in social decision making and problem solving. Today, under the rubric of *problem representation*, it is a central research interest of cognitive psychology. Given a particular environment of stimuli, and a particular background of previous knowledge, how will a person organize this complex mass of information into a problem formulation that will facilitate his solution efforts? How did Newton's experience of the apple, if he had one, get represented as an instance of attraction of apple by Earth?

Phenomena like these provided the central theme for *Administrative Behavior*. That study represented "an attempt to construct tools useful in my own research in the field of public administration." The product was actually not so much a theory as prolegomena to a theory, stemming from the conviction "that decision making is the heart of administration, and that the vocabulary of administrative theory must be derived from the logic and psychology of human choice." It was, if you please, an exercise in problem representation.

On examination, the phenomenon of subgoal identification proved to be the visible tip of a very large iceberg. The shape of the iceberg is best appreciated by contrasting it with classical models of rational choice. The classical model calls for knowledge of all the alternatives that are open to choice. It calls for complete knowledge of, or ability to compute, the consequences that will follow on each of the alternatives. It calls for certainty in the decision maker's present and future evaluation of these consequences. It calls for evaluation of these consequences. It calls for the ability to compare consequences, no matter how diverse and heterogeneous, in terms of some consistent measure of utility. The task, then, was to replace the classical model with one that would describe how decisions could be (and probably actually were) made when the alternatives of search had to be sought out, the consequences of choosing particular alternatives were only very imperfectly known both because of limited computational power and because of uncertainty in the external world, and the decision maker did not possess a general and consistent utility function for comparing heterogeneous alternatives.

Several procedures of rather general applicability and wide use have been discovered that transform intractable decision problems into tractable ones. One procedure already mentioned is to look for satisfactory choices instead of optimal ones. Another is to replace abstract, global goals with tangible subgoals, whose achievement can be observed and measured. A third is to divide up the decision-making task among many specialists, coordinating their work by means of a structure of communications and authority relations. All of these, and others, fit the general rubric of "bounded rationality," and it is now clear that the elaborate organizations that human beings have constructed in the modern world to carry out the work of production and government can only be understood as machinery for coping with the limits of man's abilities to comprehend and compute in the face of complexity and uncertainty.

This rather vague and general initial formulation of the idea of bounded rationality called for elaboration in two directions: greater formalization of the theory, and empirical verification of its main claims. During the decade that followed the publication of *Administrative Behavior*, substantial progress was made in both directions, some of it through the efforts of my colleagues and myself, much of it by other research groups that shared the same Zeitgeist.

B. *Empirical Studies*

The principal source of empirical data about organizational decision making has been straightforward "anthropological" field study, eliciting descriptions of decision-making procedures and observing the course of specific decision-making episodes. Examples are my study, with Guetzkow, Kozmetsky, and Tyndall (1954), of the ways in which accounting data were used in decision making in large corporations; and a series of studies, with Richard Cyert, James March, and others, of specific nonprogrammed policy decisions in a number of different companies (see Cyert, Simon, and Donald Trow). The latter line of work was greatly developed and expanded by Cyert and March and its theoretical implications for economics explored in their important work, *A Behavioral Theory of the Firm*.

At about the same time, the fortuitous availability of some data on businessmen's perceptions of a problem situation described in a business policy casebook enabled DeWitt Dearborn and me to demonstrate empirically the cognitive basis for identification with subgoals, the phenomenon that had so impressed me in the Milwaukee recreation study. The businessmen's perceptions of the principal problems facing the company described in the case were mostly determined by their own business experiences - sales and accounting executives identified a sales problem, manufacturing executives, a problem of internal organization.

Of course there is vastly more to be learned and tested about organizational decision making than can be dealt with in a handful of studies. Although many subsequent studies have been carried out in Europe and the United States, this domain is still grossly undercultivated (for references, see March, 1965; E. Johnsen, 1968; G. Eliasson, 1976). Among the reasons for the relative neglect of such studies, as constrasted, say, with laboratory experiments in social psychology, is that they are extremely costly and time consuming, with a high grist-to-grain ratio, the methodology for carrying them out is primitive, and satisfactory access to decision-making behavior is hard to secure. This part of economics has not yet acquired the habits of patience and persistence in the pursuit of facts that is exemplified in other domains by the work, say, of Simon Kuznets or of the architects of the MIT-SSRC-Penn econometric models.

C. Theoretical Inquiries

On the theoretical side, three questions seemed especially to call for clarification: what are the circumstances under which an employment relation will be preferred to some other form of contract as the arrangement for securing the performance of work; what is the relation between the classical theory of the firm and theories of organizational equilibrium first proposed by Chester Barnard; and what are the main characteristics of human rational choice in situations where complexity precludes omniscience?

The Employment Relation. A fundamental characteristic of modern industrial society is that most work is performed, not by individuals who produce products for sale, nor by individual contractors, but by persons who have accepted employment in a business firm and the authority relation with the employer that employment entails. Acceptance of authority means willingness to permit one's behavior to be determined by the employer, at least within some zone of indifference or acceptance. What is the advantage of this arrangement over a contract for specified goods or services? Why is so much of the world's work performed in large, hierarchic organizations?

Analysis showed (Simon, 1951) that a combination of two factors could account for preference for the employment contract over other forms of contracts: uncertainty as to which future behaviors would be advantageous to the employer, and a greater indifference of the employee as compared with the employer (within the former's area of acceptance) as to which of these behaviors he carried out. When the secretary is hired, the employer does not know what letters he will want her to type, and the secretary has no great preference for typing one letter rather than another. The employment contract permits the choice to be postponed until the uncertainty is resolved, with little cost to the employee and great advantage to the employer. The explanation is closely analogous to one Jacob Marschak had proposed for liquidity preference. Under conditions of uncertainty it is advantageous to hold resources in liquid, flexible form.

Organizational Equilibrium. Barnard had described the survival of organizations in terms of the motivations that make their participants (employees, investors, customers, suppliers) willing to remain in the system. In *Administrative Behavior,* I had developed this notion further into a motivational theory of the balance between the inducements that were provided by organizations to their participants, and the contributions those participants made to the organizations' resources.

A formalization of this theory (Simon, 1952; 1953) showed its close affinity to the classical theory of the firm, but with an important and instructive difference. In comparing the two theories, each inducement-contribution relation became a supply schedule for the firm. The survival conditions became the conditions for positive profit. But while the classical theory of the firm assumes that all profits accrue to a particular set of participants, the owners, the organization theory treats the surplus more symmetrically, and does not predict how it will be distributed. Hence the latter theory leaves room, under conditions of monopoly and imperfect competition, for bargaining among the participants (for example, between labor and owners) for the surplus. The survival conditions—positive profits rather than maximum profits—also permit a departure from the assumptions of perfect rationality.

Mechanisms of Bounded Rationality. In *Administrative Behavior*, bounded rationality is largely characterized as a residual category—rationality is bounded when it falls short of omniscience. And the failures of omniscience are largely failures of knowing all the alternatives, uncertainty about relevant exogenous events, and inability to calculate consequences. There was needed a more positive and formal characterization of the mechanisms of choice under conditions of bounded rationality. Two papers (Simon, 1955; 1956a) undertook first steps in that direction.

Two concepts are central to the characterization: *search* and *satisficing*. If the alternatives for choice are not given initially to the decision maker, then he must search for them. Hence, a theory of bounded rationality must incorporate a theory of search. This idea was later developed independently by George Stigler in a very influential paper that took as its example of a decision situation the purchase of a second-hand automobile. Stigler poured the search theory back into the old bottle of classical utility maximization, the cost of search being equated with its marginal return. In my 1956 paper, I had demonstrated the same formal equivalence, using as my example a dynamic programming formulation of the process of selling a house.

But utility maximization, as I showed, was not essential to the search scheme--fortunately, for it would have required the decision maker to be able to estimate the marginal costs and returns of search in a decision situation that was already too complex for the exercise of global rationality. As an alternative, one could postulate that the decision maker had formed some *aspiration* as to how good an alternative he should find. As soon as he discovered an alternative for choice meeting his level of aspiration, he would terminate the search and choose that alternative. I called this mode of selection *satisficing*. It had its roots in the empirically based psychological theories, due to Lewin and others, of aspiration levels. As psychological inquiry had shown, aspiration levels are not static, but tend to rise and fall in consonance with changing experiences. In a benign environment that provides many good alternatives, aspirations rise; in a harsher environment, they fall.

In long-run equilibrium it might even be the case that choice with dynamically adapting aspiration levels would be equivalent to optimal choice, taking the costs of search into account. But the important thing about the search and satisficing theory is that it showed how choice could actually be made with reasonable amounts of calculation, and using very incomplete information, without the need of performing the impossible--of carrying out this optimizing procedure.

D. *Summary*

Thus, by the middle 1950s, a theory of bounded rationality had been proposed as an alternative to classical omniscient rationality, a significant number of empirical studies had been carried out that showed actual business decision making to conform reasonably well with the assumptions of bounded rationality but not with the assumptions of perfect rationality, and key components of the theory--the nature of the authority and employment relations, organizational equilibrium, and the mechanisms of search and satisficing--had been elucidated formally. In the remaining parts of this paper, I should like to trace subsequent developments of decision-making theory, including developments competitive with the theory of bounded rationality, and then to comment on the implications (and potential implications) of the new descriptive theory of decision for political economy.

III. The Neoclassical Revival

Peering forward from the late 1950s, it would not have been unreasonable to predict that theories of bounded rationality would soon find a large place in the mainstream of economic thought. Substantial progress had been made in providing the theories with some formal structure, and an increasing body of empirical evidence showed them to provide a far more veridical picture of decision making in business organizations than did the classical concepts of perfect rationality.

History has not followed any such simple course, even though many aspects of the Zeitgeist were favorable to movement in this direction. During and after World War II, a large number of academic economists were exposed directly to business life, and had more or less extensive opportunities to observe how decisions were actually made in business organizations. Moreoever, those who became active in the development of the new management science were faced with the necessity of developing decision-making procedures that could actually be applied in practical situations. Surely these trends would be conducive to moving the basic assumptions of economic rationality in the direction of greater realism.

But these were not the only things that were happening in economics in the postwar period. First, there was a vigorous reaction that sought to defend classical theory from behavioralism on methodological grounds. I have already commented on these methodological arguments in the first part of my talk. However deeply one may disagree with them, they were stated persuasively and are still influential among academic economists.

Second, the rapid spread of mathematical knowledge and competence in the economics profession permitted the classical theory, especially when combined with statistical decision theory and the theory of games due to von Neumann and Morgenstern, to develop to new heights of sophistication and elegance, and to expand to embrace, albeit in highly stylized form, some of the phenomena of

297

uncertainty and imperfect information. The flowering of mathematical economics and econometrics has provided two generations of economic theorists with a vast garden of formal and technical problems that have absorbed their energies and postponed encounters with the inelegancies of the real world.

If I sound mildly critical of these developments, I should confess that I have also been a part of them, admire them, and would be decidedly unhappy to return to the premathematical world they have replaced. My concern is that the economics profession has exhibited some of the serial one-thing-at-a-time character of human rationality, and has seemed sometimes to be unable to distribute its attention in a balanced fashion among neoclassical theory, macroeconometrics, and descriptive decision theory. As a result, not as much professional effort has been devoted to the latter two, and especially the third, as one might have hoped and expected. The Heartland is more overpopulated than ever, while rich lands in other parts of the empire go untilled.

A. Search and Information Transfer

Let me allude to just three of the ways in which classical theory has sought to cope with some of its traditional limitations, and has even sought to make the development of a behavioral theory, incorporating psychological assumptions, unnecessary. The first was to introduce search and information transfer explicitly as economic activities, with associated costs and outputs, that could be inserted into the classical production function. I have already referred to Stigler's 1961 paper on the economics of information, and my own venture in the same direction in the 1956 essay cited earlier.

In theory of this genre, the decision maker is still an individual. A very important new direction, in which decisions are made by groups of individuals, in teams or organizations, is the economic theory of teams developed by Jacob Marschak and Roy Radner. Here we see genuine organizational phenomena--specialization of decision making as a consequence of the costs of transmitting information--emerge from the rational calculus. Because the mathematical difficulties are formidable, the theory remains largely illustrative and limited to very simple situations in miniature organizations. Nevertheless, it has greatly broadened our understanding of the economics of information.

In none of these theories--any more than in statistical decision theory or the theory of games--is the assumption of perfect maximization abandoned. Limits and costs of information are introduced, not as psychological characteristics of the decision maker, but as part of his technological environment. Hence, the new theories do nothing to alleviate the computational complexities facing the decision maker--do not see him coping with them by heroic approximation, simplifying and satisficing, but simply magnify and multiply them. Now he needs to compute not merely the shapes of his supply and demand curves, but, in addition, the costs and benefits of computing those shapes to greater accuracy as well. Hence, to some extent, the impression that these new theories deal with the hitherto ignored phenomena of uncertainty and information transmission is illusory. For many economists, however, the illusion has been persuasive.

B. *Rational Expectations Theory*

A second development in neoclassical theory on which I wish to comment is the so-called "rational expectations" theory. There is a bit of historical irony surrounding its origins. I have already described the management science inquiry of Holt, Modigliani, Muth, and myself that developed a dynamic programming algorithm for the special (and easily computed) case of quadratic cost functions. In this case, the decision rules are linear, and the probability distributions of future events can be replaced by their expected values, which serve as certainty equivalents (see Simon, 1956; Henri Theil, 1957).

Muth imaginatively saw in this special case a paradigm for rational behavior under uncertainty. What to some of us in the HMMS research team was an approximating, satisficing simplification, served for him as a major line of defense for perfect rationality. He said in his seminal 1961 *Econometrica* article, "It is sometimes argued that the assumption of rationality in economics leads to theories inconsistent with, or inadequate to explain, observed phenomena, especially changes over time... Our hypothesis is based on exactly the opposite point of view: that dynamic economic models do not assume enough rationality" (p. 316).

The new increment of rationality that Muth proposed was that "expectations, since they are informed predictions of future events, are essentially the same as the predictions of the relevant economic theory" (p. 316). He would cut the Gordian knot. Instead of dealing with uncertainty by elaborating the model of the decision process, he would once and for all--if his hypothesis were correct--make process irrelevant. The subsequent vigorous development· of rational expectations theory, in the hands of Sargent, Lucas, Prescott, and others, is well known to most readers (see, for example, Lucas, 1975).

It is too early to render a final verdict on the rational expectations theory. The issue will ultimately be decided, as all scientific debates should be, by a gradual winnowing of the

299

empirical evidence, and that winnowing process has just begun. Meanwhile, certain grave theoretical difficulties have already been noticed. As Muth himself has pointed out, it is rational (i.e., profit maximizing) to use the "rational expectations" decision rule if the relevant cost equations are in fact quadratic. I have suggested elsewhere (1978a) that it might therefore be less misleading to call the rule a "consistent expectations" rule.

Perhaps even more important, Albert Ando and Benjamin Friedman (1978, 1979) have shown that the policy implications of the rational expectations rule are quite different under conditions where new information continually becomes available to the system, structural changes occur, and the decision maker learns, than they are under steady-state conditions. For example, under the more dynamic conditions, monetary neutrality--which in general holds for the static consistent expectations models--is no longer guaranteed for any finite time horizon.

In the recent "revisionist" versions of consistent expectations theory, moreover, where account is taken of a changing environment of information, various behavioral assumptions reappear to explain how expectations are formed--what information decision makers will consider, and what they will ignore. But unless these assumptions are to be made on a wholly *ad hoc* and arbitrary basis, they create again the need for an explicit and valid theory of the decision-making *process* (see Simon, 1958a; B. Friedman, 1979).

C. *Statistical Decision Theory and Game Theory*

Statistical decision theory and game theory are two other important components of the neoclassical revival. The former addresses itself to the question of incorporating uncertainty (or more properly, risk) into the decision-making models. It requires heroic assumptions about the information the decision maker has concerning the probability distributions of the relevant variables, and simply increases by orders of magnitude the computational problems he faces.

Game theory addresses itself to the "outguessing" problem that arises whenever an economic actor takes into account the possible reactions to his own decisions of the other actors. To my mind, the main product of the very elegant apparatus of game theory has been to demonstrate quite clearly that it is virtually impossible to define an unambiguous criterion of rationality for this class of situations (or, what amounts to the same thing, a definitive definition of the "solution" of a game). Hence, game theory has not brought to the theories of oligopoly and imperfect competiton the relief from their contradictions and complexities that was originally hoped for it. Rather, it has shown that these difficulties are ineradicable. We may be able to reach consensus that a certain criterion of rationality is appropriate to a particular game, but if someone challenges the consensus, preferring a different criterion, we will have no logical basis for persuading him that he is wrong.

D. Conclusion

Perhaps I have said enough about the neoclassical revival to suggest why it has been a highly attractive commodity in competition with the behavioral theories. To some economists at least, it has held open the possibility and hope that important questions that had been troublesome for classical economics could now be addressed without sacrifice of the central assumption of perfect rationality, and hence also with a maximum of a priori inference and a minimum of tiresome grubbing with empirical data. I have perhaps said enough also with respect to the limitations of these new constructs to indicate why I do not believe that they solve the problems that motivated their development.

IV. Advances in the Behavioral Theory

Although they have played a muted role in the total economic research activity during the past two decades, theories of bounded rationality and the behavioral theory of the business firm have undergone steady development during that period. Since surveying the whole body of work would be a major undertaking, I shall have to be satisfied here with suggesting the flavor of the whole by citing a few samples of different kinds of important research falling in this domain. Where surveys on particular topics have been published, I will limit myself to references to them.

First, there has been work in the psychological laboratory and the field to test whether people in relatively simple choice situations behave as statistical decision theory (maximization of expected utilities) say they do. Second, there has been extensive psychological research, in which Allen Newell and I have been heavily involved, to discover the actual microprocesses of human decision making and problem solving. Third, there have been numerous empirical observations--most of them in the form of "case studies"--of the actual processes of decision making in organizational and business contexts. Fourth, there have been reformulations and extensions of the theory of the firm replacing classical maximization with behavioral decision postulates.

A. Utility Theory and Human Choice

The axiomatization of utility and probability after World War II and the revival of Bayesian statistics opened the way to testing

301

empirically whether people behaved in choice situations so as to maximize subjective expected utility (SEU). In early studies, using extremely simple choice situations, it appeared that perhaps they did. When even small complications were introduced into the situations, wide departures of behavior from the predictions of SEU theory soon became evident. Some of the most dramatic and convincing empirical refutations of the theory have been reported by D. Kahneman and A. Tversky, who showed that under one set of circumstances, decision makers gave far too little weight to prior knowledge and based their choices almost entirely on new evidence, while in other circumstances new evidence had little influence on opinions already formed. Equally large and striking departures from the behavior predicted by the SEU theories were found by Howard Kunreuther and his colleagues in their studies of individual decisions to purchase or not to purchase flood insurance. On the basis of these and other pieces of evidence, the conclusion seems unavoidable that the SEU theory does not provide a good prediction - not even a good approximation - of actual behavior.

Notice that the refutation of the theory has to do with the *substance* of the decisions, and not just the process by which they are reached. It is not that people do not go through the calculations that would be required to reach the SEU decision - neoclassical thought has never claimed that they did. What has been shown is that they do not even behave as *if* they had carried out those calculations, and that result is a direct refutation of the neoclassical assumptions.

B. *Psychology of Problem Solving*

The evidence on rational decision making is largely negative evidence, evidence of what people do not do. In the past twenty years a large body of positive evidence has also accumulated about the processes that people use to make difficult decisions and solve complex problems. The body of theory that has been built up around this evidence is called information processing psychology, and is usually expressed formally in computer programming languages. Newell and I have summed up our version of this theory in our book, *Human Problem Solving*, which is part of a large and rapidly growing literature that assumes an information processing framework and makes use of computer simulation as a central tool for expressing and testing theories.

Information processing theories envisage problem solving as involving very selective search through problem spaces that are often immense. Selectivity, based on rules of thumb or "heuristics," tends to guide the search into promising regions, so that solutions will generally be found after search of only a tiny part of the total space. Satisficing criteria terminate search when satisfactory problem solutions have been found. Thus, these theories of problem solving clearly fit within the framework of bounded rationality that I have been expounding here.

By now the empirical evidence for this general picture of the problem solving process is extensive. Most of the evidence pertains to relatively simple, puzzle-like situations of the sort that can be brought into the psychological laboratory for controlled study, but a great deal has been learned, also, about professional level human tasks like making medical diagnoses, investing in portfolios of stocks and bonds, and playing chess. In tasks of these kinds, the general search mechanisms operate in a rich context of information stored in human long-term memory, but the general organization of the process is substantially the same as for the simpler, more specific tasks.

At the present time, research in information processing psychology is proceeding in several directions. Exploration of professional level skills continues. A good deal of effort is now being devoted also to determining how initial representations for new problems are acquired. Even in simple problem domains, the problem solver has much latitude in the way he formulates the problem space in which he will search, a finding that underlines again how far the actual process is from a search for a uniquely determined optimum (see J.R. Hayes and Simon).

The main import for economic theory of the research in information processing psychology is to provide rather conclusive empirical evidence that the decision-making process in problem situations conforms closely to the models of bounded rationality described earlier. This finding implies, in turn, that choice is not determined uniquely by the objective characteristics of the problem situation, but depends also on the particular heuristic process that is used to reach the decision. It would appear, therefore, that a model of process is an essential component in any positive theory of decision making that purports to describe the real world, and that the neoclassical ambition of avoiding the necessity for such a model is unrealizable (Simon, 1978a).

C. Organizational Decision Making

It would be desirable to have, in addition to the evidence from the psychological research just described, empirical studies of the process of decision making in organizational contexts. The studies of individual problem solving and decision making do not touch on the many social-psychological factors that enter into the decision process in organizations. A substantial number of investigations have been carried out in the past twenty years of the decision-making process in organizations, but they are not easily summarized. The difficulty is that most of these investigations

have taken the form of case studies of specific decisions or particular classes of decisions in individual organizations. To the best
of my knowledge, no good review of this literature has been published, so that it is difficult even to locate and identify the
studies that have been carried out.[3] Nor have any systematic
methods been developed and tested for distilling out from these
individual case studies their implications for the general theory of
the decision-making process.

The case studies of organizational decision making, therefore,
represent the natural history stage of scientific inquiry. They
provide us with a multitude of facts about the decision-making
process--facts that are almost uniformly consistent with the kind
of behavioral model that has been proposed here. But we do not
yet know how to use these facts to test the model in any formal
way. Nor do we quite know what to do with the observation that
the specific decision-making procedures used by organizations
differ from one organization to another, and within each organization, even from one situation to another. We must not expect from
these data generalizations as neat and precise as those incorporated in neoclassical theory.

Perhaps the closest approach to a method for extracting theoretically relevant information from case studies is computer simulation. By converting empirical evidence about a decision-making
process into a computer program, a path is opened both for testing the adequacy of the program mechanisms for explaining the
data, and for discovering the key features of the program that
account, qualitatively, for the interesting and important characteristics of its behavior. Examples of the use of this technique
are G.P.E. Clarkson's simulation of the decision making of an
investment trust officer, Cyert, E.A. Feigenbaum, and March's
simulation of the history of a duopoly, and C.P. Bonini's model of
the effects of accounting information and supervisory pressures
in altering employee motivations in a business firm. The simulation methodology is discussed from a variety of viewpoints in
Dutton and Starbuck.[4]

D. Theories of the Business Firm

The general features of bounded rationality--selective search,
satisficing, and so on--have been taken as the starting points for
a number of attempts to build theories of the business firm incorporating behavioral assumptions. Examples of such theories
would inlcude the theory of Cyert and March, already mentioned;
William Baumol's theory of sales maximization subject to minimum
profit constraints; Robin Marris' models of firms whose goals are
stated in terms of rates of growth; Harvey Leibenstein's theory of
"X-inefficiency" that depresses production below the theoretically
attainable; Janos Kornai's dichotomy between supply-driven and

demand-driven management; Oliver Williamson's theory of trans-
actional costs; the evolutionary models of Richard Nelson and
Sidney Winter (1973); Cyert and Morris DeGroot's (1974) models
incorporating adaptive learning; Radner's (1975a,b) explicit satisficing models; and others.

Characterized in this way, there seems to be little commonality among all of these theories and models, except that they
depart in one way or another from the classical assumption of
perfect rationality in firm decision making. A closer look, however, and a more abstract description of their assumptions, shows
that they share several basic characteristics. Most of them
depart from the assumption of profit maximization in the short
run, and replace it with an assumption of goals defined in terms
of targets--that is, they are to greater or lesser degree satis
ficing theories. If they do retain maximizing assumptions, they
contain some kind of mechanism that prevents the maximum from
being attained, at least in the short run. In the Cyert-March
theory, and that of Leibenstein, this mechanism can be viewed as
producing "organizational slack," the magnitude of which may
itself be a function of motivational and environmental variables.

Finally, a number of these theories assume that organizational
learning takes place, so that if the environment were stationary
for a sufficient length of time, the system equilibrium would
approach closer and closer to the classical profit-maximizing
equilibrium. Of course they generally also assume that the environmental disturbances will generally be large enough to prevent the classical solution from being an adequate approximation
to the actual behavior.

The presence of something like organizational slack in a model
of the business firm introduces complexity in the firm's behavior
in the short run. Since the firm may operate very far from any
optimum, the slack serves as a buffer between the environment
and the firm's decisions. Responses to environmental events can
no longer be predicted simply by analyzing the "requirements of
the situation," but depend on the specific decision processes that
the firm employs. However well this characteristic of a business
firm model corresponds to reality, it reduces the attractiveness of
the model for many economists, who are reluctant to give up the
process-independent predictions of classical theory, and who do
not feel at home with the kind of empirical investigation that is
required for disclosing actual real world decision processes.

But there is another side to the matter. If, in the face of
identical environmental conditions, different decision mechanisms
can produce different firm behaviors, this sensitivity of outcomes
to process can have important consequences for analysis at the
level of markets and the economy. Political economy, whether

descriptive or normative, cannot remain indifferent to this source of variability in response. At the very least it demands that - before we draw policy conclusions from our theories, and particularly before we act on those policy conclusions--we carry out sensitivity analyses to test how far our conclusions would be changed if we made different assumptions about the decision mechanisms at the micro level.

If our conclusions are robust--if they are not changed materially by substituting one or another variant of the behavioral model for the classical model--we will gain confidence in our predictions and recommendations; if the conclusions are sensitive to such substitutions, we will use them warily until we can determine which micro theory is the correct one.

As reference to the literature cited earlier in this section will verify, our predictions of the operations of markets and of the economy are sensitive to our assumptions about mechanisms at the level of decision processes. Moreover, the assumptions of the behavioral theories are almost certainly closer to reality than those of the classical theory. These two facts, in combination, constitute a direct refutation of the argument that the unrealism of the assumptions of the classical theory is harmless. We cannot use the in vacua version of the law of falling bodies to predict the sinking of a heavy body in molasses. The predictions of the classical and neoclassical theories and the policy recommendations derived from them must be treated with the greatest caution.

V. Conclusion

There is a saying in politics that "you can't beat something with nothing." You can't defeat a measure or a candidate simply by pointing to defects and inadequacies. You must offer an alternative.

The same principle applies to scientific theory. Once a theory is well entrenched, it will survive many assaults of empirical evidence that purports to refute it unless an alternative theory, consistent with the evidence, stands ready to replace it. Such conservative protectiveness of established beliefs is, indeed, not unreasonable. In the first place, in empirical science we aspire only to approximate truths; we are under no illusion that we can find a single formula, or even a moderately complex one, that captures the whole truth and nothing else. We are committed to a strategy of successive approximations, and when we find discrepancies between theory and data, our first impulse is to patch rather than to rebuild from the foundations.

In the second place, when discrepancies appear, it is seldom immediately obvious where the trouble lies. It may be located in the fundamental assumptions of the theory, but it may as well be merely a defect in the auxiliary hypotheses and measurement postulates we have had to assume in order to connect theory with observations. Revisions in these latter parts of the structure may be sufficient to save the remainder.

What then is the present status of the classical theory of the firm? There can no longer be any doubt that the micro assumptions of the theory--the assumptions of perfect rationality--are contrary to fact. It is not a question of approximation; they do not even remotely describe the processes that human beings use for making decisions in complex situations.

Moreover, there is an alternative. If anything, there is an embarrassing richness of alternatives. Today, we have a large mass of descriptive data, from both laboratory and field, that show how human problem solving and decision making actually take place in a wide variety of situations. A number of theories have been constructed to account for these data, and while these theories certainly do not yet constitute a single coherent whole, there is much in common among them. In one way or another, they incorporate the notions of bounded rationality: the need to search for decision alternatives, the replacement of optimization by targets and satisficing goals, and mechanisms of learning and adaptation. If our interest lies in descriptive decison theory (or even normative decision theory), it is now entirely clear that the classical and neoclassical theories have been replaced by a superior alternative that provides us with a much closer approximation to what is actually going on.

But what if our interest lies primarily in normative political economy rather than in the more remote regions of the economic sciences? Is there then any reason why we should give up the familiar theories? Have the newer concepts of decision making and the firm shown their superiority "for purposes of economic analysis"?

If the classical and neoclassical theories were, as is sometimes argued, simply powerful tools for deriving aggregative consequences that held alike for both perfect and bounded rationality, we would have every reason to retain them for this purpose. But we have seen, on the contrary, that neoclassical theory does not always lead to the same conclusions at the level of aggregate phenomena and policy as are implied by the postulate of bounded rationality, in any of its variants. Hence, we cannot defend an uncritical use of these contrary-to-fact assumptions by the argument that their veridicality is unimportant. In many cases, in fact, this veridicality may be crucial to reaching correct conclusions about the central questions of political economy. Only a comparison of predictions can tell us whether a case before us is one of these.

307

The social sciences have been accustomed to look for models in the most spectacular successes of the natural sciences. There is no harm in that, provided that it is not done in a spirit of slavish imitation. In economics, it has been common enough to admire Newtonian mechanics (or, as we have seen, the Law of Falling Bodies), and to search for the economic equivalent of the laws of motion. But this is not the only model for a science, and it seems, indeed, not to be the right one for our purposes.

Human behavior, even rational human behavior, is not to be accounted for by a handful of invariants. It is certainly not to be accounted for by assuming perfect adaptation to the environment. Its basic mechanisms may be relatively simple, and I believe they are, but that simplicity operates in interaction with extremely complex boundary conditions imposed by the environment and by the very facts of human long-term memory and of the capacity of human beings, individually and collectively, to learn.

If we wish to be guided by a natural science metaphor, I suggest one drawn from biology rather than physics (see Newell and Simon, 1976). Obvious lessons are to be learned from evolutionary biology, and rather less obvious ones from molecular biology. From molecular biology, in particular, we can glimpse a picture of how a few basic mechanisms--the DNA of the Double Helix, for example, or the energy transfer mechanisms elucidated so elegantly by Peter Mitchell--can account for a wide range of complex phenomena. We can see the role in science of laws of qualitative structure, and the power of qualitative as well as quantitative explanation.

I am always reluctant to end a talk about the sciences of man in the future tense. It conveys too much the impression that these are potential sciences which may some day be actualized, but that do not really exist at the present time. Of course that is not the case at all. However much our knowledge of human behavior falls short of our need for such knowledge, still it is enormous. Sometimes we tend to discount it because so many of the phenomena are accessible to us in the very activity of living as human beings among human beings that it seems commonplace to us. Moreover, it does not always answer the questions for which we need answers. We cannot predict very well the course of the business cycle nor manage the employment rate. (We cannot, it might be added, predict very well the time of the next thunderstorm in Stockholm, or manage the earth's climates.)

With all these qualifications and reservations, we do understand today many of the mechanisms of human rational choice. We do know how the information processing system called Man, faced with complexity beyond his ken, uses his information processing capacities to seek out alternatives, to calculate consequences, to

308

resolve uncertainties, and thereby--sometimes, not always--to find ways of action that are sufficient unto the day, that satisfice.

Footnotes

* Herbert A. Simon from Carnegie Mellon University, is indebted to Albert Ando, Otto A. Davis, and Benjamin M. Friedman for valuable comments on an earlier draft of this paper.

1. The phrase "that works" refutes, out of hand, Friedman's celebrated paean of praise for lack of realism in assumptions. Consider his example of falling bodies (pp. 16-19). His valid point is that it is advantageous to use the simple law, ignoring air resistance, when it gives a "good enough" approximation. But of course the conditions under which it gives a good approximation are not at all the conditions under which it is unrealistic or a "wildly inaccurate descriptive representation of reality." We can use it to predict the path of a body falling in a vacuum, but not the path of one falling through the Earth's atmosphere. I cannot in this brief space mention, much less discuss, all of the numerous logical fallacies that can be found in Friedman's 40-page essay. For additional criticism, see Simon (1963) and Samuelson (1963).

2. In a footnote, Becker indicates that he denotes as irrational "[A]ny deviation from utility maximization." Thus, what I have called "bounded rationality" is "irrationality" in Becker's terminology.

3. For leads into the literature, see March and Simon; March; Johnsen; J.M. Dutton and W.H. Starbuck. However, there are large numbers of specific case studies, some of them carried out as thesis projects, some concerned with particular fields of business application, which have never been recorded in these reference sources (for example, Eliasson, 1976).

4. In addition to simulations of the firm, there are very interesting and potentially important efforts to use simulation to build bridges directly from decision theory in political economy. See G. Orcutt and S. Caldwell, R. Wertheimer, and Eliasson (1978).

References

A.A. Alchian, "Uncertainty, Evolution and Economic Theory," *Journal of Political Economy*, June 1950, 58, 211-21.

A. Ando, "On a Theoretical and Empirical Basis of Macroeconometric Models," paper presented to the NSF-NBER Conference on Macroeconomic Modelling, Ann Arbor, October 1978.

Chester I. Barnard, *The Functions of the Executive*, Cambridge, Mass. 1938.

William Baumol, *Business Behavior, Value and Growth*, New York 1959.

G.S. Becker, "Irrational Behavior and Economic Theory," *Journal of Political Economy*, February 1962, 70, 1-13.

Charles P. Bonini, *Simulation of Information and Decision Systems in the Firm*, Englewood Cliffs, 1963.

Alfred Chandler, *Strategy and Structure*, Cambridge, Mass. 1962.

N.C. Churchill, W.W. Cooper, and T. Sainsbury, "Laboratory and Field Studies of the Behavioral Effects of Audits," in C.P. Bonini et al., eds., *Management Controls*, New York 1964.

G.P.E. Clarkson, "A Model of the Trust Investment Process," in E.A. Feigenbaum and J. Feldman, eds., *Computers and Thought*, New York 1963.

John R. Commons, *Institutional Economics*, Madison 1934.

R.M. Cyert, E.A. Feigenbaum, and J.G. March, "Models in a Behavioral Theory of the Firm," *Behavioral Science*, April 1959, 4, 81-95.

_____ and M.H. DeGroot, "Rational Expectations and Bayesian Analysis," *Journal of Political Economy*, May/June 1974, 82, 521-36.

_____ and _____ "Adaptive Utility," in R.H. Day and T. Groves, eds., *Adaptive Economic Models*, New York 1975, 233-46.

_____ and James G. March, *A Behavioral Theory of the Firm*, Englewood Cliffs, 1963.

_____ and H.A. Simon, "Theory of the Firm: Behavioralism and Marginalism," unpublished working paper, Carnegie-Mellon University 1971.

_____ and _____ and D.B. Trow, "Observation of a Business Decision," *Journal of Business, University of Chicago*, October 1956, 29, 237-48.

D.C. Dearborn and H.A. Simon, "Selective Perception: The Identifications of Executives," *Sociometry*, 1958, 21, 140-144; reprinted in *Administrative Behavior*, ch. 15, 3rd ed., New York 1976.

J.M. Dutton and W.H. Starbuck, *Computer Simulation of Human Behavior*, New York 1971.

G. Eliasson, *Business Economic Planning*, New York 1976.

_____, *A Micro-to-Macro Model of the Swedish Economy*, Stockholm 1978.

B.M. Friedman, "Optimal Expectations and the Extreme Information Assumptions of 'Rational Expectations' Macromodels," *Journal of Monetary Economics*, January 1979, 5, 23-41.

_____, "A Discussion of the Methodological Premises of Professors Lucas and Sargent," in *After the Phillips Curve: The Persistence of High Inflation and High Unemployment*, Boston 1978.

Milton Friedman, *Essays in Positive Economics*, Chicago 1953.

J.R. Hayes and H.A. Simon, "Understanding Written Problem Instructions," in W. Gregg, ed., *Knowledge and Cognition*, Potomac 1974, 167-200.

A.O. Hirschman, *Exit, Voice and Loyalty*, Cambridge, Mass. 1970.

Charles C. Holt, Franco Modigliani, John F. Muth, and Herbert A. Simon, *Planning Production, Inventories and Work Force*, Englewood Cliffs 1960.

Y. Ijiri and H.A. Simon, *Skew Distributions and the Sizes of Business Firms*, Amsterdam 1977.

E. Johnsen, *Studies in Multiobjective Decsion Models*, Lund 1968.

311

D.W. Jorgenson and C.D. Siebert, "A Comparison of Alternative Theories of Corporate Investment Behavior," *American Economic Review*, September 1968, 58, 681-712.

D. Kahneman and A. Tversky, "On the Psychology of Prediction," *Psychological Review*, July 1973, 80, 237-51.

Janos Kornai, *Anti-Equilibrium*, Amsterdam 1971.

Howard Kunreuther et al., *Disaster Insurance Protection: Public Policy Lessons*, New York 1978.

Harvey Leibenstein, *Beyond Economic Man*, Cambridge, Mass. 1976.

J. Lesourne, *A Theory of the Individual for Economic Analysis*, Vol. 1, Amsterdam 1977.

R.E. Lucas, Jr., "An Equilibrium Model of the Business Cycle," *Journal of Political Economy*, December 1975, 83, 1113-44.

_____, "On the Size Distribution of Business Firms," *Bell Journal of Economics*, Autumn 1978, 9, 508-23.

James G. March, *Handbook of Organizations*, Chicago 1965.

_____ and H.A. Simon, *Organizations*, New York 1958.

Robin Marris, *The Economic Theory of "Managerial" Capitalism*, London 1964.

Jacob Marschak, "Role of Liquidity under Complete and Incomplete Information," *American Economic Review Proceedings*, May 1949, 39, 182-95.

_____ and Roy Radner, *Economic Theory of Teams*, New Haven 1972.

Alfred Marshall, *Principles of Economics*, 8th ed., New York 1920.

E.S. Mason, "Comment," in Bernard T. Haley, ed., *A Survey of Contemporary Economics*, Vol. II, Homewood, 1952, 221-22.

J.M. Montias, *The Structure of Economic Systems*, New Haven 1976.

J.F. Muth, "Rational Expectations and the Theory of Price Movements," *Econometrica*, July 1961, 29, 315-53.

          , "Optimal Properties of Exponentially Weighted Forecasts," *Journal of American Statistical Association*, June 1960, 55, 299-306.

R.R. Nelson and S. Winter, "Toward an Evolutionary Theory of Economic Capabilities," *American Economic Review Proceedings*, May 1973, 63, 440-49.

          and   , "Neoclassical vs. Evolutionary Theories of Economic Growth," *Economic Journal*, December 1974, 84, 886-905.

Allen Newell and Herbert A. Simon, *Human Problem Solving*, Englewood Cliffs 1972.

          and   , "Computer Science as Empirical Inquiry: Symbols and Search," *Communications of the ACM*, March 1976, 19, 113-26.

G. Orcutt and S. Caldwell and R. Wertheimer II, *Policy Exploration through Microanalytic Simulation*, Washington 1976.

A. Papandreou, "Some Basic Problems in the Theory of the Firm," in Bernard F. Haley, ed., *A Survey of Contemporary Economics*, Vol. II, Homewood 1952.

E.H. Phelps-Brown, "The Meaning of the Fitted Cobb-Douglas Function," *Quarterly Journal of Economics*, November 1957, 71, 546-60.

R. Radner, (1975a) "A Behavioral Model of Cost Reduction," *Bell Journal of Economics*, Spring 1975, 6, 196-215.

          , (1975b) "Satisficing," *Journal of Mathematical Economics*, June-September 1975, 2, 253-62.

David R. Roberts, *Executive Compensation*, Glencoe 1959.

P.A. Samuelson, "Discussion: Problems of Methodology," *American Economic Review Proceedings*, May 1963, 53, 231-36.

Henry Schultz, *The Theory and Measurement of Demand*, Chicago 1938.

Herbert A. Simon, *Administrative Behavior*, New York 1947; 3rd ed., 1976.

          , "A Formal Theory of the Employment Relation," *Econometrica*, July 1951, 19, 293-305.

_____, "A Comparison of Organization Theories," *Review of Economic Studies*, No. 1, 1952, 20, 40-48.

_____, "A Behavioral Model of Rational Choice," *Quarterly Journal of Economics*, February 1955, 69, 99-118.

_____, "Rational Choice and the Structure of the Environment," *Psychological Review*, March 1956, 63, 129-38.

_____, "Dynamic Programming under Uncertainty with a Quadratic Criterion Function," *Econometrica*, January 1956, 24, 74-81.

_____, *Models of Man*, New York 1957.

_____, "The Compensation of Executives," *Sociometry*, 1957, 20, 32-35.

_____, "Theories of Decision Making in Economics and Behavioral Science," *American Economic Review*, June 1959, 49, 223-83.

_____, "Discussion: Problems of Methodology," *American Economic Review Proceedings*, May 1963, 53, 229-31.

_____, "From Substantive to Procedural Rationality," in Spiro J. Latsis, ed., *Methodological Appraisal in Economics*, Cambridge 1976.

_____, (1978a) "Rationality as Process and as Product of Thought," *American Economic Review Proceedings*, May 1978, 68, 1-16.

_____, (1978b) "On How to Decide What to Do," *Bell Journal of Economics*, Autumn 1978, 9, 494-507.

_____, G. Kozmetsky, H. Guetzkow, and G. Tyndall, *Centralization vs. Decentralization in Organizing the Controller's Department*, New York 1954; reprinted Houston, 1978.

_____ and F.K. Levy, "A Note on the Cobb-Douglas Function," *Review of Economic Studies*, June 1963, 30, 93-94.

G.J. Stigler, "The Economics of Information," *Journal of Political Economy*, June 1961, 69, 213-15.

H. Theil, "A Note on Certainty Equivalence in Dynamic Planning," *Econometrica*, April 1957, 25, 346-49.

John von Neumann and Oscar Morgenstern, *Theory of Games and Economic Behavior*, Princeton 1944.

A.A. Walters, "Production and Cost Functions: An Econometric Survey," *Econometrica*, January-April 1963, 31, 1-66.

Oliver Williamson, *Markets and Hierarchies: Analysis and Antitrust Implications*, New York 1975.

S. Winter, "Satisficing, Selection, and the Innovating Remnant," *Quarterly Journal of Economics*, May 1971, 85, 237-61.

Part Nine   What is Wrong and Right with Economics?

We want to end the reader with a few readings that sum up several of the points and arguments which appeared in the other parts of this volume. Most economists would neither condemn nor accept all aspects of how economists explain. Most economists believe that there are topics or ideas which could be modified or even abandoned to improve the methodology of economics. The articles in this section attempt to identify the areas needing improvement and to suggest possible remedies.

In the first two articles Wassily Leontief argues that the empirical foundation of economics has lagged behind the phenomenal output of economic theory which he believes often has no real world counterpart. In particular he argues that much use of mathematics by economists merely serves to hide the weak empirical foundations on which the assumptions of this mathematics are based. He is equally as harsh on the uncritical use of econometrics as he points out that the development of statistical techniques can serve to hide the weakness of much of the data that economists use. To improve this situation, Leontief makes two suggestions: (i) the development of more interdisciplinary research ventures, and (ii) the production and distribution of more and better data. His methodological position can be summed up in his statement:

> True advances can be achieved only through an iterative process in which improved theoretical foundation raises new empirical questions and the answers to these questions lead to new theoretical insights.

G.D. Worswick, in his presidential address to Section F of the British Association in 1971, has taken a methodological position similar to Leontief. We recommend this article to the readers as a complement to Leontief's essay. The overuse of mathematics and econometrics comes in for harsh criticism from Worswick also on the grounds that they have little reference to any actual situations and many assumptions are accepted uncritically. He argues that in many universities theory and technique courses are often stressed to the exclusion of the courses in content and "data." He worries that if the private sector economist perceives that much theory and technique are unrelated to the actual world, he may dismiss most economics as useless. Worswick's recommendations to economists for improving the situation are: (i) to spend more time critically examining their data while remembering that the context of a model can change, (ii) to direct their studies to more practical areas, and (iii) to expand their interest to include normative or value judgment areas rather than just predicting the outcomes of certain policy options because economists are better trained than most laymen to decide which policy should be followed.

It would be worthwhile to draw the reader's attention to a few developments in econometrics and in microeconomics that have taken place, which might lessen some of the shortcomings of economics alluded to above. For example, many new estimation techniques, which are alternatives to least squares, have been developed in the seventies under the heading of "robust regression." These developments should provide solutions to the problems of outliers and thick tails (non-normality) found most commonly in the empirical distributions of economic variables. A review of these developments can be found in Huber (1981) and references therein. Furthermore, the theoretical development of the "(new)^2 welfare economics," to use Reiter's (1977) terminology, suggests that economists are increasingly showing concern for the practical features of a system of economic organization such as cost of operation and administrative feasibility within entire classes of organizations. Louis L. Wilde (1981) has forcefully argued that the use of laboratory experiments in economics, which has increased markedly in recent years (as evidenced in published articles in the economics journals) has a potential for providing a rather inexpensive "implementation and testing of theoretical developments in the "(new)^2 welfare economics." The reader who is interested in a complete description of the methodology and functions of laboratory experiments in economics should consult Vernon L. Smith (1982).

Walter Heller, taking a more positive stance than either Leontief or Worswick, recognizes that various criticisms have been leveled against economics. After providing an overview or catalogue of these criticisms by academic and other economists, he tries to show that the quality of inputs into the economics "industry" has improved and the demand for the services of economists has increased. Heller then does two case studies, one for public finance, and the other for economics of inflation; he shows the progress which economists have made in these two areas of economics. Heller's article attempts to offset or balance the essentially negative tone of the previous articles.

In a similar manner, Donald MacDougall, then President of the Royal Economics Society, argues that it is misplaced to emphasize only what is wrong with economics. We strongly recommend this article to the readers as a complement to Heller's essay. He recognizes that there are problems which should be addressed, but argues that economics has advanced since World War II. He takes issues raised in four areas, notes the criticisms, and shows that some of these are overstated or that they must be put against or balanced by progress. The four areas are: (1) the basic assumptions of economics, (2) the balance of economic research, (3) the predictive power of economics, and (4) unsolved economic problems. In this evaluation, MacDougall deals with the familiar issues of econometrics, mathematics, realism, and faulty data, but tries to be fair to both sides of each debate.

Besides the views of these four economists, a large number of others have mused on what is right or wrong with economics. The interested reader should consult some of those noted in the suggested readings to this part: Hahn, Phelps Brown, Blackman, Maisel, Bergmann, Sweezy, and Galbraith for the negative, and Johnson, Schultze, Solow, and Tobin for the positive.

The reader would also benefit by reading Chapter 12 in Boland's (1982) textbook referenced in the introduction to this volume wherein he makes a case for a problem-dependent methodology. He points out that there are many methodologies instead of an all-purpose methodology and the choice among them is based best on one's objective. He has argued that Instrumentalism (of Friedman and his followers) is the most appropriate methodology if one's objective is to solve present short-run practical problems. Similarly, Conventionalism (of Koopmans and Samuelson among others) with emphasis on generality, is more appropriate if one's objective is longer-run problem solving and cataloguing. Finally, Popper's methodology, which emphasizes disagreements, criticism and reformulation of the problem, is more suitable when one's objective is learning for learning's sake.

16 Theoretical Assumptions and Nonobserved Facts

Wassily Leontief*

Economics today rides the crest of intellectual respectability and popular acclaim. The serious attention with which our pronouncements are received by the general public, hard-bitten politicians, and even skeptical businessmen is second only to that which was given to physicists and space experts a few years ago when the round trip to the moon seemed to be our only truly national goal. The flow of learned articles, monographs, and textbooks is swelling like a tidal wave; *Econometrica*, the leading journal in the field of mathematical economics, has just stepped up its publication schedule from four to six issues per annum.

And yet an uneasy feeling about the present state of our discipline has been growing in some of us who have watched its unprecedented development over the last three decades. This concern seems to be shared even by those who are themselves contributing successfully to the present boom. They play the game with professional skill but have serious doubts about its rules.

Much of current academic teaching and research has been criticized for its lack of relevance, that is, of immediate practical impact. In a nearly instant response to this criticism, research projects, seminars and undergraduate courses have been set up on poverty, on city and small town slums, on pure water and fresh air. In an almost Pavlovian reflex, whenever a new complaint is raised, President Nixon appoints a commission and the university announces a new course. Far be it from me to argue that the fire should not be shifted when the target moves. The trouble is caused, however, not by an inadequate selection of targets, but rather by our inability to hit squarely any one of them. The uneasiness of which I spoke before is caused not by the *irrelevance* of the practical problems to which present day economists address their efforts, but rather by the palpable *inadequacy* of the scientific means with which they try to solve them.

If this simply were a sign of the overly high aspiration level of a fast developing discipline, such a discrepancy between ends

Reprinted by permission from the American Economic Association. The article appeared in the *American Economic Review*, 61 (1971), 1-7.

and means should cause no worry. But I submit that the consistently indifferent performance in practical applications is in fact a symptom of a fundamental imbalance in the present state of our discipline. The weak and all too slowly growing empirical foundation clearly cannot support the proliferating superstructure of pure, or should I say, speculative economic theory.

Much is being made of the widespread, nearly mandatory use by modern economic theorists of mathematics. To the extent to which the economic phenomena possess observable quantitative dimensions, this is indisputably a major forward step. Unfortunately, any one capable of learning elementary, or preferably advanced calculus and algebra, and acquiring acquaintance with the specialized terminology of economics can set himself up as a theorist. Uncritical enthusiasm for mathematical formulation tends often to conceal the ephemeral substantive content of the argument behind the formidable front of algebraic signs.

Professional journals have opened wide their pages to papers written in mathematical language; colleges train aspiring young economists to use this language; graduate schools require its knowledge and reward its use. The mathematical model-building industry has grown into one of the most prestigious, possibly the most prestigious branch of economics. Construction of a typical theoretical model can be handled now as a routine assembly job. All principal components such as production functions, consumption and utility functions come in several standard types; so does the optional equipment as, for example, "factor augmentation"-- to take care of technological change. This particular device is, incidentally, available in a simple exponential design or with a special automatic regulator known as the "Kennedy function." Any model can be modernized with the help of special attachments. One popular way to upgrade a simple one-sector model is to bring it out in a two-sector version or even in a still more impressive form of the "n-sector," that is, many-sector class.

In the presentation of a new model, attention nowadays is usually centered on a step-by-step derivation of its formal properties. But if the author--or at least the referee who recommended the manuscript for publication--is technically competent, such mathematical manipulations, however long and intricate, can even without further checking be accepted as correct. Nevertheless, they are usually spelled out at great length. By the time it comes to interpretation of the substantive *conclusions*, the assumptions on which the model has been based are easily forgotten. But it is precisely the empirical validity of these *assumptions* on which the usefulness of the entire exercise depends.

What is really needed, in most cases, is a very difficult and seldom very neat assessment and verification of these assumptions in terms of observed facts. Here mathematics cannot help and because of this, the interest and enthusiasm of the model builder suddenly begins to flag: "If you do not like my set of assumptions, give me another and I will gladly make you another model; have your pick."

Policy oriented models, in contrast to purely descriptive ones, are gaining favor, however nonoperational they may be. This, I submit, is in part because the choice of the final policy objectives--the selection and justification of the shape of the so-called objective function--is, and rightly so, considered based on normative judgment, not on factual analysis. Thus, the model builder can secure at least some convenient assumptions without running the risk of being asked to justify them on empirical grounds.

To sum up with the words of a recent president of the Econometric Society, "... the achievements of economic theory in the last two decades are both impressive and in many ways beautiful. But it cannot be denied that there is something scandalous in the spectacle of so many people refining the analysis of economic states which they give no reason to suppose will ever, or have ever, come about.... It is an unsatisfactory and slightly dishonest state of affairs."

But shouldn't this harsh judgment be suspended in the face of the impressive volume of econometric work? The answer is decidedly no. This work can be in general characterized as an attempt to compensate for the glaring weakness of the data base available to us by the widest possible use of more and more sophisticated statistical techniques. Alongside the mounting pile of elaborate theoretical models we see a fast-growing stock of equally intricate statistical tools. These are intended to stretch to the limit the meager supply of facts.

Since, as I said before, the publishers' referees do a competent job, most model-testing kits described in professional journals are internally consistent. However, like the economic models they are supposed to implement, the validity of these statistical tools depends itself on the acceptance of certain convenient assumptions pertaining to stochastic properties of the phenomena which the particular models are intended to explain; assumptions that can be seldom verified.

In no other field of empirical inquiry has so massive and sophisticated a statistical machinery been used with such indifferent results. Nevertheless, theorists continue to turn out model after model and mathematical statisticians to devise complicated procedures one after another. Most of these are relegated to the stockpile without any practical application or after only a perfunctory demonstration exercise. Even those used for a while soon fall out of favor, not because the methods that supersede them perform better, but because they are new and different.

Continued preoccupation with imaginary, hypothetical, rather than with observable reality has gradually led to a distortion of the informal valuation scale used in our academic community to assess and to rank the scientific performance of its members. Empirical analysis, according to this scale, gets a lower rating than formal mathematical reasoning. Devising a new statistical procedure, however tenuous, that makes it possible to squeeze out one more unknown parameter from a given set of data, is judged a greater scientific achievement than the successful search for additional information that would permit us to measure the magnitude of the same parameter in a less ingenious, but more reliable way. This despite the fact that in all too many instances sophisticated statistical analysis is performed on a set of data whose exact meaning and validity are unknown to the author or rather so well known to him that at the very end he warns the reader not to take the material conclusions of the entire "exercise" seriously.

A natural Darwinian feedback operating through selection of academic personnel contributes greatly to the perpetuation of this state of affairs. The scoring system that governs the distribution of rewards must naturally affect the make-up of the competing teams. Thus, it is not surprising that the younger economists, particularly those engaged in teaching and in academic research, seem by now quite content with a situation in which they can demonstrate their prowess (and incidentally, advance their careers) by building more and more complicated mathematical models and devising more and more sophisticated methods of statistical inference without ever engaging in empirical research. Complaints about the lack of indispensable primary data are heard from time to time, but they don't sound very urgent. The feeling of dissatisfaction with the present state of our discipline which prompts me to speak out so bluntly seems, alas, to be shared by relatively few. Yet even those few who do share it feel they can do little to improve the situation. How could they?

In contrast to most physical sciences, we study a system that is not only exceedingly complex but is also in a state of constant flux. I have in mind not the obvious change in the variables, such as outputs, prices or levels of employment, that our equations are supposed to explain, but the basic structural relationships described by the form and the parameters of these equations. In order to know what the shape of these structural relationships actually are at any given time, we have to keep them under continuous surveillance.

By sinking the foundations of our analytical system deeper and deeper, by reducing, for example, cost functions to production functions and the production functions to some still more basic relationships eventually capable of explaining the technological change itself, we should be able to reduce this drift. It would, nevertheless, be quite unrealistic to expect to reach, in this way, the bedrock of invariant structural relationships (measurable parameters) which, once having been observed and described, could be used year after year, decade after decade, without revisions based on repeated observation.

On the relatively shallow level where the empirically implemented economic analysis now operates even the more invariant of the structural relationships, in terms of which the system is described, change rapidly. Without a constant inflow of new data the existing stock of factual information becomes obsolete very soon. What a contrast with physics, biology or even psychology where the magnitude of most parameters is practically constant and where critical experiments and measurements don't have to be repeated every year!

Just to keep up our very modest current capabilities we have to maintain a steady flow of new data. A progressive expansion of these capabilities would be out of the question without a continuous and rapid rise of this flow. Moreover, the new, additional data in many instances will have to be qualitatively different from those provided hitherto.

To deepen the foundation of our analytical system it will be necessary to reach unhesitatingly beyond the limits of the domain of economic phenomena as it has been staked out up to now. The pursuit of a more fundamental understanding of the process of production inevitably leads into the area of engineering sciences. To penetrate below the skin-thin surface of conventional consumption functions, it will be necessary to develop a systematic study of the structural characteristics and of the functioning of households, an area in which description and analysis of social, anthropological and demographic factors must obviously occupy the center of the stage.

Establishment of systematic cooperative relationships across the traditional frontiers now separating economics from these adjoining fields is hampered by the sense of self-sufficiency resulting from what I have already characterized as undue reliance on indirect statistical inference as the principal method of empirical research. As theorists, we construct systems in which prices, outputs, rates of saving and investment, etc., are explained in terms of production functions, consumption functions and other structural relationships whose parameters are assumed, at least for arguments' sake, to be known. As econometricians, engaged in what passes for empirical research, we do not try, however, to ascertain the actual shapes of these functions and to measure the magnitudes of these parameters by turning up new factual information. We make an about face and rely on indirect statistical inference to derive the unknown structural relationships from the observed magnitudes of prices, outputs and other variables that, in our role as theoreticians, we treated as unknowns.

Formally, nothing is, of course, wrong with such an apparently circular procedure. Moreover, the model builder in erecting his hypothetical structures is free to take into account all possible kinds of factual knowledge and the econometrician in principle, at least, can introduce in the estimating procedure any amount of what is usually referred to as "exogenous" information before he feeds his programmed tape into the computer. Such options are exercised rarely and when they are, usually in a casual way.

The same well-known sets of figures are used again and again in all possible combinations to pit different theoretical models against each other in formal statistical combat. For obvious reasons a decision is reached in most cases not by a knock-out, but by a few points. The orderly and systematic nature of the entire procedure generates a feeling of comfortable self-sufficiency.

This complacent feeling, as I said before, discourages venturesome attempts to widen and to deepen the empirical foundations of economic analysis, particularly those attempts that would involve crossing the conventional lines separating ours from the adjoining fields.

True advance can be achieved only through an iterative process in which improved theoretical formulation raises new empirical questions and the answers to these questions, in their turn, lead to new theoretical insights. The "givens" of today become the "unknowns" that will have to be explained tomorrow. This, incidentally, makes untenable the admittedly convenient methodological position according to which a theorist does not need to verify directly the factual assumptions on which he chooses to base his deductive arguments, provided his empirical conclusions seem to be correct. The prevalence of such a point of view is, to a large extent, responsible for the state of splendid isolation in which our discipline nowadays finds itself.

An exceptional example of a healthy balance between theoretical and empirical analysis and of the readiness of professional economists to cooperate with experts in the neighboring disciplines is offered by Agricultural Economics as it developed in this

326

country over the last fifty years. A unique combination of social and political forces has secured for this area unusually strong organizational and generous financial support. Official agricultural statistics are more complete, reliable, and systematic than those pertaining to any other major sector of our economy. Close collaboration with agronomists provides agricultural economists with direct access to information of a technological kind. When they speak of crop rotation, fertilizers, or alternative harvesting techniques, they usually know, sometimes from personal experience, what they are talking about. Preoccupation with the standard of living of the rural population has led agricultural economists into collaboration with home economists and sociologists, that is, with social scientists of the "softer" kind. While centering their interest on only one part of the economic system, agricultural economists demonstrated the effectiveness of a systematic combination of theoretical approach with detailed factual analysis. They also were the first among economists to make use of the advanced methods of mathematical statistics. However, in their hands, statistical inference became a complement to, not a substitute for, empirical research.

The shift from casual empiricism that dominates much of today's econometric work to systematic large-scale factual analysis will not be easy. To start with, it will require a sharp increase in the annual appropriation for Federal Statistical Agencies. The quality of government statistics has, of course, been steadily improving. The coverage, however, does not keep up with the growing complexity of our social and economic system and our capability of handling larger and larger data flows.

The spectacular advances in computer technology increased the economists' potential ability to make effective analytical use of large sets of detailed data. The time is past when the best that could be done with large sets of variables was to reduce their number by averaging them out or what is essentially the same, combining them into broad aggregates; now we can manipulate complicated analytical systems without suppressing the identity of their individual elements. There is a certain irony in the fact that, next to the fast-growing service industries, the areas whose coverage by the Census is particularly deficient are the operations of government agencies, both federal and local.

To place all or even the major responsibility for the collection of economic data in the hands of one central organization would be a mistake. The prevailing decentralized approach that permits and encourages a great number of government agencies, non-profit institutions and private businesses engaged in data gathering activities acquitted itself very well. Better information means more detailed specialized information can be best collected by those immediately concerned with a particular field. What is, however, urgently needed is the establishment, maintenance and enforcement of coordinated uniform classification systems by all agencies, private as well as public, involved in this work. Incompatible data are useless data. How far from a tolerable, not to say, ideal state our present economic statistics are in this respect, can be judged by the fact that because of differences in classification, domestic output data cannot be compared, for many goods, with the corresponding export and import figures. Neither can the official employment statistics be related without laborious adjustments to output data, industry by industry. An unreasonably high proportion of material and intellectual resources devoted to statistical work is now spent not on the collection of primary information but on a frustrating and wasteful struggle with incongruous definitions and irreconcilable classifications.

Without invoking a misplaced methodological analogy, the task of securing a massive flow of primary economic data can be compared to that of providing the high energy physicists with a gigantic accelerator. The scientists have their machines while the economists are still waiting for their data. In our case not only must the society be willing to provide year after year the millions of dollars required for maintenance of a vast statistical machine, but a large number of citizens must be prepared to play, at least, a passive and occasionally even an active part in actual fact-finding operations. It is as if the electrons and protons had to be persuaded to cooperate with the physicist.

The average American does not seem to object to being interviewed, polled, and surveyed. Curiosity, the desire to find out how the economic system (in which most of us are small gears, and some, big wheels) works might in many instances provide sufficient inducement for cooperation of this kind.

One runs up, of course, occasionally against the attitude that "what you don't know can't hurt you" and that knowledge might be dangerous: it may generate a desire to tinker with the system. The experience of these years seems, however, to have convinced not only most economists--with a few notable exceptions--but also the public at large that a lack of economic know ledge can hurt badly. Our free enterprise system has rightly been compared to a gigantic computing machine capable of solving its own problems automatically. But any one who has had some practical experience with large computers knows that they do break down and can't operate unattended. To keep the automatic, or rather the semi-automatic, engine of our economy in good working order we must not only understand the general principles on which it operates, but also be acquainted with the details of its actual design.

A new element has entered the picture in recent years--the

adoption of methods of modern economic analysis by private business. Corporate support of economic research goes as far back as the early 1920s when Wesley Mitchell founded the National Bureau. However, it is not this concern for broad issues of public policies or even the general interest in economic growth and business fluctuations that I have in mind, but rather the fast-spreading use of advanced methods of Operations Research and of so-called Systems' Analysis. Some of the standard concepts and analytical devices of economic theory first found their way into the curricula of our business schools and soon after that, sophisticated management began to put them into practice. While academic theorists are content with the formulation of general principles, corporate operations researchers and practical systems' analysts have to answer questions pertaining to specific real situations. Demand for economic data to be used in practical business planning is growing at an accelerated pace. It is a high quality demand: business users in most instances possess first-hand technical knowledge of the area to which the data they ask for refer. Moreover, this demand is usually "effective." Profit-making business is willing and able to pay the costs of gathering the information it wants to have. This raises the thorny question of public access to privately collected data and of the proper division of labor and cooperation between government and business in that fast-expanding field. Under the inexorable pressure of rising practical demand, these problems will be solved in one way or another. Our economy will be surveyed and mapped in all its many dimensions on a larger and larger scale.

Economists should be prepared to take a leading role in shaping this major social enterprise not as someone else's spokesmen and advisers, but on their own behalf. They have failed to do this up to now. The Conference of Federal Statistics Users organized several years ago had business, labor, and many other groups represented among its members, but not economists as such. How can we expect our needs to be satisfied if our voices are not heard?

We, I mean the academic economists, are ready to expound, to any one ready to lend an ear, our views on problems of public policy: give advice on the best ways to maintain full employment, to fight inflation, to foster economic growth. We should be equally prepared to share with the wider public the hopes and disappointments which accompany the advance of our own often desperately difficult, but always exciting intellectual enterprise. This public has amply demonstrated its readiness to back the pursuit of knowledge. It will lend its generous support to our venture too, if we take the trouble to explain what it is all about.

Footnote

*   Presidential address delivered at the eighty-third meeting of the American Economic Association, Detroit, Michigan, December 29, 1970.

Reference

F.H. Hahn, "Some Adjustment Problems," *Econometrica,* January 1970, 38, 1-2.

17 Academic Economics

Wassily Leontief

"A dismal performance... What economists revealed most clearly was the extent to which their profession lags intellectually" (1). This editorial comment by the leading economic weekly (on the 1981 annual proceedings of the American Economic Association) says, essentially, that the "king is naked." But no one taking part in the elaborate and solemn procession of contemporary U.S. academic economics seems to know it, and those who do don't dare speak up.

Two hundred years ago the founders of modern economic science--Adam Smith, Ricardo, Malthus, and John Stuart Mill-- erected an imposing conceptual edifice based on the notion of the national economy as a self-regulating system of a great many different but interrelated, and therefore, interdependent, activities; a concept so powerful and fruitful that it gave impetus to Charles Darwin's pathbreaking work on his theory of evolution.

The central idea of what is now being referred to as Classical Economics attracted the attention of two mathematically trained engineers. Leon Walras and Vilfredo Pareto, who translated it with considerable refinement and elaboration into a concise language of algebra and calculus and called it the General Equilibrium Theory. Under the name of neo-classical economics this theory now constitutes the core of undergraduate and graduate instruction in this country.

As an empirical science, economics dealt from the outset with phenomena of common experience. Producing and consuming goods, buying and selling, and receiving income and spending it are activities engaging everyone's attention practically all the time. Even the application of the scientific principle of quantification did not have to be initiated by the analyst himself--measuring and pricing constitute an integral part of .the phenomena that he sets out to explain. Herein lies, however, the initial source of the trouble in which academic economics find itself today.

By the time the facts of everyday experience were used up,

Reprinted by permission of the American Association for the Advancement of Science. The letter originally appeared in *Science*, 217 (1982), 104-07.

331

economists were able to turn for bits and pieces of less accessible, more specialized information to government statistics.
However, these statistics--compiled for administrative or business, but not scientific purposes--fall short of what would have
been required for concrete, more detailed understanding of the
structure and the functioning of a modern economic system.

Not having been subjected from the outset to the harsh discipline of systematic fact-finding, traditionally imposed on and
accepted by their colleagues in the natural and historical sciences, economists developed a nearly irresistible predilection for
deductive reasoning. As a matter of fact, many entered the field
after specializing in pure or applied mathematics. Page after page
of professional economic journals are filled with mathematical
formulas leading the reader from sets of more or less plausible
but entirely arbitrary assumptions to precisely stated but irrelevant theoretical conclusions.

Nothing reveals the aversion of the great majority of the
present-day academic economists for systematic empirical inquiry
more than the methodological devices that they employ to avoid or
cut short the use of concrete factual information. Instead of
constructing theoretical models capable of preserving the identity
of hundreds, even thousands, of variables needed for the concrete description and analysis of a modern economy, they first of
all resort to "aggregation." The primary information, however
detailed, is packaged in a relatively small number of bundles
labeled "Capital," "Labor," "Raw Materials," "Intermediate
Goods," "General Price Level," and so on. These bundles are
then usually fitted into a "model," that is, a small system of
equations describing the entire economy in terms of a small
number of corresponding "aggregative" variables. The fitting, as
a rule, is accomplished by means of "least squares" or another
similar curve-fitting procedure.

A typical example of a theoretical "production function" intended to describe the relationship between, say, the amount of
steel produced, y_1, and the quantities of the four different
inputs, y_2, y_3, y_4, and y_5 needed to produce it is, for instance,
described as follows (2):

$$y_1^{\rho_1} = a_1 |G^2|^{\rho_1} + (1 - a_1) |G^3|^{\rho_1}$$

where

$$-G^2 = [a_2 |y_2|^{\rho_2} + (1 - a_2) |y_3|^{\rho_2}]^{1/\rho_2}$$

$$-G^3 = [a_3 |y_4|^{\rho_3} + (1 - a_3) |y_5|^{\rho_3}]^{1/\rho_3}$$

or alternatively,

$$\ln |G^2| = \tfrac{1}{2} \ln |y_2| + \tfrac{1}{2} \ln |y_3|$$

$$\ln |G^3| = \tfrac{1}{2} \ln |y_4| + \tfrac{1}{2} \ln |y_5|$$

or, finally:

$$\ln y_1 = a_1 \ln |G^2| + (1 - a_1) \ln |G^3|$$

To ask a manager of a steel plant or a metallurgical expert for information on the magnitude of the six parameters appearing in these six equations would make no sense. Hence, while the labels attached to symbolic variables and parameters of the theoretical equations tend to suggest that they could be identified with those directly observable in the real world, any attempt to do so is bound to fail: the problem of "identification" of aggregative equations after they have been reduced--that is, transformed, as they often are--for purposes of the curve-fitting process, was raised many years ago but still has not found a satisfactory solution. In the meantime, the procedure described above was standardized to such an extent that, to carry out a respectable econometric study, one simply had to construct a plausible and easily computable theoretical model and then secure--mostly from secondary or tertiary sources--a set of time series or cross section data related in some direct or indirect way to its particular subject, insert these figures with a program of an appropriate statistical routine taken from the shelf into the computer, and finally publish the computer printouts with a more or less plausible interpretation of the numbers.

While the quality and coverage of official statistics have recently been permitted to deteriorate without eliciting determined protest on the part of their potential scientific users, masses of concrete, detailed information contained in technical journals, reports of engineering firms, and private marketing organizations are neglected.

A perusal of the contents of the *American Economic Review*, the flagship of academic economic periodicals over the last 10 years, yields the picture in Table 1.

These figures speak for themselves. In a prophetic statement of editorial policy, the managing editor of the *American Economic Review* observed (3) 10 years ago that "articles on mathematical economics and the finer points of economic theory

Table 1. Percentages of different types of articles published in the *American Economic Review*.

Type of article	March 1972 to December 1976	March 1977 to December 1981
Mathematical models without any data	50.1	54.0
Analysis without mathematical formulation and data	21.2	11.6
Statistical methodology	0.6	0.5
Empirical analysis based on data generated by the author's initiative	0.8	1.4
Empirical analysis using indirect statistical inference based on data published or generated elsewhere	21.4	22.7
Empirical analysis not using indirect statistical inference based on data generated by author	0.0	0.5
Empirical analysis not using indirect statistical inference based on data generated or published elsewhere	5.4	7.4
Empirical analysis based on artificial simulations and experiments	0.5	1.9

occupy a more and more prominent place than ever before, while articles of a more empirical, policy-oriented or problem-solving character seem to appear less frequently."

Year after year economic theorists continue to produce scores of mathematical models and to explore in great detail their formal properties; and the econometricians fit algebraic functions of all possible shapes to essentially the same sets of data without being able to advance, in any perceptible way, a systematic understanding of the structure and the operations of a real economic system.

How long will researchers working in adjoining fields, such as demography, sociology, and political science on the one hand and ecology, biology, health sciences, engineering, and other applied physical sciences on the other, abstain from expressing serious concern about the state of stable, stationary equilibrium and the splendid isolation in which academic economics now finds itself? That state is likely to be maintained as long as tenured members of leading economics departments continue to exercise tight control over the training, promotion, and research activities of their younger faculty members and, by means of peer review, of the senior members as well. The methods used to maintain intellect-

334

ual discipline in this country's most influential economics departments (4) can occasionally remind one of those employed by the Marines to maintain discipline on Parris Island.

References

1. *Business Week*, 18 January 1982, p. 124.

2. L.R. Christensen, D.W. Jorgenson, L.J. Lau, "Transcendential logarithmic production functions," *Review of Economic Statistics*, 55, 28 (1972).

3. G.H. Borts, *American Economic Review*, 62, 764 (1972).

4. M.W. Reder, *Journal of Economic Literature*, 20, 1 (1982).

18 What's Right With Economics?

Walter W. Heller*

I come here with no eye-opening report from the frontiers of economics, no stirring cry for reform of conventional economics, no closely reasoned analysis of an economic dilemma or puzzle, no scathing or reproachful scolding of the profession for its technical preciousness or moral blindness, no report on painstaking research results, no valedictory on a lifetime of theoretical or empirical contributions. The AEA presidential addresses have been all of these things.

But tonight, going against our current fashion of telling the world what's wrong with economics, I offer a modest contribution to the immodest subject of what's right with economics--and, in particular, what's right with economics as a guide to public policy. In doing so, I won't ignore the dark side of the moon--indeed, I can't, since I will deal at some length with the bedeviling subject of inflation. But believing that it is at least as reasonable to judge a discipline by its successes as by its failures, I intend to accentuate the positive.

I. The Critical Look Inward

In recent years, as I shall illustrate in a moment, we have instead accentuated the negative. In good part, this has taken the becoming form of *mea culpa* or rather *nostra culpa*. We have, for example, readily confessed that the inflationary shocks of 1973-74 caught not just the economy but the economist by surprise. On this and other fronts, the chorus of self-criticism has risen to a new crescendo. It is almost as if we take pride in our humility. Nietzsche must have been thinking of economists when he observed that "he who despises himself nevertheless esteems himself as a self-despiser."

This is not to imply that economists' criticisms are all self-inflicted wounds. Far from it. Often among our colleagues' favorite targets are the shortcomings of mainstream economics, the misuse of modern techniques, the fallacies of conventional wisdom --in each case, the target is not the critic's but his colleagues' brand of economics, not *mea culpa* but *eorum culpa*.

Reprinted by permission from the American Economic Association. The article appeared in the *American Economic Review*, 65 (1975), 1-26.

In any event, he who comes to praise economics risks being buried in the barrage of indictments that economists have brought against themselves and their brethren. Let me give you a sampling of some that will be ringing in my ears as I follow the parlous path of economic virtue.

Ceremonial occasions--presidential, memorial, or inaugural addresses--in particular seem to evoke musings on the troubled or even dismal state of our science. For the AEA faithful, I need only recall John Kenneth Galbraith condemning neoclassical and neo-Keynesian economics for ignoring power and thus losing contact with the real world; Wassily Leontief attacking mathematical economics for building a showy superstructure on weak empirical foundations and unverifed assumptions, and thus losing contact with the real world; Kenneth Boulding assailing welfare economics for its reliance on that holiest of holies, Pareto optimality--when in fact "our lives are dominated by precisely this inter-dependence of utility functions which the Paretian optimum denies"-- thus also losing contact with the real world.

In one form or another, variations on Leontief's lament have been heard in many another presidential address, to wit:

By F.H. Hahn (Econometric Society, 1968), who decried "the spectacle of so many people refining the analysis of economic states which they give no reason to suppose will ever, or have ever, come about..."

By G.D.N. Worswick (Section F of the British Association, 1971), who viewed the performance of economics as "curiously disappointing," suggesting that it has "a marvelous array of pretend tools which would perform wonders if ever a set of facts should turn up in the right form."

By E.H. Phelps Brown (Royal Economics Society, 1971), who judged the usefulness of current work in economics as "not equal to its distinction" because it is "built upon assumptions about human behavior that are plucked from the air."

By James H. Blackman (Southern Economic Association, 1971), who noted that models with sufficiently intriguing mathematical properties can achieve lives of their own even if they lead the investigator further away from reality and yet, "the profession's incentive system tends perversely to reward this kind of endeavor and to deflect the attention of gifted economists from the exploration of concrete problems and the dirty work that entails."

By Sherman Maisel (American Finance Association, 1973), who concluded that most of the literature of monetary economics is "non-operational" since its prescriptions are too often based on limited or false assumptions, it by-passes critical operational problems, and it ascribes too great validity to its statistical tests.

By Barbara Bergmann (Eastern Economic Association, 1974), who prefaced her plea for more microsimulation to incorporate "realistically messy information" in our economic data base with a few roundhouse swings at the economics profession and the pointed observation that instead of studying the real nature of decision making, we typically rush to make assumptions "whose purpose in life is to let the theorem emerge, all neat and provable."

Another favorite line of criticism and attack focusses on the implicit value premises of conventional economics. Gunnar Myrdal and Robert Heilbroner chide us for concealing the value judgments that inevitably enter into our selection of problems for study, choice of approach, definition of concepts, and even gathering of data. So a "value-free" economics is an illusion-- they urge economists to specify their values and thus avoid biases and make research more realistic.

Radical economists simply reject the whole value system of conventional economics--as they see it,. the neoclassical paradigm in its very bone and marrow enthrones acquisitiveness and enshrines the existing order. Paul Sweezy accuses mainstream economists "of hiding the facts, of making the uncontrollable appear under control, of rationalizing a system which condemns hundreds of millions of people to lives of despair and starvation...."

Inflation is the latest source of critical volleys, and I will get to these in due course. Meanwhile, the sampler of economic masochism I have already provided should serve as ample insurance against complacency or smugness in considering "what's right with economics." At the same time, it strongly suggests that economics, more than any other social science, is afflicted with the common scold.

I recognize that such a quick sampling and cryptic quotes, selected to highlight criticism, do a certain injustice to economics and to some of the quoted economists whose kindlier observations have been neglected in the process. But I am also aware that my litany omitted a number of familiar flaws, for example, our impounding of tastes and preferences in ceteris paribus; the shortcomings of the maximization principle in explaining consumer and producer behavior, especially in the short run; and our limited ability to bring the claims of future generations into our social utility functions.

Were I to serve as defense counsel for the profession on this wide variety of indictments, I would urge that we plead guilty or take the Fifth on some, take to the defense on others, and take offense at the rest. Having paid my respects to the critics, I intend no point-by-point evaluation or rebuttal. This has been ably undertaken by others.[1] Rather, my object is to gain a more balanced perspective by focussing on the quality, role, and contributions of economics, especially to public policy. In that undertaking, the first step is to examine the flank we expose to the public.

II. The Economist and the Public

When we turn from inside to outside critics, the focus changes. We may think, rightly, that freely confessing our weaknesses and airing our differences stimulate responses and adaptations that strengthen economics. Yet, wearing our purple hearts on our sleeves has its price. It nourishes the darkest suspicions about our art and supplies live ammunition to outside critics who have declared open season on economists. Witness the open sesame to the oped pages for such recent thrusts as Bergmann's assault on economists in general and Friedrich von Hayek's attack on Keynesians in particular. With everything from off-the-cuff phrases about being "caught with our parameters down" to tracts for the *Times*, we feed the hand that bites us.

This is not a plea to do our self-flagellating in secret or to mute our disputes and conflicts. Open controversies, openly arrived at, are part of the therapy that keeps our profession healthy. Rather, my plea is to the media and the opinion makers to understand that appearances are deceiving, that hard give-and-take is indeed a symbol of strength, and that our areas of agreement and consensus are vastly larger than our areas of difference.

On the first point, observers from the other disciplines are often astonished at how hard economists go at each other, how readily they run the gauntlet of their colleagues' criticisms with no quarter asked and none given--and, with few exceptions, all this within the framework of professional respect and friendship. As Charles Frankel put it, unlike other social sciences, economics seems to have achieved "a working etiquette which allows people to disagree vigorously without engaging in recrimination about 'unscientific' or 'unprofessional' behavior" (quoted in Johnson (1973)).

What accounts for this? Part of it, one can unblushingly say, is simply that so many competent, tough, and rigorously trained minds have been drawn into economics in response not just to challenging policy problems but to the quantitative revolution since World War II. And part of it is that the participants can draw on a hard core of economic theory and methodology, together with a growing body of empirical knowledge, to provide standards for testing the validity (though not necessarily the relevance and reality) of ideas, analysis, and empirical findings. The result is not only a relentless intellectual policing of the profession that soon exposes the fool, the quack, and the charlatan, but a growing capacity "to participate in adversary debate over public policy issues without jeopardizing scientific integrity and freedom" (Johnson (1973)).

That brings me to the second point, the impression we give outsiders of a house divided, not to say splintered. It is worth reminding ourselves and our critics of several factors that drive a wedge between image and reality.

One, instead of laying aside our differences and living contentedly together, we economists tend to lay aside our agreements and live contentiously together. We focus our private and public debates on unsolved policy problems, tough analytical nuts, and issues on which we have rival theories, contradictory evidence, or strong ideological differences. Just as these are the questions that intrigue us, they are the ones that attract the attention of press and public. What we know--and they may not-- is that beneath the visible tip of disagreement and rivalry lies no huge iceberg of divisiveness.

Two, it is only occasionally that our areas of consensus are brought to the surface in a newsworthy way. One such occasion was the White House "summit conference" on inflation last September. Two dozen leading economists from across a wide spectrum of American economics (not wide enough, the radicals would say) signed a statement which called on the President and Congress to eliminate twenty-two restrictive laws and practices that inhibit competition, inflate costs, and prop up prices. Only a tiny minority held out (if any minority that includes Galbraith can be called "tiny"). Even more striking, in a sense, was that while the customary and largely ideological clashes among, say, Galbraith, Milton Friedman, and Paul Samuelson caught the public eye, the real story lay in the minimal dissent among the participants on (a) the forecast of a soggy or sagging economy, (b) the urgency of providing relief to the victims of inflation and the casualties of recession, (c) the need to ease monetary restraint, (d) the small anti-inflationary payoff on moderate ($5 to $10 billion) budget cuts, and (e) the advisability of resisting popular demands for reimposing full-scale wage and price controls.

Three, even where disagreement flourishes--most visibly, perhaps, between Keynesians and monetarists--the public may not discern that the analytical and empirical ties that bind us are far stronger than the forces that divide us. Our controversies take place within the context of basic consensus on the nature and methods of economic theory and inquiry, on the content of the disagreement, and on the kinds of tests that may one day resolve the conflict. "Such disagreement within agreement lies at the heart of the process of normal development of a science" (Benjamin Ward, p.12).

Four, much of what the public perceives as a clash of economic concepts and findings is in fact a clash of ideology and values. Given the way technical economics and ethical preferences are packaged in policy debates (and given our lapses in identifying which is which), this is hardly surprising. Thus, whoever opens the package labeled "monetarist" typically finds not just money supply in full flower, but a dedication to minimum government intervention, small budgets, reliance on rules rather than authority, and price stability. Contrasting correlations appear in the Keynesian package. So outsiders can be excused for slipping into the fallacy of association and attributing the split to our unresolved analytical conflicts rather than to divergent evaluations of social priorities and competing philosophies of government. These associational chains are not linked together by an inexorable logic--in part, they seem to be an accident of birth as in the case of the Chicago twins of monetarism and *laissez-faire* rules. A belief in the supremacy of monetary over fiscal tools could quite logically go hand-in-hand with avid interventionism. But this escapes the jaundiced eye of the outside observer, who takes the ideological lineup as further evidence that economics is riven to its core.

Five, there is an ironic but substantial inverse correlation between the degree of consensus among economists and the degree of public acceptance of their findings. Thus, in the macroeconomic sphere of stabilization policy, where debate and disputes among economists flourish, their imprint on public policy is undeniable. But in the considerably more peaceful realm of microeconomics and allocative efficiency--where a reliable analytical apparatus coupled with solid quantitative work, especially on costs and benefits, has led the great majority of disinterested economists to an agreed diagnosis and prescription--the policy box score shows few hits, fewer runs, and lots of runners left on base. Economists widely, in some cases almost uniformly, favor tougher antitrust policy, freer trade, deregulation of transportation, pollution taxes in place of most prohibitions, and tax reform to remove income tax shelters. They oppose fair trade laws, restrictive labor and management practices, distortive zoning laws and building codes, import quotas, ceilings on interest rates, maritime subsidies, and pure (or impure) pork barrel projects.

Granted, the diffuse and inchoate consumer interest has been no match for the sharply focussed, articulate, and well-financed efforts of producer groups. But the economist is beginning to pick up some allies. Public interest groups are increasingly giving focus and force to the consumer and general public interest. And the march of events is providing some windfalls: Among the apples that have dropped in our laps are flexible exchange rates, the dethroning of agricultural price supports, inroads on import quotas, and moves to end percentage depletion. Under the pressure of virulent inflation, government actions that erode productivity and boost costs and prices are being subjected to new and searching scrutiny. So perhaps, on these micro-economic issues where economists sing in reasonably close harmony, the outside world will no longer quite tune us out. In macro-economic policy, where cacaphony prevails, we can be sure that the world will tune us in.

It may also be useful to draw attention--especially the attention of those who interpret us to the public--to certain other misperceptions and roadblocks that thwart good economics and tend to put economists in bad repute.

First, much of our economic analysis and the uncommon sense growing out of it fly in the face of "common sense," for example: that budget deficits need not spell inflation, nor national debt a burden on our grandchildren; that thriftiness can be a mixed virtue; that while exploding oil prices inflate costs, they *de*-flate demand; that in an overheated economy, greater taxes can be the lesser evil; and so on. Behind every false dictate of common sense lies a primitive and misbegotten economic theory--and for most of our pains to correct it, we can expect to get the back of everyman's hand.

Second, a related cross to bear can be characterized by Kermit Gordon's apt phrase, "virtue is so much easier when duty and self-interest coincide." Not only does that foredoom action on may microeconomic fronts, as already noted, but it puts roadblocks in the path of efforts to make fiscal policy a two-way street. For forty years, Congress has enacted major tax increases only under the whiplash of war. The resulting reliance on tight money to fight peacetime excess demand, coupled with expansionary fiscal policy to fight recession and slack, have had an unmistakeable ratchet effect that has tilted the system toward tighter money and easier budgets. (Small wonder, by the way, that many economists and policy makers are unwilling to give up, via indexing, the increases in effective income tax rates "legislated" by inflation.)

343

Third, the public sees economists as the bearers of hard and unpalatable truths. And often we are, by the very nature of our sometimes dismal discipline. Except when idle resources can be put to work or productivity increased, our message is the stern one of tradeoffs, benefits at a cost, and no one-dimensional daydreaming. Even worse, at times economics has to bring the bad tidings that for some problems there are no satisfactory solutions. For some thirty years, we have warned that full employment, price stability, and full freedom of economic choice cannot coexist in a world of strongly organized producer groups. More recently, economic analysis has brought home the unromantic truth that failure to cure some of our social ills traces less to a failure of will, or "rightwing villains," or a calloused "establishment," or powerlessness of the people, than it does to the prosaic facts that the problems are tough and complex and the goals we seek may be irreconcilable--in short, trace more to conflicts in our national objectives than to conflicts among social groups. Welfare reform is a case in point: no solution can simultaneously provide a decent minimum income for all, preserve work incentives, cut no one's benefits, and avoid huge budget costs (see Schultze (1972); Rivlin (1973)). We may view such work as a contribution to straight thinking and rational choice. Our critics are more likely to view it, at worst, as a counsel of defeat (which it is not) or at best a counsel of inescapable compromise (which it is).

Since the foregoing misperceptions and roadblocks thwart the translation of good economics into good policy, one could justify, in cold cost-benefit terms, a sizeable investment to overcome or reduce them. The most obvious implication is that the country needs to invest more in formal economic education at all levels. But an equally pressing need is for economists to invest more of their time and effort in making themselves understood to the public and policy maker--and that in turn requires recognition of this skill in the academic reward system. This might serve as a useful antidote to the influence of mathematics and econometrics which, while heightening the precision of professional thinking and internal communication, have apparently dulled the appetite and eroded the facility to communicate with the public in intelligible English prose.

In a very real sense, this confronts the press with an unusual opportunity and challenge, perhaps even a responsibility, to serve as a translator and interpreter of economics and its offerings. But believing (probably rightly) that their readers and listeners prefer to hear of fights and failures, crises and controversies, rather than of quiet contributions and consensus, the conventional or electronic press is not very likely to rise to this challenge. So it is still up to economists. But I must not carry this too far. Just as I am eschewing any Cassandra-like pronouncements tonight, so I have promised myself to suppress the oracular and even the avuncular (Dutch-type) mood evoked by these occasions. So I shall press on.

III. Standards of Judgment

From the foregoing, it is evident that I feel, first, that economists have gone beyond beguiling humility and welcome self-criticism to the point of almost neurotic self-rebuke, and second, that press and public have all too lustily taken up the cry--in part taking us at our word, in part misinterpreting us, and in part reflecting their belief that, after the high promise of the 1960s, we have failed them in not foreseeing and forestalling the crises of the 1970s: stagflation, energy shortage, and the environment.

In my quest for a more balanced perspective on the state of economics, the next task is to set up some standards for judging the quality and performance of economists. Since we have developed no measures of output or allocative efficiency, no capital-output or cost-benefit ratios, for the economics "industry," I will have to fall back on more subjective and less quantitative measures in judging its quality and contributions.

My mixed bag of criteria inclues (1) the quality of inputs; (2) the demands for our services; (3) as a proxy for a measure of outputs, the record of accomplishment in a given field (public finance); (4) finally, the cruelest test, our handling of the economics of inflation.

The *potential* of economics for informing and improving public policy depends on the stock of human capital, technology and tools at its command. Here, economics had no difficulty in holding its head high, especially in terms of the striking advances of the past three or four decades.

Harry Johnson may be a trifle extravagant in his assessment that the United States now has "perhaps fifty economic departments of an average quality comparable to the average quality of the four or five best departments in the whole world in the pre-World War II period ..." (1973), but only a trifle. Another attest to professional quality, already referred to, might be put this way: Show me another field that has enough inner strength to confess so much remaining weakness (and to carry on so much open controversy). Humility where we have things to be humble about (and we do) is a becoming trait. But coupling it with pride where we have things to be genuinely proud about is hardly a deadly sin.

Accompanying the growth in the quantity and quality of

345

economic brainpower have been striking advances in the techniques and tools with which economists work. For this audience, I can speak in shorthand about the strengthened analytical base of micro- and macroeconomics; the methodological revolution that moved us from the rationalist-historical approach into the age of quantification, with its insistence on systematic measurement of the shapes of economic functions and empirical testing of hypotheses and its use of econometrics and simulation techniques (with a powerful assist from the computer); and such conceptual advances as those in the economics of human capital, of cost-benefit relations, of uncertainty, of control, of transactions and information costs, of "second best," and of the allocation of time.

In normative economics and the analysis of value-laden social problems, new frontiers in the study of economic behavior are being opened up by survey research techniques (especially by the Michigan Survey Research Center), by efforts to measure nonmarket benefits or values (especially by the National Bureau of Economic Research) and by "controlled" social experimentation (for example, by the Brookings Institution and the University of Wisconsin Institute for Research on Poverty). These newer tools and the institutions that nurture them constitute part of the rich and expanding resources of economics.

Economics can also draw on a broad data base, especially in federal statistics. But here, the quantity, timeliness, and even the quality of the data are not keeping pace with either the problems requiring analysis or the capacity of our quantitative techniques. Responding to policy needs and mounting self-criticism, the profession has opened many new fronts in the search for realistic micro-data to link up with macro-data, for cross-section data to help overcome the curse of collinearity in time-series analysis, and for custom-built data developed by survey and experimental techniques.

That the human, analytical, and quantitative resources of economics provide a huge potential for solving problems seems undeniable. That more of these powerful resources than ever before are being put at the disposal of economic policy makers also seems undeniable. What we do not know is what proportion is being misdirected into arid puzzles, sterile proofs, and recreational mathematics while the world's pressing economic and social problems go begging for answers. Here, we can only match one observer's impression against another's. The profession itself has not come to grips with *this* question of allocative efficiency.

A second test in appraising the state of economics, one not unknown to economics, is that of the market place. This takes several forms, none very robust, but none trivial. The first is the upsurge in enrollments in economics courses, especially in

346

introductory economics, that has occurred in the academic years 1973-1974 and 1974-75. The second is the oft-reported high ranking of economists' salaries in business, government and academic life. A third is the strong and growing demand for economists' inputs into the policy-making process--either as staff members or as expert witnesses for congressional committees, individual congressmen, and the executive branch.

With students, business, and government beating a path to our door, we can infer that something must be right with economics, or wrong with the economy, or both. Either we are building a better mousetrap or there are more and bigger mice threatening our customers. Perhaps it is simply that we have the only mousetraps in town.

But there must be more to it than that. Take the policy maker, for example. What he finds congenial is that he can hand an economist a problem--relating to changes in taxation, regulations, budget proposals, pollution control, poverty, social security, public service jobs, gasoline taxes, oil prices, and so on-- and be reasonably sure of getting a useful appraisal of alternative paths to his objectives, of costs and benefits, and of distributional, allocative, and stabilization impacts. Many of these judgments will come with orders of magnitude or reasonably precise numbers attached. He may not trust our GNP forecasts, but he has come to respect our hardheaded analysis and numbers on the myriad problems of economic choice with which he is faced.

It seems fair to draw another inference: notwithstanding the current wave of self criticism and public criticism, even lampooning, of economists and despite our highly visible public debates and highly vulnerable participation in policy making, economics continues to maintain its standing as a science. Signs of a reported crisis of public confidence or of a "recession of self-confidence" are few and far between. Reports of the demise of our discipline are grossly exaggerated.

IV. The "Outputs" of Public Economics

Having considered some indicators of the quality of our inputs and of the revealed preferences for our outputs, let me continue this exercise in casual (and congenial) empiricism by taking an unscientific but not unrepresentative sample of the outputs of economics, especially those bearing on policy. For this purpose, I draw on my chosen field of public finance, or public economics, to illustrate the telling conceptual and empirical advances of economics in recent decades and the resulting enrichment of its offerings to the policy maker. Indeed, such an appraisal offers so many healthy antidotes to "what's wrong with economics" that I was tempted to devote my whole discourse to it tonight. But I resisted the temptation because, first, much of it has already been done in carefully documented depth in survey volumes by Brookings and the National Bureau;[2] second, I figured it might test your patience and mine; and third, it would have left no room for a confrontation with inflation. So I offer instead a miniaturized assessment of the achievements of public economics as viewed through the policy prism.

Public Expenditures

Consider first the striking contributions economics has made in the past generation to clear thinking and better informed decisions on public expenditures. Partly, this reflects advances in economic science, for example, in the theory of public goods and human capital, and partly, creative new applications of the economist's characteristic way of looking at problems of choice, namely, through the lens of opportunity costs, benefits, and alternative paths to a stated goal.

Economics can offer much more concrete guidance on efficient ways of allocating resources to achieve stated governmental objectives than it can on what the public-private sector division of resources should be. That may be a good thing in that presidents and congressmen view the fixing of goals for public health, housing, welfare, and the like as what *they* were elected for, yet at the same time seek, or at least accept, economic guidance on the choice among competing methods of achieving these goals.

Nonetheless, rapid progress in the theory of public goods since the appearance of the Samuelson classic on "The Pure Theory of Public Expenditures" just twenty years ago has vastly improved on the simplistic theory it replaced. It has facilitated straight thinking on the derivation of conditions for efficient public-sector allocations from private evaluations and on the articulation of social priorities through the political process.

Interwoven with the newer thinking about public goods has been a resurgent interest in externalities or spillover effects. In a sense, the pure collective good is a case of total externality—all of its benefits are external and nonmarketable since nobody can be excluded from them. That may clarify thinking but gives little policy guidance.

Yet, the externality concept translates into hard-headed policy advice in such disparate areas as pollution, federal aid, and the law. When pollution became a national concern, economists quickly drew on their tool kit to develop proposals for antipollution taxes (within the context of target air and water

348

quality standards). Tax penalties of so much per unit would put price tags on use of the public's air and water, thus internalizing external costs and using market incentives to accomplish depollution rather than relying on the less efficient route of regulation.

When local governments supply education and public health services to a mobile population, many of the benefits spill over to other units. An important rationale for federal grants flows from these externalities, namely, that to get local units to produce enough education and health service to achieve a national, not just a local, cost-benefit optimum requires conditional grants from the federal purse.

Further, since externalities in the form of damage to third parties lie at the heart of many problems in legal justice, economics is able to make an important contribution in this area.

When we turn to the empirical outputs that are now illuminating problems of public choice, we find the past decade bristling with new thinking, new techniques, and new measurements. These offer the decision maker important new guides in the selection and evaluation of government programs and new insights into alternative systems of delivering government services:

Measurement of cost-benefit ratios has developed from the early metrics of water projects into, first, a sophisticated cost-benefit calculus for tangible investments like dams, roads, pollution-control pro-jects and, second, cost-benefit estimates for intangible investments in human brainpower, skills, and health. Shadow pricing has been one of the useful tools in this connection. Cost-benefit analysis, even with its limits of quantification and its inability to shed light on distributional and value questions, is an important aid to informed decisions.

A related advance is the development of new and tougher standards for judging government programs. The former criteria centered on the question: Is the program put into effect quickly and with high fidelity to the congressional intent? Now, the accountability question is: Does it deliver the goods? Does it accomplish the objectives? Inputs used to be stressed--if they conformed with the intent of the legislation, they .tended to be judged a success. But now we try to measure outputs, a tougher and more elusive standard. (The parallel with judging the performance of economics and economists is painfully obvious). Antipoverty programs, which were among the first to be evaluated by these stringent standards, seem to have borne the brunt of the evaluation boom. By the old inputs standard, a program like Head Start would have fared much better.

The reach of cost-benefit analysis will be lengthened if a broad range of new research efforts in nonmarket sectors of economic activity pays off. I refer not only to the exciting work on measurement of the returns on investments in human capital (T.W. Schultz), but to efforts to measure the output of the medical industry, to measure the relations between crime and punishment, and to measure the value of nonmarket economic activity conducted within firms and households.

The new technique of controlled social experimentation on proposed welfare and housing measures, health insurance, and education vouchers is yielding important insights. As a result of experiments on negative income taxation, for example, the equity versus efficiency, or equality versus incentives, controversy will never be conducted in a vacuum again (Rivlin, 1973). In spite of some limitations, the New Jersey experiment yielded strong evidence that fears of fatal incentive effects of a negative income tax were grossly overblown.

Another focus of fruitful thinking relates to alternative strategies for delivering social services. The in-cash versus in-kind choice is a basic one. Economists are predisposed toward the in-cash approach on grounds that one can generally depend on people to follow their own best interests. But there are significant exceptions where consumer sovereignty is limited or specific goods externalities exist or some explicit social values take priority.

Out of economics also comes the attempt to develop "market analogs" to serve as substitutes for market incentives in reconciling public with private interests, decentralized individual decisions with social goals. Pollution taxes are a case in point. Performance standards for teacher pay would be another. Putting medical insurance programs on an efficiency-based reimbursement basis would be a third. The big gap is in the redesign of incentives and institutions to guide decentralized government decision making more systematically toward the aims of our social programs (Schultze, 1971). Thus far, the government, like the economics profession, is largely in the dark about its own production function.

Taxation

What strikes an old public finance functionary as forcibly as any change in the field of public finance is the way in which modern thinking has knocked the props out from under the neat and primitive theories of tax incidence of a generation ago. The property tax provides a particularly instructive case in point. The textbooks of the 1930s and 1940s told us confidently that the tax on land (fixed supply) was capitalized and on dwellings (sup-

350

ply responsive) fell like an excise tax on the occupant, the consumer of housing services. The policy lesson was clear: Given the declining proportion of income spent on housing services as income rises the tax was hopelessly regressive. Today? It is recognized that the old incidence analysis was wrong, even on its own terms.

The modern theory of incidence (defined as the impact on distribution of private real income) draws on general equilibrium theory, distinguishes between sources-of-income and uses-of-income effects, and disentangles the concepts of specific, differential, and balanced-budget incidence. The resulting analysis indicates that much of the aggregate burden of the property tax falls on owners of capital and hence tends to be progressive – and this progressivity is enhanced by the particular "excise-type" effects of this tax (Henry Aaron). In short, error has been exposed and though the debate is not over, we are now in transit toward truth.[3] It is hard to put down the knee-jerk reaction that prefixes "property tax" with "regressive." And it will take some time before policy makers accept the proposition that, at the very least, the property tax is now in the unexpected position of "innocent until proved guilty." But the implications for policy are profound.

Economists have long been useful and influential contributors to the design of the federal tax structure and of particular taxes. Again, elementary concepts we now take for granted--for example, horizontal versus vertical equity, Richard Musgrave's three branches of distribution, allocation, and stabilization, the lagged effect of tax changes, and automatic versus discretionary tax changes were not even part of our vocabulary in the pre-World War II period. Yet, all of these are now factored into our economic advice on taxation.

Even more directly impinging on policy are the empirical advances. One thinks of searching studies of particular taxes and tax components (especially in the Brookings Studies on Government Finance), and of the relentless identifying and quantifying of federal income tax preferences or "loopholes." Much of the thrust of economists' recent work on these "tax expenditures" has been (a) to identify the beneficiaries and specify the size of the government subsidies provided in the form of preferential tax treatment, (b) to define the inequities, both horizontal and vertical, that they create, and (c) to estimate the distortions in resource flows caused by preferential treatment of oil and gas, housing, real estate partnerships, and the like, and measure the resulting welfare loss. Though the congressional response has been slow and halting, progress has been made along the lines plotted by economists, and a solid base has been laid for the further tax reform that is surely coming.

351

Out of the countless other advances, one stands out, namely, the highly informative work done on the distributional impacts of taxation with the aid of the powerful tool of micro-unit data files (for example, the MERGE file developed by Joseph Pechman and Benjamin Okner). Such micro-unit files are a new-generation statistical missile, MIRVed so that they can simultaneously hit multiple revenue-estimating and burden-distribution targets. With their help, for example, economists have measured the growing burden of income, payroll, and consumption taxes on the lower income groups and developed techniques for removing them --most recently, in the context of the impact of inflation on the same groups.

One should add that if revolution rather than reform becomes the order of the day in the federal tax structure, the economist is ever ready with reasonably sophisticated analytics and a fair amount of empirical information on such major alternatives as a value-added tax, a progressive expenditure tax, and a net-worth tax. One of the next stages in tax research, a highly complex one, will be the general equilibrium analysis of such sweeping changes in the tax system as, say, the substitution of a value-added tax for the corporate income tax or for part of the payroll tax. Or, if stimulation of private saving becomes a compelling objective, perhaps the substitution of an expenditure tax for part of the income tax will become a live issue. The skills of the economist will be front and center in any such redesign of the tax system.

The negative income tax story is relevant here. The concept and its rudimentary principles were developed and discussed among economists in the early 1940s. Some of us were already using it as a teaching device in the mid-1940s. A quarter-century after its origin, it became the basis for the Family Assistance Plan developed by Mr. Nixon's economists. And a more limited version of the plan seems again to be rustling in the leaves.

Fiscal Policy

In the domain of fiscal policy, it is harder to answer the question, "What have you economists done for us lately?" with a sparkling array of examples. Much of the theoretical ferment in this field is associated with the flowering of Keynesian macroeconomics in the late 1930s and 1940s, the very period when the microeconomics of tax incidence and public expenditures languished.

Conceptual advances have continued throughout the past twenty-five years, but they have been more in the nature of a fleshing out and consolidation of the original breakthroughs with the aid of the powerful tools of mathematics and econometrics. Multiplier analysis, for example, has moved from the theoretical realm into large computer models of the economy--with the tax cut of 1964 and the surtax of 1968 providing empirical grist for the mill. While the models differ on the exact value of the multiplier, "a fiscal policy planner will not often be led astray if he uses a multiplier of 2" for government spending (see Blinder and Solow).

Coupled with multiplier studies is the even more subtle study of the structure of the "outside lags," of the timing of responses in the economy to changes in fiscal policy. Though the empirical efforts and debates go on apace, the behavior of the cumulative multipliers in a clutch of economic models suggest that for any given change in fiscal policy, "at least 75 percent, probably much more, of the ulimate effect is felt within the first year after the initiation of the policy" (Blinder and Solow). Although intractable questions remain concerning investment responses to fiscal policy changes, enough has been learned about aggregate demand responses to provide two broad generalizations about fiscal policy:

One, the conditions for intelligent fiscal policy are met if economic forecasting can answer two not-very-exacting questions: Do projected economic conditions in the ensuing six to nine months call for restraint or stimulus? Is the required dosage large or small?

Two, given the limited margin for error in a high-employment economy, it is better to rely on many smaller monetary-fiscal moves than a few large ones.

Implicit in these two generalizations is a third one: Given both the internal shifts and the external shocks with which stabilization policy has to cope, a discretionary policy that makes efficient use of feedback information will be more effective than an automatic policy that locks in on fixed fiscal and monetary targets.

Development of a simplified measure of fiscal impact revolving around the "full employment surplus" (FES) concept is another example of the typical process by which economists expose error, develop approximations of truth, but continue the vigorous debate on further improvements. First, policy makers had to be weaned away from the annually balanced budget and the cyclically balanced budget as policy targets and from actual deficits or surpluses (especially in budgets other than the national income accounts budget) as measures of budget stimulus or restriction. It was not easy. It took almost a quarter of a century before a Democratic president was converted (in 1961) and another decade to capture a Republican White House.

But success on the policy frontier has its own pitfalls, both political and economic. What was intended as a measure of policy was instead taken as a goal, namely, a balanced budget at full employment, a "self-fulfilling prophecy" as the Nixon Administration called it. This erroneously implied that the fiscal target should remain fixed regardless of changes in monetary policy and significant shifts in private demand, for example, a plant-and-equipment boom. Apart from trying to correct such misconceptions, economists have had to wrestle with the problem of the overstatement of the full employment surplus when inflation expands revenues faster than expenditures, not to mention the problem of weighting for differing multipliers if tax or expenditure components change sharply. In brief, the advances over the bad old days of the annually balanced budget are enormous, but economists are aware of the limitations of the FES measure and are struggling to resolve them.

Just as economics relegated erroneous budget concepts to the dustbin, so it has cast a shadow over such former favorites (of mine, among others) as federal capital budgeting and the "shelf of public works." The initial enthusiasm for the capital budget concept (in the context of a Congress seeking to balance the budget annually) was dispelled by second-thought analysis showing that (a) it rested on some faulty parallels with private finance, (b) the implicit fiscal policy rule of always financing capital projects by borrowing is in error, and (c) it would bias government capital spending toward bricks and mortar instead of brainpower and people. In the public works case, the concept ran afoul the findings of prosaic economic research: recent studies show that the public works program launched in 1963 to speed recovery was far from completed before excess demand overtook us in the 1966-69 period. This is not to rule out the use of certain types of "public works" that are nimble on their feet, such as road and forest maintenance work, for stabilization purposes. Nor does it rule out speeding up or delaying the launching of projects that are to be undertaken for sound cost-benefit reasons in any event. But it is fair warning not to expect very much stabilization help from the public works sector (not to be confused with public service employment).

In the conscious use of taxes for stabilization purposes, the huge 1964 income tax cut delivered economic expansion and a balanced budget on schedule without inflation by mid-1965, just before the Vietnam escalation struck the economy. The temporary 1968 surtax, buffeted by powerful demand forces and monetary easing, left a more ambiguous econometric trail. Subsequent fiscal policy thinking emphasizes the advantages of temporary tax changes that embody not just income effects but intertemporal substitution effects. For example, lowering the prices of investment goods in a recession via a clearly temporary increase in the investment credit, or temporary cuts in consumption taxes on durable goods (or lacking these, temporary purchase subsidies), would constitute a powerful incentive to purchase those goods before the price went up again.

Further work is needed to measure the cost-push effects of anti-inflationary tax increases that offset part of their demand-damping effect. In recession, the cost-easing and demand-push effects work in happy harmony. They work at cross purposes in tax increases (though not in expenditure cuts) to curb inflation. The question of how large the offsetting cost-push effects, or aggregate supply effects, may be, is unresolved. In a high-inflation economy, this is a serious gap in our fiscal policy knowledge.

Other Aspects

This kaleidoscope of contributions, long as it is, leaves out a whole string of developments in budget concepts, techniques, and processes--efforts that were crowned by the congressional budget reforms recently put into effect. Much of the guidance and momentum for these reforms was provided by economic analysis and by a succession of five economist-budget directors throughout the 1960s. Also omitted is the conceptual work on the economics of the bureaucratic process, of how government works. Other omissions include the rebirth of interest and great advances in the economics of state-local finance, the rapid growth of the important new field of urban economics--with its contributions to regional economics, location research, and analysis of the city as an economic system--and the enriched economics of fiscal federalism. I have even eschewed an assessment of revenue sharing, the rationale and form of which were developed by economists. With little imperialism, economists can also cite the firm quantitative evidence being developed to demonstrate the adverse economic effects of many public regulatory activities.[4]

For all the advances, the agenda of unresolved conceptual questions and unfinished empirical business is huge. But even this truncated review of progress and current output in public economics makes clear that the contributions of recent decades have enormously enriched this field not only conceptually but as a source of hard practical advice to decision makers who want to shape a better tax system, do justice to the poor, improve social programs, reform budget procedures, fight unemployment, and so on. And in the process, the frontiers of normative economics, both theoretical and empirical, have been pushed out into the areas of education, health, racism, crime, family behavior, and even political behavior.

As a result, we have plunged ever deeper into the realm of

355

values. Not that it was a value-free inquiry to ask the traditional questions about the effect of a given policy on material
output. But surely the testing of policies by the costs they incur
and how effective they are in meeting some generally accepted
criteria of social welfare or general welfare involves economics
directly in value and distributional problems.   And it enables
economics to say important things on social policy issues within
the framework of the conventional economic paradigm and with
rigor of the non-mortis variety.

We are becoming interdisciplinary in spite of ourselves. When
we do it, of course, we don't think of it as cross-sterilization
of disciplines. But here is an area where modesty becomes us.
For if we confine ourselves too narrowly to economics, we are far
too likely to attribute to economic variables the behavior and
results that are really a response to social variables. Fearing
just that, one observer has been unkind enough to suggest that
we ought to stick to inflation problems where we all know what to
say.

V. The Economist and Inflation

Inflation may no longer be "Public Enemy Number One" now that
severe recession is upon us, but it is surely "Economists' Enemy
Number One." Among the charges of, by, and against economists
that have been touched off by double-digit inflation and reported
in the public prints are these:

> Economists have confessed (I plead guilty) that 1973 was "the
> year of infamy in inflation forecasting" and, as already
> noted, that "we were caught with our parameters down."

> Aaron Gordon puts it more explicitly when he says that "the
> forecasters fell flat on their faces in predicting price changes
> because they didn't have any way of estimating sectoral
> supply scarcity" and adds that we have not "even started to
> develop a theory of aggregate supply."

> Leontief scolds macroeconomists more generally: "There is a
> lot of fancy methodology, but the macroeconomists get in-
> digestion if you give them facts."

> We are reminded *ad nauseam* that the "new economists" of
> the 1960s had promised to fine-tune inflation out of their full
> employment economy (a clear-cut triumph of caricature over
> fact since Keynesians time and again warned of precisely the
> opposite danger).

> Myrdal and Heilbroner have pointed to stagflation as Exhibit A
> that economists typically lag rather than lead their targets,

that being "behind its time" is "the regular methodological weakness of establishment economics."

Von Hayek recently reentered the fray to lay the blame for worldwide inflation squarely at the door of economists, particularly those "who have embraced the teachings of Lord Keynes."

Apart from the charge that Keynesian economists have *caused* inflation (which is much like saying that the cause of forest fires is trees), the bill of particulars against macroeconomics runs something like this: First, it did not forewarn the body politic that it would have to pay such a high price in endemic inflation for the attainment of high employment. Second, its progress in solving some important puzzles of endemic inflation relating, for example, to the Phillips curve, wage inflation, expectations, and uncertainty is much too slow. Third, there is no articulated general theory of inflation as such. Fourth, economists failed to foresee the 1973-74 epidemic inflation because their forecasting models lacked the central supply and price parameters. Fifth, macroeconomics is helpless in the face of epidemic or external-shock inflation—indeed, it has not satisfactorily explained the co-existence of inflation and recession, or stagflation. Without attempting a point-by-point assessment of these complaints, I will touch on all of them in the following sympathetic interpretation of how economists are coping with inflation's tough analytic and empirical challenges.

Addressing myself for a moment to our reproachful public, let me simply say to them: "We never promised you a rose garden without thorns." Over most of the past thirty years, macroeconomists have warned again and again, first, that aggressive fiscal and monetary policy to manage aggregate demand was bound to generate inflationary pressures once the economy entered the full employment zone, and second, that while full employment spells inflation, recessions run into price and wage rigidities that thwart deflation, an asymmetry bound to produce a ratchet effect on the price level. Keynes himself foresaw the basic problem in his little book, *How to Pay for the War*, in 1940. Abba Lerner and William Beveridge also wrote of the problem in the early 1940s. And it has been discussed in the stabilization theory and policy literature, in congressional hearings, and in other policy forums ever since.

This country finally embraced activist fiscal policies for full employment in the 1960s, most explicitly in the 1964 tax cut. Following the canons of Keynesian economics, focussing on the economy's full employment potential as their target, and steadfastly rejecting a spate of "structural" explanations of unemployment, economists were at first alone in prescribing tax cuts as a tonic for the stagnant economy. Enacted early in 1964, the tax cut delivered the promised expansion and budget balance without inflation. By August 1965, when Vietnam escalation began, unemployment had been brought to 4.4 percent with only the faintest stirring of the inflationary beast (i.e., with consumer prices rising at less than a 2 percent annual rate).

In a very real sense, economists have been victims of their own success. Macroeconomic policy, capped by the tax cut, was the major force holding the postwar economy on a vastly higher plane than the prewar economy.[5] On one hand, the high employment, limited-recession economy forged with our macro-economic policy tools is indeed an inflation-prone economy--the formula for successful management of high-pressure prosperity is far more elusive than the formula for getting there. Yet on the other hand, success bred great expectations on the part of the public that economics could deliver prosperity without inflation and with ever-growing material gains in the bargain. The message got through that we had "harnessed the existing economics... to the purposes of prosperity, stability, and growth," and that as to the role of the tax cut in breaking old molds of thinking, "nothing succeeds like success" (Heller). *The Economist* unkindly corrected me: "Nothing exceeds like success."[6]

To be sure, critics and converts alike ignored our caveats that the goal of "prosperity without a price-wage spiral" had "eluded not only this country but all of its industrial partners in the free world," that "the margin for error diminishes as the economy reaches the treasured but treacherous area of full employment...," and that "the 'new economics' promises no money-back guarantees against occasional slowdowns or even recessions" (Heller).

All too soon, Vietnam blew the economy off-course. Economists found that in the political arena fiscal policy was not a two-way street and that the much delayed surtax adopted in mid-1968 was no match for surging inflation. Nor was the induced recession of 1969-70. It took a combination of the 1971 shock therapy of tight wage-price controls and the stimulus of tax cuts to subdue inflation and energize expansion. It is worth noting that economists analyzed and projected the effects of this "new economic policy" with exceptional precision. That the tax cuts, coupled with controls and devaluation, would generate a surging expansion at very moderate rates of inflation in 1972 was widely and accurately forecast.

But the period from August 1971 to January 1973 was in the nature of a remission from the inflationary disease, clearly not a cure. The 1969-70 recession brought home the worsening problem of persistent inflation in the face of slowdown and recession. It presented new empirical puzzles for the analysts of the Phillips curve, wage equations, and expectational inflation. And it began to prompt the public mutterings that are being intensified by the 1974-75 stagflation: "All right, so you did not promise us a rose garden without thorns--but the thorns without the rose garden?"

Keenly aware of these problems, economists have long been at the drawing boards on this problem of endemic inflation. In a close parallel with research on cancer, economists are working on various pieces of the inflation puzzle and producing useful insights and guidance for policy purposes. But as economists, we would be the first to underscore that these puzzles are far from being fitted into an articulated and holistic theory of inflation. Inflationary analysis appears as an appendage to Keynesian and monetarist theories. But as yet, the Keynesian apparatus cannot tell us how any given change in aggregate demand is divided between changes in real output and changes in prices. Nor has monetarist theory unlocked the puzzle of how the effects of monetary changes are divided between output and price level changes. And no big breakthrough is in sight.

Does this mean that the economist has to stand mute in the meanwhile? Not at all. He is pushing ahead on the various pieces of basic research on the cancer of inflation and isolating and prescribing effectively for particular forms of the cancer even without having a complete explanation of the disease. Let me come back to the sustained and systematic research efforts on endemic inflation after examining the 1973-74 epidemic and the economist's responses to it. Since the epidemic is an over-layer on the endemic base, the distinctions won't be clear-cut--but they are nonetheless useful for viewing what the economist is able to contribute to policy.

The food-fuel price bulge generated over half of the 1973-74 inflation--and of economists' woes as well. Yet, it is asking a lot of economists to expect them to have foreseen that the oil cartel would quadruple oil prices, that the world would suffer widespread and successive crop failures, that the Peruvian anchovies would go into hiding, and that the Soviets would "solve our surplus grain problem" overnight.

Several unpleasant policy surprises also beset the inflation forecasters. First, just when a new rash of inflation was breaking out early in 1973, the reasonably effective Phase II controls were abruptly dropped in favor of the weak and ineffective Phase III. Second, six months later, after inflation had changed into a commodity-driven structural phenomenon involving a drastic readjustment of relative prices, the White House (to the pained surprise of economists inside and outside the administration) prescribed just the wrong medicine, a new wage-price freeze. A third policy surprise was that the dollar was allowed to sink like a stone: At its low point in the summer of 1973 (just before a substantial rebound), relative prices of imports had risen 10 percent in six months. About a quarter of the 1973 inflation has been attributed to these policy developments (see William Nordhaus and John Shoven).

It is worth noting that unexpected twists and turns of federal policy--which might be terms "internal shocks" in contrast with the "external shocks" of the food-fuel price explosion--are a continuing bane of the forecaster's existence. The about-face of the Federal Reserve in 1974 is another painful case in point. The sharp turn from ease to tightness in the first quarter of the year was a major factor in transforming prospects of recovery into recession in the second half of 1974. It is not quite clear why economists should be better at anticipating these shocks, especially the external ones, than society as a whole, or other professional specialists, or practical men of the world. Nothing in statistical methodology or economic science enables us to predict random shocks. What *can* be expected of us is that when they occur, we will spot them quickly, identify them, and analyze their significance for policy.

It is also worth remembering that democratic governments, by their nature, are pressure-responders rather than problem-anticipators. This carries two implications for political economists. On one hand, if an idea's time has not yet come, or if a problem has not yet become a crisis, the economist's call for action is likely to go unheeded. On the other, spotting emergent problems early can perhaps hasten an idea's time and alert the policy makers to impending danger.

Economists can more readily be faulted for being caught by surprise by the shortages of materials and primary processing capacity that caused the economy to bump against its ceiling sooner than expected and by the worldwide economic boom that put severe pressure on raw commodity supplies and prices. On the first point, we suffered both from information failure--the official capacity indexes simply did not reveal how close the economy was to its output ceilings--and from analytic limits. While identifying the causes, economists have been unable to pinpoint the relative significance of the shortfall of investment that began in the late 1960s, of underinvestment caused by price controls, of delays induced by environmental policies, and of the surge in foreign demand touched off by devaluation. However, I should add that the shortages problem is meat and drink for economists, and they are responding (especially in the energy field) with new analyses of price elasticities, investment needs, and the like. All of a sudden, price theory is back in vogue, and elasticities have replaced multipliers as the badge of a policy maker's *savoir faire*.

Delays in perceiving that the U.S. economic expansion was part of a worldwide upsurge can again be laid more to lack of an adequate information system than to any inability to understand the underlying principles. Still, a better sense of history and of the emerging worldwide imbalance between growing aspirations and growing incomes on one hand and inelastic resource supply and lagging technology on the other would have made us more conscious and cautious. We are considerably less likely to be caught by surprise in the future in view of the new worldwide data networks that are being developed by Project LINK at the University Pennsylvania and by Otto Eckstein and his colleagues at Data Resources Incorporated (DRI).

Without absolving economists, one should apply this operational test: With proper foresight, would tighter monetary and budget policy have been able to damp inflation? It is worth recalling, first, that the full employment budget was making a swing of over $10 billion towards restraint between fiscal 1973 and fiscal 1974 (from a $2 billion deficit to a $10 billion surplus under the old 4 percent unemployment standard) and that monetary policy pushed interest rates into the double-digit region; second, that there was little that an aggregate demand squeeze could have done to push world commodity prices down. So the answer is clear: Even tougher fiscal and monetary policy would have had limited scope in holding inflation down.

This is not to deny that generating a larger full employment surplus would have been the prudent course in calendar 1973. But it is worth noting that to offset the food and fuel price explosions--which were triggered by forces largely immune to U.S. fiscal and monetary policy--would have required a *reduction* of 3 percent in all other prices. Such a target implies depression-inducing doses of fiscal and monetary restriction, an unthinkable "solution."

Looking toward the future, many economists draw the lesson not that one should keep the economy's motor idling, but rather that one should provide it with safety devices and heavy-duty shock absorbers, for example, stock-piling of foodstuffs, oil, and basic raw materials, careful tracking of commodity exports, distant early warning systems to spot shortages-in-the-making, and conservation and development measures to limit dependence on foreign raw materials cartels. In other words, it is a call for better planning, better data, and faster conversion of knowledge into policy.

Another criterion of economists' responses to inflationary shocks is how quickly they adapted (read, "disaggregated") their macromodels, large and small, to incorporate new supply and price parameters that had previously been judged of second or third order importance and hence relegated to Marshall's *ceteris paribus* pound. Some of the mongrel pups impounded there turned out to be full blooded huskies, for example, food prices, the exchange value of the dollar, oil and other raw material supplies and prices. At first most economists were slow and the big models sluggish in their responses. After all, for two decades prices had moved in tandem with wages, with a year-by-year percentage-point differential of 2 3/4 ± 1. So most models relied on wage trends, with some adjustment for productivity and capacity behavior, to give them a fix on price trends. Their eyes were on labor market indicators rather than commodity supplies, exchange rates, and the like. After some initial delays, the model building scrambled to disaggregate, to build microelements into their macromodels. For example, DRI now has a good stage-of-processing models that absorb the impacts of food and energy explosions. Price elasticities are being built into the macromodels to reflect the impact of massive relative price changes on the macrodimensions of the economy.

The whole experience reminds us of the role and limits of econometric forecasting models. First, the combination of computers, mathematics, and econometrics cannot produce the miracles that the uninitiated may expect of them––there is no way of replicating reality with its 3 million equations, all of them nonlinear. Second, their indispensable function is to bring us closer to reality and help the mind manage the previously unmanageable ––they permit us to release vastly more animals from the *ceteris paribus* pound than we could manage without these tools. Third, they have to be constantly adjusted to plug in common sense, adjust the length of the lags, and bring in new dimensions of the problem. Else, they will lock out things that a more judgmental approach would include, and will fail to respond quickly to changes in order of importance.

So the inflation-shock experience has brought home the need not just to watch supply but to watch *all* the pieces lest the model prevail over the mind, rather than having the model help the mind prevail over matter. The macro-stalactites have to reach toward the micro-stalagmites, and vice versa. I hope that metaphor is not a portent of the pace at which the advance toward macro-micro fusion will proceed.

Economists who use judgmental models have shown us how to be the master rather than the slave of the computer. A case in point was the early analysis (especially by George Perry) of the macro-impact of the oil price increases. A year ago, his work had already brought out the oil paradox--the *in*flation of costs and hence prices, leading to a *de*flation of aggregate demand--and had provided some estimates of both. The insight that some $15 to $20 billion of consumer purchasing power would be siphoned off into the hands of oil producers and royalty collectors without any early return to the economy in the form of demand for imports or investment goods had important implications for demand-management policy--implications that were ignored until severe recession was full upon us.[7]

These important insights into the macro-economic policy implications of oil prices fit into the broader efforts of economists to disentangle the sources of the current inflation and identify the appropriate remedies. They differentiate among (1) excess demand, which had spent most of its force by early in 1974, (2) the price-wage-price spiral, which began to turn more rapidly in 1974, and (3) external-shock of special-sector inflation, in particular, the commodity-price surges that permeate the present inflation and account for its special character and ferocity.

The first responds rather readily to monetary-fiscal pressure, the second responds more reluctantly, and the third is highly resistant to the demand-management measures of any given country. For the second and especially the third types, therefore, high costs in unemployment and foregone output have to be incurred for small gains in curbing inflation. So the distinction is an instructive one for policy--even when the instructions are ignored. As we meet here tonight, the economic lessons that were so long ignored are being painfully driven home by severe recession and unemployment coupled with continuing inflation. A much-belated consensus that fiscal and monetary stimulus can now be undertaken with minimal inflationary risk is rapidly forming.

The economists' three-ply classification of inflation sources is also useful in driving home another point: In most U.S. inflations consisting of the first two types, one person's price is another person's income, so that in spite of some reshuffling, there is no net loss in real income. Not so in 1973-75. Commodity inflation has transferred tens of billions of dollars of *real* income out of the pockets of urban consumers and wage earners into the hands of farmers and foreigners where it is beyond the reach of the collective bargaining process. From this, several important inferences can be drawn:

Point for point, this inflation *cum* relative price changes is harsher in its impact than previous postwar inflations.

In this "no-win" inflation, the wage earner's loss has not generally been the employer's gain; hence, if the wage "catch-up" process succeeds in recouping the *full* rise in the cost of living, much of the wage increase will pass through to prices and thereby give the wage-price spiral another self-defeating turn.

It follows, as various economists urged throughout 1974, that tax cuts to bolster the real income of labor, if put in the context of a social contract, might well relieve some of the pressure for higher wages.

In this respect, today's situation contrasts rather sharply with the 1950-51 inflation when a similarly rapid run-up in world commodity prices was accompanied by a rapid rise in profit margins side-by-side with vigorous federal policies to boost capacity. The ensuing combination of ebbing world market prices and wage increases that could be granted without generating higher product prices resulted in a remarkable four-year period of price stability from 1952 to 1956.

A closely allied economic insight goes to the nature of the inflationary process. It explains in good part why inflation is so stubborn even in the face of overly restrictive monetary-fiscal policy and rapidly mounting unemployment and slack in the economy. It is the sharp run-up in *relative* prices of food, fuel, and imported goods--coupled with the downward rigidities of wages and prices--that is the key to most of our stagflationary malaise today.

These downward rigidities are a striking example of the way in which economic solutions create their own problems and move the economist relentlessly from one new frontier to another. Once macroeconomics gave governments the know-how and tools of modern demand-management to avoid depression, and once the public caught on that even recessions are essentially man-made--chiefly by That Man in the White House, whoever he is, together with the Congress and the Federal Reserve Board--it became part of the politics of survival to hold employment high and keep recessions in check. Absent the fears of mass unemployment and prolonged recession, the risks of not cutting prices and not accepting lower wages are minimized. Having put the Great Depression of the 1930's far behind us, will we therefore have to live with the Great Inflation of the 1970s?

Essentially, the economist answers that, given the ratchet behavior of wages and prices, the level can only float upward to accommodate the massive relative price increases of oil, grains, certain raw materials, and imported goods. These sharp changes in the composition of supply touch off reverberating price increases throughout the economy as prices in the scarce-supply sectors become costs in the less-scarce ones. The reverberations go on--in substantial part independent of the state of aggregate demand and hence of monetary and fiscal policy--until the prices of the initiating goods have risen sufficiently farther than prices in general to accomplish the necessary realignment of relative prices. This is the process going on now. It takes time, but not forever. It has much to do with double-digit inflation, but it does not condemn us to Weimar Republic inflation.

Solow (1975) reminds us that the supply-shift phenomenon bears a close relationship to the demand-shift analysis of the creeping inflation of the mid-1950s. At that time, the parallel process was touched off by an investment boom that put excess demand pressures on capital goods industries even when there was no excess aggregate demand in the economy. Given the downward rigidity and cost-oriented nature of wages and prices in areas of excess market power, the price level had to float upward to accommodate those relative price changes (see Schultze, 1959).

John Dunlop and other economists have emphasized that there is a closely related phenomenon on the wage side known as "scale wages" or "wage relativities" or even a "just wage" (see Robert Hall and Michael Piore). If the relative wage scale is thrown out of kilter by an outsized wage settlement in one industry, the others will writhe, twist, and turn until the old relationships are reestablished. There is only one way the wage structure can move to accommodate this process: Up. Again, the process burns itself out only when a new equilibrium has been established on a higher plateau.

The policy implications of the supply-shift, demand-shift, and wage-shift insights are reasonably clear. One is the limited scope of repressive monetary-fiscal policy in coping with this process. Another is that the key to a successful wage-price policy for these circumstances is to establish and effectuate norms for the pace-setters and thus thwart the wage-wage and price-price spirals and the interacting wage-price spiral. Once the process is launched, the role of the wage-price watchdog with teeth would be to see to it that the adjustment process is a limited and straightforward one, not a leapfrogging sequence that will prolong the agony of adjustment. Again, understanding the economics of the process is the *sine qua non* for shaping the right policy to fit the particular type and phase of inflation that is beleaguering us.

Let me return now, before closing, to several of the abiding problems of endemic inflation that are engaging the attention and efforts of economists.

An important but elusive question for the policy maker concerns the costs of inflation. Can the economist tell him anything useful and definitive on this subject? Useful, perhaps. Definitive, no. First, the economist would remind him that people continually blame inflation for crimes it does not commit. They are sure that every increase in their pay envelope is a reward for merit, every increase in prices an inflationary theft. Especially pertinent to our present shock-spiral is the observation that people "blame inflation for changes in relative prices and in real incomes that stem from market forces that have nothing to do with the course of the general price level" (Edward Foster).

Second, studies show that in a typical U.S. inflation, the poor have gained more in jobs and incomes than they have lost in higher prices. But in the present inflation, prices have shifted sharply against the poor, and any initial gains they may have made in jobs and income in 1973 have been more than offset by the losses incurred in the deepening 1974-75 recession induced to fight inflation.

Third, at the rates of inflation experienced prior to the 1973-75 explosion, most economists find it difficult to believe that the costs of inflation--mostly in redistributional effects, but with some distortion in resource allocation--hold a candle to the welfare losses of substantial add-ons to unemployment. Fourth, however, when inflation reaches double-digit levels, the costs in terms of the social conflicts and tensions it generates and the uncertainties and loss of confidence in the dollar yardstick it may breed are important intangibles that economists cannot ignore, yet have not been able to quantify. We need to understand far more about what unsettles and upsets people about inflation, how this affects their economic behavior, and what economic costs result. Clearly, in an economy where inflation is endemic, the balance between its gains and losses deserves intensive further study.

Another important question is this: How much of the present run-up in prices of foodstuffs, oil, and raw materials is a transitory phenomenon, how much is a one-time shift to a new plateau, and how much represents a new upward trend? Economists have trained the guns of price theory and price elasticity estimation on these questions in the case of oil and several other basic materials. They generally come up with more optimistic answers for five to ten years hence than for the near-term. But much of the answer lies in geo-political, meteorological, and similar puzzles-- for example, the effectiveness of oil and other raw material cartels, the pace of world population increases and income growth, and the possibility of a dry, cold phase in world weather--that lie largely or wholly beyond the reach of economic analysis.

What we do know is this: The 1950s and the 1960s were a

period of gently declining or roughly stable world prices for raw materials or foodstuffs. Now, rising population, industrialization, income, and aspirations may put such pressure on the world's supply capabilities that while we are not nearing any Club-of-Rome ultimate limits, we may for some time exceed the speed limits of stable expansion. If so we may have passed an inflection point in the price trends of basic inputs to the economy (see Walt Rostow). The mild downward trend of the 1951-71 period facilitated the rise in real incomes of urban workers side-by-side with rising profits. If this trend is reversed, rising income claims will generate greater strains, and the Phillips curve tradeoff will take place around a higher inflation constant. Economic analysis of long-run supply prices of basic commodities using alternative assumptions regarding world political, weather, and economic trends could be a useful aid to rational economic planning.

Coming back into the domain of economics as such, one should take account of the important new thinking and efforts now being devoted to the continuing mysteries of industrial pricing policies and the role of fixed-rule (generally, mark-up) pricing as a shield against uncertainty. Answering the question of how, and how fast, supply-shifts in the auction markets or market-oriented sector are transmitted through the rule-determined sector--where certain relativities seem to be maintained in the structure of prices (and wages)--is essential to an understanding of structural inflation (see Piore).

In turn, this analysis will strongly influence thinking on government intervention in private wage-price and perhaps also supply-demand decisions. If the wage-price structure is indeed fairly rigid and if supply- and demand-shifts set off an inflationary spiral, the "natural market forces" will not readily make the necessary supply-demand adjustment in any case. Wage-price restraint or controls would not be supplanting some supple and efficient resource allocation mechanism, yet would insert a circuit breaker into the inflationary spiral. This view of the world would also suggest that government action to stimulate supply and suppress demand at certain pressure points in the economy might well pass the test of economic efficiency. In pursuing these questions and hypotheses, the economist will be laying a firmer conceptual and empirical foundation for specifying the areas and circumstances in which intervention may be the lesser evil.

One should not leave the subject of economists' contributions to analysis and prescription on the inflation problem without mention of the intriguing attempt of the Brookings Panel on Economic Activity to bring the best analytical and empirical efforts of economists to bear directly on the problems and puzzles that confront the policymaker. In relation to inflation, the Panel has focussed much of its attention on such questions as the structure of labor markets, the Phillips curve relationship and wage equations, the costs of unemployment, price behavior in specific sectors like foodstuffs and oil, and the role of fiscal and monetary policies. Apart from the significant contributions that have been made to understanding these problems, and to bringing academic work into closer contact with current policy problems, the Brookings Panel is an interesting and perhaps unique exercise in "continuing confrontational econometrics." Responding to the kinds of criticisms quoted earlier in my remarks, the Brookings Panel combines rigorous quantitative testing with continuing surveillance by one's peers to assure that the investigator (1) looks beyond mathematics and makes his assumptions and relations conform to common sense, (b) spells out the implications of his econometrics and, if they are implausible, tries again, and (c) constantly keeps asking questions of the model. With the Panel now going into its sixth year of thrice-yearly meetings, previous analyses become not undisturbed museum pieces, but grist for the mill of constant retesting under the harsh light of reality and peer-group criticism.

I have dealt at some length with the substance of economists' work and findings on inflation because mere assertions of progress would hardly suffice to demonstrate what's right with economics in this most vulnerable area. The fact that there are no final or comprehensive answers has not kept economists from making significant distinctions, analyses, and measurements that equip policy makers with better means of judging the policy tradeoffs and determining how to improve the fit of policy-to-problem for the different types and stages of inflation. When policy makers fail to heed these lessons, as in 1974, both the economy and the economist feel the backlash.

Throughout this discourse, I have time and again been tempted to kick over the traces I fastened on myself and give voice to my own criticisms, dissatisfactions, and admonitions. But since an unholy (and unwitting) alliance of my colleagues and outside critics has amply and ably taken care of this, I felt it best to stay within my constraints in the interest of doing what I could do to redress the balance. As economists, we have many sins, none deadly, to confess. But these are far outweighed by the virtues, all quite lively, that we can legitimately profess.

Footnotes

*   Presidential address delivered at the eighty-seventh meeting of the American Economic Association, San Francisco, Cali-

fornia, December 29, 1974. The address was abridged for oral delivery. I owe particular thanks for the many conversations I held with Francis Boddy, Otto Eckstein, Edward Foster, Arthur Okun, Joseph Pechman, George Perry, Robert Solow, and James Tobin. I also wish to thank Gardner Ackley, Kenneth Arrow, Walter P. Heller, John R. Meyer, Franco Modigliani, Alice Rivlin, Paul Samuelson, Charles Schultze, Christopher Sims, and George Stigler, for contributions to the adult education that underlies this address. The errors of course are mine.

1. Among those who have sprung to the defense with varying degrees of fervor are Harry Johnson (1968), Donald MacDougall, Charles Schultze (1972), Robert Solow (1970, 1971), and James Tobin (1973, 1974). For more general appraisals of the criticisms and the state of economics, see Blackman and Nancy Ruggles.

2. See Alan Blinder and Robert Solow et al. This is the capstone volume of the Brookings Studies on Government Finance, directed by Joseph A. Pechman, which has produced 35 books in the past decade. See also Carl Shoup et al. This was one of several survey volumes under the general heading, *Economic Research: Retrospect and Prospect*, based on the Bureau's Fiftieth Anniversary Colloquia.

3. Those who view decisions to locate in a particular community as a conscious choice of one particular bundle of public services over others conclude that the property tax on housing is a benefit tax, a payment for benefits received.

4. As an example of the "Age of Quantification," George Stigler cites the sea. of studies on regulatory practices and their costs and benefits in the past dozen years, where there was a vacuum before. He notes that thirty-six "quantitative studies of effects of laws" were reported in two journals alone during this period, the *Journal of Law and Economics* and the *Journal of Political Economy*. These are promoting a broader consensus within the profession, informing decision makers, and posing challenges that will make policy failures easier to identify. (Personal correspondence).

5. As gauges of the contrast between prewar and post-war performance: unemployment averaged 18.8 percent in the decade of depression (1931-40) in contrast with 4.8 percent in the twenty-eight years since World War II; the prewar peak annual rate was 24.9 percent, the postwar peak was 6.8 percent. Annual real GNP dropped 30 percent from 1929 to

1933; since the war, mild declines have occurred only in three years (1949, 1954, and 1970), though 1974-75 may add two more. Consumer prices in 1940 were 18 percent below 1929; from 1948 to 1974, they increased 106 percent.

6. Macroeconomists were not alone in their exuberance in the mid-1960's. On this rostrum a decade ago, George Stigler, after reviewing the great promises and early accomplishments of the "Quantitative Revolution in Economics," was moved to say, "I am convinced that economics is finally at the threshold of its Golden Age--nay, we already have one foot through the door. ...Our expanding theoretical and empirical studies will inevitably and irresistibly enter into the subject of public policy, and we shall develop a body of knowledge essential to intelligent policy formulation. And then, quite frankly, I hope that we become the ornaments of democratic society whose opinions on economic policy shall prevail."

7. Late in 1974, Perry undertook a more searching econometric probe with the benefit of actual rather than projected oil price data and with the aid of the large scale formal models. His analysis shows that the purchasing power loss had reached $37 billion (annual rate) by the third quarter of 1974 and that the rise in the deflator attributable to the oil price jump was 3.8 percent. His analysis embraced not only the real-income effect (the transfer of real-income from consumers to producers), but also the monetary-policy effect (the reduction of the real value of the money stock and the rise in interest rates stemming from the highly inelastic short-run demand for petroleum products), the automobile-demand effect (higher saving), and the induced-inflation effect (the price-wage-price effect) of the oil price rise on the macro-economy.

References

H. Aaron, "A New View of Property Tax Incidence," *American Economic Review Proceedings*, May 1974, 54, 212-21.

B.R. Bergmann, "Economist, Poll Thy People," *New York Times*, "Points of View," November 3, 1974.

W.H. Beveridge, *Full Employment in a Free Society*, London 1944.

J.H. Blackman, "The Outlook for Economics," *Southern Economic Journal*, April 1971, 37, 385-95.

A.S. Blinder and R.M. Solow et al., "Analytical Foundation of Fiscal Policy," *Economics of Public Finance*, Washington 1974, 3-118.

K. Boulding, "Economics As a Moral Science," *American Economic Review*, March 1969, 59, 1-12.

H.R. Bowen, "Toward a Humanist Economics," *Nebraska Journal of Economics and Business*, Autumn 1972, 11, 9-24.

E. Foster, "Costs and Benefits of Inflation," *Federal Reserve Bank Minneapolis*, March 1972.

J.K. Galbraith, "Power and the Useful Economist," *American Economic Review*, March 1973, 63, 1-11.

F.H. Hahn, "Some Adjustment Problems," *Econometrica*, January 1970, 38, 1-17.

Robert E. Hall, "The Process of Inflation in the Labor Market," *Brookings Papers*, Washington 1974, 2, 343-410.

Robert L. Heilbroner, "Economics as a 'Value-Free' Science," *Social Research*, Spring 1973, 40, 129-43.

W.W. Heller, *New Dimensions of Political Economy*, Cambridge, 1966.

H.G. Johnson, "The Economic Approach to Social Questions," *Economica*, February 1968, 35, 1-21.

——— , "Scholars as Public Adversaries: The Case of Economics," in C. Frankel, ed., *Social Science Controversies and Public Policy Decisions*, ch.12, forthcoming.

J.M. Keynes, *How to Pay for the War*, London 1940.

W. Leontief, "Theoretical Assumptions and Nonobserved Facts," *American Economic Review*, March 1971, 61, 1-7.

A.P. Lerner, "Functional Finance and the Federal Debt," *Social Research*, February 1943, 10, 38-51.

D. MacDougall, "In Praise of Economics," Presidential address to the Royal Economic Society, June 1974.

S.J. Maisel, "The Economics and Finance Literature and Decision Making," *Journal of Finance*, May 1974, 29, 313-22.

R.A. Musgrave, *The Theory of Public Finance*, New York, 1959.

G. Myrdal, *Asian Drama: An Inquiry into the Poverty of Nations*, Vol. I, New York 1968.

W. Nordhaus and J. Shoven, "Inflation 1973: The Year of Infamy," *Challenge*, May-June 1974, 17, 14-22.

A.M. Okun, *The Political Economy of Prosperity*, Washington 1969.

J.A. Pechman and B.A. Okner, *Who Bears the Tax Burden?* Washington 1974.

G.L. Perry, "The Petroleum Crisis and the U.S. Economy," prepared for the Brookings Conference on the Impact of Higher Oil Prices on the World Economy, November 1974 (to be published).

E.H. Phelps Brown, "The Underdevelopment of Economics," *Economic Journal*, March 1972, 82, 1-10.

M. Piore, "Curing Inflation with Unemployment, Outmoded Notions of Supply and Demand," *New Republic*, November 2, 1974, 27-31.

A.M. Rivlin, "Why Can't We Get Things Done?" *Brookings Bulletin*, Spring 1972, 9, 5-9.

_____, "Social Experiments: The Promise and the Problem," *Evaluation*, 1973, 1, 77-78.

_____, Systematic Thinking for Social Action, Washington 1971.

M.J. Roberts, "On the Nature and Condition of Social Science," *Daedalus*, Summer 1974, 103, 47-64.

W.W. Rostow, "Political Economy in a Time of Scarcity: How to Get from Here to There," *Naval War College Review*, September-October 1974, 27, 32-45.

N. Ruggles, *Economics*, Englewood Cliffs, 1970.

C.L. Schultze, "Is Economics Obsolete? No, Underemployed," *Saturday Review*, January 22, 1972.

_____, *Recent Inflation in the U.S.*, Joint Economic Committee, working paper No. 1, Congress of the United States, Washington 1959.

_____, "The Reviewers Reviewed," *American Economic Review Proceedings*, May 1971, 61, 45-52.

T.W. Schultz, et al., "Human Capital: Policy Issues and Research Opportunities," in his *Human Resources*, Vol. VI, New York 1972.

C.S. Shoup et al., *Public Expenditures and Taxation*, New York 1972.

R.M. Solow, "Science and Ideology in Economics," *Public Interest*, Fall 1970, 21, 94-107.

_____, "The State of Economics - Discussion," *American Economic Review Proceedings*, May 1971, 61, 63-68.

_____, "What the Intelligent Citizen Should Know About Inflation," *Public Interest*, forthcoming 1975.

G.J. Stigler, "The Economist and the State," *American Economic Review*, March 1965, 55, 1-18.

P. Sweezy, "Capitalism, for Worse," *Monthly Review*, February 1974, 25, 1-7.

J. Tobin, *The New Economics One Decade Older*, Princeton 1974.

_____, "Cambridge (U.K.) vs. Cambridge (Mass.)," *Public Interest*, Spring 1973, 31, 102-09.

F.A. von Hayek, "Inflation and Unemployment," *New York Times*, "Points of View," November 15, 1974.

B. Ward, *What's Wrong with Economics?* New York 1972, p.12.

G.D.N. Worswick, "Is Progress in Economic Science Possible?" *Economic Journal*, March 1972, 82, 73-79.

Suggested Readings

Part One **The Nature of Economics**

Textual Materials

M. Blaug. *The Methodology of Economics* (London: Cambridge University Press, 1980), pp. 46-52.

H. Katouzian. *Ideology and Method in Economics* (New York: New York University Press, 1980).

I.M.T. Stewart. *Reasoning and Method in Economics* (Toronto: McGraw-Hill, 1979).

Other Readings

W.J. Cahnman. "Max Weber and the Methodological Controversy in the Social Sciences." In *Sociology and History*, ed. by W.J. Cahnman and A. Boskoff (New York: Free Press, 1964), pp. 103-27.

S. Gordon, "Social Science and Value Judgements." *Canadian Journal of Economics,* 10 (1977), pp. 529-46.

T.W. Hutchison. *'Positive' Economics and Policy Objectives* (Cambridge: Harvard University Press, 1964), pp. 21-120.

K. Klappholz, "Value Judgements and Economics." *British Journal for the Philosophy of Science,* 15 (1964), pp. 97-104.

F. Machlup. *Methodology of Economics and Other Social Sciences* (New York: Academic Press, 1978).

R.L. Meek, "Value Judgements in Economics." *British Journal for the Philosophy of Science,* 15 (1964), pp. 84-96.

G. Myrdal. *Objectivity in Social Research* (London: Gerald Duckworth, 1970), pp. 14-56.

Part Two **Economics and Value Judgment**

Textual Materials

M. Blaug. *The Methodology of Economics* (London: Cambridge University Press, 1980), pp. 46-52.

L.A. Boland. *The Foundations of Economic Method* (London: George Allen and Unwin, 1982), pp. 13-43.

H. Katouzian. *Ideology and Method in Economics* (New York: New York University Press, 1980), Chapter 1.

I.M.T. Stewart. *Reasoning and Method in Economics* (Toronto: McGraw-Hill, 1979), pp. 4-8.

Other Readings

M. Brodbeck. "Methodological Individualism: Definition and Reduction." In *Modes of Individualism and Collectivism,* ed. by J. O'Neill (London: Heinemann, 1973), pp. 287-311.

I. Krimerman. *The Nature and Scope of Social Science. A Critical Anthology* (New York: Meredith, 1969).

F. Machlup. *Methodology of Economics and Other Social Sciences* (New York: Academic Press, 1978), Chapter 6.

E. Nagel, "Assumptions in Economic Theory." *American Economic Review.* Papers and Proceedings (May 1963), pp. 211-19.

K. Popper. *An Essay of Historicism* (London: Routledge and Kegan Paul, 1957).

L. Robbins. *An Essay on the Nature and Significance of Economic Science* (London: Macmillan, 2nd ed., 1935), Part One.

P. Winch. *Idea of a Social Science* (London: Routledge & Paul, 1958).

Part Three   The Goal of Economics as a Hard Science

<u>Textual Materials</u>

A.R. Bergstrom. *The Construction and Use of Econometric Models* (London, England: English University Press, 1967).

M. Blaug. *The Methodology of Economics* (London: Cambridge University Press, 1980), pp. 260-262.

D.F. Hendry, A.R. Pagan and J.D. Sargan. "Dynamic Specification," in Z. Griliches and M.D. Intriligator (eds.) *Handbook of Econometrics* (Amsterdam: North Holland, 1982).

T.C. Koopmans. *Three Essays on the State of Economic Science* (New York: McGraw-Hill, 1957).

I.M.T. Stewart. *Reasoning and Method in Economics* (Toronto: McGraw-Hill, 1979), Chapter 9.

<u>Econometrics Textbooks</u>

P. Kennedy. *A Guide to Econometrics* (Cambridge, Massachusetts: The M.I.T. Press, 1980). A Supplement to Econometrics text.

E. Malinvaud. *Statistical Methods and Econometrics.* Second English Edition (Amsterdam: North Holland, 1970).

D.G. Mayes. *Applications of Econometrics* (Toronto: Prentice-Hall International, 1981), Chapter 10. Computer packages.

J. Stewart. *Understanding Econometrics* (London, England: Hutchinson and Co. Ltd., 1976). A Supplement to Econometrics text.

<u>Other Readings</u>

R. Frisch, "Econometrics in the World Today," in W. Eltis, M. Scott and J. Wolfe, *Induction, Growth and Trade* (Oxford: Oxford University Press, 1970).

C.W.J. Granger and M.W. Watson, "Time Series and Spectral Methods in Econometrics" in Z. Griliches and M.D. Intriligator (eds.) *Handbook of Econometrics* (Amsterdam: North Holland Pub. Co., 1982).

B. Kantor, "Rational Expectations and Economic Thought." *Journal of Economic Literature,* 17 (1979), pp. 1422-1441.

E. Leamer. *Specification Searches* (New York: John Wiley and Sons, 1978).

R.E. Lucas, Jr., "Econometric Testing of the Natural Rate Hypothesis," in *The Econometrics of Price Determination* (Washington, D.C.: Board of Governors of the Federal Reserve System, 1972), pp. 50-59.

R. Maddock and Michael Carter, "A Child's Guide to Rational Expectations," *Journal of Economic Literature,* 20 (1980), pp. 39-51.

T.J. Sargent, "A Classical Macroeconometric Model for the United States." *Journal of Political Economy,* 84 (1976), pp. 207-237.

T.J. Sargent and Neil Wallace, "Rational Expectations and Dynamics of Hyperinflation." *International Economic Review,* 83 (1975), pp. 241-55.

C.A. Sims, "Macroeconomics and Reality." *Econometrica,* 48 (1980), pp. 1-48.

E. Streissler. *Pitfalls in Econometric Forecasting* (London: Institute of Economic Affairs, 1970).

P.A.V.B. Swamy, J.R. Barth and P.A. Tinsley, "The Rational Expectations Approach to Economic Modelling," *Journal of Economic Dynamics and Control,* 4 (1982), pp. 125-147.

G. Tintner, "The Definition of Econometrics," *Econometrica,* 21 (1953), pp. 31-40.

G. Tintner, "Some Thoughts About the State of Econometrics," in S. Krupp, *The Structure of Economic Science* (Englewood Cliffs, N.J.: Prentice-Hall, 1966).

A. Zellner. "Statistical Analysis of Econometric Models." *Journal of the American Statistical Association,* 74 (1979), pp. 628-43.

Part Four   Should Prediction be the Goal of Economics?

L. Boland, "Friedman's Methodology vs. Conventional Empiricism: A Reply to Rotwein." *Journal of Economic Literature*, 18 (1980), pp. 1555-57.

L.A. Boland. *The Foundations of Economic Method* (London: George Allen and Unwin, 1982, Chapters 1, 7 and 8).

M. Friedman. *The Methodology of Positive Economics* (Chicago: University Press, 1953), pp. 3-43.

T.C. Koopmans, *Three Essays on the State of Economic Science* (New York: McGraw-Hill, 1957).

T.C. Koopmans, "Economics Among the Sciences." *American Economic Review*, 69 (1979), pp. 1-13.

R. Lucas, "Methods and Problems in Business Cycle Theory." *Journal of Money, Credit and Banking*, 12 (1980), pp. 696-715.

J. Melitz, "Friedman and Machlup on the Significance of Testing Economic Assumptions." *Journal of Political Economy*, 73 (1965), pp. 37-60.

E. Nagel, "Assumptions in Economic Theory." *American Economic Review*. Papers and Proceedings, 53 (May 1963), pp. 211-19.

A.G. Papandreau, "Theory Constructions and Empirical Meaning in Economics." *American Economic Review*, 53 (May 1963), pp. 205-10.

E. Rotwein, "Friedman's Critics: A Critic's Reply to Boland." *Journal of Economic Literature*, 18 (1980), pp. 1553-55.

P. Samuelson, "Problems of Methodology: Discussion." *American Economic Review*, 53 (1963), pp. 231-36.

Part Five   The Role of Empiricism in Economics

D.V.T. Bear and D. Orr, "Logic and Expediency in Economic Theorizing." *Journal of Political Economy*, 75 (1967), pp. 188-96.

L. Boland. *The Foundations of Economic Method* (London: George Allen and Unwin, 1982), Chapters 9 and 12.

M. Bronfenbrenner. "A Middlebrow Introduction to Economic Methodology." In *The Structure of Economic Science,* ed. by S.R. Krupp (Englewood Cliffs: Prentice-Hall, 1966), pp. 5-24.

F. Machlup. "Operationalism and Pure Theory in Economics." In *The Structure of Economic Science,* ed. by S.R. Krupp (Englewood Cliffs: Prentice-Hall, 1966), pp. 53-67.

D.P. O'Brien, "Whither Economics?" *Economics,* 11 (1975), pp. 75-98.

L. Robbins. *An Essay on the Nature and Significance of Economic Science* (London: Macmillan, 2nd ed., 1935).

I.M.T. Stewart. *Reasoning and Method in Economics* (Toronto: McGraw-Hill, 1979), Chapter 6.

Part Six How Theories are Verified

M. Blaug. *The Methodology of Economics* (London: Cambridge University Press, 1980), Chapter 4.

R.E. Engle. "Wald, Likelihood Ratio and Lagrange Multiplier Tests in Econometrics" in Z. Griliches and M.D. Intriligator (eds.), *Handbook of Econometrics* (Amsterdam: North Holland, 1982).

H. Katouzian. *Ideology and Method in Economics* (New York: New York University Press, 1980), Chapter 3.

James G. MacKinnon. "Model Specification Tests against Non-Nested Alternatives," paper presented at the Canadian Economic Association Meetings, Ottawa, 1982, forthcoming in *Econometric Review.*

Part Seven Some Aspects of Model Building
  and Policy Making Role

W. Baumol. "Economic Models and Mathematics." In *The Structure of Economic Science,* ed. by S. Krupp (Englewood Cliffs: Prentice-Hall, 1966), pp. 88-101.

K.E. Boulding. *Economics as a Science* (New York: McGraw-Hill, 1970), Chapter 4.

E. Devons. *Essays in Economics* (London: George Allen and Unwin, 1961).

M. Friedman, "A Monetary and Fiscal Framework for Economic Stability." *American Economic Review*, 38 (1948), pp. 245-264.

H. Katouzian. *Ideology and Method in Economics* (New York: New York University Press, 1980), Chapter 7.

R.E. Lucas, Jr. "Rules Discretion, and the Role of the Economic Advisor." In *Rational Expectations and Economic Policy*, ed. Stanley Fischer (Chicago: The University Press, 1980), pp. 199-210. Reprinted in Studies in Business Cycle Theory (Cambridge, Massachusetts: The MIT Press, 1981), pp. 248-61.

F. Machlup. *Methodology of Economics and Other Social Sciences* (New York: Academic Press, 1978), Chapter 6.

E. Malinvaud, "Econometrics Faced with the Needs of Macroeconomic Policy." *Econometrica*, 49 (1981), pp. 1363-75.

E. Rotwein. "Mathematical Economics: The Empirical View and an Appeal for Pluralism." In *The Structure of Economic Science*, ed. by S. Krupp (Englewood Cliffs: Prentice-Hall, 1966), pp. 102-113.

I.M.T. Stewart. *Reasoning and Method in Economics* (Toronto: McGraw-Hill, 1979), pp. 142-50.

J. Tinbergen, "The Use of Models: Experience and Prospects." *American Economic Review*, special issue, (December, 1981), pp. 17-22.

Part Eight **Pattern Modelling, Storytelling, Holism, and Behavioral Requirements**

Institutionalism

C. Craypo, "Collective Bargaining in the Multinational, Conglomerate Corporation: Litton's Shutdown of Royal Typewriter". *Industrial and Labour Relations Review*, 29 (1975), 3-25.

P. Diesing, *Patterns of Discovery in the Social Sciences* (Chicago: Aldine-Atherton, 1971).

J.K. Galbraith, *Economics and the Public Purpose* (Boston: Houghton Mifflin, 1973).

A.G. Gruchy, "The Current State of Institutional Economics."
The American Journal of Economics and Sociology, 41 (1982),
225-41.

A. Kaplan, *The Conduct of Inquiry* (San Francisco:
Chandler Publishing Co., 1964).

W.F. Mueller, "Antitrust in a Planned Economy." *Journal of
Economic Issues,* 9 (1975), 159-80.

G. Myrdal, "Institutional Economics." *Journal of Economic
Issues,* 12 (1978), 771-83.

W.J. Samuels, "Interrelations between Legal and Economic Processes." *Journal of Law and Economics,* 14 (1971), 435-50.

Scientific Revolutions

M. Blaug, *The Methodology of Economics* (London: Cambridge
University Press, 1980), Chapter 1 and 2.

M. Bronfenbrenner, "The Structure of Revolutions in Economic
Thought." *History of Political Economy,* 3 (1971), 136-51.

T.W. Hutchison, *Knowledge and Ignorance in Economics*
(Chicago: The University of Chicago Press, 1977).

, *On Revolutions and Progress in Economic Knowledge*
(Cambridge: Cambridge University Press, 1978).

H. Katouzian, *Ideology and Method in Economics* (New
York: New York University Press, 1980), Chapter 4.

T.S. Kuhn, *The Structure of Scientific Revolutions*
(Chicago, 1970).

S.J. Latsis, ed. *Method and Appraisal in Economics*
(Cambridge: Cambridge University Press, 1976).

D.C. North, "Structure and Performance: The Task of Economic
History." *Journal of Economic Literature,* 16 (1978), 963-78.

D.N. McCloskey, "Does the Past Have Useful Economics?"
Journal of Economic Literature, 14 (1976), 434-61.

G.E. Peabody, "Scientific Paradigms and Economics: An Introduction." *The Review of Radical Political Economics,* 3
(1971), 1-16.

G.J. Stigler, "Does Economics Have a Useful Past?" *History of Political Economy,* 1 (1969), 217-30.

Part Nine **What is Wrong and Right with Economics?**

B.R. Bergmann, "Economist, Poll Thy People." *New York Times,* Nov. 3, 1974.

J.H. Blackman, "The Outlook for Economics." *Southern Economic Journal,* 37 (1971), 385-95.

J.K. Galbraith, "Power and the Useful Economist." *American Economic Review,* 63 (1973), 1-11.

F.H. Hahn, "Some Adjustment Problems." *Econometrica,* 38 (1970), 1-17.

P.J. Huber, *Robust Statistics* (Toronto: John Wiley and Sons Canada Ltd., 1981).

H.G. Johnson, "The Economic Approach to Social Questions." *Economica,* 35 (1968), 1-21.

D. MacDougall, "In Praise of Economics." *Economics Journal,* 84 (1974), 773-86.

S.J. Maisel, "The Economics and Finance Literature and Decision Making." *Journal of Finance,* 29 (1974), 313-22.

E.H. Phelps Brown, "The Underdevelopment of Economics." *Economic Journal,* 82 (1972), 1-10.

C.L. Schultze, "Is Economics Obsolete? No, underemployed." *Saturday Review,* January 22, 1972.

V.L. Smith, "Microeconomic System as an Experimental Science." Discussion Paper 81-32, College of Business and Public Administration, University of Arizona, Tucson, Arizona, February 1982 (to appear in the *American Economic Review*).

S. Reiter, "Information and Performance in the '(new)[2] Welfare Economics'," *American Economic Review,* 67 (1977), pp. 226-234.

R.M. Solow, "Science and Ideology in Economics." *Public Interest,* 21 (1970), 94-107.

P. Sweezy, "Capitalism, for Worse." *Monthly Review,* 25 (1974), 1-7.

J. Tobin, "Cambridge (U.K.) vs. Cambridge (Mass.)." *Public Interest*, 31 (1973), 102-09.

L.L. Wilde, "On the Use of Laboratory Experiments in Economics," in J.C. Pitt (ed.), *Philosophy in Economics* (London: D. Reidel Publishing Company, 1981, 137-48).

G.D.N. Worswick, "Is Progress in Economic Science Possible?" *Economic Journal*, 82 (1972), 73-79.

Glossary

A

Ad Hoc Hypothesis Arbitrary proposition or set of propositions used to account for observations not explained by a theory.

Analytic (of statements) Derived from logical analysis or investigation of the constituent elements of a material or abstract entity (contrast synthetic).

Analytical School School of economic methodologists whose analyses proceed from propositions the material truth of which is intuitively known.

Antecedent Existing or going before; prior in time.

Anthropomorphism Reasoning in which human attributes are ascribed to inanimate objects.

Apodictic (of a proposition) Logically certain or necessarily true, having been demonstrated or being demonstrable.

A Posteriori Based upon empirical data, actual observations (contrast A Priori).

A Priori Based upon deduction from initial premises to conclusions without reference to observed phenomena.

Appeal to Authority References to the pronouncements of experts, the principles of law, etc. in support of an argument.

Apriorism Reliance upon a priori reasoning (See A Priori).

Argument by Analogy A form of reasoning by which the similarity of two things in one respect is inferred from observed similarities between the two things in other respects.

Argumentum Ad Hominem Attacking the character rather than the argument of an opponent.

Assumption That which is assumed for the sake of argument without reference to its validity.

Atomism The theory that minute, discrete and indivisible elements ultimately constitute all phenomena. (contrast Stolism).

385

Auxiliary Hypothesis   A supplementary proposition or set of propositions used to explain and predict the occurrence of specified objects or events (See Hypothesis).

Axiom   A proposition or statement which is self-evident and universally accepted without proof.

B

Beg the Question (also Petitio Principii)   To assume the truth of the very point being questioned.

C

Casual Empiricism   Off-hand or systematic observation.

Categorical   An unqualified or conditional statement.

Causal Explanation   An explanation implying that one event was caused by a previous event or series of events.

Circular Reasoning   Reasoning which assumes that which is to be proven.

Conditional   Subject to or dependent upon the existence or occurrence of certain things or events.

Confirmation   The act of establishing the truth, accuracy, or validity of a hypothesis through empirical testing.

Consequent   That which follows or progresses logically.

Construct   A complex notion or idea formed from a series of simpler notions or ideas.

Contingent Statement   A statement which is neither logically necessary nor logically impossible so its truth or falsity can be determined only by empirical observation.

Control   A parallel experiment used as a standard of comparison in which the factor whose effect is being studied is withheld.

Conventionalism   A method of selecting, through deductive logic, the 'best' theory according to generally accepted criteria.

D

Deduction   Reasoning in which the conclusion is derived logically from the stated premises.

Determinism Doctrine that human choices and decisions are pre-determined.

Deterministic (of hypotheses) Assertions about the entire population being studied free of perturbation (antonym: stochastic).

E

Empirical Relying on experience or observation.

Enumeration, 100 Per cent The study of an entire population rather than a sample of that population.

Epistemology The study of the origin, nature, methods, and limits of human knowledge.

Exact Sciences Sciences that deal with specific and objective facts, e.g. the physical sciences with a higher level of predictive accuracy or wholly deductive disciplines such as mathematics, etc.

Experiment A test or trial designed to investigate observed phenomena.

F

Fallacy Erroneous reasoning that renders an argument logically inconsistent.

Fallacy of Composition Fallacious reasoning which assumes that truths concerning the part can be extended to the whole.

Falsification To disprove a hypothesis by empirical testing (contrast Verification).

H

Heuristic A method or argument involving the intuitive discovery rather than rigorous proof of hypotheses.

High-Level (of statements in a theory) Relating to general rules, laws, or principles.

Historicism Doctrine that immutable laws rather than human actions determine the course of history.

Holism Doctrine that whole entities have an existence greater than the sum of their parts (contrast Atomism).

Hypostatization The treatment of concepts or ideas as distinct substances or realities.

387

Hypothesis A proposition or set of propositions used to explain and predict the occurrence of specified objects or events.

Hypothetical (noun) Alternative term for conditional.

Hypothetico - Deductive Method A research methodology consisting of the following stages:
1) the deduction of predictions from hypothesis;
2) the testing of predictions using empirical observations;
3) the revision of hypothesis in light of the empirical evidence;
4) the deduction and empirical testing of revised predictions. (Cf. V.J. Tarascio, *A study in the History of Some Scientific Aspects of Economic Thought* (Chapel Hill, N.C.: University of N.C. Press, 1966).

I

Ignorance Lack of knowledge or information.

Induction Reasoning which derives general principles from empirical observations (contrast Deduction).

Instrumentalism Doctrine that the value of scientific theories is determined by their usefulness in predicting the occurrence of objects or events.

Instrumentation The utilization of instruments to assist in the measurement of observable phenomena.

Intersubjectivity Agreement among a number of scientists on the conduct and interpretation of empirical research.

Introspection The attempt at gathering evidence on human behavior, attitude, etc., by examination of oneself.

L

Law (in science) A statement of a sequence of phenomena invariable under the same conditions.

Law of Large Numbers Doctrine that individual deviations from the norm will tend to offset each other as the sample size increases.

Logic The study of the principles of correct or reliable inference.

Logical 'Truth' (of statements) A statement accepted as 'true' in a deductive argument regardless of its empirical validity.

Low-Level (of statements in a theory) Relating to rules or principles of restricted generality.

M

Major Premise The predicate or major term of the conclusion in a syllogism (compare Minor Premise).

Material Truth A statement accepted as empirically 'true'.

Mechanistic Explanation See Causal Explanation.

Metaphysical Concerned with abstract unverifiable thoughts or ideas.

Methodological Individualism Doctrine that group behavior can only be understood in the context of the actions of its individual members.

Methodology A set of rules, methods, or principles regulating the conduct of theoretical and empirical investigation.

Minor Premise The subject or minor term of the conclusion in syllogism (compare Major Premise).

Model A system of relations among economic phenomena derived from a specified set of axioms.

Monism Doctrine that all phenomena can be explained in terms of one principle (contrast Pluralism).

N

Naturalims (also Physicalism) Doctrine that only natural forces and elements, excluding the supernatural or spiritual, compromise all observable phenomena.

Natural or Physical Sciences Sciences dealing with objects or processes observed in nature.

Nomological Concerned with discerning scientific "laws".

Normative (of statements) Based on personal values or preferences (contrast Positive).

O

Objective Probability A relative frequency value that a specific outcome has been observed to occur in the long run.

Occam's Razor Maxim that assumptions used to explain an object or event must not be multiplied beyond necessity.

P

Pluralism Doctrine that different phenomena can be explained only in terms of different principles (contrast Monism).

Plurality of Causes (usually in phrase 'principle of ...') Doctrine that one observed event may have many causes.

Positive (of statements) Based on empirical fact rather than personal preferences (contrast Normative).

Positivism Doctrine that positive facts and phenomena, not speculation upon ultimate causes, are relevant in scientific investigation.

Possibility Chance of occurrence of an event.

Post Hoc Ergo Propter Hoc Fallacious reasoning which accepts event A as a cause of event B merely because event A occurred earlier in time.

Postulate Statement assumed without proof as a basis for reasoning (see Axiom).

Pragmatic Concerned with practicality.

Prediction Forecast of future events.

Premise Postulate supporting a conclusion in conjunction with other postulates.

Probability The likelihood or chance of an object's or event's occurrence.

Proposition of Regularity (Uniformity) Proposition which states the conclusions drawn from observed cases can be extended to unobserved cases.

Protocol (also Protocol Statement) Statement reporting an observation exactly without interpretation.

R

Rationalism Doctrine that reason alone, unaided by empirical observation, is the source of all knowledge.

Reductionism Doctrine that ideas should be expressed in the terms most amenable to empirical testing.

S

Social Sciences Sciences dealing with society or social behavior.

Statistical (of hypotheses) ehrefer about some members of a sample.

Subjective Probability A probability estimate based on personal belief and experience of a particular situation without the benefit of a priori or a posteriori evidence.

Subjectivism Doctrine that all knowledge is limited to personal experiences.

Syllogism A deductive argument whose conclusion is supported by two premises (see Major and Minor Premises).

Synthetic (of Statements) Reasoning process in which the conclusion is arrived at directly from the stated propositions or principles (contrast Analytic).

T

Tautology Statement that can be shown using certain basic rules to be true irrespective of observed events (contrast Contingent Statement).

Taxonomic Concerned with identification and classification.

Teleological Explanation Argument that one event was designed or intended to make another event occur (Contrast Causal Explanation).

Term (in syllogistic reasoning) The subject or predicate in a syllogy.

Testing Process in which predictions are compared with empirical observations to assess their accuracy.

Theorem Idea, belief, or statement deduced from a set of premises or assumptions.

Theory System of general propositions or principles used to explain a class of phenomena.

U

Uncertainty Doubt or hesitancy concerning the occurrence of an event, often expressed as a statistical probability.

Universal (of Statements) Applicable to all members of a class.

V

Validation To substantiate or confirm a hypothesis and hence the theory using the probabilistic results of empirical observations.

Verification To prove a hypothesis by empirical testing (contrast Falsification).

Author Index

393

F (cont'd)

Friend, I. - 60, 62, 65
Frisch, R. - 52, 65, 92, 93,
  95, 100, 377

G

Galbraith, J.K. - 240, 243,
  253, 254, 256, 260, 261,
  264, 269, 319, 338, 341,
  371, 381, 383
Gamaletos, T. - 225
Gibson, Q. - 80, 88
Gillespie, C.C. - 277
Goldberger, A.S. - 225
Gordon, A. - 356
Gordon, D. - 278
Gordon, K. - 343
Gordon, S. - 26, 375
Gramm, W. - 271
Granger, C.W.J. - 41, 378
Gregg, W. - 311
Griliches, Z. - 57, 65, 378,
  380
Grossack, I. - 271
Groves, T. - 310
Gruchy, A. - 240, 243, 267, 268,
  270, 382
Guetzkow, H. - 293, 314

H

Hahn, F.H. - 319, 330, 338, 371,
  383
Haley, B.F. - 313
Hall, R. - 196, 365, 371
Harrison, R.S. - vi, 239, 240, 243
Harrod, R.F. - 278
Hayes, J.R. - 303, 311
Heilbroner, R.L. - v, 25, 27,
  84, 248, 249, 261, 269, 339,
  356, 371
Heller, W.W. - vi, 318, 319,
  337, 358, 371
Hempel, C.G. - 85, 98, 149,
  246, 268
Hicks, J.R. - 225, 282

Hill, F.G. - 256
Hill, L. - 271
Hirsch, A. - 272
Hirschman, A.O. - 311
Hollis, M. - x, 268
Holt, C. - 289, 299, 311
Howrey, E.P. - 51, 65
Huber, P.J. - 318, 383
Hume, D. - 67
Hurwicz, L. - 282
Hutchison, T.W. - 24, 26,
  69, 84, 155, 181, 187,
  191, 195, 196, 197, 241,
  277, 375, 382
Hutt, W.H. - 279
Hymans, S. - 51, 65

I

Ijiri, Y. - 287, 311
Infeld, L. - 181
Intriligator, M.D. - 378,
  380
Irwin, M. - 271

J

James, W. - 70, 85, 86, 180,
  181
Jevons, S. - 85
Johnsen, E. - 294, 309, 311
Johnson, H.G. - 99, 222,
  225, 319, 340, 341, 345,
  369, 371, 383
Johnston, J. - 221, 225
Jorgensen, D.W. - 286, 312,
  335

K

Kahneman, D. - 302, 312
Kantor, B. - 41, 378
Kantorovich, L. - 289
Kaplan, A. - 240, 252, 256,
  262, 263, 264, 268, 269,
  270, 271, 272, 382
Kapp, K.W. - 243, 260, 261,
  267, 269, 271

K (cont'd)

Kassalow, E. - 271
Katouzian, H. - ix, x, 155,
  201, 241, 375, 376, 380,
  381, 382
Kaufman, F. - 172, 176, 182
Kelley, A.M. - 267
Kelsen, H. - 22
Kelvin, Lord - 12
Kennedy, P. - 377
Keynes, J.M. - 58, 65, 276,
  278, 357, 371
Keynes, J.N. - 34, 35, 69, 84,
  85, 106, 150,
Kirzner, I.M. - 86
Klappholz, K. - 26, 44, 48,
  195, 375
Klein, L.R. - 223, 225
Klein, P. - 267
Knight, F.H. - 80, 88, 179
Koopmans, T.C. - 40, 67, 68,
  116, 117, 118, 122, 130, 155,
  183, 185, 189, 190, 191, 192,
  193, 194, 195, 197, 225, 289,
  319, 377, 379
Kornai, J. - 304, 312
Kozmetsky, G. - 293, 314
Krimerman, I. - x, 376
Krupp, S.R. - 87, 151, 152, 154,
  201, 380, 381
Kuh, E. - 61, 64
Kuhn, T.S. - 27, 33, 37, 38,
  61, 65, 87, 98, 240, 241,
  249, 273, 274, 275, 276,
  277, 278, 382
Kunreuther, H. - 302, 312
Kuznets, S. - 294

L

Lakatos, I. - 241
Latsis, J.J. - x, 241, 382
Lau, L.J. - 335
Leamer, E. - 41, 57, 65, 378
Leeman, W.A. - 179
Leibenstein, H. - 304, 305,
  312

Leontief, W. - vi, 37, 55,
  57, 59, 60, 65, 206, 225,
  230, 238, 251, 317, 318,
  321, 338, 356, 371
Lerner, A.P. - 357, 371
Lesourne, J. - 312
Lester, R.A. - 139, 268
Levy, F.K. - 287, 314
Lewin, G. - 296
Lindbeck, A. - 37
Lingard, J. - 226
Lipsey, R. - 69, 70, 74, 76,
  77, 78, 80, 82, 84, 86,
  87, 88, 195, 197, 269
Little, J.M.D. - 239, 247,
  268
Loasby, B.J. - 222, 225
Longley, J.W. - 210, 226
Lovell, M. - 50, 52, 65
Lowe, A. - 37, 38
Lower, M. - 271
Lucas, R.E. - 41, 68, 200,
  287, 299, 312, 378, 379,
  381

M

MacDougall, D. - 318, 319,
  369, 371, 383
Machlup, F. - v, vi, x, 1,
  3, 22, 26, 46, 48, 84,
  87, 132, 139, 140, 141,
  142, 143, 146, 151, 152,
  153, 154, 155, 157, 182,
  201, 283, 375, 376, 380,
  381
Macmillan, H. - 233
Maddock, R. - 41, 378
Mahoney, M. - 52, 62, 65
Maisel, S.J. - 319, 339,
  372, 383
Malinvaud, E. - 40, 201,
  226, 282, 377, 381
Malthus, T. - 331
March, J.G. - 293, 294,
  304, 305, 309, 310, 312
Margenau, H. - 165, 176,
  179, 182

M (cont'd)

Markowitz, H. - 193, 198
Marris, R. - 37, 304, 312
Marschak, J. - 295, 298,
  312
Marshall, A. - 34, 35, 71,
  85, 150, 281, 312, 362
Marx, K. - 34, 35, 37, 260
Mason, E. - 283, 312
Mayer, T. - v, 39, 49, 51,
  62, 65
Mayes, D.G. - 377
McClelland, P. - 243, 268
McClements, L.D. - vi, 200,
  201, 203, 226
McCloskey, D.N. - 241, 382
McCormick, B.J. - 84
Means, G. - 256
Meek, R.L. - 25, 26, 375
Melitz, J. - 120, 121, 130,
  148, 379
Menger, C. - 176, 183
Mill, J.S. - 34, 35, 85, 136,
  149, 150, 152, 155, 162,
  180, 331
Mini, P.V. - 268
Mitchell, P. - 308
Mitchell, W.C. - 56, 65, 245,
  267, 269, 272
Modigliani, F. - 289, 299, 311
Montias, J.M. - 312
Morgenstern, O. - 40, 88, 193,
  198, 231, 238, 297, 315
Morrison, J.L. - 209, 226
Mosak, J.L. - 205, 226
Mueller, W.F. - 240, 253, 254,
  269, 382
Muggeridge, M. - 229
Musgrave, R.A. - 351, 372
Muth, J. - 289, 299, 311, 312,
Myrdal, G. - 26, 37, 240, 243,
  256, 260, 261, 339, 356, 372,
  376, 382

N

Nagel, E. - 25, 27, 37, 85,
  122, 129, 130, 148, 178, 206,
  226, 277, 379

Nath, S.K. - 46, 48
Nell, E. - x, 268
Nelson, R. - 305, 313
Nerlove, M. - 206
Newell, A. - 301, 302, 308,
  313
Newton, I. - 165, 245, 254,
  255, 292
Ng, Y.-K. - v, 25, 43
Nordhaus, W. - 372
North, D.C. - 241, 266, 382

O

O'Brien, D.P. - 131, 380
Okner, B.A. - 352, 372
Okun, A. - 372
Olmstead, A. - 61
Oppenheim, P. - 85, 246,
  268
Oppenheimer, R. - 5
Orcutt, G. - 309, 313
Orr, D. - 85, 120, 121,
  129, 132, 143, 144, 145,
  146, 154, 379

P

Papandreau, A.G. - 283,
  313, 379
Pareto, V. - 85, 331
Patinkin, D. - 60, 65
Peabody, G.E. - 241, 382
Pechman, J.A. - 352, 369,
  372
Perry, G.L. - 362, 370, 372
Phelps-Brown, E.H. - 287,
  313, 319, 338, 372, 383
Phillips, A.W. - 233, 238
Piore, M. - 365, 367, 372
Planck, M. - 13, 22, 61
Polanyi, M. - 33, 38, 179
Pope, D. - v, 67, 89, 95
Pope, R. - v, 67, 89, 95
Popper, K. - 1, 49, 66, 70,
  85, 120, 241, 274, 319,
  376
Prescott, J. - 299
Pycke, S. - 62, 63

About the Authors...

BALDEV RAJ is Professor of Economics at *Wilfrid Laurier University*, Waterloo, Ontario, Canada. He received his B.A. and M.A. from *Delhi University*; M.A. and Ph.D. from *The University of Western Ontario*. He has held visiting appointments at *The University of Western Ontario* and the *Indian Statistical Institute*. Dr. Raj is the author of numerous research papers in econometrics, statistics, managerial economics, finance and monetary economics. Recently he co-authored the book *Econometrics: A Varying Coefficients Approach*.

WILLIAM MARR is Professor of Economics at *Wilfrid Laurier University*, Waterloo, Ontario, Canada. He received his B.A. from *McMaster University* and his M.A. and Ph.D. from *The University of Western Ontario*. He is the author of "Labour Market and Other Implications of Immigration Policy for Ontario" for the Ontario Economic Council, and co-author of *Canada: An Economic History*. He is the author of articles in economic history, Canadian immigration, and internal labour migration.